DESCARTES' MEDITATIVE TURN

Cultural Memory in the Present

Hent de Vries, Editor

DESCARTES' MEDITATIVE TURN

Cartesian Thought as Spiritual Practice

Christopher J. Wild

STANFORD UNIVERSITY PRESS
Stanford, California

Stanford University Press
Stanford, California

© 2024 by Christopher J. Wild. All rights reserved.

Printed in the United States of America on acid-free, archival-quality paper

Cataloging-in-Publication Data available upon request.
Library of Congress Control Number: 2023040306
ISBN: 9781503638280 (cloth), 9781503638594 (paper), 9781503638600 (ebook)

Cover design: Lindy Kasler
Cover art: René Descartes, French, 17th Century, engraving on laid paper sheet (trimmed within plate mark): 7 5/8 x 5 7/16 in. Gift of John O'Brien, 1991.208.39

Contents

	Introduction: Descartes' Meditative Turn and the Tradition of Spiritual Exercises	1
1	Founding First Philosophies: Descartes' Conversion	27
2	Method and Meditation: The Cartesian Art of Turning	74
3	The Discernment of Ideas and the Evidence of the *Cogito*	121
4	Cartesian Ceroplastics: Meditating the Mediality of the Mind	161
5	*Adversio*, *Animadversio*, and *Attentio*: Turning toward God	187
6	"To Gaze with Wonder and Adoration": *Contemplatio Dei* and Meditative Ascent	222
	Acknowledgments	259
	Notes	261
	Bibliography	307
	Index	331

Introduction: Descartes' Meditative Turn and the Tradition of Spiritual Exercises

The Question of Descartes' Spirituality

Why did René Descartes, the founding father of early modern rationalist philosophy, choose "meditations," a practice and genre associated with religious piety and devotion at the time, for the title of his *magnum opus* that lays the metaphysical foundations for his reform of all knowledge, including mathematics and science? Similarly, why did Descartes preface the *Meditations* with a letter to the Theological Faculty of the Sorbonne in which he claims that he has discovered a new way to convert unbelievers by rational and, therefore, more reliable means? Or why does his meditator at the end of the Third Meditation, at the almost exact center of the text, engage in an almost ecstatic visionary experience, resembling those described by Saint Augustine, Bernard of Clairvaux, or Bonaventure, before they begin turning back toward the sensory world?

Most modern readers, whether professional or casual, don't pose these kinds of questions, let alone answer them in a comprehensive and convincing manner. As a consequence, most scholars understand "meditating" merely as a synonym for concentrated and sustained thinking, stripping it of its devotional provenance and failing to account for its specific character as an intellectual and spiritual practice. Similarly, the prefatory letter to the Faculty of the Sorbonne is either entirely ignored or is explained—with a palpable embarrassment—as a transparent attempt by Descartes to placate the religious authorities to avoid Galilei's fate of censorship and persecution.

Accordingly, his claim that the *Meditations* is a new and universal tool in the Catholic Church's *propaganda fidei* is read as a calculated dissimulation on Descartes' part and does not reflect his true beliefs. Finally, the aforementioned passage of a beatific vision at the end of the Third Meditation gets simply passed over by the entire Descartes scholarship so that there are not even a handful of serious attempts at explicating this enigmatic passage, a fact that is even more puzzling, as the passage reads like the climactic moment of the meditator's "interior journey."

These three instances of omission in reading the *Meditations* accurately and attentively are part of a more general trend to downplay the religious and spiritual dimension of Descartes' thought. Taking these passages seriously and examining them in their wider context would mean unsettling the common narrative that Descartes is the main protagonist in the early modern project of reforming knowledge by emancipating philosophy and science from their medieval servitude to theology. While this narrative of Descartes as the founding father of modern secular philosophy goes back all the way to Kant and German idealism,[1] modern analytic philosophy has been even more radical in stripping Descartes of any cumbersome baggage belonging to an earlier "unenlightened" era and reducing his thought to issues of interest to modern mainstream philosophers, such as nature of the mind, the epistemological foundation of knowledge, or philosophy as a method for the sciences. What has emerged as a consequence is the image of Descartes as an epistemologist who is primarily interested in determining what if anything can be known for certain. In the last decades this view has been complemented or displaced by the image of Descartes as a scientist whose metaphysics is wholly subservient to his building of a new scientific system that encompasses the entire universe and is capable of explaining everything within the natural world. But Descartes the scientist is as secular as Descartes the epistemologist, and any religious atavisms, for instance, his talk of God and the immortality of the soul, have been readily jettisoned as disposable philosophical ballast. Not surprisingly, these two dominant perspectives of Descartes focus on epistemological and scientific questions that herald modern and contemporary philosophy and science. Thereby, Descartes becomes a mere gateway to the present, eclipsing the complex historical context of his thought.

Of course, the rendition I gave of Descartes' image in modern philosophy is a caricature. Like any caricature it is exaggerated, but it is also true enough to be recognizable; and it is true enough to have prompted the aforementioned omissions by modern Descartes scholarship and, more generally, to have shaped the dominant mode of understanding the *Meditations* as an ensemble of philosophical arguments scrutinized for their propositional content and validity. One of the implicit premises of reading for argument is the assumption that Descartes' manner of presentation is more or less transparent and that the language and rhetorical style, generic form, narrative organization, grammatical structures, and lexical choices of the *Meditations* do not affect the validity of their claims and effect on their readers. This could not be further from the truth. Throughout his life Descartes was extraordinarily deliberate about how he communicated his ideas and discoveries to the European Republic of Letters. In fact, Descartes systematically experimented with various philosophical genres over the course of his career, carefully coordinating propositional content, textual form, and communicative function. *Descartes' Meditative Turn* is, therefore, guided by the heuristic assumption that Descartes was convinced that the immortality of the soul and the existence of God, which the text promises to demonstrate, could be made self-evident only through meditating and that he deliberately chose the genre of meditation to lay the metaphysical foundations for his philosophy and science.

The Spiritual Dimension of Philosophy

If most modern readers of Descartes fail to take seriously the religious dimension of his thought, we should not make the opposite mistake of overseeing philosophy's contribution to the history of meditative thought and practice. Pierre Hadot and Michel Foucault remind us that meditation or, more precisely, spiritual exercises were integral to the practice of philosophy in antiquity. Ancient philosophy, according to Hadot, was a "form of life defined by an ideal of wisdom."[2] Indeed, all of the philosophical schools were distinguished by their own characteristic form of life, which included devising their own specific regime of exercises to guide the self on the path toward wisdom as the ultimate goal. Philosophy was not primarily about teaching abstract theories or interpreting texts but about a set of practices. If we are to achieve wisdom, philosophy demands the "metamorphosis of our personality" and the "transformation of our vision of the world" (PWL 82)—in short, the conversion of the self. In a sense, conversion was the beginning and the end of philosophy, for only when the self achieves its telos of wisdom is its conversion complete. Like meditation, conversion was thus not exclusively a religious phenomenon but had deep roots in the ancient philosophy that informed its Christian variants as well.

The self's transformation occupies a similarly pivotal place in Foucault's account of ancient philosophy, developed at length in his lectures on the *Hermeneutics of the Subject*. Conversion is the most radical form of transformation of the self, undertaken "so as to be able to have access to the truth."[3] Conversion "to the self" implies "constituting oneself as an object and domain of knowledge (*connaissance*)" (HS 253). It is characteristic of ancient philosophy from Plato on, according to Foucault, that the subject must pay a "price" to have access to truth, and that price is its transformation. This fundamental principle of ancient philosophy holds true for Christianity as well, with the difference that truth in the latter case is mediated by a sacred text and its understanding depends on paying the price. Foucault identifies this work of the self on itself with the phrase *epimeleia heautou*, which he interprets as "care of the self, attending to oneself, being concerned with oneself" (HS 2) and which was translated into Latin as *cura sui*. In contrast, following Foucault, the self's unmediated access to the truth (of itself) is captured in the Delphic injunction to "know thyself," or *gnōthi seauton*, which owing to Socrates became the founding expression of Western philosophy. Significantly, meditation or spiritual exercise, in Greek *meletē*, the etymological root of *epimeleia* (HS 11), is not linked with the self-reflectivity of the *gnōthi seauton* but with the care of the self. Meditation is essentially the work that the philosophical subject must undertake to gain access to truth and reach wisdom and complete its conversion.

Despite significant differences, Pierre Hadot and Michel Foucault are united in their effort to unearth what Hadot calls "philosophy as a way of life," and Foucault the "care for the self," from the layers of sediment under which it has been buried by the subsequent history of philosophy and its historiography. In the very first lecture of the *Hermeneutics of the Subject*, Foucault asks: "Why did Western thought and philosophy neglect the notion of *epimeleia heautou* (care of the self) in its reconstruction of its own history" and instead "accorded so much privilege, value, and intensity to the 'know yourself'"? (HS 12). A few pages later Foucault renames the adversaries in more familiar terms. *Gnōthi seauton* stands in for philosophy, and *epimeleia heautou* for spirituality. Foucault's question thus becomes: How did philosophy so completely displace spirituality? Hadot poses the same question in distinguishing between the "*discourse about* philosophy and *philosophy itself*" (PWL 266), noting that "historians of philosophy pay little attention to the fact that ancient philosophy was, first and foremost, a way of life" (269). In the historians' view philosophy is above all philosophical discourse. And the question for Hadot is how to account for this prejudice taking root.

For Hadot and Foucault the answer to this question is that it occurred much earlier than expected with the emergence of philosophy as a university discipline in the Middle Ages. Initially, Christianity understood itself as the true heir of ancient philosophy, the *vera philosophia*. The Christian Apologists of the second century, in particular Justin, were the first to conceive of Christianity as philosophy and, more precisely, as the definitive philosophy. The church fathers who had received a philosophical education spoke of "our philosophy" or "the philosophy according to Christ" (PWL 129).[4] When monasticism emerged as the perfection of a Christian way of life, it could similarly style itself as a quest for wisdom. As Jean Leclercq has shown, monastic writers throughout the Middle Ages continued designating their form of life with the term *philosophia*.[5] This easy embrace of ancient philosophy by early Christianity can be explained by the fact that the former was never abstract but a way of life and a practice of wisdom. And not surprisingly, its practical dimension, that is, the spiritual exercises, could be easily assimilated by Christianity because they presented no conflict with different doctrinal positions. It was as a consequence of theology's consolidation as a discipline at medieval universities that "the confusion which had existed in primitive Christianity between theology, founded on the rule of faith, and traditional philosophy, founded on reason" (PWL 270), ended and the segregation of philosophy and spirituality came about. Philosophy was no longer the royal way to wisdom, the ultimate goal of all human striving, but was demoted to the "handmaiden" of theology, supplying the latter with conceptual and logical tools for use in its higher calling. Concomitantly, spiritual exercises or, more generally, the practice of spirituality, became the domain of pious devotion and mysticism. Ceasing to be holistic, philosophy was no longer a way of life but became a "purely theoretical and abstract activity" (270). This despiritualization of philosophy was reinforced by its status as a university discipline. Those who engaged in philosophy did so not for the sake of *Bildung*, that is, self-transformation, and the intention of those who taught it was not to direct others toward wisdom but to produce specialists who in turn would produce another generation of specialists. It is not surprising that the philosophy of the Middle Ages became known as "Scholasticism," that is, philosophy of and for *scholae* (school) and not *vitae* (for life). And it is also no coincidence that Scholasticism was identified with the name of Aristotle, the ancient philosopher for whom, as Foucault observed, "the question of spirituality was least important" (HS 17).

While Foucault by and large agrees with Hadot's assessment of Scholasticism's role in despiritualizing philosophy,[6] it is the advent of the modern age, "when knowledge itself and knowledge alone gives access to the truth" (HS 17), that puts the nail in the coffin of the practice of spirituality. While he calls this *epochē* half-jokingly the "Cartesian moment," he does not pin it on Descartes alone.[7] The work of "requalifying the *gnōthi seauton* and of discrediting the *epimeleia heatou*" (14) begins long before Descartes and continues until this day. In fact, his statements about Descartes' role in this process, scattered across his lectures, are inconsistent and contradictory,[8] evidencing the power of his reception by the philosophical tradition rather than reflecting his actual intellectual practice. On the one hand, Foucault sees the "Cartesian approach" place self-evidence (*l'évidence*) at the "origin" of philosophizing. The *cogito*, that is, the Cartesian *gnōthi seauton*, is immediately self-evident and gives access to truth without any precondition, thereby making the spiritual transformation of the self obsolete. On the other hand, Foucault concedes that the concept of meditation "not as the game the subject plays with his thought but as the game thought plays on the subject, is basically exactly what Descartes was still doing in the *Meditations*, and is indeed precisely the meaning he gave to 'meditation'" (358). This characterization of the *Meditations* recalls Foucault's more nuanced assessment of Descartes' place in the history of spirituality expressed ten years earlier in his reply to Derrida's critique of the *History of Madness*. Here Foucault holds a very different view of Cartesian meditation, one much closer to the *epimeleia heatou* at the center of his later work. Meditation transforms the self and, thereby, gives it access to truth: "A 'meditation' produces, as so many discursive events, new utterances that carry with them a series of modifications of the enunciating subject: through what is said in meditation, the subject passes from darkness to light, from impurity to purity, from the constraint of passions to detachment, from uncertainty and disordered movements to the serenity of wisdom, and so on."[9] Like the student of ancient philosophy, Descartes' meditator has "to pay a price" and let themselves be transformed by using the *Meditations* to experience the self-evidence of the *cogito* and thereby have access to truth. The inconsistencies or contradictions in Foucault's account reflect Descartes' Janus-faced position within philosophy and the history of knowledge more generally, in the discrepancy between his historical reception, on the one hand, and his actual philosophical practice, on the other. They point, moreover, to the need for a fuller explanation of how it is that Descartes' reform of thought, which revives an older practice of knowledge, ushers in the new modern and scientific era.

Viewed before the backdrop of the history of spirituality, *Descartes' Meditative Turn* is an attempt to reverse the turn taken by philosophy in the Middle Ages and to recover and reboot its lost spiritual practices. That Descartes' comprehensive reform of knowledge was directed against Scholastic Aristotelianism is well documented and researched, with historians of philosophy usually focused on their diverging arguments. But Descartes' reform of knowledge concerned not only its contents—his mechanistic physics, materialistic psychology, or intellectualistic epistemology—but also its practice, in both the narrower sense of his method and the wider sense of a way of life. In contrast to his scientific method, which is by and large innovative, breaking sufficiently with the past for Descartes to be commonly construed as the founding father of modern philosophy and one of the principal protagonists in the scientific revolution, his practice as a way of life harks back to older traditions of thought that had been crowded out or displaced by Scholastic Aristotelianism. Put succinctly, Descartes' campaign against Scholasticism always also involves the repatriation of wisdom, which had been relegated to theology in the Middle Ages, to philosophy, as well as the reevaluation of philosophical practice. For instance, Descartes' programmatic preface to the French edition of his own textbook of philosophy, the *Principia philosophiae*, with which he intended to replace its Scholastic predecessors, begins by redefining philosophy (in the sense of "defining back"): "The word 'philosophy' means the study of wisdom, and by 'wisdom' is meant not only prudence in our everyday affairs but also a perfect knowledge of all things that mankind is capable of knowing, both for the conduct of life and for the preservation of health and the discovery of all manner of skills" (CSM I 179; AT IXB 2).[10] For Descartes philosophy is not theoretical but, quite to the contrary, practical knowledge, knowledge that enables us to live the "good life." The famous image Descartes offers a little later to illustrate his program of knowledge reform reinforces his holistic understanding of philosophy:

> The whole of philosophy is like a tree. The roots are metaphysics, the trunk is physics, and the branches emerging from the trunk are all the other sciences, which may be reduced to three principal ones, namely, medicine, mechanics and morals. By "morals" I understand the highest and most perfect moral system, which presupposes a complete knowledge of the other sciences and is the ultimate level of wisdom. (CSM I 186; AT IXB 14)

In Descartes' eyes, philosophy should not be limited to solving formal and logical problems, leaving the big questions concerning the human condition to other disciplines. On the contrary, as noted, Descartes' commitment to philosophy is *sed vitae*, as opposed to the Scholasticism dominating European universities throughout the early modern period.[11]

Given that the telos of philosophy is to reach the ultimate level of wisdom, it should not come as a surprise that the beginning of philosophy, its act of foundation, began for Descartes with a dramatic conversion in the famous stove-heated room during his travels through southwestern Germany in the winter of 1619. *Descartes' Meditative Turn* argues that the turn toward meditation allowed him to operationalize this discovery. The spiritual and cognitive exercises, derived from ancient philosophy and the Christian meditative tradition, that Descartes deployed in the *Meditations* enable readers to discover for themselves the immortality of the soul and the idea of God's essence and existence—with the same degree of self-evidence with which Descartes did during his own conversion. The "meditative turn" of the book's title, therefore, refers not only to Descartes' turn to meditation as textual genre but also to the turn enacted by the meditator and, thus, the reader of the *Meditations*, away from the sensory world and toward the self, its innate ideas, and the indwelling natural light implanted by God. By formulating a new brand of "metaphysical meditations," which was the title of the authorized French translation, Descartes followed in the footsteps of so many founders of philosophical schools and religious movements, from Plato and Augustine to Luther and Ignatius, who codified the spiritual insights they gained in their conversion through their own brand of spiritual and cognitive practices. By activating the inherent metaphoricity of conversion (from the Latin *convertere*, "to turn over"), Descartes' *Meditations* articulates its own version of the "art of turning," 'Socrates' famous definition of philosophy in the allegory of the cave from Plato's *Republic*.[12] Descartes' meditative turn brings to a culmination his lifelong preoccupation with the practice or craft of thinking, commonly known as the Cartesian method. By joining meditation to method the *Meditations on First Philosophy* becomes the founding document for Cartesianism, a new practice of both thought and life.

The Surge of Spirituality in Early Modern Europe

Descartes was not alone in his rediscovery of meditation and spiritual practice, as late medieval and early modern Europe saw a surge of spirituality. It sprang from the pervasive and unnerving lack of confidence among the laity and even many clerics in the ability of traditional religious institutions and media or, put less abstractly, of the church's representatives and sacraments, to communicate salvation to the faithful in the face of a myriad of crises. This soteriological insecurity led to various reform movements both within the Catholic Church and beyond, ultimately resulting in the emergence of the religious denominations of the Reformation. A common response to this crisis of religious mediation and communication,[13] and one with the advantage of requiring no institutional framework, was to turn inward. All people could take care of their soul and its salvation. All could pay heed to their spiritual life without relying on traditional mediators and media of salvation. Frequently, this turn toward the interior self, when accompanied by an intensification of faith and devotion, was understood and represented as a conversion. And just as frequently, this renewal of the inner self involved a regime of spiritual practices and meditative techniques that helped effect and stabilize it.

One of the most prominent examples of this renewed inwardness, and one germane to the cultural and historical context of Descartes, was the so-called modern devotion, or *devotio moderna*, a late medieval movement of religious reform that flourished in the Low Countries and Northern Germany and came to an end with the Reformation.[14] The *devotio moderna* began as a movement among dissatisfied laity that promoted spiritual reform and the intensification of personal piety by focusing on inner devotion and meditation. The principal practice was methodical prayer in coordination with exercises arranged day by day and week by week.[15] This methodical approach to meditative prayer spread throughout Europe as far as Spain. By way of Garcia de Cisneros, the abbot of Montserrat, the meditative methods of the *devotio moderna* reached Ignatius of Loyola, whose own exercises were influenced by his compatriot's book *Ejercitatorio de la vida spiritual* (Exercises of the spiritual life). By the time the movement was absorbed into the Reformation, it had become part of lay spirituality across a considerable expanse of Europe. Thus, the turn toward the interior self of the late medieval reform movements went hand in hand with the "secularization" of monastic meditation (in the sense that it was no longer the exclusive "property" of monastic orders), as meditative practices jumped the cloister walls to become part of lay devotion.

It should come as no surprise that the sundry Evangelical reform movements borrowed liberally from older meditative and spiritual practices as well. Luther was intimately acquainted with the spiritual practices of the Augustinian order to which he initially belonged.[16] Two seminal meditative texts of the *devotio moderna*, Gerard Zerbolt's *De spiritualibus ascensionibus* (Of spiritual ascents) and Johannes Mauburnus's *Rosetum exercitiorum spiritualium et sacrarum meditationum* (Rose garden of spiritual exercises and sacred meditations), were important enough to him to merit being singled out by name, the latter, contrary to habit, even with page numbers, evidencing a deep knowledge of their spiritual practices. Significantly, meditation played a pivotal role in the so-called tower experience, his breakthrough in understanding justification, following the pattern of a classical conversion by reading. Plagued by a "fierce and troubled conscience" Luther found respite in scripture: "At last, by the mercy of God, meditating day and night, I gave heed to the context of the words, namely, 'In it the righteousness of God is revealed,' as it is written, 'He who through faith is righteous shall live.'"[17] By enacting the principal scriptural endorsement of meditative practice in the injunction of Psalm 1:2 "to meditate day and night," Luther follows John Cassian's advice to use the verse to remember God whenever the mind strays. Luther's conversion is not only brought about by meditation, but meditation helps him stabilize and replicate it in the practice of meditative Bible reading that was shaped by Luther's hermeneutic conversion.

In the Evangelical context, meditative practices may have been not as systematically regimented, lest they appear as a form of good works, and are therefore more circumstantial. But they were no less widespread. Joseph Hall's *Occasional Meditations* (1630), to which I turn in Chapter 4, inaugurated a new meditative genre that could be integrated into one's daily routine and, consequently, became extremely popular across confessions and borders. In general, it is important to note the confessional versatility and fluidity of spiritual exercises. Whereas doctrine and ritual were the focal points of intense confessional conflict, spiritual practices were much less fraught, so borrowing led to commonalities often outweighing differences. In the way the spiritual exercises of ancient philosophy remained implicit and tacit knowledge, as a result attracting little scholarly attention, the spiritual exercises of religious devotion largely escaped confessional controversy.

The best-known example for such a regimen of spiritual exercises is undoubtedly Ignatius's *Exercitia spiritualia* (*Spiritual Exercises*), which became the foundation for the institutional and artistic practice of the Jesuit order and decisively influenced Catholic spirituality in early modern Europe and beyond. In the Ignatian exercises, the relationship between meditation and conversion (discussed in detail in Chapters 1 and 2) is especially tight. For their purpose is to aid the exercitant in making an election, modeled on Christianity's "big" conversions of Saint Matthew and Saint Paul; and their conversive mechanics are informed by Ignatius's own experience of conversion. Rendering the exercitant a virtual eyewitness of the life and suffering of Christ, the exercises formed the basis of the order's apostolic mission to convert heathens in the new world and to reconvert Protestants at home.

As the principal means for reconverting Protestants was education, the Societas Jesu set up a network of colleges across Europe. In some parts of the Catholic territories the Jesuits had a near monopoly on the education of the political and cultural elites.[18] Combining piety and erudition (*pietas et eruditio*), Jesuit education was informed by the order's distinct spirituality. Students often underwent the spiritual exercises to some degree, albeit mostly in abbreviated form. Nonetheless, the Jesuit spiritual practices permeated many other parts of their education. For instance, the plays in which the most advanced students performed in the context of the rhetoric curriculum advanced the cause of the Catholic faith and staged key tenets of Jesuit spirituality. In fact, their performance was, in a way, a spiritual exercise in its own right, designed to aid the students in absorbing what they had learned.[19] In short, students at Jesuit colleges were always also "inspired" by Ignatian spirituality, including Descartes, who would have been extensively and intensively exposed to Jesuit spiritual and intellectual culture during his eight years at the College of La Flèche, whether or not he actually underwent the Ignatian exercises.[20] Thereby, he would have been acquainted with many of the spiritual techniques of the Societas Jesu, which often had no exclusive claim on them, as they were part of the repertoire of late medieval and early modern piety. Until the end of his life Descartes acknowledged his intellectual debt and expressed gratitude for his Jesuit education.

While the Jesuits were an overwhelming influence shaping the spiritual milieu of early modern Europe, which is true in particular of Descartes, they were not the only ones. A plethora of Catholic reform movements were to be found in France. One of the most important ones, the Congregation of the French Oratory devoted to the reform of Catholic clergy, was spearheaded by Cardinal Pierre de Bérulle.[21] Bérulle was not only a major meteorological force in the spiritual climate of France but also may have intervened more directly in Descartes' spiritual and intellectual evolution.[22] Adrien Baillet tells of a semipublic event at the residence of the Papal Nuncio in 1628, at which Cardinal Bérulle, Marin Mersenne, and other savants were present and at which Descartes had his intellectual "coming out" in offering a refutation of an anti-Aristotelian lecture given by the alchemist Chandoux while reaffirming his critique of Scholasticism. According to Baillet, it was Bérulle who subsequently encouraged Descartes to elaborate his claims about providing a more solid foundation for philosophy.

It is tempting to explain Descartes' move to the Netherlands, and the "beginning of metaphysics" that he wrote there, with Bérulle's advice, but the documentary basis is thin and thus largely speculation. We will probably never know for certain whether Bérulle was Descartes' "director of conscience," as Baillet claims, but we can safely note that Bérulle was part of the young philosopher's intellectual and spiritual milieu and a powerful figure within the wider revival of spirituality in early modern France. Another major force in the same spiritual climate was Saint Francis of Sales. A close acquaintance of Cardinal Bérulle, he underwent the same education as

Descartes at the Jesuit Collège de Clermont in Paris and experienced a dramatic conversion that closely resembled Descartes' and thus may have served as one of its models (discussed in Chapter 1). His *Introduction to the Devout Life*, also known as "Philothea," became an instant success upon publication in 1608, furthering Francis's spiritual project to overcome the separation of cloister and world and facilitate the realization of a devout life in the world, in opposition to the view that monastic life was the only way to operationalize conversion and make it permanent. The *Introduction to the Devout Life* provides the individual self with a set of spiritual exercises to devote one's life to God without retreating from the secular world.

Not surprisingly, Salesian spirituality exerted significant influence across confessions and borders. But for spiritual influences on Descartes, we need not even travel as far afield as Francis of Sales. Marin Mersenne, Descartes' closest interlocutor, was also educated at La Flèche, before studying theology and joining the Minim order.[23] Matt Hettche has argued that Mersenne was a significant influence on Descartes in matters of meditation. In 1623 Mersenne began his career as an author by writing two short spiritual works, one of which, *L'usage de la raison* (The use of reason), aligns itself with Francis of Sales in promoting the complete spiritualization of everyday life. We don't know whether Descartes actually read Mersenne's early spiritual writings, but we can safely assume that he noted the effortless alacrity with which his intellectual companion moved between theology, philosophy, science, and spiritual practice.

Not only the religious sphere saw a surge of spiritual practice. Philosophy, too, experienced a surge or, better, a resurgence of spirituality. The rediscovery of many of the major works of ancient philosophy by European humanists went hand in hand with the revival of its regime of spiritual exercises. Access to the panoply of ancient philosophical schools, from the pre-Socratics through Plato to late Hellenistic philosophers, loosened Aristotle's hold on philosophy, paving the way not only for the emergence of early modern science but also for the respiritualization of philosophy. In particular, the Neostoic revival of Stoicism brought to the fore a textual corpus (works by Tacitus, Seneca, Marcus Aurelius, and Epictetus)—that resonated deeply with the political and cultural situation of the time for having been written under similar political circumstances where monarchies were producing turmoil and uncertainty rather than peace and stability. Neostoicism's seminal role for the political and intellectual culture of early modern Europe is well documented and researched,[24] while little attention has been given to the accompanying revival of spiritual practices.[25] Yet it was the regime of spiritual exercises that made Neostoicism such an effective *remedium* against the political and cultural malaise at the time.

Neostoicism was an essential part of Descartes' intellectual and spiritual milieu. Not only were the Low Countries and France the centers of the Stoic revival in early modern Europe, but Stoic texts were widely used in the educational curriculum of Jesuit colleges.[26] The philologist and philosopher Justus Lipsius, like Descartes a product of Jesuit education, found in Stoic wisdom an alternative to the excessive subtlety and abstraction of contemporary philosophy and fashioned on that basis a compelling reconciliation of Christian faith and Stoic wisdom.[27] He was made famous by *De constantia*, rendered in English as *Two Books of Constancy*,[28] which was no ordinary philosophical treatise but a contribution to the genre of philosophical consolation, a genre well established by the likes of Seneca and Boethius and designed to provide a philosophical answer to loss and suffering. Conceiving constancy as a virtue and habitus in times of war and political and social turmoil, Lipsius delineated a set of exercises to assist coping with the profound moral and cultural crisis gripping and crippling central Europe. Inspired by Lipsius, Guillaume du Vair articulated a distinctly French brand of Neostoicism in *Traité de la constance*, purportedly written in response to the Siege of Paris in 1590.[29] Like *De constantia*, du Vair's book proved enormously popular. And his Neostoicism, like that of Lipsius, was decidedly practical, a philosophy not for school but for a life under threat. A final figure of note in the spiritual milieu around 1600 was Pierre Charron, who reached back beyond Aristotle and Plato to merge ancient philosophy with Christianity, using Pyrrhonian skepticism as a tool to critique secular rationality.[30] Indeed, in his main philosophical work, *De la sagesse* (On wisdom), he developed a practice of doubt that adumbrated Descartes' own. By emptying itself of all dubious knowledge, the self prepares to be illuminated by God. Yet when the self is not guided by divine light, it must follow nature. Thus, for Charron, similar to the Stoics, wisdom consists in living and acting in accordance with nature. In *De la sagesse* he amalgamates Catholicism, philosophical skepticism, and Neostoicism to create his own unique form of spiritual practice.

Just as in the case of the Ignatian exercises, there is compelling evidence that Descartes came into direct contact with Stoicism and its spiritual practices. While the Stoic influences in Descartes' moral theory are no longer subject of debate,[31] their significance for his epistemology has gone largely unnoticed. As I detail in the following chapters, the spiritual and cognitive practices of ancient Stoicism are an important influence for Descartes' practice of doubt and discernment in the *Meditations*. Stoic echoes can also be heard in the maxims comprising the provisional moral code that Descartes designed for himself so as not to be "indecisive in [his] actions" for the period in which his search for truth remained incomplete (CSM I 122; AT VI 22). The second maxim, for instance, draws on the Stoic virtue of constancy by enjoining one to follow "even the most doubtful opinions," once adopted, "with no less constancy than if they had been quite certain" (CSM I 123; AT VI 24). By remaining steadfast in one's opinion and judgment, the self "could free [it]self from all the regrets and remorse which usually trouble the consciences of those weak and faltering spirits who allow themselves to set out on some supposedly good course of action which later, in their inconstancy, they judge to be bad" (CSM I 123; AT VI 25). As it is for Lipsius and du Vair, constancy for Descartes is instrumental for achieving and maintaining tranquility of mind by keeping the self on course and not being thrown to and fro. In Descartes' third maxim the Stoic echoes are even louder. He pledges to himself "to try always to master myself rather than fortune, and change my desires rather than the order of the world."

In general I would become accustomed to believing that nothing lies entirely within our power except our thoughts, so that after doing our best in dealing with matters external to us, whatever we fail to achieve is absolutely impossible so far as we are concerned. This alone, I thought, would be sufficient to prevent me from desiring in future something I could not get, and so to make me content. (CSM I 123–24; AT VI 25)

Descartes limits what is in our power even more radically than the Stoics by confining it essentially to the range of the *cogito*. But the maxim remains a transparent variation on the Stoic injunction to discern continually those things that depend on the self from those that do not and to get invested only in the former. Likewise Stoic is his understanding that recognizing the validity of the maxim and living it are two different things. The "secret of [the Stoic] philosophers," writes Descartes, lay precisely in their regime of spiritual exercises that enabled them "to become accustomed to seeing everything in that light" (CSM I 124; AT VI 26–27).

In his correspondence with Elisabeth of Bohemia and Queen Christina of Sweden Descartes plays spiritual guide to his royal patronesses by slipping into the role of these "ancient philosophers." Responding to Elisabeth's fit of melancholy, he promises relief through writing about "the means which philosophy provides for acquiring that supreme felicity which common souls vainly expect from fortune, but which can be acquired only from ourselves" (CSM III 256; AT IV 252). As a starting point he suggests that they examine together what the ancients had to say on this topic and read and discuss Seneca's *De vita beata*. Elisabeth proves herself an astute and critical interlocutor who pushes Descartes to go far beyond their ancient forebear and to articulate his own concept of the good life.

In the fall of 1647 Queen Christina asks Descartes to "expound to her [his] view of the supreme good understood in the sense of the ancient philosophers" (CSM III 324; AT V 81–82). Descartes, of course, answers that "God is the supreme good" (CSM III 324; AT V 82), but the supreme good that is attainable in this life is "a firm will to do well and the contentment it produces" (CSM III 324; AT IV 82). Descartes' reasoning is again Stoic: "For the goods of the body and of fortune do not depend absolutely on us; and those of the soul can all be reduced to two heads, the one being to know, and the other to will, what is good. But knowledge is often beyond our powers; and so there remains only our will, which is absolutely within our disposal" (CSM III 325; AT V 83). And the good use of the free will "produces the greatest and most solid contentment in life" (CSM III 325; AT V 83). Stoic philosophy was not an abstract theory for Descartes but of relevance to the daily lives of himself and his patronesses.

In this brief historical sketch I have tried to indicate, albeit provisionally, that there were a lively traffic and exchange in the period between different religious movements, as well as between religion and philosophy, when it came to spiritual practices. Not surprisingly, doctrines were often controversial, but spiritual practices were in a way like *adiaphora* (although never labeled as such explicitly), which is to say indifferent doctrinally, allowing them to fly under the radar. While scholars have tried to connect Descartes to a particular brand and tradition of religious meditation and spiritual exercise, it has been largely overlooked that via Neostoicism he also had access to the spiritual exercises of ancient philosophy (for the one notable exception, see the following section). As I have cursorily sketched, the spiritual milieux of France and the Low Countries, in which Descartes dwelled over the course of his adult life, were vibrant and variegated, affording him a rich ensemble of spiritual practices to craft his own "art of turning."

Descartes' Meditative Turn: Method and Argument

Descartes' Meditative Turn is the first book-length study that examines the role and significance of the tradition of meditation and spiritual exercises in Descartes' philosophy. A fair number of scholarly articles have explored the relevance of particular meditative traditions for specific aspects of Descartes' thought, beginning in 1955 when Pierre Mesnard pointed to the Jesuit practice of meditating on devotional emblems as an influence on Descartes; and Martial Gueroult countered that the more seminal tradition of meditation was the one going back to Saint Augustine, particularly his *Soliloquies*.[32] Since then, the debate between these two camps has not abated, one arguing for the importance of the Jesuit tradition and the other for the resurgence of Augustinian spirituality in early modern France as the more decisive influence on Descartes. The champions of Jesuit influence point to Descartes' exposure to the society's spiritual practices at the College of La Flèche, arguing that his thought more generally and the *Meditations* in particular were informed by Ignatius's *Spiritual Exercises*.[33] Some members of that camp have been more precise about the textual lineage in noting that students at La Flèche would probably not have undergone the full set of Ignatian exercises, let alone known the text of the *Spiritual Exercises*, which was reserved for the spiritual director. Students instead did the exercises described in the *Manuale Sodalitatis* of François Véron,[34] Descartes' professor of philosophy. Despite this qualification, they claim Descartes firmly for camp Ignatius. The other camp locates Descartes in the resurgence of Augustinian spirituality in early modern France and beyond.[35] Camp Augustine has several factions arguing for more concrete and specific influences such as Mersenne's, who was a monk of the Minim order,[36] or for the relevance of Victorine spirituality and the continued importance of Neoplatonism for the tradition of meditation,[37] while agreeing that the Augustinian tradition of meditation is more decisive than Jesuit influences for Descartes' practice of thought.³⁸ A third group of articles has argued in a more general way for relevance of the medieval meditative tradition for the *Meditations* by highlighting certain passages or features.³⁹

Despite their indisputable merits, all of these studies fall short in important ways. First, their scope is necessarily limited, as they generally focus on one or several particular spiritual practices and select passages of the *Meditations*. None develop a comprehensive methodological and hermeneutical framework that theorizes metaphysical or philosophical thinking as meditating and accounts for the specificity of this cognitive practice. Second, none of them take into account the importance of the philosophical tradition of spiritual exercises for Descartes' thought. The only exception in regard to the last issue is Matthew Jones's *Good Life in the Scientific Revolution*,⁴⁰ which devotes two chapters to the relevance of the spiritual exercises of ancient philosophy for Descartes' science (the rest of the book examines Pascal and Leibniz). He correctly claims that Descartes put forward a "therapeutic model of philosophy" that pursues the cultivation of the self and the realization of a good and long life.⁴¹ However, Jones foregrounds Descartes' natural philosophy and science, focusing primarily on the *Rules for the Direction of the Mind* and the *Discourse on the Method*. While he shows convincingly that Descartes conceived mathematics as a form of cognitive exercise, he does not consider the *Meditations* and the importance of the religious tradition of spiritual exercise and meditation.⁴² What emerges is the well-worn scientific and secular Descartes advanced by the brunt of scholarship in the last decades. Third and last, the identified similarities between the invoked meditative tradition and Descartes' thought are frequently superficial, selective, or arbitrary, particularly given that Descartes suffered from severe "anxiety of influence" and deliberately covered his tracks.⁴³

However, the fact that Descartes concealed his intellectual models does not mean that there were none or that the relationship was superficial. Quite the contrary, the discursive work he invested in masking the true lines of influence indicates their importance, going even as far as disavowing possible models when his correspondents and interlocutors called him on it.⁴⁴ A prime example is the feigned ignorance and irritation he displayed when Mersenne and Colvius drew his attention to Augustine's version of the *cogito* in *De civitate Dei* (11.26).⁴⁵ In his letter to Colvius he writes that he looked up the passage in the "library of his town [Leyden] to read it," even though Mersenne had mentioned it to him two years earlier, insinuating that he was only now learning of this parallel. Furthermore, he misrepresents Augustine's arguments to make the differences between them appear more significant. Given his training in La Flèche it seems not very credible that he would not have become acquainted with at least one of the passages in which Augustine articulates his version of the *cogito*.[46] Clearly, as he felt compelled to feign ignorance, there was much at stake here for Descartes. Yet this wasn't just a psychological block. Nor was it motivated by simple political calculation. It was necessitated by the logic and economy of his program of reforming knowledge. Self-sufficiency and autonomy made up the *conditio sine qua non* of his philosophical project. The *cogito* for Descartes isn't true because it has Augustine's authority to vouch for it but because it is self-evident; and this self-evidence is the effect of each and every mind experiencing, thinking it for itself. In fact, the *cogito* is true only when and as long as an individual mind thinks it. And meditation is the genre best suited to induce in its reader the self-evidence of the *cogito*: put simply, to bring readers to think the *cogito* for themselves.

Because the obvious allegiance to and emulation of a particular model would have undercut the self-reliance and autonomy crucial to his reform, Descartes avoided patently following a single model of spiritual exercises in his *Meditations*. Rather, he picked and chose from the whole long and rich tradition and concealed specific and concrete inspirations. Attempts of previous scholarship to identify a dominant model to the exclusion of others are thus not only doomed to failure but also run counter to Descartes' self-proclaimed intellectual project. Rather than pinpoint a single brand of spiritual exercises and meditation, each of the following chapters traces the history of one or more specific spiritual exercises that Descartes adapts to empower his readers to enact the meditative turn and to come to their own insight. Thus, *Descartes' Meditative Turn* presents an intellectual history of Descartes' meditative practice that is as sensitive to semantic shifts as it is to the emergence of new philosophical ideas.

Taking seriously that Descartes conceives thinking as meditating foregrounds its pragmatic dimension, prompting a series of questions about the nature of thinking. First and foremost, we need to ask what it means that Descartes—at the dawn of the modern age—conceives of thinking as a practice. Put differently, what does it mean to understand thinking as an activity, a doing that can be practiced, exercised, rehearsed, trained, resulting in its alteration and improvement? How does it change our conception of thinking when we foreground its practice and performance rather than its content and correctness? While Pierre Hadot's and Michel Foucault's work on the ancient tradition of spiritual exercises does provide guidance in answering these questions, it is Mary Carruthers's work on medieval monastic meditation that has gone furthest in conceptualizing meditative thought as a practice. In her seminal study *The Craft of Thought* she defines meditation as a "craft of thinking," more specifically the "craft of making thoughts about God."[47] In monastic meditation the crucial issue is not so much the mimetic quality and truth content of thoughts and images but "their cognitive utility ... by means of which the human mind can build its compositions, whether these be thoughts or prayers."[48] We tend to conceive of thinking, in part as a result of Descartes' notion of ideas as mental "images" (*imagines*), as representing the world, our emotions and inner states, or our cognitive operations (willing, judging, etc.), but not as a doing, as an activity. Thereby, we overlook how thoughts and ideas are made; how they are wielded; the effects of thinking on our minds and selves; how thinking transforms itself in the process of thinking.[49] But as I will demonstrate, Descartes had a lifelong preoccupation with such questions and, more generally, the pragmatic dimension of thought, evidenced in the articulation of his method and culminating in his adoption of meditating for the metaphysical foundation of his philosophy.

Focusing on meditative thinking as a practice has significant implications for approaching Descartes' philosophizing. It shifts the attention from the content to the form or shape of thought, raising two sets of questions concerning how ideas represent rather than what they represent. The first set pertains to how Descartes imagines the operation, the form, and the mediality of thought. Throughout the study I therefore pay close attention to how Descartes conceives and describes the operation of meditative thought with what I term "conceptual metaphorics": metaphors that illustrate but also shape his thinking about thinking.[50] The second set of questions concerns the textual form that Descartes' meditative thinking takes in the process of its articulation and communication. Even though the *Meditations* is conceived as an interior discourse, each is articulated and communicated in the form of a written and printed text. The inescapable textuality of Descartes' thought, thus, raises twin questions: How does thinking take shape in Descartes' texts? And, in turn, how does textuality shape (his) thought? Answering these questions calls for careful examination of the textual dimension of the practice and genre of meditation. In contrast to most modern scholars of Descartes, who tend to focus on the propositional and argumentative content of a philosophical text and to neglect its other features, I closely attend to Descartes' lexical choices, the grammatical structures of his text, its rhetorical features, its narrative organization, and its generic form. Thus, *Descartes' Meditative Turn* follows a two-pronged approach. On the one hand, it carefully examines the language and rhetorical style with which the *Meditations* stages thinking, and on the other, it situates Descartes' philosophy within the tradition of spiritual exercises and meditation. Thus, the individual chapters toggle between close readings of Descartes' writings and synchronic and diachronic reconstructions of various meditative practices.

While the focus of this study is the *Meditations* (1641), it draws its textual evidence from Descartes' entire oeuvre, from his earliest notebooks and the unpublished *Rules on the Direction of the Mind* through the *Discourse on the Method* (1637) and his letters all the way to the *Principles of Philosophy* (1644) and his final philosophical treatise, the *Passions of the Soul* (1649). After the first two chapters lay the groundwork by examining Descartes' conversion and the Cartesian art of turning, the remaining four chapters trace the reader's path of discovery of the self and God, starting with their turn away from the outside world and culminating in their contemplation of God in an ecstatic vision at the end of the Third Meditation. Thus, *Descartes' Meditative Turn* follows the meditative journey that the *Meditations* stages.

Following a suggestion by Anthony Grafton, the first chapter interprets the famous three dreams that came to Descartes in his stove-heated room during his travels through southwestern Germany as a classical conversion experience, modeled on famous forebears from Paul to Augustine to Ignatius. Close textual analysis of the summary of Descartes' account by his first autobiographer, Adrienne Baillet, identifies the salient features of his conversive turn and the various components of his discovery of the "foundations of a marvelous science." Elements from Descartes' conversion that inform Cartesian method, and are later reenacted by the *Meditations*, include the practice of universal doubt, the distinction of dreaming and waking, the discernment of good and evil spirits as the source of ideas, the problem of intellectual orientation, an early version of the *cogito*, and illumination by natural light. My reading of Descartes' three dreams during the fateful night of November 10, 1619, as a conversion lays the groundwork for reconceptualizing his philosophy as an "art of turning," which makes his discovery of "foundations of a marvelous science" replicable and communicable to others.

The second chapter traces Descartes' lifelong preoccupation with the pragmatic dimension of thinking, that is, thinking as a cognitive activity that—while innate—can be practiced, improved, and refined. I argue that Descartes' reform of knowledge is more about the how than the that of thinking and knowing—much like Socrates, who notes that the "art of turning" is not about imparting knowledge but using the mind in such a way that it is turned in the right direction to find truth. Commonly, this dimension of Cartesian thought is linked to the widespread attempts among late medieval and early modern natural philosophers to articulate a universal method. This chapter demonstrates that the tradition of spiritual and mental exercises from antiquity to early modernity is equally important to the Cartesian art of turning. Drawing on texts from Epictetus and Seneca, through Augustine and John Cassian, to Jean Gerson and Ignatius, the chapter asks what it means when thinking is understood as a practice or craft that needs to be exercised and rehearsed in order to operate optimally. From this perspective, a trajectory emerges in Descartes' oeuvre that is somewhat different from that in traditional accounts. Beginning with his early unfinished and unpublished *Rules for the Direction of the Mind*, Descartes displays a keen interest not only in the pragmatic aspect of thinking but, just as important, in the communication of clear and certain ideas or, to put it more technically, their generic packaging. The adoption of the meditative form for his *opus magnum* thus addresses the problem not only of how to experience incontrovertible self-evidence but also how to communicate it to his readers.

Chapter 3 brings to fruition the spadework of the first two chapters by showing how meditational practices are integral to the initial turn away from the world and toward the self, leading to the first act of foundation staged and effected by the *Meditations*, the discovery of the *cogito*. Taking as its starting point the text's frequent invocations of painting as a model of ideation, it demonstrates that the structure and operation of the imagination in Ignatius's *Spiritual Exercises* inform what I call Descartes' "meditative matrix," a model of the production of mental images or ideas that will prove intrinsically self-reflexive. In a second step, it shows that Descartes' practice of doubt is modeled on a spiritual exercise going back to ancient Stoicism, known as the "use of appearances" (*chresis phantasion*) and popularized by Ignatius as the "discernment of spirits," which subjects all mental representations to systematic testing. Already the Ignatian discernment of spirits lacks a reliable criterion to ascertain their provenance and veracity so that it is but a small step for Descartes, the student of the Jesuit College of La Flèche, to reject all mental representations as possible projections of a malicious demon and, thus, false. In a final step, I demonstrate how the evacuated meditative matrix serves as the substrate for the Cartesian *cogito*. What remains when all thoughts and images generated by the meditative matrix have become profoundly problematic are the positions of projector and spectator or, more generally, the process of representation itself, pure evidence.

The fourth chapter centers on a passage in the Second Meditation that has long frustrated philosophers: the meditation on a piece of wax, which apparently contributes little to Descartes' philosophical argument. In one of his Replies Descartes emphasizes that the wax meditation has the function of making evident the "nature"—not only the existence—of the mind as a thinking thing. Since Descartes' meditator tells the reader very little about the "nature of the mind," the wax meditation must be interpreted as a demonstration by doing. Not coincidentally, the activity in question is meditating in the generic form of an occasional meditation on the vanity of things. The *inspectio mentis* that Descartes' meditator is performing here is conditioned not only by the generic form but also by the cultural and historical semantics of the wax as a metaphor of the mind. By meditating on a seemingly random piece of wax, the meditator addresses and counters the dilemma of the constitutive invisibility of the mediality of the mind whose nature can be apprehended only in its forms, its ideas. Since the mediality of the mind can be cognized only indirectly, Descartes' meditator takes an allegorical detour via the material medium and metaphor of wax. By pyrotechnically de- and unforming it and, thus, stripping away all its qualities, Descartes' long meditative gaze reveals the mere mediality of the wax and, indirectly, the mind.

Chapter 5 turns to the second part of Descartes' stated project, the demonstration of the existence of God, and takes as its point of departure the puzzling fact that the *Meditations* contains no less than three separate and different proofs of God. Given that the proof of a benevolent and truthful God is of absolute epistemological importance, the multiplication of proofs seems counterproductive, undermining rather than enhancing the certainty of the insight. A closer look reveals that this multiplication is conditioned by a pragmatic problem: the problem of the mind's limited attention span. As Descartes argues in the *Regulae*, deductions or logical proofs are dependent on the—potentially faulty—memory, if they contain too many individual steps to be kept present to the mental eye. Careful analysis of the wording of the *Meditations* reveals for the first time Descartes' deliberate and systematic deployment of different modes of attention, which are informed by various spiritual exercises designed to improve and extend the mind's attention span. I argue that attention is essential to the Cartesian art of turning, as it has the function of keeping the mind steadily on track during its meditative journey inward. In the tradition of Stoic *prosochē*, attention keeps Descartes' meditator from flagging in their doubt of all mental representations. Similarly, the *cogito* is clear and certain only as long as the mind attends to its act of thinking. Finally, discovering the idea of God within the mind and thus recognizing his existence depends on turning the "whole attention to him" (CSM II 38; AT VII 54). Thus, this chapter demonstrates that the cultivation of the mind that Descartes' philosophy champions and endeavors to bring about consists essentially in attending to itself and its innate ideas in the natural light of reason.

Chapter 6 focuses on the final brief passage of the Third Meditation, in which Descartes' meditator engages in the contemplation of God. While scholars have by and large ignored this passage, as it adds nothing to the philosophical argument of the *Meditations*, my reading reveals it to be the culmination and pivot of Descartes' meditative turn. By contextualizing Descartes' *contemplatio Dei* within the meditative practice of ancient philosophy and the Christian West, the chapter demonstrates that it forms the telos of the spiritual journey commonly known as "meditative ascent." Therefore, the movement of Descartes' text echoes the tripartite structure of classical devotional meditation: *cogitatio—meditatio—contemplatio*. Descartes' first three meditations effect the purgation and illumination necessary to achieving the contemplative vision of God (at the almost exact center of the text as a whole). What Descartes' meditator sees is not God in his essence (as in a classical beatific vision) but the divine light in the form of the *lumen naturale* (natural light) that dwells in every human mind. With the vision of the natural light, the medium of clear and distinct cognition, Descartes' meditator completes the reenactment of the evidentiary experience of their conversion. For the natural light is the descendant of the *scintilla animae* (spark of the soul) that the young Descartes beheld in his second dream on the night of November 10, 1619. Thus, this final chapter harks back to the first chapter and thus demonstrates that Descartes draws on the practice of meditation to replicate and communicate the insights won during his conversion.

By tracing how readers are guided to enact Descartes' meditative turn and invited to discover the "foundations of a marvelous science" for themselves, this study is concerned with the role meditation plays in the metaphysical foundation of Cartesian philosophy. By focusing on the singularity of this moment and its subsequent operationalization across the rest of Descartes' philosophy, it attends to what Descartes wrote in a letter to his royal patron Princess Elisabeth of Bohemia:

I believe that it is very necessary to have properly understood, once in a lifetime, the principles of metaphysics, since they are what gives us the knowledge of God and our soul. But I think also that it would be very harmful to occupy one's intellect frequently in meditating upon them, since this would impede it from devoting itself to the functions of the imagination and the senses. I think the best thing is to content oneself with keeping in one's memory and one's belief the conclusions which one has once drawn from them, and then employ the rest of one's study time in thoughts in which the intellect co-operates with the imagination and the senses. (CSM III 228; AT III 695)

1

Founding First Philosophies: Descartes' Conversion

Conversion between Philosophy and Religion

Founders of religious movements or philosophical schools from Plato and Paul to Luther and Ignatius have grounded their new ways of thinking in a conversion, and Descartes, the founder of modern rationalism and science, was no exception. Anthony Grafton has shown that in the early modern "world of learned practice, conversion . . . played a vital role, offering a new way of representing the path to method and knowledge,"[1] and he urges us to take seriously the suggestion of Meric Casaubon, the keen critic of religious enthusiasm, that "the new philosophical sect that Descartes created owed much of its ideological force and unity to the technologies of conversion that he ingeniously secularized and applied to systems of ideas."[2] I want to do exactly that in this chapter by examining in detail the "machinery" of Descartes' conversion in pursuit of a better understanding of the role it played in the institution and operation of his new way of philosophizing. This analysis of the scene of Descartes' conversion will lay the groundwork for the argument in subsequent chapters that much of his thought can be understood as an operationalization of the evidentiary experience of conversion. For the role of conversion in the founding of new movements and schools is not restricted to the beginning but lives on, be it in followers emulating the founder's pious life or a body of philosophical thought elaborating on the original insight.

The first fact any examination of Descartes' conversion has to confront is its split and doubled representation, for he gave two very different accounts of the events of that momentous night from the tenth to the eleventh of November 1619, which resulted in his election of a life in the pursuit of truth. The rather terse account given in the *Discourse of the Method* is the most well-known and was written years after the event. Having "spent some years pursuing... studies in the book of the world and trying to gain some experience," he writes, he "resolved one day to undertake studies within myself too and to use all the powers of my mind in choosing the paths I should follow" (CSM I 116; AT VI 11). Setting the scene, he continues,

I was in Germany, where I had been called by the wars that are not yet ended there. While I was returning to the army from the coronation of the Emperor, the onset of winter detained me in quarters where, finding no conversation to divert me and fortunately having no cares or passions to trouble me, I stayed all day shut up alone in a stove-heated room, where I was completely free to converse with myself about my own thoughts. (CSM I 116; AT VI 11)

Due to this unexpected liberation Descartes is able to enter into a conversation with himself, in the course of which he resolves to "reform" these very thoughts he is having "and construct them upon a foundation which is all my own." The task famously requires one "to abandon all the opinions one has hitherto accepted" and, in his case, to follow only "the method I had prescribed for myself" (CSM I 118; AT VI 15).

This description from the hindsight of the *Discourse of the Method* conforms closely to a classical account of a philosophical conversion, in which thoughts are turned inward on the self, away from the world of the senses. Any student of ancient philosophy—and so every learned person of the time—would have readily recognized Descartes' move, along with the building and pathfinding metaphors he uses to convey it. Particularly noteworthy about this account are the serene atmospherics of a primarily intellectual affair in which the self enters into a relaxed conversation with itself. Concomitantly, Descartes portrays his conversion not as much a radical break with his past but as the natural outcome of his earlier doubts about traditional learning in committing to a life in the service of "cultivating my reason and advancing as far as I could in the knowledge of truth" (CSM I 124; AT VI 27). His conversion is thus more a conscious decision than an event befalling him.[3]

In a notebook Descartes kept at the time, aptly titled *Olympica*, he paints a very different picture of this momentous experience. This account comes down to us in a six-page paraphrase by his biographer Adrien Baillet, who still had access to the now-lost notebook. Even more than in the *Discourse of the Method*, Descartes describes the scene as one of foundation, but this time in the guise of a classical religious conversion, which is to say, a profound and dramatic crisis and its (partial) resolution through divine intervention. Having discovered, at the end of the whole day spent in deep thought, the "foundations of a marvelous science" (*mirabilis scientiae fundamenta*), Descartes is sent into transports of enthusiasm, leaving his overheated imagination susceptible to divine visitations. In the style of so many Judeo-Christian call narratives,[4] Descartes experiences "three consecutive dreams in the same night," which, Baillet reports, "he imagined could have come only from on high."[5] And as in so many instances in the Old and New Testaments, the dreams' divine origin is confirmed by a prior announcement:[6] "The Spirit who had aroused in him the enthusiasm with which he had felt his brain on fire for the past several days had predicted these dreams before he had gone to bed" (Cole 39; AT X 186). Thus, it makes perfect sense that Baillet uses the word *songes* to denote Descartes' dreams, as it is the usual French translation for *somnium*, the technical term for prophetic dreams Macrobius uses in his *Commentary on Scipio's Dream*.[7]

Not only are the dreams sent "from on high," but they also stage encounters with transcendent powers, good as well as evil. In the first dream, Descartes' oneiric self is tempted by evil spirits and in the second is descended on by the spirit of truth. These nightly visions and visitations culminate in the third dream, in which Descartes was persuaded "that it was the Spirit of Truth that had wanted to open unto him the treasures of all the sciences" (Cole 37; AT X 184–85). In the face of such busy spiritual traffic it is only logical that Descartes would actively and repeatedly seek divine assistance. After the first dream he prays to God to "protect him from the evil effects of his dream" (Cole 34; AT X 182), and at the end of the experience he similarly "had recourse in prayer to God, so that He might make known His will to him, enlighten him, and guide him in the search for truth" (Cole 39; AT X 186). Not surprisingly, given the Jesuits' privileged relation to the Holy Virgin, Descartes turns next to the "Blessed Mother of God," "laying before her his affair, which he considered the most important in his life" (Cole 39; AT X 186), and even raising the stakes "to interest the Blessed

Mother of God in a more pressing way" (Cole 39; AT X 186) by vowing to make a pilgrimage on foot to the "Notre Dame of Loretto," a vow he fulfills several years later during a journey to Italy.

As the Santa Casa di Loreto was a site officially patronized by the Society of Jesus,[8] Descartes' vow, like the other elements in the *Olympica* account, is utterly conventional. The spiritual techniques employed in his interpretations of the dreams he knew from his time at La Flèche, where he encountered the spiritual exercises of Ignatius of Loyola.[9] And in the climactic third dream, his oneiric self engages in an aleatory opening of a book clearly patterned on Augustine's conversion. This incomplete list of religious elements to which Descartes had recourse will be filled out in the rest of this chapter, but it is enough to show that the conversion narrated in Descartes' early notebook differs radically from the one hinted at in the *Discourse of the Method*. Whereas in the latter the self deliberately breaks with the past in favor of turning inward, in the former divine revelations come to the self in the form of dreams and visions such that Descartes concludes "that his human mind had nothing to do with them" (Cole 39; AT X 186). Thus, in purging all religious elements from his revised account in the *Discourse of the Method*, Descartes is deliberately disavowing them and concomitantly styling his conversion as a philosophical event.[10]

Such textual dissimulation must have been what Descartes meant when he resolved in the first aphorism of another section of the same early notebook, titled *Praeambula*, to go forth into the world masked.[11] At the same time, this "duplicity" in regard to his conversion is historically grounded, since it was from the start as much a philosophical phenomenon as it was a religious one. Indeed, going back to Plato's allegory of the cave in Book Seven of the *Republic*, which is conceived as an "image of our nature in its education and its want of education" (514a),[12] education has been understood as a turning of the soul around from the shadows to the source of light. It is in this sense that Werner Jaeger concludes that "the essence of philosophical education is 'conversion.'"[13] Not only the *paideia* allegorized by Plato starts with a conversion; many of the biographies narrated by Diogenes Laertius begin with a momentous experience through which the future philosopher breaks with his old life and turns toward philosophy. For Plato philosophy as such is "an art of this turning around" (*technē tes periagogeis*; *Republic* 518d), and as Michel Foucault has demonstrated in his lectures on the *Hermeneutics of the Subject*, Hellenistic and Roman philosophy has followed his lead.[14] In claiming to be the *vera philosophia*, Christianity inherited from ancient philosophy its spiritual practices,[15] including its technologies of conversion. And, indeed, Christianity's claim to be a religion of universal truth and appeal hinges on its conversive force, which with the increasing Christianization of Europe was directed inward in the founding of monastic orders and religious reform movements in which conversion is figured as an intensification of piety. And as the examples of Luther, Ignatius, and many others indicate, conversion was hardly a thing of the distant past in early modern Europe.

Despite important differences between philosophical and religious conversions, the traffic between them was busy in both directions. In fact, for almost every criteria used to define a conversion as either philosophical or religious, counterexamples can be found. For instance, Augustine's long process of conversion culminating with the opening of a passage from Paul's Letter to the Romans began with a momentous encounter with Cicero's *Hortensius*, a protreptic work that turned him toward philosophy and the pursuit of wisdom (*Confessions* 3.4.7–8).[16] Conversely, the calling that prompted many philosophers of antiquity to devote their life to wisdom often came from a divine source. The greatest example, of course, is Socrates, who, in one telling, was directed by an oracular command from the Delphic priestess Pythia (in the famous "Know thyself!") to undertake a life in search of self-knowledge.[17] Grafton shows in the example of Athanasius Kircher that conversion's ambidexterity, in appearing to vacillate between philosophy and religion while belonging exclusively to neither, was alive and well in the early modern Republic of Letters. The great Jesuit polymath believed he was given his scholarly vocation directly by God, who he believed had placed a copy of Herwart von Hohenburg's *Thesaurus hieroglyphicus* in his path.[18] In this light, the question becomes all the more imperative to know what precisely is at stake for Descartes when he later decides to mask his conversion as a purely intellectual and philosophical event. The answer, of course, goes to the very foundation of Descartes' philosophy, because Conversion with a capital *C*, in its religious as well as its philosophical form, is foundational. In that respect the two accounts given by Descartes concur. In the later narrative he accomplishes his "reform" of thought by constructing "a foundation all his own." In the *Olympica* version the dreams were sent to him "from on high" to authenticate "the discovery of the foundations of a wonderful science" he had made earlier that day.

Conversion is capable of playing this foundational role because of its evidentiary quality. The acts of thought, mental images, movements of the will, and emotions of which conversion is made up are self-validating. They appear to the subject as absolutely self-evident. In other words, conversion is as much a true experience as an experience of truth. Self-validating, it isn't grounded in other thoughts or experiences but, to the contrary, grounds them. One could call this the epistemological dimension of conversion: it climaxes in a moment of insight of absolute self-evidence. Even in Descartes' two most important models, the conversions of Augustine and Ignatius, one can find moments in which this epistemological dimension is foregrounded. For Ignatius at the banks of the Cardoner River, "the eyes of his understanding began to be opened: not that he saw some vision, but understanding and knowing many things, spiritual things just as much as matters of faith and learning, and this with an enlightenment so strong that all things seemed new to him."[19] What makes this illumination so remarkable in Ignatius's eyes is not its content. In fact, he is unable to specify "the particular things he understood then." It is the "great clarity" that came with the opening of the "eyes of his understanding" that will be with him for the rest of his life, imparting certainty to all his thoughts and actions. This does not mean, of course, that Ignatius will be free of doubts in his life but rather that the illumination at the banks of the river provided him with a standard of evidence, an experience of truth that became the reference point for future thought and action. Similarly, Augustine's conversion of the will in Book Eight of the *Confessions* is preceded by the conversion of the intellect in Book Seven, culminating in several beatific visions that, although ultimately unstable, are self-validating: "The person who knows the truth knows it, and he who knows it knows eternity" (*Confessions* 7.10.16).

Simultaneously and paradoxically, conversion is for all three thinkers an experience of truth that is to a certain extent incomprehensible. On the one hand, it is characterized by complete lucidity, and on the other, it remains inexplicable and opaque. The most dramatic example is surely Paul's conversion, portrayed in the first two accounts in the Acts of the Apostles as a traumatic experience—in that it is not understood in the moment when it happens.[20] Paul literally loses his senses of sight and hearing, as reported variously in the three accounts, and only with their restoration does understanding return. This is perhaps to be expected because as a symptom and effect of a psychological and epistemological crisis, conversion marks a breakdown of human reason. Precisely because the self is lost, it is at a loss to explain how this sudden certainty comes about. In fact, conversion's foundational nature is predicated on the fact that the truth experienced cannot be explained and, thus, grounded by recourse to another experience of truth.[21] Conversion, in not being part of the causal continuum of a self's thoughts or actions, is also beyond the self's control. It is not a solely immanent process and cannot be brought about willingly and deliberately. It happens to the self whether the self wants it or not. Theologically speaking, religious conversion is effected by divine grace and thus experienced as a call from beyond. For Augustine, the *tolle, lege* (pick up and read) literally comes "from a nearby house" outside the garden in which the drama of his conversion takes place (*Confessions* 8.12.29).[22] Similarly, Ignatius turns toward the divine only when he is able to distinguish which thoughts are his own and which are sent by God (or the devil)—when, in other words, he recognizes the divine call as a divine call and not as one of his own thoughts.

What distinguishes Descartes' two accounts is this question of conversion's immanence or transcendence, necessity or contingency. The question arises as a symptom of the structural dilemma haunting all acts of foundation.[23] If systems of culture and thought could control the conditions of their foundations, they would already be operating prior to their founding and thus presuppose what is being brought about. Whatever happened before the system's inception is the "blind spot" of its self-representation because it can describe itself only from within and so to an extent must remain incomprehensible—thus, the "tricks" surrounding the inception of new systems that cannot be fully rationalized immanently.

For systems that invoke a transcendent power, the question is not particularly problematical. Since the power driving toward the new system is not part of it, it can operate before the system's inception. And theological speculation often ascribes the incomprehensibility of the origin to God's—by definition—incomprehensible nature. Theological speculation thus enjoys a double advantage. On the one hand, the incomprehensibility of both creator and creation reinforce each other reciprocally. On the other hand, the incomprehensibility of the origin is assigned to the beginning of time so that any possible confusion is contained and the smooth evolution and operation of the system ensured. For systems with no resort to a transcendent power to account for their foundation, things are more difficult. They inevitably get caught up in systemic and representational paradoxes and contradictions and therefore spend an extraordinary amount of energy in concealing their constitutive openness. Either they cannot account for their beginnings or they have to presuppose what they seek to establish and thus operate on both sides of the *caesura*.

Conversion, as a figure and operation of foundation, partially "addresses" this dilemma by acknowledging both sides and establishing a functional relation between them. After all, conversion represents a special case in being a beginning that is not absolute. It is a beginning in the middle, in particular, as conversions usually happen later in life. Rarely do children undergo a conversion (because they have not been sufficiently "perverted" yet). While saints such as Antony and Benedict, the forefathers of medieval monasticism, showed their saintliness already during childhood, they underwent their decisive turn toward God only when they had entered adulthood. Conversions, rather than starts, are restarts by which a program of thought and/or action is reloaded. For this reason the new self cannot be cut off completely from its older version by conversion, and the converted self ignores its old habits of thought and action only at the peril of relapsing, of being perverted again. To avoid falling back, conversion needs not only to acknowledge its former state but to continually renew the turn toward its new self. A conversion doesn't happen once and for all. It becomes permanent only by being made permanent, by being continually repeated and operationalized. Thus, conversion functions much like the *creatio continua* Descartes postulated in the Third Meditation in which God's creative hand does not rest after completing the world and everything in it, because it would fall back into nothingness if he did not re-create it in every moment (CSM II 33; AT VII 49). Similarly, conversion must be continually renewed and operationalized so that the self can stay "turned."

Even though conversion to a certain extent operates on both sides of the break, the question of who or what initiates the reloading remains open and imperative. Otherwise, it appears unmotivated or contingent. Plato's allegory of the cave, for instance, remains entirely silent on the circumstances of self's liberation from its bonds. In numerous ancient anecdotes philosophers are prompted by a shipwreck to adapt to a new mode of life and thought, so conversion comes about unpredictably and as contingently as the behavior of the element they have just survived. Accounts of religious conversions solve the problem by ascribing conversion's authorship to God, but only seemingly, since God's hand is experienced as miraculous and unfathomable. Contingency and predestination are the two alternatives for motivating conversion, with human agency as the *tertium non datur*.

We should be in a better position now to understand what was at stake for Descartes in portraying his conversion as a religious or philosophical, transcendent or immanent event. For the "reloading" of philosophy that Descartes was attempting to launch, the question of how and by whom it is initiated is also the question of religious modes of thought and practice in the foundation of modern philosophy and science. After all, Descartes meant the *Meditations* to ground his physics and thus any further scientific inquiry into the world. It is the question whether modern philosophy and science can found themselves autonomously. Answering this question will also help us account for the mode of thought the *Meditations* enacts and presents and their ambiguous generic belonging between religion and philosophy. Finally, it is also the question about the relation of the *Discourse of the Method* and the *Meditations*, which, after all, cover much of the same argumentative ground but in very different ways. This chapter cannot answer all these questions, but it can take a first step by looking at the scene of foundation of Descartes' reform of philosophy. We need to examine the conversion Descartes experienced during that fateful night of November 10, 1619, to begin to understand how this evidentiary experience is continually re-created in and by his later thought. The following close reading of the account of the *Olympica*, thus, has a twofold aim:[24] I examine the religious traditions available to Descartes for the construction of his conversion and try to understand which role his "technology of conversion" had for the mechanism of foundation.

Lost in Thought

Descartes' three dreams come to him at a critical juncture in his project to reform his thought, when he undertakes to purge his mind of all thoughts and images to make way for new ones. "But very soon he noticed that even destruction, when it is a matter of a man ridding himself of his prejudices, is not as easy as burning down one's house." Already aware of the need to renounce old ways of thinking,

> he had nevertheless to suffer as if it were a matter of stripping himself of himself. He believed that he had come to the end. And, in truth, it was enough that his imagination presented his mind to himself entirely naked, to make him believe that he had really stripped it bare. Nothing was left but the love for Truth, the pursuit of which was to be his sole occupation of the rest of his life. (Cole 32; AT X 180)

The dreams come to him while he is in transit, not only physically exploring the "book of the world" but also mentally. As in Christianity's most seminal conversion, of Saul on the road to Damascus, Descartes' happens while he is under way, betwixt and between in the liminal space of travel. Similar to Ignatius, Descartes is an "errant knight,"[25] whose life is changed when the military campaign that had taken him to southwest Germany is suspended for the winter and he finds himself unexpectedly immobilized. Ignatius, confined to bed after his legs had been shattered by a cannonball during the siege of Pamplona, was likewise physically immobilized when the divine call reached him.

After "stripping himself of himself" Descartes is left only with his naked self,[26] which, in being emptied of all thoughts, seems to anticipate the *cogito*. But the self is not altogether empty because in the mental vacuum that results there remains a "love for Truth," a yearning and intuition born from the mind's emptiness. As a vacuum will inevitably be filled, the emptied mind attracts new thoughts and images. Awake, Descartes' conscious self is still in control, examining every new thought regarding its truth value. But asleep, once the discipline is relaxed, the mind becomes receptive to visitations and visions. That it is the imagination that presented Descartes' mind to himself "entirely naked" makes sense in terms of the pivotal role this mental faculty played for the young Descartes.[27] The Ignatian exercises that he was likely exposed to as a student at the Jesuit College of La Flèche were designed to harness the exercitant's imagination in the service of devotion, training the exercitant in a poetics of the imagination through which their mind is emptied out and systematically refilled with mental images drawn from the Gospel narratives—twin operations that strikingly resemble practice described by Descartes. No wonder then that the imagination is for Descartes a medium not only for the production of mental images but also for the reception of divine visions.[28] Engaged in intense intellectual work,

Founding First Philosophies 37

Descartes, when he is having his *visions*, is thinking with/in images, or, put differently, by evoking these tropes of rhetorical and meditative composition he figures philosophical system building as a *poesis* of laying foundations.[29] The search for truth becomes a search for the ways to find truth, the pursuit of which, in turn, "agitated his mind violently" so that he falls "into a sort of enthusiasm," which in combination with the mental vacuum puts "him in the condition to receive the impressions of dreams and visions" (Cole 33; AT X 181).

The first dream stages and works through the errancy that Descartes was practicing in real life, both physically in his traveling and intellectually in his pursuit of truth. In Baillet's summary, the plot goes as follows:

> After he fell asleep, his imagination felt itself struck by the representation of some ghosts who presented themselves to him and who so frightened him that, thinking that he was walking down the streets, he had to lean to his left side in order to be able to reach the place where he wanted to go, because he felt a great weakness on his right side, so that he could not hold himself upright. Because he was ashamed to walk in this way, he tried to straighten up, but he was buffeted by gusts that carried him off in a sort of whirlwind that spun him around three or four times on his left foot. Even this was not what alarmed him. His difficulty in dragging himself along meant that he thought he would fall at each step until, noticing a school [*un collège*] open along his way he entered in search of a refuge and remedy for his trouble. He tried to reach the school church, where his first thought was to say his prayers. However, having noticed that he had passed an acquaintance without greeting him, he wanted to retrace his steps to pay his respects, and he was thrust back by the wind that was blowing against the church. . . . What surprised him more was to see that those who clustered around that person in order to talk with him were upright and steady on their feet, although he was still bent over and unsteady on the same ground. Having almost knocked him down many times, the wind had greatly abated. (Cole 33–34; AT X 181)

While in his agitated state, Descartes could find "diversion neither in walking nor in human company" (Cole 32; AT X 181), and it is as if he is diverted to walk in the dream. The French *divertissement* derives from "diversion," the turning aside (*of* anything) from its due or ordinary course or direction, both in the literal and the figural sense. In the latter sense the "turning aside" concerns the mind and its thoughts. *Divertissement*, then, is the mind's turning away from fatiguing and sad thoughts toward distraction and entertainment in order to be refreshed and ready to return to its former occupation. It is a calculated digression from a particular path that has proved itself impassible to make the self fit again for returning to its original path. Awake, Descartes does not permit himself to be diverted and wander aimlessly. But in contrast to his waking mind, which cannot let up on its obsession to find the right way to truth, his sleeping mind becomes inattentive and as a result is allowed to wander. In the first dream Descartes' oneiric self wanders both literally and figuratively, insofar as the wandering occurs in the dream's movie-like images.

It is no coincidence, of course, that Descartes' oneiric self is continually diverted in his first dream. *Divertissement* belongs to the same family of words as "conversion," which from its beginning in ancient philosophy and Judeo-Christian religion has been figured as a movement and thus has had a spatial or topological dimension. Literally, *conversio* means "to rotate, to revolve, to turn around or upside down." Its Greek equivalent *epistrophē* (together with *metanoia*) similarly signifies a "turn" or "return" or, more generally "a change in direction" or "reorientation." Conversion implies a change of position or location, a movement or more precisely, the initiation of a movement. Plato uses the cognates of *strephein* to describe perfect circular motions, motions that return in on themselves.[30] Perfect motion not only is found in the cosmological realm but also characterizes the movement of the soul, which is destined to return in on itself. Neoplatonism, and more pertinently, Augustine both figure conversion as a return from exile, from the "region of unlikeness" (*regio dissimilitudinis*; *Confessions* 7.10.16). For Augustine the notion is prefigured in the Old Testament in the repeated narratives of the apostasy and alienation of the people of Israel from God and their return. Consequently, *epistrophē* and related terms were used to translate the Hebrew words describing this reversal and return.

In Christianity, conversion is the first step of a journey, the journey of life and spirit that ends ideally at the gates of heaven. This notion of man as *homo viator*, as wayfarer, is as old as Christian thought.[31] In Psalm 39:12, "I am a stranger with thee, and a sojourner, as all my fathers were." Man is homeless in this world, biding his time until he is allowed to return to his true home.[32] Pilgrimage becomes a figure for the *conditio humana*—with actual pilgrimages, like the one Descartes vowed to undertake to Our Lady of Loreto, replicating and anticipating the wandering and homecoming that are humankind's postlapsarian destiny. In a spiritual sense, pilgrimage was understood as the soul's interior journey toward a higher state of being in the attainment of absolute truth or uniting with the divine. Bonaventure's meditative treatise *Itinerarium Mentis in Deum* (*Journey of the Mind in God*), for instance, details the steps taken by the soul in its systematic ascent toward God. As much a literal and physical journey as it was a figural and spiritual or mental one, pilgrimage was understood in ways that allowed both dimensions, real and figural, to overlap and blend into each other. Traveling to Jerusalem or Rome was a spiritual journey; and a spiritual or mental journey like Descartes' clearly also had a physical dimension. We see this also in Ignatius's life and piety, with pilgrimage in this double dimension playing an eminent role. He refers to himself in his autobiography as "the pilgrim," and the book became known among Jesuits as the *Pilgrimage Journal* or *The Pilgrim's Story*. Already very early in his conversion Ignatius fantasized "about going to Jerusalem barefoot" (*Acta* § 8, p. 15) as a way to imitate the lives of Christ and the saints about which he had read. He tried repeatedly to realize the fantasy of a pilgrimage to Jerusalem, and it remained a constant in his further spiritual development. Jerusalem became the preoccupation of the small group of companions who gathered around Ignatius and formed the core of the future Society of Jesus. The outbreak of the war between Venice and the Turks in 1537 made it impossible for Ignatius and his companions to put into practice the vow they had made years earlier in Paris, to go to Jerusalem and preach the Gospel of Christ "in the service of souls" and to effect the conversion of Muslims. They traveled instead to Rome and put themselves at the disposition of the pope, who convinced them that "Italy is a good and true Jerusalem,"[33] and he prompted them to form a religious order. As John Olin concludes, "The Jesuits ... came into being as the substitution for the actual pilgrimage to Jerusalem Ignatius and his friends had intended to make. The Grand Turk in league with the pope, so to speak, had effected this historic change.... His original notion of a chivalrous pilgrimage to the East had evolved into a religious order."[34] Indeed, the unifying ideal of the early community of Jesuits (before they called themselves that) as well as the later order was that of a "Jerusalem apostolate,"[35] and the idea of pilgrimaging to Jerusalem became central to the order's spiritual program. Instead of going to Jerusalem physically, the exercitant in the *Spiritual Exercises* is directed to travel there mentally by envisioning themself at the different locales of the Gospel narrative.

The centrality of the pilgrimage to Jerusalem also explains the importance of Loreto for the Society of Jesus and indirectly for its product, René Descartes.[36] At the turning point of the *Spiritual Exercises* at the beginning of the second week, the exercitant begins their contemplation of the Incarnation of Christ by seeing the place, the *compositio loci*, "which here will be to see the great extent of the round earth with its many different races; then, in the same way, see the particular house of Our Lady and its rooms in the town of Nazareth in the province of Galilee" (SE § 103, p. 303). This place, which metonymically stands in for the womb that carried the savior, could be experienced *in vivo* at the Santa Casa di Loreto.[37] Instead of having to transport oneself to Nazareth, off limits at the time because of the Ottoman occupation, Nazareth had been teleported miraculously to believers in Loreto. The holy site, so central to the sacred topography of the Jesuit order, was as mobile as the imagination of its members. And this permanent spiritual mobility accompanied the physical mobility that remained characteristic of the Jesuit order, whose members, much like the apostles, were expected to spread the Gospel of Christ "unto the ends of the earth" (Acts 1:8). As the *Constitutions* prescribed, a Jesuit "should always be ready to travel about in various regions of the world."[38] Jesuits were supposed to be, as Olin terms it, "pilgrim priests."[39] Throughout his life, Descartes practiced a similar itinerancy, both literally and figuratively. He was always on the move, not to spread the Gospel but to find truth and eventually make it known to everyone.

Going on a journey or pilgrimage entails discerning, knowing, and following the right way, since the wrong way leads the pilgrim astray and directly to hell. Ignatius confronts this dilemma repeatedly in his *Autobiography*, with God always ultimately intervening to point him in the right direction. Given that the text is an account of how Ignatius, much like Augustine, has been guided by God throughout his life, the interventions were happening even before he knew it. Since not everyone could count on being guided directly by God, there was a need for help in his spiritual navigation. Among the manuals devoted to the task was Antoine Sucquet's *Via vitae aeternae* (*Path to Eternal Life*), an immensely popular devotional treatise consisting of meditative images (engraved by Boetius à Bolswert), accompanied by brief annotations explaining the individual components, and followed by three chapters guiding the viewer/reader in their contemplation.[40] The annotation to the first image (Fig. 1) begins with a motto that is as much title as exhortation to the reader: "Consider, O man, your end and your ways" (*Considera, ô homo, finem tuum & vias tuas*).[41]

FIGURE 1. Imago 1, engraved by Boëtius à Bolswert, in Antoine Sucquet, *Via vitae aeternae. Iconibus illustrata per Boëtium A Bolswert* (Antwerp: Typis Martini Nutij, 1620), 2v. Courtesy of the University of Chicago Library's Hanna Holborn Gray Special Collections Research Center.

The image shows a solitary man who, like the viewer/reader, beholds the scene unfolding before him. The inscription to the right of his head reads "Behold the end: Whither, on which side goest thou?" (*En finis: quò, quà vado?*). The man is confronted with an existential choice between two "ends": hell on the left (D) and heaven on the right (C). While the closest destination is clearly hell, heaven can be reached by three different paths (all marked G) representing the three different "states of life" (*triplex vitae status*). The shortest and most direct path to heaven belongs to the *religiosus* who puts his life in the service of reclusive prayer and devotion. The middle path, which is "oblique" and slightly curved, is for the regular clergy (*ecclesiasticus*); and the longest route, full of sinuous twists and turns, is reserved for the laity (*saecularis*), represented by the couple. These three paths further represent the *via purgativa* for beginners, the *via illuminativa* for intermediates, and the *via unitiva* for the perfect, which is a way of living as much as meditating.

The everyman depicted is at a critical juncture, at the crossroads of life at which he can either turn away from God or toward him, in other words, either pervert or convert. What this image and many others in Sucquet's *Via vitae aeternae* make evident in a oversimplified manner is that conversion is an act of (re)orientation that involves navigation, albeit not necessarily in either a conscious or controlled way. It shows that the conversional change of direction presupposes there to be at least two alternatives or, more realistically, a multiplicity of paths and ways. Nor are all paths made equal. There must be right and wrong paths, paths that lead away from the destination and paths that lead toward it, long winding paths studded with temptations and diversions and short straight ones that transport the self expeditiously to the end. In this engraving orientation seems rather simple given that ultimately there are only two choices. The only reminder of the unpredictability and inconstancy of life and world is the shipwreck on the left, making the point that piloting is a more daunting challenge than the rest of the image suggests. Only selves that are lost and heading down the wrong path are in need of redirection, and it is precisely such a loss of orientation and wandering on wrong paths that Descartes' first dream stages. Returning to the "text" of Descartes' dream, his oneiric self is represented as "walking down the streets," in other words, in transit, and being assaulted by ghosts or spirits. As the second plate (Fig. 2) in Sucquet's *Via vitae aeternae* demonstrates, seduction and/or coercion by the enemy further complicate orientation and navigation.

FIGURE 2. Imago 2, engraved by Boëtius à Bolswert, in Antoine Sucquet, *Via vitae aeternae. Iconibus illustrata per Boëtium A Bolswert* (Antwerp: Typis Martini Nutij, 1620), 98v. Courtesy of the University of Chicago Library's Hanna Holborn Gray Special Collections Research Center.

Humans may have free choice of which path to follow in life, but the alternatives are presented in a distorted and tempting fashion so that orientation becomes even more problematical. The ability of Descartes' oneiric self to move about freely and follow its chosen path is severely compromised by his encounter with spirits. All three dimensions are equally affected: right/left, forward/backward, up/down.[42] Baillet writes, "Because he felt a great weakness on his right side" that forced him "to lean to his left side," Descartes has not only difficulty maintaining his balance, compromising his ability to walk a straight line and thus follow the chosen direction, but holding himself upright. A little later the wind blows so hard that he has trouble staying upright as well as moving forward (or backward, since he is trying to retrace his steps). In the context of Descartes' search for the "right" way, these spatial dimensions must be read figuratively.[43] Lexicographically such a reading is warranted, since the Western intellectual tradition has always connected "right" and "left" spiritually and morally with good and evil, virtuous and sinful.

We saw in the first engraving from Sucquet's *Via vitae aeternae* that the right way is the "right" way because it leads to heaven and the left way is the wrong way because it goes straight to hell. The symbolics of upright posture were similarly common and conventional.[44] Spiritually coded, erect bipedality signified corporeal and moral integrity, human dignity and superiority, and was an index of man's higher calling and divine likeness. Conversely, the lack of uprightness was understood as a symptom of man's fallenness, making it no coincidence that Descartes' oneiric self feels "ashamed to walk in this way" and tries "to straighten up," given that shame, as Genesis 3:7–8 makes clear, is a direct result of the fall. Descartes' dream stages this fallenness quite literally and corporeally. The gusts of wind combined with the "great weakness on his right side" not only make it difficult for Descartes' oneiric self to hold itself upright but also cause it to "fall at each step." Its gait is so compromised that each step is a fall, repeating the original sin that Adam and Eve passed on to the human race. And the devil himself limped. In his *Sermons on the Song of Songs* Bernard of Clairvaux writes that man lost his steady gait by his *imitatio diaboli* even though his soul retained its divine image. "But he limps, as it were, on one foot, and has become an estranged son."[45]

With his stumbling walk Descartes is also following a more immediate exemplar, Ignatius of Loyola, who, as noted, had both legs severely wounded by a cannonball at the siege of Pamplona. Even following numerous surgeries, one leg was left shorter than the other so that Ignatius would limp for the rest of his life. Ignatius's ambulatory defect signals that he belongs to Adam's progeny, but it also evokes examples of founding figures, such as Jacob and Aeneas.[46] The lameness of these "founding fathers" is all the more surprising in the face of the itinerancy issuing from it: on the one hand, the repeated exile and errancy of the chosen people and, on the other, Aeneas's protracted wanderings until he finally reaches the place where the eternal city is to be established. Similarly, the physical and spiritual mobility of the Jesuit order is born from its founder's limping gait. It seems as if one has to fall first in order to walk steadily, as if a firm footing has to be preceded by falling and fumbling just as a firm foundation has to be preceded by doubt and destruction. Descartes' stumbling and falling would, then, be not only rehearsing the mental errancy of having lost the right way in his search for truth but also preparing for the discovery of the *mirabilis scientiae fundamenta*.

But we are not quite there yet. Just as the dreaming Descartes is attempting "to straighten up," he is "buffeted by gusts that carried him off in a sort of whirlwind that spun him around three or four times on his left foot." If *epistrophē* or *conversio* consists in a reorientation or turning, then the spinning can be seen, in its exaggeration and pointlessness, as a parody or, more etymologically appropriate, as its perversion. This spinning around doesn't result in a change of direction and reorientation of the self; it doesn't relocate the self or bring it any closer to the place it wants to reach. Spinning in circles, Descartes' oneiric self ends up where it began and fails to move along on the path toward truth. That the left foot is the pivot of this spinning motion further reinforces the conclusion that this *conversio*, this turning, is sinful and thus actually a *perversio*.[47]

Just as Descartes is thinking in his dream that he is about to fall, he notices "a school" (*un collège*) "open along his way" (*son chemin*). Given that he interprets the first dream as referring to his past, it is not far-fetched to equate *un collège* with La Flèche. The school is linked to Descartes' path, even though it is not his original destination. He enters a school "in search of a refuge and a remedy for his trouble" (Cole 33; AT X 181), possibly believing that education and knowledge will help him right himself and find his way back to the right path. Following a long tradition going back at least to

Hugh of Saint Victor's *Didascalicon*, the Society of Jesus held that humanistic education provided a remedy for the symptoms of original sin.[48] The fact that it is a "school church" that Descartes' oneiric self is trying to reach to seek divine assistance through prayer further underscores the spiritual nature of his affliction. He feels that his weakness and concomitant temptability will be remedied by learning only if it is supported by divine grace. Not coincidentally, in the dream Descartes is distracted and diverted again both literally and figuratively. Having passed an acquaintance without greeting him, he wants to reverse course to pay his respects but is "thrust back by the wind that was blowing against the church." Instead of acting as a hostile force throwing him down and steering him off course, the wind now blows him toward the originally intended destination. Despite being pushed toward the church, Descartes is still unable to take the path he wants to take. Walking and standing "on the same ground" as everyone else, Descartes feels demonstrably singled out for his fallenness.

Just as the wind dies down and he finally finds some relief, Descartes wakes up. The "real pain" he feels makes him fear that his oneiric imaginings "had been the work of some Evil Spirit who had wanted to seduce him," giving the ghosts and the wind a spiritual meaning and understanding the dream as staging a temptation.[49] The pain doesn't function simply as a physiological cause but also as a clue that he had been subject to a temptation by some evil spirit, a temptation that was made possible in the dream by his oneiric self's "great weakness on his right side." Even though he is no longer dreaming, he remains within its topologic in that he "turned over onto his right side, for he had slept and dreamed on his left side."[50] But just as this improper sleeping position has to be understood as much figurally as literally, so must his turning from one side to the other. For it is in response to his lack of righteousness that he leans to the left and wrong side. Now that he is awake, fear overcomes him and he turns literally as well as figuratively to the right side—or, in other words, he converts.[51] If we thus follow the topologics of conversion staged in this first dream, we cannot but locate the turning point here. This is where the conversion happens. We should note that it happens as Descartes is waking up, suggesting that it has to be enacted by the waking self. If conversion is akin to the process of awakening, then it cannot happen during sleep and in a dream.

Descartes turns to the right side once he recognizes that an evil spirit had wanted to seduce him in the dream, that the falling is not simply a physical but rather a spiritual event. "Evil spirit" refers here not only to the "representation of some ghosts" that frighten him at the beginning but also to the wind that assaults Descartes' oneiric self. Such a figural reading is suggested by Descartes himself in a series of notes titled *Praeambula* contained in the very same notebook: "The things which are perceivable by the senses are helpful in enabling us to conceive of Olympian matters. The wind signifies spirit; movement with the passage of time signifies life; light signifies knowledge" (CSM I 5; AT X 218). This passage confirms not only Descartes' own identification of wind with spirit but moreover our interpretation that "the movement with the passage of time" staged by this dream "signifies [Descartes'] life." In the more synoptic interpretation Descartes offers of the dreams following the third one, he elaborates on this kind of "spiritual" understanding: "The wind that pushed him toward the school church, when he had trouble with his right side, was nothing other than the Evil Spirit who was trying to throw him by force into a place that he intended to enter by his own free will. This was why God did not permit him to advance any farther even into a holy place or let him be carried away by a Spirit whom He had not sent. Nevertheless, he was firmly convinced that it had been the Spirit of God that had made him take the first steps toward that Church" (Cole 38; AT X 185). Insofar as the windblown wanderings of Descartes' oneiric self represent a scene of temptation and perversion, orientation and navigation, or more concretely, the choice between right and left (wrong) is a matter of what is called the discernment of spirits, a technique or practice associated primarily with Ignatius of Loyola but that can be traced back to the desert fathers. Descartes would have been very familiar with this psychotechnique from his schooling at La Flèche, as it is an essential component of the Ignatian exercises.

In the *Spiritual Exercises* the discernment of spirits constitutes the second mode of three ways of making an election (or decision). The first mode of election is what is commonly called conversion "when God Our Lord so moves and attracts the will that without doubting ... a dedicated soul follows what is shown, just as St Paul and St Matthew did" (SE § 175, p. 317); and the third mode is the "tranquil time" when "the soul is not disturbed by different spirits and can use her natural powers freely and calmly" (§ 177, p. 318). In the prefatory remarks Ignatius distinguishes three different thought processes: "one sort which are properly mine and arise simply from the free will and choice, and two other sorts which come from outside, one from the good spirit and the other from the bad" (§ 32, p. 291). The movements of the soul induced by the good spirit are consolatory and are called "consolations." In contrast, movements induced by the evil spirit are called "desolations." Whereas consolation is "any interior movement [that] is produced in the soul that leads her to become inflamed with the love of her Creator and Lord" (§ 316, p. 348), desolation consists of all the contrary things like "darkness and disturbance in the soul, attraction toward what is low and of the earth, anxiety arising from various agitations and temptations" (§ 317, p. 349). Therefore, the self should refrain from making any decision while in a desolate state and thus under the sway of the evil spirit. As simple as this sounds, the problem is that "it is characteristic of the bad angel to assume the form of 'an angel of light'" (§ 332, p. 352); in other words, feelings of consolation and spiritual joy may be induced by the enemy in order to move the self to do something pious only to seduce it later. In Chapter 3, we return to the issue of Ignatius's "more advanced ways of discerning the spirits." To be noted here is how Descartes proves himself to be a product of Jesuit education in recognizing that the wind pushing him toward the school church is not an angel of light but the evil spirit,[52] who has highjacked his movement of the will that was initially induced by the divine spirit.

Ignatius discovered this spiritual practice during his conversion. In response to his reading of Jacobus de Voragine's *Legenda aurea* and Ludolf of Saxony's *Vita Christi* he imagines himself emulating the deeds and lives of the saints: "'How would it be, if I did this which St Francis did, and this which St Dominic did?' And thus he used to think over many things which he was finding good, always proposing to himself difficult and laborious things" (*Acta* § 7, p. 15). Unexperienced in spiritual matters and still in thrall to chivalric ideals, Ignatius would find his old habits of thought returning to intrude on his pious meditations, "imagining what he was to do in the service of a certain lady: the means he would take so as to be able to reach the country where she was, the witty love poems, the words he would say to her, the deeds of arms that he would do in her service" (§ 6, pp. 14–15). Soon he discovered a difference between his various trains of thought:

That when he was thinking about that worldly stuff he would take much delight, but when he left it aside after getting tired, he would find himself dry and discontented.

But when about going to Jerusalem barefoot, and about not eating except herbs, and about doing all the other rigours he was seeing the saints had done, not only used he to be consoled while in such thoughts, but he would remain content and happy even after having left them aside. But he wasn't investigating this, nor stopping to ponder this difference, until one time when his eyes were opened a little, and he began to marvel at this difference in kind and to reflect on it, picking it up from experience that from some thought he would be left sad and from others happy, and little by little coming to know the difference in the kind of spirits that were stirring: the one from the devil, and the other from God. (§ 8, p. 15)

Regarding this passage, the editor/author of Ignatius's biographical narrative, Luis Gonçalves de Câmara,[53] adds in a note: "This was the first reflection he made on the things of God; and later, when he produced the Exercises, it was from here that he began to get clarity regarding the matter of the difference in spirits" (§ 8, p. 15).

The insight about differing forms of thought not only laid the foundation for the later elaboration of this psychotechnique in the *Spiritual Exercises*, but it can also be considered the decisive turning point in Ignatius's conversion. To be sure, the first encounter with devotional literature has a profound effect on Ignatius, but he keeps perverting these texts by reading them through the hermeneutical lens of chivalric romance, invalidating any spiritual progress he had made up to that point. Only when he is able to cease indiscriminately mixing spiritual and worldly thoughts by distinguishing different kinds of thoughts by their origin does he begin to head in the right direction in a controlled and sustained manner. It is the discernment of spirits that makes the reading of spiritual texts soteriologically productive. That the conversion so far had been rather superficial is indicated by the fact that the discernment of spirits and the recognition that God was intervening in his thoughts awaken the reflection on his sinful past and the desire for penance or *metanoia* in Ignatius.[54] Now, in contrast to a mere change of reading matter, Ignatius's sense of self is profoundly transformed. Before, all the pious meditations were little more than fickle and aimless musings of the mind, but once the discernment of spirits comes into play, the mind is able to orient itself in the spiritual landscape, much like Saint Antony being tempted by visions and visitations in the desert, and navigate the many and persistent digressions and temptations. Put more simply, the discernment of spirits simultaneously springs from the conversion and brings it about.

Once Descartes begins to discern the spirits, distinguishing right from wrong paths, and concomitantly understanding the dream as staging and enacting his mental errancy and potential perversion, he can initiate his turn. At this point Descartes is beginning to recognize that God (as well, of course, as the evil spirit) is communicating with him and to recognize the divine call as a divine call. His affective response to this recognition is fear (and shame), as the turn toward God was traditionally accompanied by a turn toward the sinful self.[55] No doubt as a consequence of Descartes' Jesuit education, the spiritual discernment and orientation found in and after the first dream prompt him in a similar manner to reflect on his sinful past and pray to God for deliverance. Thus, his turn toward God involves a reflection on himself, a reflection that is facilitated by the introjection of the divine gaze. Later, in the synoptic interpretation, Descartes will return to the theme, reiterating that his past life "could not have been as innocent in the eyes of God as in those of man" (Cole 38; AT X 186). As it did for Ignatius, the discernment of spirits and attendant fear move Descartes to true *metanoia*. It is only now, as quoted earlier, that "he turned over onto his right side." Having recognized the divine address as divine address, Descartes can now directly turn to God: "He prayed that God would protect him from the evil effects of his dream and preserve him from all of the miseries that could threaten him as his punishment for his sins" (Cole 34; AT X 182).

Descartes' *Synderesis*

The answer to his prayers comes in and with the second dream, which is extremely short, consisting, in fact, in nothing more than "a sudden, loud noise, which he took for thunder" and from which he awakes "terrified" (Cole 34; AT X 182). In other words, the dream amounts to nothing more than waking up, which is the point. It is a dream of awakening and, in that sense, purely transitional between the two more substantive dreams framing it. This is not to say that it is insignificant, in particular as in his synoptic interpretation of all three dreams Descartes understands the second one to be the turning point within the tropic motion that is his conversion. In the emotional ductus of the three dreams it marks the transition from terror and desolation to calm and consolation. Descartes is "terrified" when the thunder awakens him, and opening his eyes, he "noticed many sparks of fire scattered around the room." After some philosophical meditation on the vision

Founding First Philosophies 51

and some practical perceptual exercises, "he saw that his terrors faded away, and he fell asleep again quite calmly" (Cole 35; AT X 182).

Correspondingly, after being assailed by the evil spirit in the first dream, in the second he believes it is "the Spirit of Truth descending to take possession of him." This inspiration comes to him following two hours spent praying to God and contemplating his sins, which he confessed to being "great enough to call down upon his head thunderbolts of heaven" (Cole 34; AT X 182). The dream of thunder literalizes and realizes these metaphoric "thunderbolts of heaven," even as the "thunder" heard in the dream signifies doubly: It confirms the sinfulness upon which Descartes has just spent two hours reflecting. And the thunder is the response to his confession and prayer. The "thunderbolts from heaven" are God's answer to his turn, and this divine communication occurs because he has acknowledged his sinfulness. By confessing his sinfulness he also comes to recognize his innate goodness and deiformity. Descartes thought as much since "the fear with which he had been struck in the second dream marked in his opinion, his *synderesis*, that is, remorse of conscience concerning the sin that he could have committed in the course of his life to date" (Cole 38; AT X 186).

Synderesis is a technical term from moral theology of medieval Scholasticism, which made a rather sudden appearance in the twelfth century and gained renewed significance in the philosophical debates of the early modern period.[56] It refers to the innate principle supposed to exist within every self inclining it toward the good and restraining it from evil. As such, it is closely linked to the notion of conscience, prompting much debate among Scholastic theologians about their distinction and relation. The link between Descartes' interpretation that the fear marked his *synderesis* and the actual dream consists in the "sparks of fire scattered around the room" he sees upon waking up from the thunderclap. Baillet writes that he "had experienced this phenomenon on many other occasions, and it did not seem too strange to him, when he awoke in the middle of the night, that his eyes sparkled enough that he could make out the objects closest to him" (Cole 35; AT X 182). Although Baillet's account clearly states that Descartes was awake when he beheld the sparks, they are more closely associated with the thunderclap in his dream than with the waking world, particularly as Descartes does not perceive them as an objective phenomenon of the external world but as a condition affecting his eyes. At the very least, they unsettle the distinction between dream and waking. The linkage between *synderesis* and sparks goes back to an enigmatic passage in Jerome's *Commentary on Ezekiel* (1.7) in which he identifies the four living creatures of the prophet's vision of God's throne with the four parts of the soul. *Synderesis* is the fourth part, "that spark of conscience which was not even extinguished in the breast of Cain after he was turned out of Paradise."[57] Once the term became part of the *Glossa ordinaria*, the standard commentary of scripture that was printed as part of editions of the Bible, it was widely distributed well into the early modern period.

Being "above and beyond" the other parts of the soul described by Jerome, *synderesis* is figured as a kind of meta-faculty. As it is "not mixed up with the other three," it can make them the object of reflection as well as correction and, in doing so, distinguishes not only true reason from "imitation" but good from evil. As Thomas Aquinas writes in *De veritate* 16–17, *synderesis*'s job "is to murmur back in reply to evil and turn us towards what is good."[58] Following Augustine, he defines *synderesis* as a "natural tribunal" (in the sense of the Greek *krinein*, "to judge" and "to distinguish"),[59] and in exercising this critical function *synderesis* serves as the basis for the *discretio spirituum*, the discernment of spirits. This ability of discernment, to use Jerome's pyrotechnical metaphorics, is inextinguishable. Even expulsion from paradise and repeated sinning will not snuff out the *scintilla conscientiae* that God has implanted in each individual soul and that connects it to its prelapsarian state. *Synderesis* functions as a guide that can, if heeded, help the self find its way back to paradise or, to put it more technically, bring about its salvation. In other words, *synderesis* is the principle of spiritual orientation and navigation on which errant souls such as Descartes can rely even in the face of temptation. Citing Psalm 4:6,[60] Thomas Aquinas similarly understands the "light of natural reason, whereby we discern what is good and what is evil" as "nothing else than the imprint on us of the Divine light" (ST I–II, q. 91).[61] However dim the divine light may have become in man, it is still strong enough to throw into relief the difference between good and evil, right and wrong. Thus, *synderesis* enables the self to orient itself toward God. In *The Journey of the Mind to God* Bonaventure identifies the "spark of synderesis" with the *apex mentis*, "summit of the mind," the sixth and highest of the soul's power by which it ascends "from the lowest things to the highest things, from things outside us to those that are within, and from the temporal to the eternal" (1.6).[62] Once the soul has completed its ascent and arrives at its apex, it can behold the Godhead in a *visio beatifica*.[63] Thus, Descartes' *lumen naturale* is connected via the *scintilla conscientiae* of *synderesis* to the *lumen supernaturale* emanating from the Godhead itself.

As this brief excursion evidences, *synderesis* occupies the nodal point in a densely woven web of metaphors and concepts. The images of the divine spark and the seeds of knowledge, the metaphorics of imprinting and illumination, the notions of the *imago Dei* and the *visio beatifica*, as well as the faculties of discernment and judgment are all closely linked to *synderesis* and ensured that this Scholastic term lived on in different guises long after Scholasticism lost its dominance.[64] It therefore seems hardly a coincidence that sparks make an appearance at the decisive turning point of Descartes' conversion. By literally seeing sparks, Descartes externalizes, materializes, and thus literalizes the metaphor of the *scintilla conscientiae* linked to *synderesis*. More generally, he actualizes the metaphorics of illumination that play such a prominent role in conversion narratives—above all in Paul's vision of the resurrected Christ on the road to Damascus. Finally, the illumination of his surroundings by the "sparks of fire" reflects the waking up staged by the dream itself. As Descartes wrote in the context of the full conversion narrative, the first two dreams "conceive of Olympian matters," for just as the "wind signifies spirit" and "movement with the passage of time signifies life" in the first dream, in the second dream "light signifies knowledge" (CSM I 5; AT X 218), which was bestowed on him by the descent of the "Spirit of Truth." In another note from the *Olympica* Descartes elaborates this mode of thought:

Just as the imagination employs figures in order to conceive of bodies, so, in order to frame ideas of spiritual things [*ad spiritualia figuranda*], the intellect makes use of certain bodies which are perceived through the senses, such as wind and light. By this means we may philosophize in a more exalted way, and develop the knowledge to raise our minds to lofty heights. (CSM I 4; AT X 217)[65]

The intellect uses the images of material and sensible things to figure spiritual matters, most notably "wind and light," which play such an important role in the first two dreams. Contrary to expectation, the mind is elevated, not dragged down, by resorting to material and sensible things as meditative media. Descartes figures philosophical thought, or at least its ideal, as an ascent in the tradition of spiritual meditation and contemplation. "To raise [the mind] to lofty heights," the self needs the help of tools, mental media or machines.⁶⁶ Here and elsewhere he stresses the point that traditional philosophy has failed to provide the necessary tools to facilitate this ascent. Instead, as Descartes continues, it is poetry with its "serious sayings [*graves sententiae*]" crafted by "enthusiasm and the force of the imagination" that extract the "seeds of knowledge [*semina scientiae*]" lying dormant in the "flint" stones of the soul; to be more precise, it is the force of poetic or metaphoric language that brings out the sparks or seeds of knowledge, which are themselves metaphors of that inalienable participation in divine reason. What Descartes was doing when he was having his dreams and visions was thinking "poetically." Not a poet himself, he had to resort to dreaming to "philosophize in a more exalted way."

In this passage Descartes links the metaphorics of the *scintilla conscientiae* with the metaphorics of the *semina scientiae* (seeds of knowledge) from the Stoic tradition. Seneca uses this organic metaphor in one of his philosophical letters to explain to his young protégé how humans have a certain knowledge of virtue from birth: "Nature could not teach us directly; she has given us the seeds of knowledge, but not knowledge itself" (*Epistles* 120.4).⁶⁷ Cicero makes a similar argument by drawing on the affiliated metaphorics of the spark: "And in this whole discussion I want it understood that what I shall call Nature is (that which is implanted in us by Nature); that, however, the corruption caused by bad habits is so great that the sparks of fire [*igniculi*], so to speak, which Nature has kindled in us are extinguished by corruption, and vices which are their opposites spring up and are established" (*On the Laws* 1.33).⁶⁸ Surprisingly, Augustine has a much more optimistic view. In the same chapter in which he identifies the *scintilla rationis* with man's deiformity, he joins both metaphorics together in a discussion of human reproduction. Even "the fault of the first sin could not abolish the marvelous power of the seed, and the even more wonderful power by which seed produces seed."⁶⁹ Indeed, what is innate, according to Augustine, going a step further than his Stoic predecessors, is the power of replication by seed. Not only knowledge or virtue is seeded, but the power of seeding itself. It is the power to reproduce similitude, that is, the power of selves to produce images of themselves that ultimately reflect, however dimly, the image of the divine creator. Being made in the image of God means being able to reproduce this image by reproducing images of oneself. Thus, the metaphorics of the seed complemented those of imprinting and illumination to explain the retention of an original virtue and verity in the subject.

In the *Rules for the Direction of the Mind* Descartes merges these metaphorical regimes, taking recourse to the metaphorics of seed and spark to argue that "the great minds of the past were to some extent aware of" a method, "guided to it even by nature alone" (CSM I 17; AT X 376). A little later he writes:

> But I am convinced that certain primary seeds of truth [*veritatem semina*] naturally implanted in human minds thrived vigorously in that unsophisticated and innocent age—seeds which have been stifled in us through our constantly reading and hearing all sorts of errors. So the same light of mind [*mentis lumine*] which enabled them to see (albeit without knowing why) that virtue is preferable to pleasure, the good preferable to the useful, also enabled them to grasp true ideas in philosophy and mathematics, although they were not yet able fully to master such sciences. (CSM I 18; AT X 376)[70]

Like Cicero, Descartes maintains that "primary seeds of truth" are implanted by nature and are corrupted by the trappings of culture, while previously, in less sophisticated times, there was little corruption. The present age, in contrast, has seen an explosion of knowledge and, therefore, a multiplication of errors as well. The notion of "primary seeds" explains both how humans are naturally capable of finding, discerning, and recognizing truth and why they are failing to do so currently. Only the reform of knowledge being undertaken by Descartes can reverse the fallenness of understanding and restore man's originary capability. He conceives of his method as the cultivation of the naturally given "seeds of truth" buried in people's minds, enabling them to resist the corruption of knowledge. The *semina scientiae* to which Descartes refers in both his conversion account and in the *Regulae* are the seeds of Cartesian method. It is hard not to relate the "sparks of fire scattered across the room" via the *scintilla conscientiae* to the "seeds of knowledge" hidden in the "flint" of Descartes' soul and to understand the former as a visual and external manifestation of the latter. What Descartes receives, after the "Spirit of Truth has descended to take possession of him," is a vision of the innate spark dwelling in him and, thus, the confirmation that his intellect, in fact the intellect as such, naturally contains the seeds of method within itself and thus also the ability to distinguish right from wrong and truth from falsehood. This explains why Descartes understands the second dream to mark his *synderesis*.[71] Furthermore, it explains why the sparks he sees in the room turn out not to be part of the external world but are localized in his eyes or, more precisely, are a condition of his vision.[72] Despite having "experienced this phenomenon on many other occasions," Descartes wants to find "reasons drawn from philosophy," and by doing that "he was able to reassure himself about his mind." He calms himself once and for all by opening and closing his eyes to observe what is represented to him. It is as if these philosophical and perceptual exercises serve to confirm to him that it is the *lumen naturale* emanating from him that lets him perceive and discern "what was represented to him." Moreover, they permit him to understand these sensory data not simply as givens but as mental representations lit by his *lumen naturale*. In this highly self-reflexive moment Descartes recognizes not only the innate method within himself but also the access it gives him to the external and material world.

Descartes' epistemologization of these moral-theological concepts should come as no surprise, since it is anticipated in the Scholastic theorization of *synderesis*, which also had an epistemological dimension, although *scintilla* is paired with *rationis* instead of *conscientiae*. Conversely, Descartes' epistemologization never loses its moral-theological tinge. After all, in his synoptic interpretation Descartes links *synderesis* with the "fear with which he had been struck in the second dream" and identifies it with "the remorse of conscience concerning the sins that he could have committed in the course of his life to date." Such a moral-theological and spiritual inflection of epistemological issues seems strange only to an understanding of Descartes as "modern"—rather than "early modern"—rationalist. Descartes knew that "the fear of God is the beginning of wisdom," which is the reason that he chose this verse from Proverbs 9:10 as the epigram to the *Praeambula* section of his notebook.

Sortes Ausoniae

Descartes was primed for "serious sayings" when he fell asleep again and had his third dream. Its emotional coloring is very different from that of the first two in that it has "nothing frightful" about it. It commences with Descartes' oneiric self finding a book on a table without knowing who put it there. He opens it and sees that it's a dictionary even as another book, this time an anthology of poetry titled *Corpus poetarum*, appears similarly out of nowhere. Opening it, he chances upon the verse "Quod vitae sectabor iter?" (What path in life shall I follow?). Just as he reads this, he notices an unknown man who gives and recommends to him another piece of poetry that begins with the words "Est et non" (Yes and no). As the well-educated man that he is, Descartes retorts that he knows that this verse comes from one of the *Idylls* by Ausonius, which is also included in the anthology on the table. But his oneiric self is unable to locate the poem and undergoes a series of dreamlike confusions until the man and the books suddenly vanish—which is the beginning, in this quasi-wakeful state, of his interpretation of what just had presented itself to his imagination. Fully awake, Descartes continues his work of interpretation, making it as much a part of the dream as the dream is part of it.

The sententious commonplace that Descartes chanced upon in his dream is an example of what Leibniz, in a peculiar passage of the *Theodicy*, counted among the "small circumstances serving to convert or to pervert." The text is so seminal and so revealing for an understanding of Descartes' third dream that it's worth quoting at length:

> Nothing is more widely known than the *Tolle, lege* cry which St. Augustine heard in a neighbouring house, when he was pondering on what side he should take among the Christians divided into sects, and saying to himself,
>
> *Quod vitae sectabor iter?*
>
> This brought him to open at random the book of the Holy Scriptures which he had before him, and to read what came before his eyes: and these were words which finally induced him to give up Manichaeism. The good Steno, a Dane, who was titular Bishop of Titianopolis, Vicar Apostolic (as they say) of Hanover and the region around, when there was a Duke Regent of his religion, told us that something of that kind had happened to him. . . . He told us then that what had greatly helped towards inducing him to place himself on the side of the Roman Church had been the voice of a lady in Florence, who had cried out to him from a window: "Go not on the side where you are about to go, sir, go on the other side." "That voice struck me," he told us, "because I was just meditating upon religion." This lady knew that he was seeking a man in the house where she was, and, when she saw him making his way to the other house, wished to point out where his friend's room was. Father John Davidius, the Jesuit, wrote a book entitled *Veridicus Christianus*, which is like a kind of Bibliomancy, where one takes passages at random, after the pattern of

the *Tolle, lege* of St. Augustine, and it is like a devotional game. But the chances to which, in spite of ourselves, we are subject, play only too large a part in what brings salvation to men, or removes it from them.[73]

The passage appears in Leibniz's discussion "of the dispensation of the means and circumstances contributing to salvation and to damnation" (§ 85, p. 168). The problem Leibniz confronts here is the seeming suggestion in the Bible that God directly influences the will of some humans, such as when he hardened the heart of the pharaoh, and thus "inspires men with a kind of anti-grace" (§ 99, p. 178). Since this would contradict the theological premise that God's "goodness makes him contribute the least possible to that which can render men guilty, and the most possible to that which serves to save them" (§ 85, p. 169), Leibniz resorts to the somewhat questionable argument that "it all often comes down to circumstances which form a part of the combination of things" (§ 100, p. 178) in which God permits humans to be placed.

As he wrote these lines, Leibniz's memory of Augustine's *Confessions* must have been hazy, since he conflates Augustine's narrative with his memory of Descartes' lost account of his similarly dramatic conversion, in which books also played a pivotal role.[74] Nowhere in Book Eight of the *Confessions*, containing the account of Augustine's famous conversion, nor in the rest of the text does he ask himself "Quod vitae sectabor iter?" By the time the narrative reaches Book Eight, Augustine is no longer an adherent of Manichaeism. And the penultimate chapter of Augustine's autobiographical narrative is not concerned with the conversion of his intellect, which had been concluded in the previous book, but with the conversion of the will and the overcoming of his sexuality. However, "Quod vitae sectabor iter?" is, of course, the verse from a poem by Ausonius upon which Descartes' oneiric self chances in his third dream. Clearly and correctly Leibniz was reminded of Augustine when he read Descartes' account, and when he recalled Augustine's conversion for the *Theodicy*, Descartes' was not far from his mind.

Leibniz's slip of memory places Descartes within a lineage of conversions by "serious sayings," delivered in oral or textual form, that extends via Augustine as far back as the desert father Antony and includes Francis of Assisi, Petrarch, and Ignatius of Loyola, to name only its most famous examples. If Leibniz's anecdote of Steno, titular bishop of Titianopolis, is to be believed, the phenomenon was clearly alive and well in the early modern period as well. In antiquity, conversion by circumstantial and contingent "sayings" was linked to a divinatory practice called cledonomancy.[75] This form of divination understands the chance occurrence of words and other coincidences to be instances of divine communication in which words or signs, by being taken out of their original context and applied to a different occasion, are given new and personalized symbolic meaning. The most famous example in ancient literature comes from Book 20 of Homer's *Odyssey*, when Odysseus overhears a servant he happens to run into that morning uttering a general curse against the suitors, and he understands this as a sign of divine support for his planned ambush against them later that day.[76] While at first, as in this example, the practice was predominantly oral, written texts were soon brought in to formalize this divinatory practice. In the so-called *sortes Homericae* and *sortes Virgilianae*, Homer's and Virgil's epics functioned as pagan "holy books" to be consulted whenever one needed to look into the future or wanted to know what the outcome would be of a course of action. And the media technology of the codex provided an improved random generator so that the improbable occurrence of "serious sayings" could be orchestrated at will.

Christianity replaced these pagan texts with its own holy book in what came to be known as *sortes Biblicae*. *Sortilegia*, or the drawing and reading of lots, were refunctionalized in the Christian context, as they were employed less to predict the future, which was viewed as a suspect practice, than to discover and determine God's will and thus be able to conduct one's life in accordance with the divine will.[77] In that respect, biblical *sortilegia* parallel the Ignatian exercises, which are also designed to ascertain God's will concerning the decision or election the self finds itself confronted with, and are thus less about knowing the future than taking action in the present. The difference is even more apparent when a decision has already been made and the aim is to find confirmation by consulting God—as was the case with Descartes, who had already made the discovery of the *mirabilis scientiae fundamenta* earlier in the day. In fact, divining God's will makes knowing the future that is known to God in its entirety to a certain extent obsolete, because the self can rest assured that it is on the right path without knowing in detail what awaits it.

While the *sortes Biblicae* had the advantage of being available to be consulted at any time, the originary and most momentous instances of divine guidance being found in this random manner were conversions by the book such as Augustine's famous *apertio libri Paulini*.[78] In these instances, as in Descartes', the media technology of the codex plays a pivotal role in facilitating the self's primal act of orientation and navigation in affording the user ease of both access and mobility. Highly portable codices become mobile themselves and can wander outside into the garden, as in Augustine finding his copy of the Pauline Epistles in the garden at Milan. They can appear on the summit of a mountain, as did Petrarch's copy of Augustine's *Confessions* on Mont Ventoux. Or they can become uncanny apparitions that move about autonomously, as in Descartes' dreams. The coincidences that in antiquity were the domain of cledonomancy reappear in the conversions of Augustine, Ignatius, and Descartes: books that are encountered unexpectedly and with no intention. Not only can books deliver the conversionary call almost anywhere; they can also do so contingently or, using Leibniz's term, circumstantially. And perhaps more important than accommodating mobile readers, the codex also enables mobile reading. Figured as a movement, reading a scroll is linear, sequential, and continuous.[79] To get from one place to another, the reader has to "scroll" through the entire text (whether actually reading it or not). In contrast, the codex affords a mode of reading in which the reader can jump from place to place by simply flipping pages. The climactic scene of Augustine's conversion stages this media-technical feature of the codex dramatically, when he randomly opens a passage in his copy of Paul's Letter to the Romans, a passage he understands as being addressed to himself (*Confessions* 8.12.29).

The dramaturgy of Augustine's conversion illustrates the way the media technology of the codex and the mode of reading afforded by it solve the problem of conversionary address. As a religion of conversion with a claim to universal truth, Christianity addresses its "good message" (*euangelion*) to everyone. While this lack of discrimination ensures a maximization of the audience, it also means that a message addressed to everyone is really intended for no one in particular. In a sense, conversion is about making an abstract and universal truth one's own, about assimilating a belief or truth that in many cases was known to oneself beforehand, and in turn letting the self be touched and transformed by it. Another way of putting it would be to say that conversion takes place when an abstract truth becomes a personal belief, when a truth is not merely known but believed by an individual and particular self. It is to address this need to particularize and individualize Christianity's universal and abstract truth that the Acts of the Apostles juxtapose reports of mass conversions with more elaborate narratives of dramatic individual conversions. In cases such as Augustine, Ignatius, and Descartes, this particularization is experienced as a divine call addressed to one self and one self only.

The *apertio libri* achieves this particularization in generating matches between specific passages and individual readers by randomly selecting the passage from the text as a whole. It is as if the complete text contains a host of different messages addressed to a host of different recipients, so only in isolating one particular message from among the many other possibilities does it become personal. And by ruling out that the self has a hand in generating or transmitting it, the selection's randomness ensures that message comes from God.[80] For both of these operations, random generation and selection, the media technology of the codex is ideally suited. As suggested previously, by enabling jumping from place to place, the codex liberated readers from sequential scrolling that literally decontextualizes individual passages and thus isolates them from the rest of the text. Lifted from their immediate context, these passages take on a life of their own, connecting with the reader in new and unexpected ways, including disoriented and uncontrolled movements on the part of the reader. Contrary to expectation, this random selection produces a deeply personal address containing a transcendent and absolute truth, delivering a message for one recipient and one recipient only. Such unmediated communication with the divine is, as indicated earlier, at the heart of traditional cledonomancy as well as the Ignatian exercises. While cledonomancy derives its conversional efficacy from an improbable and uncontrollable set of circumstances, bibliomancy, or better codicomancy, makes improbable encounters more probable—without eliminating their constitutive improbability. Or to put it simply, as a portable random generator the media technology of the codex allows for the production of controlled circumstantiality.

Returning to Leibniz's final example of Jan David's *Veridicus Christianus*,[81] we see how late medieval and early modern piety, striving to improve and intensify personal devotion, improves the codex's random generation. *Veridicus Christianus* grew out of his earlier catechetical work, the *Wisdom of Simple Christians* (*Wijsheyt der Simpel Christenen*), published in

1593. As a catechism, it consisted of one hundred questions and answers in distichal form, which David elaborated after becoming rector of the Jesuit college at Ghent by adding commentaries supported by scriptural passages and quotations from church fathers and classical authors. In addition, David paired each entry with an emblem, including motto, image, and a trilingual subscription in Latin, Dutch, and French. In this way the final version was suited both for the education and admonition of children and laity and for meditation and devotion on the part of more learned readers and the clergy. What set Jan David's *Veridicus Christianus* apart from other devotional emblem books was the inclusion of a novel device, along with a short treatise explaining its rationale and use.[82] The so-called *Orbita probitatis*, or "disc of virtuousness," consisting of four circular rows of numbers (Fig. 3), on top of which was mounted a volvelle with four windows (Fig. 4), matched a number to an entry in the index, which in turn linked to one of the hundred emblems of the book.

By turning the volvelle, the reader generated a random reference to one of the "serious sayings," appearing in the form of mottos to the emblems, and was then directed how to meditate on them by reading the accompanying text. Adding this improved "random generator" to his devotional treatise indicates that David intended his work as a riposte to popular *sortilegia* in employing their methods and refunctionalizing them.[83] Similarly, the title *Veridicus Christianus* (from *verum dicens*, "speaking true") translates the Dutch *Waerseggher*, playing on the latter's double meaning as "fortune teller" and "truth teller" and suggesting that its *orbita* was a medium of divine communication through which God addresses individual believers and guides them toward salvation. That David conceived these meditations as conversive is evidenced by the fact that he prepended Augustine's famous "Tolle, lege; tolle, lege" as an epigraph to his treatise on the *Orbita probitatis*.[84] So it is no coincidence that Leibniz remembered David's *Veridicus Christianus* when he quoted the child's chant from the neighboring house calling Augustine to pick up and read. Furthermore, it is probable that Descartes, the student of the Jesuit College of La Flèche who had traveled in the Low Countries, had encountered David's seminal text as one of the first Jesuit emblem books, earning the author the title "father of Jesuit emblematical literature in the Southern Netherlands."[85] And this was likely the place he found the motto he chose

Founding First Philosophies   63

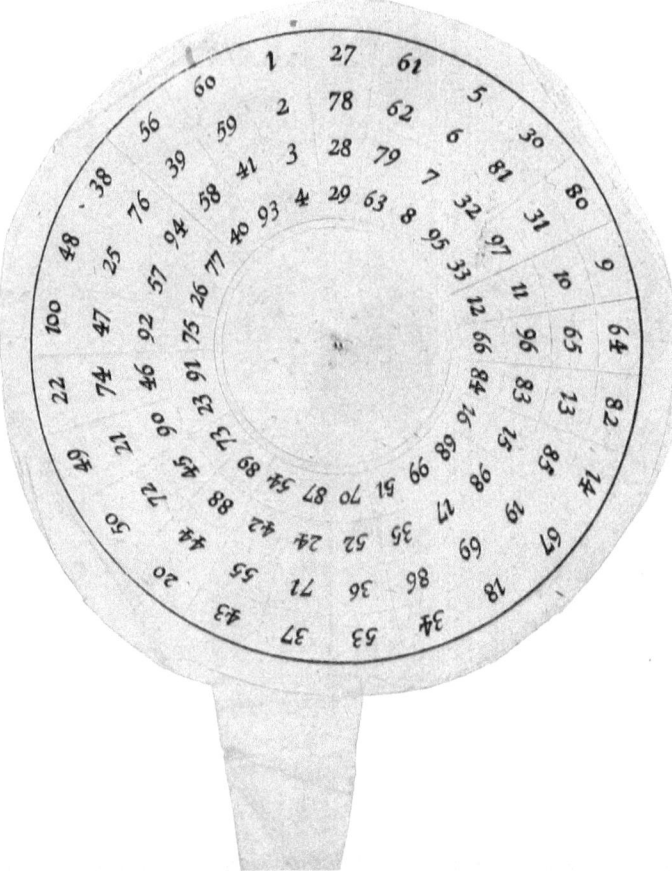

FIGURE 4. Volvelle, contained in the appendix "Orbita probitatis ad Christi imitationem veridico Christiano subserviens," in Joannes David, *Veridicus Christianus* (Antwerp: Ex officina Plantiniana, 1601), 375. Courtesy of the Getty Research Institute.

to preface his *Praeambula*, since *Initium sapientiae timor Domini* (The fear of God is the beginning of wisdom) is the title of the very first emblem in *Veridicus Christianus*.

By resorting to his own *sortes Ausoniae* Descartes inserts himself in this lineage of conversion by the book that stretches from Augustine's *Confessions* to Jan David's *Veridicus Christianus* and beyond. Accordingly, he

FIGURE 3. Lottery dial, contained in the appendix "Orbita probitatis ad Christi imitationem veridico Christiano subserviens," in Joannes David, *Veridicus Christianus* (Antwerp: Ex officina Plantiniana, 1601), 375. Courtesy of the Getty Research Institute.

interprets the verse by Ausonius that appeared in the third dream as representing "the good advice of a wise person or even Moral Theology" (Cole 37; AT X 184). In contrast to the first two dreams, which Descartes understands as "warnings and threats concerning his past life," the last dream "seemed to him to reveal the future" (Cole 38; AT X 185). The former are negative in the sense that they show something from which he is to turn away, and the latter positive in showing him what would happen in this life. In other words, Descartes believes this dream to provide guidance for the pursuit of truth, "which was to be his sole occupation for the rest of his life" (Cole 32; AT X 180), convinced him "that it was the Spirit of Truth that had wanted to open unto him the treasures of all the sciences by this dream" (Cole 37; AT X 185). The question we must ask next is thus about the role played by books or, more precisely, codices, in Descartes' discovery of a new mode of philosophical inquiry.

Recalling Descartes's claim in the *Discourse of the Method* that he had become so critical of books and the knowledge they contain that he exchanged them in favor of exploring the "book of the world" (CSM I 116; AT VI 10), it might appear strange that he would turn to an *apertio libri*—and if only in a dream—to legitimate his momentous discovery of the *mirabilis scientiae fundamenta*. Even more so, as he wrote in the previously cited passage from the *Regulae*, the "primary seeds of truth naturally implanted in human minds ... have been stifled in us through our *constantly reading* and hearing all sorts of errors" (CSM I 18; AT X 376; my emphasis). Finally, isn't the mimetic nature of Descartes' conversion at odds with the self-reliance and autonomy of thought he is otherwise cultivating and promoting? The fact that Ausonius's verse "Quod vitae sectabor iter?" is phrased as a question indicates that the third dream, rather than providing any simple answer is working through the related issues of discerning between right and wrong and making correct choices; in short, it is reflecting on methods of finding the right way and on the role books might play in this endeavor.

Striking about the third dream from this angle is the overwhelming sense of disorientation that is associated with the navigation and reading of books. Highly mobile, they appear and disappear randomly in the dream. Descartes doesn't know whence they came or where they went or who or what controls their movements. But even when he has got hold of a book, his handling is characterized by a remarkable lack of orientation. He is unable to navigate the *Corpus poetarum* even though he "boasts of knowing its order and scheme perfectly." When he loses the verse "Quod vitae sectabor iter?" while searching for the poem "Yes and No," he fails to find it again. It is as if he can find something only when he is not intentionally looking for it, that he can come upon it only by chance. In part, this lack of orientation is attributable to the way the books themselves are composed. The dictionary, symbolizing "all the sciences gathered together" (Cole 36; AT X 184), is no longer complete when it appears a second time; and the dream edition of the *Corpus poetarum* is not the same as the one that Descartes claimed to know so well.[86] And it is attributable in part to the discontinuity and contingency that characterize codical reading in bibliomancy. But in the staging of codical disorientation, Descartes' dream seems to go further than his predecessors. While Augustine's disorientation stands in the service of encountering the one passage intended for him and for him only, Descartes is left with nothing after he has lost the all-important verse. And even it—"Quod vitae sectabor iter?"—is little more than testimony to the disorientation. Descartes, the dream seems to be suggesting, in being unable to navigate books will not in those same books find the answer to the question concerning which path in life to follow, or if he does, it will be by chance.

Descartes' fruitless attempts to navigate books sound very much like the researchers without a method he describes in his *Rules for the Direction of the Mind*:

So blind is curiosity with which mortals are possessed that they often direct their minds down *untrodden paths*, in the groundless hope that they will *chance upon what they are seeking*, rather like someone who is consumed with such a senseless desire to discover treasure that he continually *roams the streets* to see if he can find any that a passer-by might have dropped. This is how almost every chemist, most geometers and many philosophers pursue their research. I am not denying that they sometimes are lucky enough in their *wanderings* to hit upon some truth, though on that account I rate them more fortunate than diligent. But it is far better never to contemplate investigating the truth about any matter than to do so without a *method*. For it is quite certain that such haphazard studies and obscure reflections blur the natural light and blind our intelligence. Those who are accustomed to *walking in the dark* weaken their eye-sight, the result being that they can no longer bear the broad daylight. (CSM I 15–16; AT X 371; my emphasis)

We find here the same metaphorics of itinerancy we have been encountering all along in connection with Descartes' conversion, whether dramatically staged as in the first dream or posed as a question in the third. It is also a metaphorics that is strongly suggested by the etymology of *methodos* as the "way or path to be followed." Method for Descartes, as I show in Chapter 2, is the art of finding one's way through the labyrinth of knowledge, not by chance but by following rules. Again, we find here the warning that any other mode of orientation runs the risk of dimming the *lumen naturale* and smothering the *scintilla rationis*. The point is clear. It is Descartes' method and not books that will provide the spiritual and intellectual orientation he is seeking.

Turning to the content of the two poems confirms and complicates this reading of Descartes' third dream.[87] "Quod vitae sectabor iter?" is the beginning of the second *Eclogue* of Ausonius, titled "A Pythagorean Reflection on the Difficulty of Choosing One's Lot in Life" (*Ex graeco pythagoricum de ambiguitate eligendae vitae*).[88] While the question implies that a choice between at least two distinct paths in life is to be made, the rest of the poem provides copious examples of how every stage and station in life, every mode of living and state of mind is equally wretched and thus to be avoided. Since "all paths in life confront you with unfavorable issues" (167), the poem directly denies the validity of the question with which it commences. It concludes pessimistically: "Therefore the opinion of the Greeks is wisest; for they say that it is good for a man not to be born at all, or, being born, to die quickly" (167). The only real difference to be found in "life" is the one between life and death, rendering the latter the only meaningful and desirable alternative to the indifference of the former. Surprisingly, the second *Eclogue* by Ausonius that appears in Descartes' dream takes a diametrically opposed position. The dichotomy of "est et non" is the ground and engine of all discourse and thought: "All the world constantly uses these familiar monosyllables. . . . In them is all, and all from them; be it a matter of business or pleasure, of bustle or repose" (171). Ausonius may deplore the way all aspects of life are conditioned by this distinction, exclaiming: "What a thing is the life of man which two monosyllables toss about!" (173); but that changes nothing about the eclogue's central claim that "est et non" is the first and fundamental distinction, the distinction inherent in all distinctions, and thus responsible for the differentiality of world and life. The two poems could not be further apart: the first postulating the elementary indifference of life and being, the second maintaining their inherent oppositionality and differentiality.

The question that then arises is what does this contradiction mean for a reading of Descartes' *apertio libri*? Can or should it be resolved? If we look at the dramaturgy of the third dream, how the two poems are staged, we may be able to dynamize and temporalize this seemingly irreconcilable contradiction. The drama begins with Descartes opening a copy of the *Corpus poetarum* and chancing on the question "Quod vitae sectabor iter?" The text of the poem replies that all paths in life are equally unattractive, that there is no difference between them, and that the question itself is therefore invalid. A stranger then gives the dreamer a piece of poetry that begins with "est et non" and argues the opposite: difference is not only relevant but constitutive of everything. By recommending the second poem as "an excellent piece," the stranger seems to be countering the "argument" of "Quod vitae sectabor iter?" Clearly sensing the challenge, and as we have seen, boasting about his prowess, Descartes is thwarted again and again, until having found nothing he was looking for, everything vanishes. As far as we know from the text, all that he is left with is the piece of poetry the stranger gave him. In this regard one could say that "est et non" has the last word. If this is the case, the differentiality in life is affirmed by this dream sent "from on high" by the "Spirit of Truth." Put differently, "Quod vitae sectabor iter?" asks whether there is a difference that makes a difference, and moreover if the *mirabilis scientiae fundamenta* constitute that difference-making difference. "Est et non" would then be the answer to this question. Or, once again, there is a difference that makes a difference and "Quod vitae sectabor iter?" is a valid question, since it has a valid answer, even though it, the right way in life to follow, is—as far as I can tell—never actually provided.

Bringing together the poems' complicated interplay of messages with the drama of codical reading staged by Descartes gives us a fuller understanding of the role of the third dream in his conversion. First, it is important to note that despite Descartes' own sense of revelation, the dream remains strangely inconclusive. Descartes is left with a question and a "yes and no." The dream seems to give him no substantive advice on which path to take to find the truth he is searching for, let alone the truth itself. The obvious and easy resolution of all this is that Descartes already discovered the *mirabilis scientiae fundamenta* well before falling asleep and dreaming. The dream, then, came as the confirmation that what he found earlier actually is the answer to the question "Quod vitae sectabor iter?" This question is actually the answer to whether the *mirabilis scientiae fundamenta* are the answer to how Descartes should spend his life in pursuit of truth. So it's a revelation after all, albeit clothed as a question. That the question is produced by the topical aleatory opening of a book—as in Augustine— underscores this conclusion. And it is further underscored by Descartes' interpretation of Ausonius's verse, as we have seen, as "representing the good advice of a wise person or even Moral Theology." Descartes interprets the question not as much as a question that yet has to be answered than as advice or an answer in its own right. But even this stops short of a more complex and profound explanation. Descartes wasn't expecting to discover the truth, since in the course of his discovery he had come to recognize that the pursuit of truth "was to be his sole occupation for the rest of his life." He was looking for confirmation that finding the truth is a question of the (correct) way to search for it—and possibly even that the *mirabilis scientiae fundamenta* would help him discern and find the right way.[89] In short, rather than discover truth, Descartes learns that methodical orientation and navigation are the key to doing so. This might seem banal, but clearly it was not for Descartes, who believed, as shown by the passage from the *Regulae*, that scientific inquiry hitherto had been coincidental and circumstantial as it paid little attention to method or the "path to be followed." Descartes thus has no need to experience a substantial revelation, that is, one bearing significant informational content, because he had already discovered the *mirabilis scientiae fundamenta*, which concern not content but method.

Descartes' conversion is unique in the sense that it does not show a right way or, more precisely, a particular right way. Instead, it makes evident that a right way exists and that it can and must be found by the subject itself. Following the directionless wanderings of the first dream, the spirit of truth descends in the second to enlighten the dreamer about the divine *scintilla rationis* buried in his mind, an innate God-given faculty of spiritual and mental orientation that enables him to distinguish between right and wrong, true and false, and thus find the correct way. Moreover, the third dream reconfirms for Descartes that books and the knowledge they contain cannot provide the orientation and navigation for which he is looking. The question posed by Ausonius's verse pertains not only to life and the pursuit of truth but also to the books at hand. Had Descartes been able to navigate the *Corpus poetarum* and to find the verse he was so certain he would find there, it would have meant that books can be successfully navigated and, moreover, provide orientation in the search for truth. At the same time, it would have suggested that there is no difference that makes a difference, as argued in the text of the poem, and that there is no right way but only many different equally wrong ways. In either case Descartes' question would have received a very different answer as Descartes confirms in his later assessment of traditional (book) learning in the *Discourse of the Method*, where he observes that after centuries of philosophical inquiry, "there is still no point in it which is not disputed and hence doubtful," deciding on that account to hold "as well-nigh false everything that was merely probable" (CSM I 114; AT VI 8). The disorientation he experienced navigating books, paired with the visualization of the innate seeds of method contained in his mind, made it evident to him that the *mirabilis scientiae fundamenta* were all he needed in his lifelong pursuit of truth. The function and significance of Descartes' *apertio libri*, therefore, differs radically from the one performed by Augustine—even though it is clearly modeled on the latter's example. Augustine opens Paul's Letter to the Romans to receive divine guidance. Descartes opens the *Corpus poetarum* to receive reconfirmation that guidance can come only from thought itself by finding the right way of thinking, that is, method.

It would be wrong to assume that Descartes' *apertio libri* simply breaks with the tradition his dream invokes. To be sure, his dream radically refunctionalizes this mode of evidentiary experience. The truth Descartes is seeking is no longer to be found in books, not even the Book of Books, the Bible, yet he nevertheless experiences a moment of truth by randomly opening a copy of the *Corpus poetarum* and chancing on the verse by Ausonius. For he continues to understand it as a divine message that tells him that henceforth he should rely on his own innate (divinely implanted) sense of orientation to choose the correct path in life and thought. Even though thought must guide itself, the guidance system has to be instituted by a higher authority. To put it more paradoxically, Descartes' method of autonomous thought still requires a divine and thus transcendent foundation and legitimation.

The Dramaturgy of Descartes' Meditative Turn

The three dreams Descartes had in the night from November 10 to 11, 1619, were "methodical" in a number of ways. First, they stage the issue of finding and following the right way. The first dream dramatizes Descartes' mental errancy, his spiritual and intellectual disorientation, which he realizes can be remedied only by correctly discerning the spirits, that is, by relying on his innate ability to distinguish good from evil, true from false. The second dream, followed by the vision of the "sparks of fire scattered around the room," made evident to Descartes that method—the art of finding and following the right way (or to put it Platonically, the art of turning around)—is buried in the flint of his soul and awaits only the "sharp blows of [poetic] imagination" to be brought to the surface and made to shine brightly. The third and most poetic of the three dreams stages this poetic extraction by having Descartes' oneiric self serendipitously encounter two poems by Ausonius. The first poem's verse "Quod vitae sectabor iter?" explicitly reflects Descartes' preoccupation with method, with finding and following the right way, and confirms the abiding urgency of this question. Furthermore, in staging the difficulty of navigating codices, the dream demonstrates that the answer to the question asked in the verse cannot be found in books. It can be answered and the right way found only by the thinking self thinking for itself.

Second, the dreams are methodical in the way that they work through the problem of finding the right way. By staging and literalizing his mental errancy and subsequent orientation, the dreams enact Descartes' conversion and in the process reflect on its logic and economy. Put differently, Descartes is converted by his oneiric self's performance and staging of conversion, which means that the dreams must be read not only representationally, that is, allegorically and symbolically, but also performatively by examining both what they signify and what they do in terms of movement and the dramaturgy that enacts the conversionary turn. The emotional ductus between the three dreams, which Descartes examined closely, makes the point clearly. The first dream shares with the second the attendant emotion of "terror and dread," prompting Descartes to interpret both dreams as "warnings and threats concerning his past life." After beholding and contemplating the sparks of fire, "his terrors faded away, and he fell asleep again quite calmly" (Cole 35; AT X 182). The second dream, together with the events and actions surrounding it, thus forms the transition and turning point, and as a result, Descartes experiences the third dream as "very soothing and very agreeable" (Cole 38; AT X 185), containing "nothing frightful" (Cole 35; AT X 182). He therefore takes it "to reveal the future" and to show "nothing but what would happen in the rest of his life" (Cole 38; AT X 185).

In classically Ignatian fashion, the dreams move from dread and desolation to hope and consolation and so follow and enact a meditative ductus. As Mary Carruthers has shown, the "rhetorical concept of ductus emphasizes way-finding by organizing the structure of any composition as a journey through a linked series of stages, each of which has its own characteristic flow (its 'mode' or 'color'), but which also moves the whole composition along."[90] With its appropriation by monastic meditation, ductus becomes "the conduct of a thinking mind on its way through composition."[91] As discussed previously, the scene of Descartes' conversion is a scene of composition, and in dreaming he is thinking visually and thus composing poetically. Such a meditative ductus begins with the "fear of God," as Augustine explains in *On Christian Teaching* (*De doctrina christiana*), so that the self is "turned . . . toward knowing His Will," ending in joy and tranquility when it has reached the seventh step of this mental ladder and attained wisdom.[92] It is perhaps not far-fetched to suppose that Descartes patterned his methodical dreams after Augustine's notion of meditative ductus. In its focus on mental orientation and navigation, the concept of ductus, as I elaborate in the next chapter, is joined by method and meditation.

Of course, Descartes has not reached wisdom yet. The concluding dream leaves him with a question that is not answered but rather affirmed in its openness and urgency—and with good reason. If thinking is moving, then the necessity of orientation and navigation never ceases. At every step, with every new turn the thinking self needs to decide anew which path to follow. It is for this reason that the conversion ends in such an inconclusive manner. Descartes did not find truth, not even the way to truth, but only the truth of the way. In staging the difficulties of finding the right path in thought and life, his conversion demonstrated to him with incontrovertible certainty the abiding importance of method as a *technē* of orientation and navigation. As this issue will remain the paramount problem of Descartes' thought, he will subsequently reach back to this momentous night. To avert aimless wandering, Descartes must continually renew and operationalize his conversion, making it no surprise that many moments of Descartes' conversion recur in his later thought and, like a mycelium, infiltrate his philosophy.[93] His lifelong obsession with method is an obvious example, but his philosophical thought is also haunted by the dreams and the striving to be free of them. The evil spirit of the first dream is reincarnated as the *genius malignus* of the First Meditation so that the discernment of spirits practiced there is refunctionalized as an epistemological operation to examine all mental representations. The *cogito* of the *Discourse of the Method* and the *Meditations* is a more formalized version of the "naked self" that presented itself to him after having stripped himself of all prejudices but before receiving his dream visions. But even small circumstantial details reappear. The way Descartes sets the scene in the *Meditations* seems to replicate the solitary conversation he had with himself by the fire of an overheated *poêle*. These and other recurring moments are taken up in the later chapters. The focus for now, and the subject of the next chapter, is Descartes' operationalization of conversion as an art of turning or, put differently, his *technē* of thought.

2

Method and Meditation: The Cartesian Art of Turning

Conversio and *Constantia*

When Descartes discovered the "foundations of a marvelous science" on that momentous day of November 10, 1619, it was only the beginning of his lifelong search for truth and knowledge. The illumination, which he literally experienced as he woke up from his second dream, showed him that the *lumen naturale*, the natural light of reason, that is, the instrument and medium of conceiving clear and distinct ideas as well as most other cognitive operations of the Cartesian method, dwelled within him by virtue of his innate deiformity. But it also was in need of constant systematic exercise to reduce obfuscation and increase its brilliance and scope. In a similar fashion, the illumination that Plato's prisoner in the allegory of the cave experiences, when he is unbound and turns away from the shadows on the cave wall and toward the light source at the cave entrance, is only the first, albeit decisive step on a long, arduous journey toward light and truth. The ascent in Plato's allegory of the cave begins with a conversion and culminates in *theoria*, an ecstatic vision of truth or the divine.[1] It is in this context that Socrates defines philosophical education—which the allegory of the cave is supposed to illustrate—as a *technē tēs periagōgēs*, "the art of turning around." At issue, says Socrates, in reference to the faculty of vision, is "the way in which this power can most easily and efficiently be turned around, not an art of producing sight in it. Rather, this art takes as given that sight is there, but not rightly turned nor looking at what it ought to look at" (*Republic* 518d).[2] This art of turning around, rather than understanding the soul as a passive receptacle into which knowledge is poured, is concerned with how the soul exercises and utilizes its innate faculties. If philosophical education were merely about communicating knowledge, the self would be enlightened once it had received that very knowledge. But intellectual enlightenment is not a question of possessing specific knowledge; it has to do with being and remaining "turned" toward the light. Any number of obstacles stand in the way of the soul staying turned, including the pain of relinquishing its sedentary position, the blindness resulting from looking directly into the unaccustomed light, the steepness of the ascent, social pressure, and, of course, resistance to changing ingrained habits.

In the Christian context it is man's fallenness that is responsible for his propensity to relapse, or better, to be "perverted" again. Indeed, in a fallen world there is really no end to conversion until the peril of perversion ends with man's death and redemption. The circumstances that threaten the permanence of a conversion essentially depend on how the latter is conceived. So, for instance, if conversion involves the withdrawal from family and community, social relations exert a pull that is difficult to resist, as shown in examples of many desert fathers. Considered as a psychological phenomenon, conversion's persistence is imperiled by distraction and/or forgetfulness (discussed in Chapter 5). If the primary objective of monastic meditation and prayer is the constant "memory of God" (*mnēmē theou*),[3] the mind's attention must not turn toward other thoughts and things or its continual recall will fail. Therefore, meditations on the vanity of the world from ancient Stoicism onward exhort the self to avert its eyes from enticements of the sensory world and stay turned toward intelligible thoughts and things.

Put simply, conversions don't happen once and for all but become permanent only by being rendered permanent, by continually being repeated and operationalized. They must be constantly renewed so that the self stays "turned." If constancy, or *constantia* (the term I propose to designate the continual perpetuation of conversion), indeed functions like a kind of Cartesian *creatio continua*, as we saw in Chapter 1, then the distinction between *conversio* and *constantia* is more heuristic than real; for constancy is also a turning, albeit a smaller quotidian and thus less dramatic one. An art of turning thus consists in the operationalization of the turn, of being able to repeat and execute it in a controlled fashion to keep on track in the pursuit of truth. In that Socrates uses the phrase to describe the nature of philosophical education, or *paideia*, the operationalization of conversion also includes its communication to others. The art of turning is not only about making the initial conversion iterable within the self's life span but also concerns its replication in others, thereby serving as the basis of philosophical schools and religious movements.

That Descartes was concerned with the operationalization of his conversion is evidenced by the repeated recurrence of its salient elements throughout his work or, to put this differently, by his deliberate and persistent return to this scene of foundation. The *Discourse on the Method*, for instance, returns to the stove-heated room to retell his "discovery of a miraculous science" as the pivotal event in Descartes' intellectual biography. Although its rendition is much less dramatic and detailed than the version in Descartes' lost notebook, *Olympica*, it nonetheless organizes the narration of his autobiography and grounds the presentation of the work's substance, that is, his new method of intellectual inquiry. Likewise, the *Meditations on First Philosophy* returns to this scene of foundation, not to retell it but this time quite literally to reenact it (a distinction to which we return later). Descartes begins his *Meditations* as follows:

> Some years ago I was struck by the large number of falsehoods that I had accepted as true in my childhood, and by the highly doubtful nature of the whole edifice that I had subsequently based on them, I realized that it was necessary, once in the course of my life [*semel in vita*], to demolish everything and start again right from the foundations [*primis fundamentis*] if I wanted to establish anything at all in the sciences that was stable and likely to last. But the task looked an enormous one, and I began to wait until I should reach a mature enough age to ensure that no subsequent time of life would be more suitable for tackling such inquiries. This led me to put the project off for so long that I would now be to blame if by pondering over it any further I wasted the time still left for carrying it out. So today I have expressly rid my mind of all worries and arranged myself a clear stretch of free time. I am here quite alone, and at last I will devote myself sincerely and without reservation to the general demolition of my opinions. (CSM II 12; AT VII 17–18)

Semel in vita—once in one's life one is called upon to tear down the edifice of one's knowledge and rebuild it from the foundations up, and in these very lines Descartes sets out to perform this demolition and reconstruction here and now, calling on the reader to do the same by meditating with him. Later on we examine in greater detail how meditation operates as a philosophical genre to afford the meditator—that is, in any given instance the reader—to re-create the author's conversive experience, particularly as the conversion is not a generic one as in Plato's allegory of the cave but a specific one, Descartes', so that the *Meditations* evokes and restages the scenario of that fateful night in November 1619, with the meditator sitting in the stove-heated room by a fire conversing with themself.

That the purpose of the *Meditations* is conversion is demonstrated by the dedicatory letter to the Faculty of the Sorbonne. Explaining that his intention is to convert unbelievers by rational means, Descartes observes that traditional modes of inducing belief in the existence of God and of an immortal soul are circular: "We must believe in the existence of God because it is a doctrine of Holy Scripture, and conversely, that we must believe Holy Scripture because it comes from God; for since faith is the gift of God, he who gives us grace to believe other things can also give us grace to believe that he exists." He then adds that "this argument *cannot be put to unbelievers* because they would judge it to be circular" (CSM II 3; AT VII 2). Faith breaks that circular logic for those who receive it from God, but those who don't remain unconverted. Instead, in his *Meditations on First Philosophy* Descartes articulated and enacted a new rational art of turning in arguing that "everything that may be known of God can be demonstrated by reasoning which has no other source but our mind" (CSM II 3; AT VII 2). Consequently, he comes to the same conclusion as Augustine that "God may be more easily and more certainly known than the things of this world" (CSM II 4; AT VII 2). By radically doubting all "things of this world" and turning inward, that is, converting, Descartes hopes to find not only the self (in the form of the *cogito*) but, again like Augustine, God.

The philosophical and religious traditions of the West prior to Descartes developed and deployed three principal means to effect *conversio* and maintain *constantia*. Rarely is one deployed in isolation, and instead all three are combined to complement and reinforce one another. The most visible and culturally formative means to make conversion permanent is institutionalization. Philosophical schools and religious movements, of which Socratic philosophy and the Franciscan order are prominent examples, have often sought to replicate or at least approximate the conversion experience of their founders. As Pierre Hadot has shown in great detail, philosophy in antiquity was a way of life.[4] Joining a particular philosophical school entailed not only acquiring a body of knowledge but also adopting a prescribed way of living; and forming a philosophical school ensured the perpetuation not only of a particular body of knowledge but this style of life as well. Similarly, entry into a monastic order meant turning away from the world and devoting one's life to divine service. By following the elaborate set of rules, or *regulae*, prescribed by the order, the monk makes his turn toward God permanent. Monastic orders give what Giorgio Agamben has called "form" to the spiritual and physical life of their members.[5] And that form is often shaped and fueled by the conversion experience of its founder.

Socrates' remark that the "virtues of the soul are somewhat close to those of the body," because they "are really not there beforehand and are later produced by habits and exercises," evidences the pivotal role of practice for the philosophy as an "art of turning around." By conceiving philosophy as an art of turning, it consists as much in knowing how as in knowing what. In antiquity philosophy is not only learned by practice but conceived as a practice. The way of life that defined a particular philosophical school was made up by a particular set of practical exercises. The form of monastic life was, similarly, regulated by a set of spiritual and corporeal practices specific to the order. Ignatius's *Spiritual Exercises* exemplifies how a regimen of spiritual practices is designed to make the founder's conversion experience replicable and communicable.

The third means consists in the material support for the institutionalization and the practices of the conversive turn. An array of media help communicate conversion as well as help the converted stay turned. The myth of Theuth at the end of Plato's dialogue *Phaedrus* indicates that the issue of mediality is central to the operationalization of turning. Socrates famously questions the efficacy of writing, in contrast to the spoken word, for improving memory, shaping the self, and ultimately attaining wisdom. In contrast, Christianity, as a religion of the book, resorts increasingly to written texts as it attempts to produce converts beyond the confines of the Jewish community and to carry its message to the ends of the earth. The complexity of the media ecology of early Christianity by the time of Augustine is expressed in the ensemble of media working together to effect his conversion. Book Eight of the *Confessions* begins with human exemplars and oral narratives, goes on to visions and the child's call from the neighboring house, and culminates in the copy of Paul's Letter to the Romans, which he takes up and opens randomly only to find his own personalized message from God. The Jesuit order in particular was extraordinarily media savvy and sensitive to the affective force of images, theater, rituals, miracles, visions, and other means to win new converts to Catholicism and strengthen the resolve of the already turned. Institutions, practices, and media thus work in consort to operationalize and stabilize the conversive turn.

Descartes was famously distrustful of traditional institutions and media of knowledge and piety. His third dream confirmed to him that books were not going to show him which way in life to follow. Similarly, the school that he enters in the first dream provides no orientation during his windblown wandering, and the school church affords him no sanctuary from the assaults of the evil spirit. In the more-detailed and systematic account of his intellectual trajectory given in the *Discourse on the Method*, Descartes relates how he abandoned the world of books in favor of his travels "in the great book of the world" (CSM I 115; AT VI 9). Thus, the turn toward the self and its power of reasoning that he performed in the course of his conversion can also be understood as a turn away from traditional sources of learning and intellectual authority or, to put it more technically, away from the traditional practices and media of conversion. The third rule in the *Rules for the Direction of the Mind* articulates this program of intellectual self-sufficiency succinctly: "Concerning objects proposed for study, we ought to investigate what we can clearly and evidently intuit and deduce with certainty, and not what other people have thought or what we ourselves can conjecture. For knowledge can be attained in no other way" (CSM I 13; AT X 366).

Instead of Descartes relying on traditional institutions and media of learning, his solution to the operationalization of the illumination he experienced during his conversion was to resort to practice and devise an "art of thinking," as Antoine Arnauld would later call it: an "art" in the sense of the Greek *technē* and in the sense that Plato understands philosophy as *technē tēs periagōgēs*, frequently comparing it to crafts such as medicine, piloting (a ship), carpentry, weaving, pottery, horsemanship, and so forth. While *technē*, in contrast to empirical practice (*empeiria*), requires knowledge (*epistēmē*), it involves a specific kind of practical knowledge, a "knowing how" rather than "knowing that."[6] Instead of knowing something, the goal of technical knowledge is to make something or to do something well.

This practical knowledge is methodical in the sense that it entails a set of rules and procedures that makes it iterable and optimizable. In that sense it is not discrete like propositional knowledge that the mind either possesses or not. As an art or a craft, *technē* requires practice to be acquired, perfected, and maintained. In the *Sophist* Plato differentiates between practical *technai* and theoretical arts such as dialectic or calculation. Where the former aim to produce a separate artifact, the latter has no separate product. Its aim is the technical skill itself. It is a kind of practical knowledge whose purpose is the production of (practical) knowledge. The effect of practice in this sense is to make thought autonomous.

Descartes' *technē* of thought is most commonly identified with his method and has, thus, not escaped scholarly notice. What has not received sufficient attention is the central role that the spiritual practices of philosophy and religious devotion play in the Cartesian *technē* of thought. Descartes' cognitive practices are consistently informed by and modeled on spiritual exercises from a variety of different traditions ranging from ancient philosophy to the resurgent piety of his own day. Indeed, the rules of method can be said to make up only the tip of an enormous iceberg of mental and spiritual practices in Descartes' work. Until the end of his life he was concerned with the pragmatic dimension of thinking, with the idea that thought is a form of doing that can be practiced and exercised. Thus, method and meditation are not antithetical but part of a larger whole. We recall Descartes writing in the preface to the French edition of *Principia philosophiae* that "the whole of philosophy is like a tree. The roots are metaphysics, the trunk is physics, and the branches emerging from the trunk are all the other sciences, which may be reduced to three principal ones, namely, medicine, mechanics, and morals" (CSM I 186; AT IXB 14–15). For Descartes, the ultimate goal and fruit of philosophy is the "highest degree of wisdom which constitutes the supreme good of human life" (CSM I 183; AT IXB 9). The "supreme good," which is to be attained through the search for truth, included as much a long life realized by medicine,[7] as it did happiness afforded by morals.[8] The search for truth and the pursuit of the supreme good became a way of life for Descartes, motivating him to withdraw from the world and, almost like an early Christian anchorite, to live in solitude and to observe a strict dietetic regimen.[9] Philosophy in this holistic and organic sense was, thus, for Descartes a lifelong practice.

The two most important and well-known conceptual metaphors with which Descartes conceives and figures thinking as practice are, of course, building and path finding, architecture and orientation.[10] Both are intimately conjoined not only in Descartes' oeuvre but in the long history of spiritual and meditational practices of the Western tradition. In fact, as I show in the following pages, these two operational metaphors are the conduits by which the tradition of spiritual exercises from antiquity to Loyola informs Descartes' practice of thinking most perceptibly.

Cartesian Edification

"Among the first" ideas "that occurred" to Descartes according to his account in the *Discourse on the Method*, when he "stayed all day shut up alone in a stove-heated room ... to converse with myself about my own thoughts," was an extended metaphor or, more precisely, an allegory of his conversion and its operationalization:

There is not usually so much perfection in works composed of several parts and produced by various different craftsmen as in the works of one man. Thus we see that buildings undertaken and completed by a single architect are usually more attractive and better planned than those which several have tried to patch up by adapting old walls built for different purposes. Again, ancient cities which have gradually grown from mere villages into large towns are usually ill-proportioned, compared with those orderly towns which planners lay out as they fancy on level ground. Looking at the buildings of the former individually, you will often find as much art in them, if not more, than in those of the latter; but in view of their arrangement—a tall one here, a small one there—and the way they make the streets crooked and irregular, you would say it is chance, rather than the will of men using reason, that placed them so. (CSM I 116; AT VI 11–12)

This is the first published version of the image that Descartes will use throughout his oeuvre to illustrate his project of reforming knowledge and understanding. It conceives of the production of knowledge, of thinking and all other mental operations involved, as building, whether of the individual production of knowledge as building a single house or its collective counterpart in building a whole city. Thinking resembles the building of an architectural structure; or, put more succinctly, thinking is edification. Descartes' initial motivation for introducing this poetic image is to account for the self-reliance and self-sufficiency of his reform project. At this point he doesn't yet explain why buildings or cities designed by a single architectural mind are more perfect than those "produced by various different craftsmen." Instead, he makes his case empirically by pointing out that they "are usually more attractive and better planned."

Conceding that it is "unreasonable for an individual to plan to reform a state by changing it from the foundations up and overturning it in order to set it up again, or again for him to plan to reform the body of the sciences or the established order of teaching them in the schools" (CSM I 117; AT VI 13), Descartes holds that one's individual edifice is another matter.[11] As far as individual knowledge is concerned, the house can be "pulled down in order to rebuild" it. Hence Descartes' resolution:

Regarding the opinions to which I had hitherto given credence, I thought that I could not do better than to undertake to get rid of them, all at one go, in order to replace them afterward with better ones, or with the same ones once I had squared them with the standards of reason. I firmly believed that in this way I would succeed in conducting my life much better than if I built only upon old foundations and relied only upon principles that I had accepted in my youth without ever examining whether they were true. (CSM I 117; AT VI 13–14)

Descartes' insistence on absolute self-sufficiency and self-reliance in epistemological matters requires that the old self be stripped entirely bare. The mental practice known as universal doubt that was already present in the *Olympica* notebook is conceived here as demolition. In contrast to ancient and early modern skepticism, the purpose of Descartes' practice of universal doubt is to discover a solid foundation, "to reach certainty—to cast aside the loose earth and sand so as to come upon rock and clay" (CSM I 125; AT VI 29). This Descartes accomplished with the discovery of the "foundations of a wonderful science" as part of his conversion, including the recognition of the foundationality of foundation.

What sets the account of the *Discourse on the Method* most distinctly apart from the narrative in the *Olympica* is Descartes' reconfiguration of his conversion as an allegory of destruction and reconstruction. Within the framework of this image, conversion becomes explicitly the laying of the foundation, which, if it is solid, translates into a stable and durable edifice, whereas a weak foundation does not. Thus, the permanence of a conversion depends on the solidity of the foundation established by that very conversion.

In the first lines of the *Meditations*, returning to the architectural metaphor elaborated in the *Discourse*, Descartes articulates this functional relationship lexically. "The whole edifice that I had subsequently based on [*postea superextruxi*]," the "falsehoods" that were "accepted as true in my childhood" (CSM II 12; AT VII 17), is literally "built on top," in Latin, *superextruere*. A few lines later Descartes observes that anything constructed upon (*superaedificatum*) a foundation that has been undermined "collapses of its own accord." He thus thinks of the edifice of knowledge as a *superaedificium* that must be understood in relation to the substructure by which it is shaped and defined. Since the building of everything else in the edifice continues the work of laying its foundation, the architectural allegory draws an intimate and functional link between Descartes' conversion and its subsequent operationalization.[12]

By figuring thinking and meditating as building, Descartes retools the West's meditational practice and discourse for the purpose of constructing a new philosophical system. Architectural structures and spaces played a pivotal work in the cognitive work of the essentially oral culture of classical antiquity, as in the mnemotechnics of ancient rhetoric, in which buildings served as templates for structuring the "storehouse of memory."[13] The author of the *Rhetorica ad Herennium* compares these templates or, more technically, backgrounds to wax tablets (*cerae*) or papyrus, and the images placed on them to writing (3.18.31).[14] Delivery then takes the form of reading aloud what is inscribed on the mnemonic tablets. The account in *Ad Herennium* insists that the backgrounds be arranged in a clearly discernible order so that the mind is not confused and can orient itself more easily. Nonetheless, the author of *Ad Herennium* advises the rhetor to choose the layout of an existing building to memorize rather imagine a fictional one,[15] although if no suitable real backgrounds are available they may create one so as to "obtain a most serviceable distribution of appropriate backgrounds" (3.29.32). Once the rhetor has constructed their own mnemonic storehouse, they can begin filling it, in some sense furnishing it with images (*imagines*) that serve to recollect either "things" (*memoria rerum*) or "words" (*memoria verborum*). The art of memory, as it was conceptualized by ancient rhetoric, consists then of two distinct but complementary operations. First the mind builds itself (as) a storehouse by memorizing an architectural plan; then it proceeds to fill it(self) with furnishings—in short, construction followed by interior decoration. Memory, in fact, the mind as a whole, is conceived as a building, and memorizing (as well as most acts of cognition such as perceiving, imagining, and thinking) as a process of constructing and decorating the house of the mind.

Paul's figural usage of edification (*oikodomē* in the Greek original and *aedificatio* in the Latin Vulgate) integrates notions from the Old Testament and Hellenistic philosophy to arrive at a genuinely Christian concept, which infuses the rhetorical practice of mnemonic construction with a number of essential new elements.[16] In doing so, he transforms rhetorical "edification" from a mental into a spiritual practice.[17] While Paul uses *oikodomē* and *oikodomein* and the various cognates quite frequently, the *locus classicus* is the following seminal passage from the First Letter to the Corinthians:[18]

> For we are labourers together with God: ye are God's husbandry, ye are God's building [*Dei aedificatio*]. According to the grace of God which is given unto me, as a wise masterbuilder [*sapiens architectus*], I have laid the foundation [*fundamentum posui*], and another buildeth thereon [*superaedificat*]. But let every man take heed how he buildeth thereupon [*superaedificet*]. For other foundation can no man lay than that is laid, which is Jesus Christ. Now if any man build upon this foundation [*superaedificat super fundamentum hoc*] gold, silver, precious stones, wood, hay, stubble; every man's work shall be made manifest: for the day shall declare it, because it shall be revealed by fire; and the fire shall try every man's work of what sort it is. If any man's work abide which he hath built thereupon, he shall receive a reward. If any man's work shall be burned, he shall suffer loss: but he himself shall be saved; yet so as by fire. Know ye not that ye are the temple of God [*templum Dei*], and that the Spirit of God dwelleth in you? If any man defile the temple of God, him shall God destroy; for the temple of God is holy, which temple ye are. (1 Cor 3:9–17)

Paul figures himself as the "wise master builder," who with the help of God's grace has established Jesus Christ as the foundation for the edifice, literally the *superaedificatio*, that the individual self erects thereupon. Only by building on this divine foundation does the self become God's *aedificatio* and *templum*.

This emphasis on the foundation sets Paul's architectural metaphorics apart from what is seen in his rhetorical forebears.[19] While they were unconcerned with the footing of their *loci*, it is decisive for Paul, as the self's salvation does not hinge on its *superaedificationes* but on the foundation that is Jesus Christ.[20] If they get destroyed, the self suffers loss yet will be saved. This means that there is no other foundation but Jesus Christ and his Gospel, which Paul is spreading. Nevertheless, once the foundation has been laid through Paul's teachings of Jesus Christ, every man builds his individual superstructures with a wide array of materials—"gold, silver, precious stones, wood, hay, stubble." Despite the common foundation, the resulting edifices will look very different and will be judged accordingly (although not in view of eternal salvation). In this point Paul departs in a second way from rhetorical edification. Whereas the *ars memoria* of ancient rhetoric foregrounds the faithfulness of reproduction (even though composition, that is, *inventio, dispositio,* and *elocutio*, is creative), Pauline construction allows for individual creativity in regard to the *superaedificationes*. Mary Carruthers emphasizes this point: "Paul uses his architectural metaphor as a trope of invention, not for storage.... From the beginning of Christianity, the architecture trope is associated with invention in the sense of 'discovery,' as well as in the sense of inventory."[21]

It is easy to see how Paul's architectural metaphor of edification, which in the Corinthian context aimed at the building of a Christian community, could be readily transferred to the individual self and, even more narrowly, to the formation of the interior, spiritual self, and in the medieval monastic context refer to the practice of meditation and spiritual exercise.[22] The construction of spiritual places within the interior self was an integral part of meditative practice. And this type of what Carruthers calls "locational memory" is still operative in Ignatius's *Spiritual Exercises*, which otherwise affords a much more delocalized and mobile imagination. Every individual meditational exercise is to begin with the *compositio loci*, that is, "seeing the place," according to Ignatius. "It should be noted here that for contemplation or meditation about visible things, e.g., a contemplation about Christ Our Lord who is visible, the 'composition' consists in seeing through the gaze of the imagination the material place where the object I want to contemplate is situated. By 'material place' I mean, e.g., the temple or a mountain where Jesus Christ or Our Lady is to be found, according to what I want to contemplate."[23] Ignatius, thus, makes explicit that meditation requires a place as its foundation.

As implied in the Ignatian *compositio loci*, which teleports the exercitant to a specific place in the Holy Land described in the Gospels in order to visualize and contemplate the story unfolding there, meditative edification usually had the function of creating pathways for the meditative self. Similarly, the aim of ancient rhetoric, the classical precursor, was not the construction and decoration of a mnemonic edifice in itself. *Memoria* was only the fourth stage of eloquence. The fifth and last was the *actio*, or delivery, that realized, that is, literally actualized, the paths prescribed by the memorized layout by "walking" from place to place, recalling the *imagines* deposited there, and verbalizing them as the end product, which was the speech itself. As Carruthers writes of monastic rhetoric, "The trope of 'steps' or 'stages' was commonly applied to the affective, emotional 'route' that a meditator was to take in the course of such composition, from 'fear' to 'joy.' . . . These 'routes,' emotional and rational, are always characterized as routes through the things in one's memory."[24] The technical term for the "conduct of a thinking mind on its way through a composition" was "ductus";[25] and we recall from Chapter 1 that the ductus of Descartes' three dreams led from fear, the beginning of wisdom, to joy in the discovery of the foundations of a wonderful science. We also recall from the long passage from the *Discourse on the Method* at the beginning of this section that Descartes was attuned to the effect that orderly design and construction of a city had on the layout of cities. Of buildings in ancient cities, he wrote, "in view of their arrangement—a tall one here, a small one there—and the way they make the streets crooked and irregular, you would say it is chance, rather than the will of men using reason, that placed them so." Thus, already the foundations, and not just the erected edifice, determine the layout of the possible paths—which brings us to the discovery Descartes made in that stove-heated room: his method.

Method and Intellectual Orientation

The "foundations of a wonderful science" that Descartes discovered in his conversion and then proceeded to spell out in his first longer text, *Rules for the Direction of the Mind*, and to elaborate further in the *Discourse on the Method*, was most likely his method. Cartesian method is usually contextualized and conceptualized within the context of early modern science and its emerging methodology,[26] and Descartes was not the only early modern natural philosopher who was intensely engaged in developing a reliable and actionable method. However, from the perspective of modern scientific practice, its actual articulation cannot but disappoint. The four "principal rules" presented in the second part and the three "rules of morals" deduced from method in the third part seem too general and, with no proposed experiments or mathematical proofs, not actionable enough to fit fully into the context of early modern experimental science.[27] No experiment could be set up; no mathematical proof could be devised implementing them. Instead, they are better read as the answer to the question posed in the third dream, "Which path in life shall I follow?" They are designed to guide a life of thought in the pursuit of truth rather than concrete scientific procedures. In the following pages I attempt to show how Descartes' method operationalizes the insights gained during his conversion and thus to resituate Descartes' method within the tradition of spiritual exercises and meditation reaching back into antiquity. As Matthew Jones has demonstrated, the tradition of spiritual exercises was integral to the practice of science in the early modern world.[28] Both were joined in the pursuit of a common goal, attaining and realizing the "good life"; and, as I have indicated cursorily, Descartes fully bought into that project. Furthermore, the practice of meditation had developed very sophisticated methods of thinking that provided Descartes with viable alternatives to the Aristotelian tradition he set out to critique and supplant. Put differently, the philosophical and religious tradition of spiritual exercise would not have appeared backward to one such as Descartes, and it had much to offer a young intellectual seeking to reform the era's modes of knowing.

Descartes' fervent and enduring concern with the issue of intellectual orientation explains why he frequently activates the latent metaphoricity of method as the path to be followed.[29] In the *Regulae ad directionem ingenii* (*Rules for the Direction of the Mind*) Descartes gives the first account of his method, describing it as a set of "reliable rules which are easy to apply, and such that if one follows them exactly, one will never take what is false to be true or fruitlessly expend one's mental efforts, but will gradually and constantly increase one's knowledge till one arrives at a true understanding [*perveniet ad veram cognitionem*] of everything within one's capacity" (CSM I 16; AT X 371–72), as the mind is directed along "the right path of truth" (CSM I 12; AT X 366) and prevented from taking wrong turns and expending unnecessary energy. "Anyone who sets out in quest of knowledge of things," warns Descartes, "must follow this rule as closely as he would the thread of Theseus if he were to enter the labyrinth" (CSM I 20; AT X 379–80). A rule, *regula*, derived from the Latin verb *regere* (to govern, direct, steer), is the tool by which the mind directs, derived from the Latin verb *diregere* (to lay straight, steer, direct), and is directed. Thus, the title *Regula ad directionem ingenii* is a *figura etymologica*, if not tautological: *per etymologiam* rules direct the mind in its search for truth. "Throughout this treatise we shall try to pursue every humanly accessible path [*vias omnes*] which leads to knowledge of the truth. We shall do this very carefully, and show the paths to be very easy, so that anyone who has mastered the whole method, however mediocre his intelligence, may see that there are no paths closed to him that are open to others" (CSM I 32; AT X 399–400).[30] It should come as no surprise that Descartes figures the discovery of the right way as a turning: "If we do not know something we are capable of knowing, this is simply because we have never discovered a way [*advertimus viam ullam*] that might lead us to such knowledge [*duceret ad talem cognitionem*]; or because we have fallen into the opposite error" (CSM I 16; AT X 372). The rules of method not only turn the mind's attention in the right direction (the Latin verb Descartes uses is *advertere*, that is, "to turn toward something, to pilot, to turn the attention"),[31] but they also stabilize the mind in its progress toward ever-greater and more accurate knowledge.

The *Discourse on the Method* employs the same itinerant metaphorics, only to a slightly different end. As indicated by the full title, *Discourse on the Method of Rightly Conducting One's Reason and Seeking Truth in the Sciences* (*Discourse de la méthode pour bien conduire sa raison, et chercher la verité dans les sciences*), it was engaged in the same project of directing the mind in its pursuit of knowledge. Consequently, metaphors of finding and losing one's way abound in the text.[32] Yet, while the *Regulae* describe and explain the rules that guided the intellect in its quest for truth, *Discourse on the Method* narrates the circuitous path that led Descartes to the discovery of his method. Instead of teaching how to follow rules, it tells how he was misdirected by his studies and teachers, by books and their authors, and how he ultimately took up a lifestyle of permanent itinerancy, physically as well as intellectually (and spiritually). This may explain the text's somewhat oxymoronic title. After all, the term "discourse" is derived from the Latin verb *discurrere*, which means "to run to and fro."[33] So while "method" refers to the path that will lead the self toward its goal and keeps it on track, "discourse" implies, at least etymologically, a certain spatial disorientation and errancy. This would also be in line with Descartes' claim that the discovery that enabled his systematic quest for knowledge came ultimately as a matter of luck, which would seem at odds with a treatise on methodical inquiry: "I consider myself fortunate to have happened upon certain paths in my youth which led me to considerations and maxims from which I formed a method whereby, it seems to me, I can increase my knowledge gradually and raise it little by little to the highest point allowed by the mediocrity of my mind and the short duration of my life" (CSM I 112; AT VI 3).

What Descartes, writing behind the mask of a rationalist philosopher, attributed to circumstance, Leibniz, the reader of Descartes' early notebook *Olympica*, called providence. So while discovering the path, the *mirabilis scientiae fundamenta*, was beyond the self's control, its systematic and sustained pursuit was the object of method. In fact, to provide guidance after the illumination has passed is precisely the function of method: "But, like a man who walks alone in the dark, I resolved to proceed so slowly, and to use such circumspection in all things, that even if I made but little progress I should at least be sure not to fall" (CSM I 119; AT VI 16–17). Proceeding slowly but systematically is the mark of method as "those who proceed but very slowly can make much greater progress, if they always follow the right path, than those who hurry and stray from it" (CSM I 111; AT VI 2). *Discourse on the Method*, thus, tells the story of errancy in search of a controlled and systematic form of locomotion and orientation. Paradoxically, it also makes it clear that Cartesian method, despite its claim to control and reliability, cannot account for its own beginnings.

Cartesian method, in sum, is a systematic practice of mental movement that represents an alternative to the aimless "wanderings [*feliciter errare*]" of contemporary science (CSM I 16; AT X 371). "For it is quite certain that such haphazard studies and obscure reflections [*meditationes obscuras*] blur the natural light and blind our intelligence," writes Descartes. "Those who are accustomed to walking in the dark weaken their eye-sight, the result being that they can no longer bear the broad daylight" (CSM I 16; AT X 371). It is hardly a coincidence that Descartes blends the metaphorics of *methodos* and illumination, putting the practitioner of Cartesian method in much the same situation as Plato's cave dweller being blinded by the light when he emerges from his prison. Descartes is claiming that by practicing his method, the mind cultivates its indwelling natural light and in the process accustoms itself to the resultant illumination of the object under investigation. His method not only directs the intellect along the path to be followed but in the process transforms the intellect itself in such way that it becomes more skilled in orientation and navigation. In contrast, those without method not only walk in the dark but also "weaken" their mental vision and, thereby, become "no longer" able "to bear" illumination. In the end, inquiry without method is worse than no inquiry at all. Even if the *a-methodoi* were to chance upon the light of truth, blinded as they are, they may not even recognize it.

As a mode of mental orientation and navigation Cartesian method is predicated on conceiving thinking as movement. This conceptualization of thought is not so pronounced in the *Discourse*, where the metaphorics of *methodos* is associated with Descartes' intellectual biography, but the *Regulae* and *Meditations* operationalize it incessantly. In the former Descartes begins by distinguishing two "actions of the intellect [*intellectus nostri actiones*]": intuition and deduction (CSM I 14; AT X 368). By intuition he understands, not

> the fluctuating testimony of the senses or the deceptive judgment of the imagination as it botches things together but the conception of a clear and attentive mind, which is so easy and distinct that there can be no room for doubt about what we are understanding. Alternatively, and this comes to the same thing, intuition is the indubitable conception of a clear and attentive mind which proceeds solely from the light of reason. (CSM I 14; AT X 368)

Whereas intuition is primarily concerned with "apprehending single propositions" (CSM I 14; AT X 369), deduction involves the "inference of something as following necessarily from some other propositions which are known with certainty" (CSM I 15; AT X 369), that is, intuitions. A deduction proceeds

> through a continuous and uninterrupted movement of thought [*per continuum et nullibi interruptum cogitationis motum*] in which each individual proposition is clearly intuited. This is similar to the way in which we know that the last link in a long chain is connected to the first: even if we cannot take in at one glance all the intermediate links on which the connection depends, we can have knowledge of the connection provided we survey the links one after the other and keep in mind that each link from first to last is attached to its neighbor. (CSM I 15; AT X 369–70)

While intuition functions like a glance that takes no time, in deduction the mind is "aware of a movement or a sort of sequence [*motus sive successio*]" (CSM I 15; AT X 370).[34] As soon as more than one clear and distinct thought (i.e., intuition) is in play, the mind is on the move; or in Descartes' own words: "Inferring one thing from another involves a kind of movement of our mind" (CSM I 37; AT X 407).[35] Descartes' metaphor of proofs as chains of individual thoughts, and deduction, similarly, as "the movement from one link to another,"[36] conjoins edification and method. The chain is constructed link by link so that the mind can readily follow the trail that is laid out. Thinking and meditating, for Descartes as well as for the tradition of spiritual exercises, consist not only in designing and constructing mental edifices but also in the actualization, by moving through them, of the routes marked out by those very structures. Building and walking are, therefore, the two main conceptual metaphors for meditative practice.

We have seen that conceiving thinking or meditating as movement is implicit in the practice of monastic meditation. Realizing a meditative route, making one's way between the individual *loci* of one's mental edifice, requires some sort of mental motion. The meditator needs to get from one place to the next in order to complete their prayer or spiritual ascent. Descartes would have known this from the very beginning of the *Spiritual Exercises*, where Ignatius makes this explicit in explaining the concept and term "spiritual exercises":

The term "spiritual exercises" denotes every way of examining one's conscience, of meditating, contemplating, praying vocally and mentally, and other spiritual activities, as will be said later. For just as strolling, walking, and running are exercises for the body, so "spiritual exercises" is the name given to every way of preparing and disposing one's soul to rid herself of all disordered attachments, so that once rid of them one might seek and find the divine will in regard to one's life for the good of the soul. (SE § 1, p. 283)

While Ignatius defines spiritual exercises very broadly—examining one's conscience, meditating, contemplating, praying—to illustrate what is common to all spiritual exercises, he compares them to "strolling, walking, and running," that is, to locomotion. Whatever the soul does when it is engaged in spiritual activities or exercises, it always also moves, is in (loco)motion spiritually and mentally, with the effect of the soul ridding itself of "all disordered attachments" and turning toward God, in averting the temporal and converting to the eternal. In short, spiritual exercises repeat conversion and make it repeatable. By operationalizing conversion, they keep the self turned and on track toward its ultimate goal of eternal salvation. In a similar way, Descartes' method operationalizes the turning that he performed in that stove-heated room away from the external, sensible world toward the internal, rational self and the illumination that he experienced when he recognized that every mind contained the *scintilla animae* or *lumen naturale* that functions as the guiding light in the search for truth.

Descartes' conceptualization of method as a mode of intellectual orientation and navigation is entirely in line with its traditional usage going back to Plato, for whom it could mean a mode of intellectual inquiry as well as doctrine or opinion.[37] Most important, method is what defines philosophy as a *technē*, or art, with art and method so closely related in ancient Stoicism that they become almost synonymous. As Neal Gilbert observes, "Only the man who has the *methodos* can be said to have a sound knowledge of an art, and it is this *methodos* which enables him to teach the art to others."[38] Its latent metaphoricity remains always present and is activated frequently. In the *Phaedrus* Socrates claims that any art without method would be like the wanderings of a blind man (270d).[39] In the Latin Middle Ages the Greek *methodos* remains relatively rare and gets translated with a host of different terms: *disciplina, doctrina, regula, via, ars*. Cicero had rendered *methodos* with *via et ratio*,[40] considerably slowing its Latinization and adaptation as a technical term well into the Middle Ages but simultaneously keeping its figurative sense alive. As a philosophical term it appears with the first translations of Greek texts in the twelfth century. Robert Grosseteste, in his translation of Eustratius's commentary on Aristotle's *Nicomachean Ethics*, is clearly well aware of the term's metaphoricity: "Method, most often translated as *doctrina*, is composed from the Greek *meta*, meaning 'after' or 'with,' and *hodos*, that is 'path,' and ... denotes a *habitus* that is guided by trailblazing reason."[41]

For Renaissance thinkers method became, as Gilbert puts it, "the party slogan,"[42] adopting as their primary reference Plato's *Phaedrus*, particularly the section in which Socrates discusses the true art of rhetoric (265d–277c). Like Socrates, Jacopo Zabarella argues that method is the mark of any true art or science: "It is manifest that every science, and every discipline is conveyed [*tradi*] by some method and cannot endure [*consistere*] without method. For, in no branch of learning can anyone teach well, unless both in disposing its parts and in clarifying every theorem, and in conveying knowledge of its hidden things, he maintains some method."[43] Method is the mode by which a science is practiced and thus rendered replicable, as well the mode by which it is communicated and taught. In short, a *technē*'s *constantia* (Zabarella uses the verb *consistere*) and *traditio* (from *tradere*) depend on method, even as it guides and controls scientific inquiry: "For indeed these are as it were ways and passages from something to something [*viae quaedam sunt et transitus ab aliquo ad aliquod*], which is the proper signification of the Greek word, *methodos*."[44] Similar to its Cartesian version, the notion of method as a *via*, *transitus*, or *processus* is predicated on conceiving intellectual inquiry as a movement: "Logical discursive movement [*logicus namque discursus*] can be considered in things, in concepts, and in words; and [as a movement] it cannot happen in a moment of time but only with some lapse [of time] and in time."[45] In contrast to signification, which for Zabarella happens in an instant, "discursive movement" takes place in time and has duration. The parallels between Descartes's "deduction" and Zabarella's "discursive movement," "intuition," and "signification" are thus apparent.

Meditation and method share a common purpose, that is, to keep the mind on track in pursuit of its goal, be it eternal salvation or truth. Or to put it differently, to be successful in operationalizing and sustaining the conversive turn, meditation always had to be methodical. Likewise, Platonic philosophy was an art of turning only insofar as it followed a method, employing what I have called a "guidance system." As Descartes' discourse and practice demonstrate, he places himself firmly in that tradition. After all, the "foundations of a wonderful science" that he discovered during his conversion were the beginnings of his method, and method remained instrumental to his lifelong search for truth. The *Meditations* in particular integrates method in such a way that *meditatio* and *methodos* merge. Thus, in contrast to Michel Foucault's claim, there is no tension between method and meditation. In Descartes, as in Plato, they are homologous. As the following chapters demonstrate, Descartes' *Meditations* invites his readers to follow a precise *methodos* and, thereby, enact his turn.

Descartes' Practice of Thought

So far we have examined the two metaphors—building and path finding—Descartes used to conceptualize and illustrate the illumination and insight he experienced during his conversion. Both conceive of thinking as a practice, so whatever the mind thinks, it either constructs an edifice of knowledge or follows the path toward truth--or both. As yet, however, these conceptual metaphors tell us little about the specific cognitive or mental practices that Descartes performed in building and exploring the edifice. For the mind does many different things when it thinks. It thinks in the narrow sense of the term, but it also perceives, imagines, remembers, judges, and wills, to name only a few operations that Descartes considers in the *Meditations* (CSM II 19; AT VII 28). He subjects many of these mental operations to systematic and sustained practice in the *Meditations* and elsewhere. Given that the spiritual and mental exercises salient to the *Meditations* will be given detailed treatment in the following chapters, the rest of this chapter touches on them in passing to focus instead on Descartes' lifelong preoccupation with the issue of mental practice. It examines two interrelated issues. The first calls for a number of questions about practice in itself. How does Descartes' practice of philosophy operationalize the illumination and insight gained during his conversion? How does he conceive of mental practice as a result; and, concretely, how does he actually practice thought? Finally, how does the practice of knowing affect knowledge, or, put differently, how does knowing how determine the knowing that? The second issue relates to the communication of the philosophical practice to others. How does Descartes communicate practice to his readers? What are the challenges involved? Is there something like a Cartesian pedagogy of philosophical practice?

The most obvious and immediate answer to the first cluster of questions is Cartesian method. It is a reasonable assumption that the "foundations of a wonderful science," discovered in the stove-heated room, was his method, and insofar as it served as the foundation of philosophical and scientific practice, it was designed to be easily replicated and refined. Consisting of a limited number of "reliable rules which are easy to apply" (CSM I 16; AT X 371–72), and unlike other famous methods of the time such as dialectics or Ramus's logic, Cartesian method was simple by design, easy to remember and keep close at hand. Its easy applicability and reliability uncouple it from specific subjects and objects of inquiry, and following the method requires no particular talent or preexisting skill. Every "human mind has within it a sort of spark of the divine, in which the first seeds of useful ways of thinking are sown, seeds which, however neglected and stifled by studies which impede them, often bear fruit of their own accord" (CSM I 17; AT X 373). In this sense, the capacity to practice method is innate. Anyone can follow and apply the rules Descartes describes in the *Regulae* and *Discourse on the Method* and enacts in the *Meditations*. Similarly, as Descartes stresses in the second part of the *Discourse*, "Since I did not restrict the method to any particular subject-matter, I hoped to apply it as usefully to the problems of the other sciences as I had to those of algebra" (CSM I 121; AT VI 21). Algebra and geometry were the two disciplines on which Descartes first tested his method because they "are simply the spontaneous fruits which have sprung from the innate principles of method" (CSM I 17; AT X 373). But the rules of method, as he writes in Rule Fourteen of the *Regulae*, are "so useful in the pursuit of deeper wisdom that I have no hesitation in saying that this part of our method was designed not just for the sake of mathematical problems; our intention was, rather, that the mathematical problems should be studied exclusively for the sake of the excellent practice which they give us in the method" (CSM I 59; AT X 442). Working through and solving mathematical problems afford Descartes the opportunity to practice and improve his method. Method is not a means but an end in itself.

Method's indifference to content ensures its formal constancy across disciplines and subject matter, and its easy applicability facilitates its replicability; or put more simply, it makes it easy to practice. After discovering it, Descartes spent the following years practicing "constantly my self-prescribed method in order to strengthen myself more and more in its use" (CSM I 122; AT VI 22).[46] His method is designed to be honed and refined, and it demands continuous and repeated exercise.[47] For the "innate principles," on which Cartesian method is based, need to be "cultivated with extreme care [*summa cura excolantur*]" (CSM I 17; AT X 373).[48] Or to spell out the two metaphors frequently employed by Descartes: The *semina scientia* or "seeds of truth naturally implanted in human minds" (CSM I 18; AT X 376) have to be grown, brought to flower, and allowed to bear fruit. The *scintilla animae*, "spark of the divine" (CSM I 17; AT X 373), must be fanned so that the *lumen naturale* shines brightly enough to illuminate truth.⁴⁹ In short, Descartes holds that reason can and needs to be practiced.

Descartes' ultimate goal of practicing his method is to make methodical thinking habitual or, to put it a bit more paradoxically, to make its "innate principles" second nature. Then the mind no longer has to apply its rules on a case-by-case basis because its very mode of operation is to enact them. In a letter to Princess Elisabeth of Bohemia Descartes expounds the importance of habituation for correct judgment:

> Besides the knowledge of truth, habituation [*l'habitude*] is also required for being always disposed to judge well. For since we cannot always be attentive to the same thing—even though we have been convinced of some truth by reason of some clear and evident perceptions—we will be able to be turned [*detournez*], afterward, to believing false appearances, if we do not, through a long and frequent meditation, imprint [*imprimée*] it sufficiently in our mind so that it turns into habit [*tournée en habitude*]. In this sense, the Schools are right to say that the virtues are habits, for one rarely makes a mistake because one doesn't have theoretical knowledge of what to do, but only because one doesn't have practical knowledge, that is to say because one doesn't have a firm habit of believing it. (CSM III 267; AT IV 295)⁵⁰

Habituation here works against the postlapsarian inclination of the mind to be turned away, literally to be perverted by false opinions and perceptions, so that it remains turned toward what it knows to be clear and evident.⁵¹ With a play on words Descartes indicates what is a stake—that the second nature of habit improves on the mind's inconstant first nature. The turn toward clear and evident perceptions must be turned into the habit of turning toward clear and evident perceptions. Thus, judgment and misjudgment are not simply a function of knowledge or the lack thereof but of practice, more precisely of an "art of turning" that must be exercised and through "long and frequent meditation" become a habit imprinted on the mind.

Already in Descartes' reference to the "Schools" in the previous passage, we see this conjunction of method and habit going all the way back to ancient philosophy. Ancient Stoicism, which adopted Plato's intimate conjunction of *technē* and *methodos*, defined the former as *hexis odopoēitikē*, that is, the "habit of making something by means of a way,"⁵² and thus derived its habituality from its etymological origin as a "path to be followed." For Zabarella this derivation still held true: "This method therefore, taken in the wide sense, appears to be nothing other than a logical habit, or an instrumental habit of [the] understanding that serves us in obtaining knowledge of things. For normally not every way and every passage is called a method, but only that which is taken by our minds as it investigates the science of things."[53] This conceptualization of method seizes on the habituating effect of the "path to be followed." Sigmund Freud, who was trained as a neurologist, called this effect *Bahnung*, "facilitation," "pathbreaking," or "breaching," as it is variously translated.[54] Modern cognitive science speaks of "priming" to describe the phenomenon of neural pathways processing more readily and efficiently as a result of being used frequently. By laying down a track, the *methodos*, or path to be followed, results in a faster and smoother ride for the train of thought than would be the case over rough and pathless terrain, and it makes it more likely that the mind will take the same route again. In the earliest articulation of his method in the *Regulae* Descartes recognized the potential of this mental "breaching": "We must therefore practice these easier tasks first, and above all methodologically, so that by following accessible and familiar paths we may grow accustomed, just as if we were playing a game, to penetrating always to the deeper truth of thing" (CSM I 36; AT X 405). In "breaching," edification and method converge and coalesce. Edification "paves the way" for methodological thought to follow.

Yet method is only half of the equation, for Descartes not only calls for a path but also demands "long and frequent meditation" so as to "imprint it sufficiently in our mind" and to turn it into habit. Repeatedly rehearsing a chain of thoughts (in Latin *iter*; again and again, *iterum*[55]), to make the path more passable and the passage into second nature, is the other half. Breaching is achieved by repeated practice, or "reiteration"; and meditation is the reiteration of the prescribed mental movements. Method requires practice, and meditation is that practice of running through certain thoughts again and again.[56]

Descartes follows a tradition going back to Plato in his use and enactment of the term "meditation," in which *meditari* and *meditatio* were used to translate their Greek counterparts, *meletan* and *meletē*. Initially, *meletan* and *meletē* had a wide semantic range, generally denoting "caring for, attending to, practicing" or even "using something," which is to say, not specifically tied to the intellectual and spiritual sphere. In his lectures on the *Hermeneutics of the Subject* Michel Foucault observes that *meletan*, often employed and coupled with the verb *gumnazein*, means to practice and train. The *meletai* are exercises, gymnastic and military exercises, military training. *Epimeleisthai* refers to a form of vigilant, continuous, applied, regular, etcetera, activity much more than to a mental attitude.... The series of words, *meletan, meletē, epimeleisthai, epimeleia*, etcetera, thus designate a set of practices. And in the Christian vocabulary of the fourth century you will see that *epimeleia* commonly has the meaning of exercise, of ascetic exercise. So we keep in mind that *epimeleia/epimeleisthai* refer to forms of activity.[57]

Yet *meletē* does not pertain to all forms or, better, every aspect of activity. It denotes the preparation for that which is later enacted by continual practice. As Per Rönnegård remarks, *meletan* in Plato "is primarily used for theoretical and mental exercises in preparation for an activity, be it technical or philosophical."[58] Like Descartes, Epictetus emphasizes that theoretical knowledge needs to be complemented by *meletē*, that is, practice: "That is why the philosophers admonish us not to be satisfied with merely learning, but to add thereto practice [*meletēn*] also, and then training [*askēsin*]" (*Discourses* 2.9.13).[59] Meditative practice aims at habituation and is predicated on the principle of "corresponding action": "Every habit [*hexis*] is confirmed and strengthened by the corresponding actions, that of walking by walking, that of running by running.... The same principle holds true in the affairs of the mind also" (2.18.1–3). *Meletē*, thus, consists in the rehearsal and repeated reflection of the canonical precepts and operations of Stoicism in order to memorize and habituate to them to be prepared for the "real thing."

The Latin verb *meditari* draws on the semantics of *meletan* but confines it to the intellectual or psychological realm. The *Thesaurus Linguae Latinae* lists four principal meanings of the term: cognition generally as in what it is "to reflect" and "to consider" (*deliberatio, consideratio*); pertaining to the will (*voluntatem*), the public process of deliberation, and the giving and taking of counsel (*consilium*); preparation (*praeparationem*) by means of exercises and meditation to learn an art or science (*meditatio de exercitationibus ad artem et scientiam*); actual performance or execution of the practice in the realm of action (*actionem*). It is in the third sense, as Irénée Hausherr notes, that *meditari* "would usually correspond best to the Greek *meletan*, as it was used by the monks and by certain philosophers."[60] The semantic range and usage of *meditatio* in Western Christianity was shaped by Jerome's translation of the Psalms, where twenty-seven of the forty-four occurrences of *meditari* and *meditatio* in the Vulgate appear.[61] Since knowledge of the precise wording of the Psalms was prerequisite for ordination to the priesthood, the Psalter formed the foundation of Christian knowledge and practice, and in becoming the official liturgy of the Roman Church, Jerome's language reached the Christian faithful at large. Already the very first Psalm highlights the importance of meditation: "Blessed is the man who meditates on the Lord's law day and night" (*Beatus vir qui . . . in lege [Domini] meditabitur die ac nocte*). Readers were enjoined to meditate incessantly on God's law by memorizing the Psalms. For the early monks this meant the repeated and audible recitation of biblical passages.[62] In building and elaborating on its patristic foundations, medieval monastic meditation added subject matter and new techniques, deeply influencing the late medieval and early modern surge of spirituality in the *Devotio moderna*. In fact, as Ignatius's *Spiritual Exercises* evidences, the later references often renewed and revitalized the spiritual insights and practices of the early monastic writers.[63] For Ignatius the meditation of scripture is still central to his program of rendering the turn toward God permanent and communicating it to others. And Luther's *lectio divina* is born from his meditative engagement with the Psalms that he seeks to replicate in the Lutheran practice of *Bibellektüre*.

What these diverse notions of meditation all have in common is the objective "to assimilate an idea, notion, or principle, and make them come alive in the soul" (PWL 112n38). Like *askēsis*, with which meditation is intimately aligned from its inception in ancient philosophy, it aims at "making the things you know your own [*facere suum*]."[64] The self appropriates precepts and doctrines in this way, putting them into practice; and this practice is the practice of meditation. Put differently, meditation facilitates the interiorization and implementation of "theoretical" knowledge.[65] It isn't enough to know on an intellectual level. This knowledge must change the whole self, its passions and actions. Only then can the self become virtuous, reach wisdom, and realize a good life. Meditation is thus the mode by which the self acquires an *epistēmē* and *technē*, be it that of an ancient philosophical school or of the *vera philosophia* of Christianity. Meditation continues the work of conversion in personalizing an abstract truth. Fortifying the self against relapse, it seeks to make the conversion permanent by enacting the turn over and over again. For early Christianity, as well as ancient philosophy, meditation was the royal road to wisdom and salvation.

It is in this sense that the mature Descartes understands the practice of meditation when he sets out to ground his "art of turning around" in the *Meditations on First Philosophy*. Every one of the principal cognitive operations treated in the *Meditations* requires practice, that is, repeated and concentrated meditation. Turning away from the sensory world and old preconceived opinions, turning toward the self, and then turning toward God require practice and thus meditation. Nor does doubting everything come easily:

> I shall stubbornly and firmly persist in this meditation; and . . . resolutely guard against assenting to any falsehoods. . . . But this is an arduous undertaking, and a kind of laziness brings me back to normal life. I am like a prisoner who is enjoying an imaginary freedom while asleep; as he begins to suspect that he is asleep, he dreads being woken up, and goes along with the pleasant illusion as long as he can. In the same way, I happily slide back into my old opinions and dread being shaken out of them, for fear that my peaceful sleep may be followed by hard labor when I wake, and that I shall have to toil not in the light, but amid the inextricable darkness of the problems I have now raised. (CSM II 15; AT VII 23)

Descartes' meditator likens themself to Plato's prisoner in the cave, preferring the dreamlike images on the cave wall to remaining turned around and facing the real world. Not unlike Plato's prisoner Descartes' meditator is all too happy to relapse and revert. For having subjected everything to doubt once is not enough. The mind needs to turn away from the sensory world more permanently. Its *a-* and *con-versio* need to be stabilized. And the means to do so is habitual practice and meditation. In the Second Set of Replies Descartes, therefore, recommends his readers "not just to take the short time needed to go through it, but to devote several months, or at least weeks, to considering the topics dealt with, before going on to the rest of the book. If they do this, they will undoubtedly be able to derive much greater benefit from what follows" (CSM II 94; AT VII 130). Only when Descartes' meditator has adequately practiced turning away from the sensory impressions and preconceived opinions is the meditator capable of cognizing the immortality of the soul and the existence of God, which are, as the subtitle claims, "demonstrated" by the *Meditations*. More generally, clear and distinct cognition as such, pertaining to all "things related to the intellect," is contingent on meditative practice. Mersenne points out in the Second Set of Objections that Descartes had achieved a high level of mastery of discerning clearly and distinctly: "You have trained your mind by continual meditations for several years, so that what seems doubtful and very obscure to others is quite clear to you; indeed you may have a clear mental intuition of these matters and perceive them as the primary and principal objects of the natural light" (CSM II 87; AT VII 122). Later, in the Seventh Set of Replies Descartes concedes that "there are, however few people who correctly distinguish between what they in fact perceive and what they think they perceive; for not many people are accustomed to clear and distinct perceptions" (CSM II 348; AT VII 511). Thus, doubt and clear and distinct cognition, the two crucial mental operations of Descartes' metaphysical project, require meditative practice.

The purpose of practicing cognitive operations is, as I have shown, both mnemonic and preparatory—which accounts for the peculiar temporality of practice. By reducing contingency and variability, practice makes an operation more readily repeatable, so one of the primary objectives of practice is to stay in practice. The "art of turning around" is thus a practice that fortifies mind and self against relapse. The practice has not only a reiterative aspect but is also oriented toward the future. Put simply, practice prepares for future performances. In the Stoics' exercise of the *praemeditatio malorum* the mind puts before its mental eye possible misfortunes and disasters so as not to be caught unprepared and be able to react appropriately, which is to say, composed and informed by reason.[66] In a similar manner, Ignatius directs exercitants to imagine the moments of their death, judgment, and sentencing by God when making their election (see SE § 184–88, p. 319). In other words, the current decision is rehearsed in the light of its future judgment.

Considering thought as practice entails focusing less on the objects of cognition and more on its operation, which is exactly what Descartes does in the *Meditations* when his meditator brackets all cognitive content as potentially false and turns their attention to the process of thinking. Repeatedly, Descartes distinguishes between thought as an act, operation, or medium and its content or objects. In his "Preface to the Reader" he counters the objection to his first proof of God—that it doesn't follow from the existence of an idea of a perfect being in the mind of the meditator that such a being actually exists—by pointing out that the word "idea" is ambiguous. It "can be taken materially, as an operation of the intellect, in which case it cannot be said to be more perfect than me. Alternatively, it can be taken objectively, as the thing represented by that operation; and this thing, even if it is not regarded as existing outside the intellect, can still, in virtue of its essence, be more perfect than myself" (CSM II 7; AT VII 8).[67] Meditating brings the operationality and materiality of thought to the fore, while its objective or representational dimension is temporarily suspended.[68] "Taken materially," an idea is a re-*presentation*; "taken objectively," it is a *re*-presentation. The former focuses on the operation of presenting, and the latter on the object that is represented. In this respect his concept and practice of meditation align closely with medieval monastic meditation as a "craft of making thoughts about God."[69] Descartes exploits the bracketing of representationality entailed by monastic meditation for his own epistemological project. His skeptical challenge of sensory ideas and, more fundamentally, his critique of mental representationalism are, in fact, made possible by his meditative turn. Given their foundational function, the focus of the *Meditations* is less on knowing particular things and more on how to know in the first place; less on knowing that and more on knowing how, not of course know-how in the common sense that pertains to the practical engagement with the real world (which has not yet been proven to exist by Descartes' meditator) but on the know-how of knowing that.

Moreover, considering meditative thought as a mental practice brings to the fore its self-reflexivity and recursivity. For whatever the object of practice is, its objective is to transform the mind so that it becomes more adept in its practice—similar to carpenters who want to become masters at their craft. When they work on their wood to transform it into a table, they not only work on the wood, but they work on working the wood. Thus, their raw materials consist of the wood and their body and mind as the agents of this work (as well as the tools). Practice is a second-order work or a meta-work: a work on work, an acting upon action. Strictly speaking, all craftmanship involves this kind of second-order work, so that by crafting a good table, a craftsperson ultimately crafts themselves. As Mary Carruthers has shown so eloquently, meditation was regarded as "a *craft* of thinking. . . . In the idiom of monasticism, people do not 'have' ideas, they 'make' them. The work (and I include both process and product in my use of this word) is not better than the skillful hand, or in this case the mind, of its user."[70] As early as the *Regulae* Descartes exploits the parallels between his practice of thought and "mechanical crafts." In Rule Ten he recommends taking on "the simplest and least exalted arts," first, "especially those in which order prevails—such as weaving and carpet-making, or the more feminine arts of embroidery, in which threads are interwoven in an infinitely varied pattern. Number games and any games involving arithmetic, and the like, belong here" (CSM I 35; AT X 404). In this passage Descartes singles out crafts that are distinguished by their orderliness, but the parallel extends much further.

What sets the mental craft of meditation apart from manual crafts (which never are strictly manual or corporeal) is that subject, object, and action coincide. This is, as Epictetus emphasizes, the premise for a meditative life: "From now on my mind [*dianoia*] is the material with which I have to work, as the carpenter has his timbers, the shoemaker his hides" (*Discourses* 3.22.20). Thinking is not only the material (the thoughts used), the product (the thoughts made), and the act of making or producing them but also the tool. As Carruthers points out, most people nowadays "buy tools ready made. But in many crafts even now, and in all crafts during the Middle Ages, an apprentice learned not only how to use his or her tools but how to make them." Or, as she puts it, "tool-making is an essential part of the orthopraxis of craft."[71] Similarly, Descartes must craft his method first, before he can use it to make discoveries, that is, find or invent things and thus produce knowledge. As he writes in the *Regulae*, his method

> in fact resembles the procedures in the mechanical crafts, which have no need of methods other than their own, and which supply their own instructions for making their own tools. If, for example, someone wanted to practice one of these crafts—to become a blacksmith, say—but did not possess any of the tools, he would be forced at first to use a hard stone (or a rough lump of iron) as an anvil, to make a rock do as a hammer, to make a pair of tongs out of wood, and to put together other such tools as the need arose.... What this example shows is that, since in these preliminary inquiries we have managed to discover only some rough precepts which appear to be innate in our minds rather than the product of any skill, we should not immediately try to use these precepts to settle philosophical disputes or to solve mathematical problems. (CSM I 31; AT X 397)

For Descartes the resemblance between his method and mechanical crafts consists in both being self-reliant. Neither presupposes anything that it cannot supply for itself. Just as the mechanical crafts, which create their own tools almost ex nihilo, Cartesian method relies only on "rough precepts," in a way "natural tools," like the hard stone or the rock hammer in his example, which are "innate in our minds." The craft or art in both cases lies in the ability to refine these rough tools or to use them to produce more refined ones. In fact, Descartes warns of applying these "rough precepts" prematurely to "philosophical disputes" or "mathematical problems," which are too complex for such simple tools. Only when the a tool's sophistication matches the sophistication of the artifact to be crafted can it be successfully employed. Thus, the *Regulae* shows us a snapshot of the early stages of Descartes' toolmaking process, and the *Discourse* represents a later, more mature stage, in which the products crafted by Cartesian method, that is, the accompanying treatises, eclipse the tools. With the *Meditations* Descartes finally arrives at the "philosophical disputes," the telos of the Cartesian craft of thought. What holds for cognitive practice in the *Regulae* holds even more so for the *Meditations*, which starts from a tabula rasa and proceeds with complete self-sufficiency.

This appears to put Descartes' meditator in a seemingly impossible position. In regard to their tools they have nothing but what is innate in their mind, and however rough they may be, they must apply them to the most sophisticated philosophical problems. Here, the difference between the art of meditation and the mechanical crafts is decisive. As noted before, in meditative thought there is no difference between the artisan, their materials, their tools, and their products. All consist of thoughts. In the case of meditative edification, the building that results even serves as a dwelling for the thinking mind. Unlike mathematics, which relies both on the corporeal imagination and physical media such as diagrams, metaphysical meditation operates without mediation. The feedback is direct, and the meditator has little resistance to contend with, unlike the mechanical craftsperson, who has to control the materiality of their material and tools, and even their own body. In short, meditative thought is unmediated work on itself. By practicing thinking, that is, by meditating, thought transforms itself. Cartesian meditation, thus, stands in the tradition of ancient spiritual exercises, which Pierre Hadot describes as "thought which, as it were, takes itself as its own subject matter, and seeks to modify itself" (PWL 81). With this, meditation continues the self-transformation that began with Descartes' conversion as a young man.

Communicating Meditative Practice

Just as meditative practice is faced with its own challenges and requires its own method, so does teaching it to others. As we know, Descartes was highly critical of traditional methods and media of communicating knowledge, and here we will see that his misgivings spring from the particular pitfalls involved in communicating the insight and illumination gained during conversion. The challenge of communicating the "art of turning" is twofold. The first aspect pertains to the teaching of an "art," that is, a spiritual practice; and the second has to do with the difficulty posed by communicating the "turning," conveying the evidentiary experience of conversion. In Descartes' case, this teaching of an art requires him to communicate his spiritual and intellectual practice, which is all about the know-how of knowing that. We recall that Plato's "art of turning around" does not bring about illumination by "putting sight into blind eyes" (*Republic* 518b) but by teaching the students to start using their power of vision properly. It is not as much about imparting new information to the mind as about changing the way the mind thinks. Similarly, the aim of Descartes' method is not to teach new knowledge but to re- and transform thinking itself. Descartes' "art takes as given that sight is there, but not rightly turned." Illumination is achieved when the mind's innate spark is fanned sufficiently for its *lumen naturale* to shine more brightly on the objects of its inquiry. As I have shown, this know-how of knowledge must be practiced, which means it is learned by doing rather than by being simply informed of its principles. In the examples of the craft of violin making and the art of violin playing, learning the principles of the respective practice is not the same as being able to master it in the sense of being able to implement and perform tasks required. Violin makers' knowledge is actualized in what they do, namely, practicing their craft; the violinists' art, in their performance. And neither, then, will try to teach their craft or art by simply reciting its principles and bringing their students to memorize them. Instead, both discover other methods of instruction, such as learning by following rules, imitating examples, bringing concentrated discipline to the task, and continually practicing it. The master uses exemplary technique and unique style to guide and shape the learning of their students, who are better thought of as apprentices, as the model is one of inculcating practice rather than Scholastic instruction.

As we have seen, Descartes understands mathematics and philosophy according to the craft model, which means that the *episteme* of these intellectual arts is of a different kind. As he points out in the Third Rule of the *Regulae*, "Even though we know other people's demonstrations by heart, we shall never become mathematicians if we lack the intellectual aptitude to solve any given problem. And even though we have read all the arguments of Plato and Aristotle, we shall never become philosophers if we are unable to make sound judgement on matters which come up for discussion" (CSM I 13; AT X 367). It is for this reason that reading "the writings of the ancients" is of limited value. We can get only so far in becoming mathematicians and philosophers by reading their demonstrations. We need to be able to produce the demonstrations by ourselves for "any given problem" and thus need to train our "aptitude."

It is not only Descartes' method, his mode of mental orientation and locomotion, that calls for a specific form of communication but also the foundational experience of illumination initiating and fueling its continuation. The challenge arises from the fact that conversion is a radically personal and subjective experience. Each self must undergo the experience of illumination and "see" for itself. As the famous injunction to Socrates by the Delphic oracle, "Know Thyself!," reminds us, conversion to a philosophical life meant first and foremost a turn toward the self. The illumination essentially consists in the self gaining knowledge about itself; and while others can provide valuable insights, "thyself" is the one who needs to undergo the knowing of it.

If the philosophical turn toward the self is radically subjective, religious conversion is no less so. Saul's experience of being struck down and called on the road to Damascus is portrayed as radically personal. His companions remain completely uncomprehending. They may be terrified by the event, but they are not touched by it. And Paul's own account makes a point of him having been singled out and elected to go to the Gentiles "to open their eyes, and to turn them from darkness to light, and from the power of Satan unto God" (Acts 26:18). Augustine similarly receives an utterly personalized message when he seemingly randomly opens his copy of Paul's Letter to the Romans and reads "the first passage on which my eyes lit" (*Confessions* 8.12.29). The passage (Rom 13:13–14) was meant for him and for him only, as it addressed his lingering attachment to the pleasures of the flesh. Once he reads the last words, "it is as if a light of relief from all anxiety flooded into my heart. All the shadows of doubt were dispelled" (*Confessions* 8.12.29). These are not the only examples of cases in which conversion is figured as a personal address, a call directed at a particular self that cannot be transferred. And we remember that Descartes understands his conversion as a similarly personalized call.

Conversion, in both its religious and philosophical versions, involves the experience of a universal truth, which, while held to be universal, still needs to be made true for a particular self. Augustine was a Christian all his life, and he knew of Christianity's doctrines long before his dramatic conversion in the garden outside Milan. But only when he recognized that its message pertained to him and when he let himself be touched and transformed by it did he fully "turn." Put succinctly, conversion is the moment when an abstract truth becomes concretized and subjectivized; it is about an individual self making an abstract and universal truth its own.

The irreducible subjectivity of conversive illumination, which makes it so difficult to communicate, persists in its operationalization—at least for Descartes. As we have seen, method, the Cartesian "art of turning," eschews external guidance and proceeds in complete self-sufficiency.[72] In the French foreword to the *Principia philosophiae* Descartes compares this imperative of self-direction with autopsy (seeing for oneself, from the Greek *aut-opsia*). "Living without philosophizing," he writes, "is exactly like having one's eyes closed without ever trying to open them; and the pleasure of seeing everything which our sight reveals is in no way comparable to the satisfaction accorded by knowledge of the things which philosophy enables us to discover" (CSM I 180; AT IXB 3). Of course, as we have repeatedly encountered in his works, Descartes is using sight as a metaphor for thought. Philosophizing is using one's own reason to guide one's thought in the pursuit of truth. Given that orientation without sight is no orientation at all, being guided by others who see is better than no guidance at all, "yet even the latter is much better than keeping one's eyes closed and having no guide but oneself" (CSM I 180; AT IXB 3). Best, however, is always going to be being guided by one's own eyes, that is, orientation springing from autopsy. In a letter to Hogelande Descartes uses a another Greek term to characterize true knowledge, *scientia*. Only insights acquired "by means of our native human intelligence ... may be called *autarchēs* [self-sufficient]" (CSM III 144; AT III 723).[73] As Descartes relates in *Discourse on the Method*, he cultivated this mode of self-guidance from very early on (see CSM I 119; AT VI 16). In fact, his conversion in the stove-heated room essentially consists in the realization that he cannot rely on others to find his own path in life. In Rule Ten of the *Regulae* Descartes details his strategy to combat the profound "anxiety of influence" he experienced in the face of overwhelming tradition:[74] "Whenever the title of a book gave promise of a new discovery, before I read further I would try and see whether perhaps I could achieve a similar result by means of a certain innate discernment. And I took great care not to deprive myself of this innocent pleasure through a hasty reading of the book" (CSM I 35; AT X 403). Instead of reading the book, the young Descartes would use his "innate discernment" to extrapolate the contents from the title, and in a way write the book himself. The frequent success of this strategy led him to articulate a set of "reliable rules" that would eventually become his method.

This possibly apocryphal little anecdote points to the dilemma posed by communicating conversive illumination and its methodical operationalization: How does one teach intellectual self-direction without violating its essence? How to direct someone to self-direct? In the appendix to the Fifth Set of Replies Descartes indicates his acute awareness of this dilemma, stressing the point that his "thought must not be the standard for others" and that he "never wanted to force anyone to follow my authority." Instead, "the thought of each person—i.e., the perception or knowledge which he has of something—should be for him the 'standard which determines the truth of the thing'" (CSM II 272; AT IXA 207–8). While Descartes eschewed other forms of instruction, such as lecturing and spiritual direction, he did resort to writing and publishing, however reluctantly and punctiliously.[75] Given his oneiric critique of the bibliographic medium, his dilemma can be reformulated: how to write a book that evades the traditional ways of self-replicating of knowledge?[76] Communicating illumination and the practice of method in the medium of writing becomes the question of genre,[77] allowing the problem to be stated yet more precisely: Which genre of philosophical writing is best suited to articulate and communicate the Cartesian "art of turning"?

That Descartes was deeply attentive to the implications of generic form over the course of his intellectual career is evidenced by the variety of philosophical and literary genres he tried out, often covering the same topics and arguments more than once. Notably, he never resorted to a particular genre more than once.[78] Descartes' use of philosophical genres also evidences a division of labor within his overall project of reforming knowledge. Different textual forms serve different communicative functions. What unites Descartes' experiments with philosophical genres, not all of which were equally successful, is his awareness of the way each one affects readers in a particular way. In that respect Descartes' writing is less akin to modern philosophical discourse—which as Jacques Derrida has shown, is largely indifferent, if not dismissive of textual form[79]—and is more closely related to the textual practices of ancient philosophy. As Pierre Hadot describes it, "Above all, the work, even if it is apparently theoretical and systematic, is written not so much to inform the reader of its doctrinal content but to form him, to make him traverse a certain itinerary in the course of which he will make spiritual progress ... in which all the detours, starts and stops, and digressions of the work are formative elements" (PWL 64). We will see in the following chapters how Descartes' *Meditations* similarly charts a spiritual and intellectual journey that the reader is expected to follow and reenact.

The instruction manual, nowadays, is the genre most often used to communicate know-how. It explains how to use a certain device, perform a certain procedure, or perhaps play a game. Descartes' first philosophical work, the *Rules for the Direction of the Mind*, can be understood in a sense as a user's manual for his method. Initially the work was conceived in three parts, each comprising twelve rules. The first set of rules concerns the main tenets of his method and its two basic operations, intuition and deduction. The second set deals with "perfectly understood problems," composite natures made up of simple and self-evident ones; and the third was foreseen as addressing "imperfectly understood problems," that is, composite natures assembled by the intellect that are deduced from other composite natures. The three parts were designed pedagogically as a carefully calibrated progression: first the exposition of the rules, then the application of those rules to problems that can be successfully settled, and finally to problems that cannot yet be fully resolved. While the stages of composition are complex and controversial,[80] only the first set was completed, the second remained unfinished, and the third was never written. What appears clear is that Descartes never finished the *Regulae* because he was unsatisfied with the approach. Instead, he turned to the composition of a small metaphysical treatise that ultimately took the form of the *Meditations*.[81]

Precisely why the *Regulae* failed where the *Meditations* succeeded remains unknown and thus subject to speculation. But it is possible to offer a few considerations. As I suggested earlier, Descartes' *Regulae* is designed to direct the mind's intellectual life—much like monastic rules guided the spiritual life of monks. Rather than convey information or propositional knowledge Descartes' ensemble of rules instills practice or know-how. The rules teach how to think and produce true knowledge. While the approach taken is different, the *Regulae* shares with the *Meditations* the same concern with imparting mental practice. The *Discourse on the Method* and its two accompanying treatises are examples of the knowledge produced by Cartesian practice but are not intended to teach the practice itself. That task falls to the *Meditations*, albeit by other means. To this extent they continue the project of the *Regulae*, which is the elaboration of the *mirabilis scientiae fundamenta* Descartes discovered during his conversion.

The *Regulae* delineates the rules of the Cartesian *technē* of thought, directing the intellect's acts of thought toward true knowledge. We recall that Descartes recognizes only two "actions of the intellect," intuition and deduction (CSM I 14; AT X 368; see also CSM I 48; AT X 425). As completely self-evident and "indubitable conceptions of a clear and attentive mind," intuitions anchor the chains of deduction and lend them certainty. Intuitions form the foundation for the whole edifice of knowledge. Because the number of intuitions is limited to the number of "simple natures" (or what Descartes would later call "innate ideas") contained in the mind, it must resort to deductions to extend the reach of its certain knowledge. By the means of deduction the mind infers "something as following necessarily from some other propositions which are known with certainty" (CSM I 15; AT X 369). Of course, it would be preferable for the mind to know everything by intuition, but as only very few things are accessible to this error-immune mode of knowing, the mind has to settle for second best in systematically linking the few intuited truths to as many ideas and thoughts as possible. The work of connecting the deductive links in the chain is the domain of method and its rules, and the bulk of the *Regulae* is devoted to the rules that govern and guide deductive reasoning. Intuitions, in their simplicity, "must occur to us spontaneously; they cannot be sought out" (CSM I 50; AT X 428), so their operation is not governed by rules and thus is not easily communicated to others.[82] It may have been this resistance to "regulation" that prompted Descartes to abandon the *Regulae* and turn to the project of devising a mode of conveying the foundations of thought, the *mirabilis scientiae fundamenta* he discovered a decade earlier.

In regard to the communication of the Cartesian *technē* of thought the *Discourse on the Method* represents a blind alley. We recall the peculiar contradiction exhibited by the title of Descartes' first publication, in which "discourse" refers to the mind's errancy in its search for truth, and "method" to the path to be followed in order to arrive at that very truth, a contradiction that puts into question whether this treatise is really intended to teach his method and its metaphysical foundation. Descartes seems to signal his reluctance in a letter to Mersenne on February 27, 1637: "I have not been able to understand your objection to the title; for I have not put *Treatise on Method* but *Discourse on Method*, which means *Preface or Notice on the Method*, in order to show that I do not intend to teach the method but only to discuss it. As can be seen from what I say, it is concerned more with practice than with theory" (CSM III 53; AT I 349). The gist of his method is pragmatic, but the *Discourse* is not the place, text, and genre to communicate and impart his intellectual practice to his readers,[83] a point made explicitly in Descartes' careful choice of "discourse" rather than "treatise" in the title, as the former is merely prefatorial or indicative, that is, pointing to its actual use but not explaining and teaching it.[84] Later, in the *Meditations*, Descartes writes that the *Discourse on the Method* was not meant to provide a full treatment of his philosophy but merely a sample so that he could learn from his readers "how I should handle these topics at a later date" (CSM II 6; AT VII 7). Employing the itinerant metaphorics noted earlier, Descartes makes a point of saying that he did not conceive the *Discourse* as a guide: "The route which I follow in explaining them [these topics] is so untrodden and so remote from the normal way, that I thought it would not be helpful to give a full account of it in a book written in French and designed to be read by all and sundry, in case weaker intellects might believe that they ought to set out on the same path" (CSM II 6–7; AT VII 7). Unlike the *Meditations*, which was written in Latin, the *Discourse* was written in French, for a wider readership and including readers whose "weaker intellect" was not suited to enter such "untrodden" and "remote" territory. The *Discourse*, as Descartes states at the beginning, is an intellectual travelogue: "I shall be glad, nevertheless, to reveal in this discourse what paths I have followed, and to represent my life in it as if in a picture, so that everyone may judge it for himself" (CSM I 112; AT VI 3–4). Descartes wants to narrate the paths he has followed. He does not want to prescribe them for his reader:

> My present aim, then, is not to teach the method which everyone must follow in order to direct his reason correctly, but only to reveal how I have tried to direct my own.... I am presenting this work only as a history or, if you prefer, a fable in which, among certain examples worthy of imitation, you will perhaps also find many others that it would be right not to follow; and so I hope it will be useful for some without being harmful to any, and that everyone will be grateful to me for my frankness. (CSM I 112; AT VI 4)

If the core of Cartesian method is the self-direction of the mind, then the *Discourse* cannot be teaching it, dictating to the reader which path to follow, because then their thoughts would not be self-directed. Descartes is not in the business of giving precepts but merely an example, and one with little force at that, since in calling it a fable, he fictionalizes and thus weakens it. Then he further diminishes its force by including negative examples whose imitation he says would be harmful. Indeed, Descartes explicitly counsels against anyone emulating his example: "My plan has never gone beyond trying to reform my own thoughts and construct them upon a foundation which is all my own. If I am sufficiently pleased with my own work to present you with this sample of it, this does not mean that I would advise anyone to imitate it.... The simple resolution to abandon all the opinions one has hitherto accepted is not an example that everyone ought to follow" (CSM I 118; AT VI 15).

Paradoxically, the *Discourse* simultaneously establishes and denies the exemplarity of Descartes' story, doing so through a mode of presentation that describes past and somewhat fictionalized events with only a loose bearing on the present situation of the reader. Descartes singles out his exercise of universal doubt as potentially setting a dangerous example that he wanted to avoid by casting the *Discourse* in its particular form. In a letter in May 1637, probably written to Silhon, Descartes spells out the pragmatics of doubting in more detail. He concedes that the *Discourse* falls short in explaining "the arguments by which I claim to prove that there is nothing at all more evident and certain than the existence of God and of the human soul" (CSM III 55; AT I 353). To do that, he would have had to engage his reader in total doubt "to show that there is no material thing of whose existence one can be certain" (CSM III 55; AT I 353). But such a demonstration requires repeated practice on the part of the reader. It is not enough that the reader be shown that all material things are doubtable but that the reader comes to that conclusion by doubting for themself. Only then does the exercise of doubt have the intended effect:

> Thus I would have accustomed the reader to detach his thought from things that are perceived by the senses, and then I would have shown that a man who thus doubts everything material cannot for all that have any doubt about his own existence. From this it follows that he, that is to say the soul, is a being or substance which is not at all corporeal, whose nature is solely to think, and that it is the first thing one can know with certainty. If you spend a sufficient time on this meditation, you acquire by degrees a very clear, dare I say intuitive, notion of intellectual nature in general. This is the idea which, if considered without limitation, represents God, and if limited, is the idea of an angel or a human soul. (CSM III 55–56; AT I 353)

Absent the personal experience of total doubt, the "intuitive notion of intellectual nature," which lies at the heart of the *cogito* as well as the cognition of God, remains unattainable. Doubt is pivotal for the turn away from the sensible world and toward the intellectual world, which is to say, the soul and God as well as other intellectual beings such as angels—and not surprisingly, this turn is meditative. Meditation is the means by which the doubt necessary for the turn is enacted, whereas the *Discourse* treats doubt in such a way that the reader merely reads about it. Descartes' letter continues: "But as for intelligent people like yourself, Sir, if they take the trouble not only to read but also to meditate in order on the same topics on which, as I reported, I meditated myself, spending a long time on each point, to see whether I have gone wrong, I trust that they will come to the same conclusions as I did" (CSM III 56; AT I 354). While reading is clearly a necessary precondition, only meditation achieves the reenactment on the part of the reader of the meditation that Descartes performs.

As we have seen, reading and meditation were intimately linked historically, so intimately that within the Christian tradition, in particular, meditation was conceived as a certain mode of reading.[85] If we revisit the passage in the light of the notion of meditative reading, it becomes apparent that for Descartes the problem is more a mode of reading divorced from meditation. He calls for meditating in addition to reading. As he writes in the preface, the *Meditations* requires a certain kind of reader:[86]

I would not urge anyone to read this book except those who are able and willing to meditate seriously with me [*serio mecum meditari*], and to withdraw their minds from the senses and from all preconceived opinions. Such readers, as I well know, are few and far between. Those who do not bother to grasp the proper order of my arguments and the connection between them, but merely try to carp at individual sentences, as is the fashion, will not get much benefit from reading this book. They may well find an opportunity to quibble in many places, but it will not be easy for them to produce objections which are telling or worth replying to. (CSM II 8; AT VII 9–10)

Similar to the exercitant in the Ignatian exercises, the reader is required to withdraw from the sensory world and set aside all prior knowledge in order to engage in serious meditation with the *I* of the *Meditations*. Similarly, Descartes asks his reader to set aside the customary mode of reading focused on "individual sentences" that treats the text as an assemblage of "places" between which the reader can jump to and fro at will. Descartes intends the *Meditations* not primarily to communicate propositional knowledge that can be condensed into "individual sentences" but rather to impart the comprehension of their inner organization and produce a more holistic understanding of the text. The intended experience of the *Meditations* is contingent on this meditative mode of reading and concomitantly on Descartes' particular mode of presentation.

Nonetheless, the question remains, How does the *Meditations* avoid the dilemma of undoing intellectual self-direction by teaching it? How is the text to convey mental practice to the reader and yet preserve the reader's autarchy? The answer is that with and in the *Meditations* Descartes found a way or method to orchestrate the reader's discovery of the truth by themself. While the text itself enacts this method rather than explains it, Descartes' Second Reply (to Mersenne) offers a more descriptive explanation. Mersenne had suggested to Descartes that he arrange his arguments in "geometrical fashion to enable the reader to perceive them 'as it were at a single glance'" (CSM II 110; AT VII 155). Descartes complies with little enthusiasm, noting that the choice of the "order" (*ordo*) and "method of demonstration" (*ratio demonstrandi*) for the *Meditations* had been deliberate. As to order, he had reasoned that "the items which are put forward first must be known entirely without the aid of what comes later; and the remaining items must be arranged in such a way that their demonstration depends solely on what has gone before" (CSM II 110; AT VII 155).[87] The method of demonstration mirrors the order in that it "shows [*ostendit*] the true way [*veram viam*] by means of which the thing in question was discovered methodically [*methodice*] and as it were a priori, so that if the reader is willing to follow it and give sufficient attention to all points, he will make the thing his own and understand it just as perfectly as if he had discovered it for himself" (CSM II 110; AT VII 155).

Descartes calls this method of demonstration "analysis."[88] In revealing the path that led Descartes to the discovery of "things," it allows the reader to retrace it. The path does the guiding, not Descartes, and the reader remains largely self-sufficient. The capacity of the "true way" to guide the reader is due to two defining characteristics: it was discovered "methodically" and it is "a priori." Its original discovery by Descartes was not haphazard but the result of his employment of his method. Because the way is a *methodos*, a path to be followed, the discovery is iterable and transferable. Descartes' usage of the term "a priori" conforms neither to the Scholastic understanding as proceeding from cause to effect nor to the modern version as knowledge independent from experience. Descartes writes *tanquam*, "as it were," indicating that he understood a priori literally: as a discovery proceeding from that which was prior, or "has gone before." Every step must be intelligible either by itself or in terms of the preceding steps. Any other procedure would involve the introduction of steps unknown and alien to the reader and thus imposed by someone else. That would put the self-discovery in jeopardy, making it difficult for the reader to make the thing discovered "their own."

Making a thought one's own applies to no cognitions more than to intuitions, and to no intuition more than to the *cogito*,[89] which is self-evident and indubitable only if and when the self thinks "it" for itself.[90] Only in the moment of its thinking can it form the foundation for the edifice of thought. Readers that join Descartes in meditating have to enact the *cogito* themselves, have to perform the cogitational act of becoming aware of their own existence as the agent of their thoughts by and for themselves.[91] The evidence and certainty of the *cogito* cannot be produced by an act of narration or description or by lodging a propositional claim.[92] It has to be experienced in being performed. At the same time, as John Lyons notes, the *cogito* is not "an imitable performance."[93] It is not Descartes' *cogito* the reader is performing, in which there would remain an irreducible distance between the imitation and the imitated. On the contrary, they need to enact their own *cogito* and experience the act of thinking of themself by themself so that it is entirely their own. In the *Meditations* Descartes stages the performance of thinking the *cogito* and invites the reader to join in this performance; and it is by joining in the performance that the *cogito* becomes their own. He does this by creating a persona or role that the reader may assume.[94] It is the *ego*, or *I*, of the meditator, the persona that Descartes adopted when writing the *Meditations*, which is the very same persona the reader adopts when in turn reading the text and joining the author in meditation.[95] By adopting the ego or persona of Descartes' meditator, the reader impersonates and enacts their own thoughts. In contrast to the *je* of the *Discourse on the Method*, which is not meant for emulation, the ego of the *Meditations* is designed to be easily adopted.[96]

The easy adoption of this persona is rooted in the linguistic structure of the first-person pronoun as a linguistic element whose meaning can be determined only in reference to the instance of discourse in which it is uttered. According to Emile Benveniste, "*I* signifies 'the person who is uttering the present instance of the discourse containing *I*.'"[97] In Descartes' case this discourse is the meditative text that is actualized in the act of reading and rereading. As Jaako Hintikka noted in a famous essay, whether the *cogito* is performed in speech, in writing, or in thought is of secondary importance.[98] Private thought acts are subject to the same logic of linguistic performance as the speech act of enunciating the *I*. Indeed, the *Meditations* can be understood to an extent as a classical soliloquy, as the self in conversation with its own thoughts.[99] Descartes often portrays thought processes as an internal discourse subject to rhetorical persuasion and deception. This means for the *Meditations* that the first-person pronoun "ego" refers first to Descartes as the writer and original meditator, but then also to anyone who takes up the text and reads it.

In linguistic terms, ego is called a shifter because it can be inhabited by anyone, so when it is inhabited by a particular reader, it is that reader who is doing the meditating.[100] Then the reader and no one else is the reference of the ego in the act of meditating. Benveniste calls the *I* "a unique but mobile sign . . . which can be assumed by each speaker on the condition that he refers each time only to the instance of his own discourse."[101] The linguistic shifter ego thus conjoins utmost generality with utmost particularity. In that regard the meditative subject mirrors the conversive subject in need of individualizing God's universal address and receiving its own personalized call in order to make the turn. Descartes' reenactment and communication of his own conversion in the *Meditations* is in part predicated on exploiting the "shiftiness" of the first-person singular. Anyone can choose to take up the text and read, but only the reader who does so will be transformed by the performance of Descartes' meditations.

Unlike the *je* of the *Discourse on the Method* that refers to Descartes' former self, the ego of the *Meditations* represents the meditator's present self, both Descartes in the act of writing and the reader in their reenactment. As Benveniste observes, the reality of the ego is the "reality" of the "present instance of discourse," that is, the time at which the ego is speaking or, in Descartes' case, reading, thinking, and meditating, and, this is important to note, each and every time it is reading, thinking, and meditating and only as long as it is engaged in these activities. Thus, the impersonation of Descartes' meditator always (again) happens in the present, in what Robert McMahon has described in regard to Anselm's meditative treatise of the *Proslogion* as the "ongoing present" that is "recreated by our reading."[102] More generally, the time and tense of meditation are what one might want to call the "meditative present." It is for that very reason that the *Meditations* is written in the present tense, in contrast to the *Discourse on the Method*, in which Descartes narrates his discoveries in the past tense.

The First Meditation famously begins with the meditator's declaration that the moment has come to radically reform their thoughts: "So today I have expressly rid my mind of all worries and arranged myself a clear stretch of free time" (CSM II 12; AT VII 17–18). In this "stretch of free time" that Descartes' meditator and reader share, the ensuing meditations unfold. Each meditation is to be performed without interruption on a single day, requiring six days for the performance of the complete set.[103] Descartes' meditator is very emphatic about the meditations needing to be performed in the proper order. Otherwise, the work they are designed to do cannot be done. The meditator expressly and repeatedly points to the temporal gaps between the individual meditations, the time that has passed in which the ego has not been meditating, highlighting its presence now that it is "live and on air" again. Similarly, the meditator pauses at the end of the Third Meditation to "spend some time in the contemplation of God." Finally, the meditator frequently emphasizes that certain habits of thought persist and others need to be repeated and rehearsed so as to become habitual, pointing to the mental work necessary for readers to make these thoughts their own and for the meditations to be successful.[104] Only once a meditation has been fully internalized is it time to proceed to the next.[105]

The intellectual and spiritual work performed in the meditations creates its own temporality. Since the reader is transformed by meditating, they change in the course of the meditations. After eliminating the sensory world through the practice of radical doubt, the ego is nothing but a thinking thing, a *res cogitans*. Thus, the ego is defined and shaped by its thoughts. Initially, it knows very little for certain, in fact, only that it is thinking, but gradually its thought and knowledge expand. In other words, the knowledge and identity of the meditator are situational (see, for instance, CSM II 93; AT VII 129). It depends on the particular stage in the sequence of the meditations—or, in linguistic terms, on the "present instance of discourse." In short, when the meditator refers to themselves, the identity of that ego can be determined only in reference to the moment of its performance. The meditator generates their own "on-going present." The meditative subject, in contrast to what we see in the *Discourse on the Method*'s narration of the childhood, schooling, and military experience of its "hero," remains bare, approximating the abstractness and generality of the grammatical ego.

Descartes contrasts the analytic method of demonstration used in the *Meditations* with what he calls "synthesis," which is the "directly opposite method," as it proceeds "a posteriori." It commences with the conclusion and then "employs a long series of definitions, postulates, axioms, theorems, and problems" to prove it beyond doubt (CSM II 111; AT VII 156). Rather than retrace and reenact the process of discovery, synthesis begins with the result and then fortifies it against objections. While analysis requires a willing and attentive reader, synthesis compels assent in the most "argumentative or stubborn" of readers (CSM II 111; AT VII 156). It is, then, not well suited to the communication of "metaphysical subjects," that is, innate ideas, and by extension to the Cartesian art of turning because it limits the autonomy and self-sufficiency of the thinking self. The primary purpose of synthetic demonstration is not designed to enable the reader in making the knowledge their own and discovering it for themself but for pedagogical settings in which the preservation of intellectual autonomy is secondary or in which students lack the necessary receptivity for analysis. According to Descartes, it was the method of demonstration used by the ancient geometers, often as a "follow-up to analysis" (CSM II 110; AT VII 156). It also bears significant resemblance to the pedagogical approach of medieval Scholasticism.

If Frans Burman is to be believed, the *Principia philosophiae*, intended by Descartes as a "summary" of his philosophy, conceived in the style of a "compendium of scholastic philosophy" (CSM III 161; AT VIII 259), is actually composed in the synthetic style (CSM III 338; AT V 153). Doubt about the reliability of the text of the *Conversation with Burman*, and Descartes never explicitly having characterized the *Principia* as synthetic, has prompted considerable debate about his claim.[106] Whether or not the *Principia* is truly synthetic, it is deliberately and expressly written in a mode unlike the *Meditations*. In a letter to Mersenne on December 31, 1640, Descartes writes that the *Principia* contains "almost the same things as the *Meditations* . . . , except that it is in an entirely different style," lacking false starts and pragmatic digressions (CSM III 167; AT III 276). The *Principia* simply presents a "series of theses" in an impersonal mode and expounds the "conclusions with the true premises" from which they are derived (CSM III 157; AT III 233).[107] Originally, Descartes planned to have the *Principia* published in tandem with a "textbook of traditional philosophy . . . with notes by me at the end of each proposition," in which Descartes wanted to "add the different opinions of others, and what one should think of them all" (CSM III 157; AT III 233). So, in this case, Descartes had no qualms telling his readers what to think about his own philosophy and that of others. The *Principia* is designed for the traditional pedagogical setting of the classroom, in which a teacher invested with intellectual authority teaches students who respect that authority. In the *Principia* Descartes is therefore much less concerned with preserving the intellectual autonomy of his readers and enabling them to make his discoveries their own.

The other text in which Descartes resorted to an overtly didactic genre to present his metaphysics was *The Search for Truth by Means of the Natural Light* (*La recherche de la vérité par la lumière naturelle*). Written in French, it was clearly intended for wider circulation, with its broad appeal indicated by the dramatis personae engaged in philosophical dialogue. At the center of the pedagogical project stands the figure of Polyander, literally, Everyman, who is unlettered but equipped with common sense and thus competent to arbitrate the debate between the two main protagonists, Epistemon (the knowledgeable) and Eudoxus (famous or of sound judgment). Polyander is represented as *un honnête homme*, that is, a cultured member of the aristocracy who is well educated but not learned.[108] He is a blank page ready to be inscribed by the ideas being presented by the two interlocutors. Epistemon is well versed in classical and Scholastic philosophy. Eudoxus is Descartes' alter ego in this match between Scholastic and Cartesian philosophy. The prize is persuading Polyander, and it should come as no surprise that Eudoxus wins handily, so the contest between the two philosophical positions ends not in reconciliation but in the triumph of the superior Cartesian one. The goal is not to have Polyander discover the truth of Cartesian thought by himself, as Eudoxus guides him in the demonstration of his superiority as a thinker in part by invalidating his opponent. In other words, *The Search for Truth* pursues a communicative and pedagogical strategy very different from that in the *Meditations*. Dependent on a negative foil, it does not proceed with the autonomy Descartes envisioned for his total reform of thought. Meditation was the genre Descartes chose both to establish the metaphysical foundations of his thinking as such and, just as important, to communicate his "art of turning" and operationalizing the act of founding for his learned readers by offering spiritual exercises designed to replicate and communicate the founder's and the movement's evidentiary experience. Thus, Descartes' *Meditations on First Philosophy* has also to be understood as an attempt to provide the founding document for Cartesianism, a new practice of both thought and life.

3

The Discernment of Ideas and the Evidence of the *Cogito*

The Meditative Turn

"Some years ago I noticed [*animadverti*] the large number of falsehoods that I had accepted as true in my childhood, and the highly doubtful nature of the whole edifice that I had subsequently based on them. I realized that it was necessary, once in the course of my life, to overturn [*evertanda*] everything and start again right from the foundations if I wanted to establish anything at all in the sciences that was stable and likely to last" (CSM II 12; AT VII 17).

Descartes' *Meditations on First Philosophy* begins with a turning (in Latin *vertere*) or, to be more precise, with tale of a turn that happened "some years ago" that the meditator proposes to reenact in the present. More precisely, it begins by the meditator's *anima*, or soul, turning toward (*adverti*) a "large number of falsehoods," resulting in the realization that it is necessary to overturn (*evertanda*) the entire edifice of knowledge to "start again right from the foundations." Both the recognition that the edifice needs to be demolished and the demolition itself are figured as turns. The *animadversio* refers to the turning of the mind's attention to the falsity of opinions based on sensory perception, and the *eversio opinionum* to the overturning of these very opinions. Descartes figures his practice of doubt not only as a turn but as one facilitating another turn, the *aversio*, or the turn away from the sensory world.

Already in the synopsis prefacing the *Meditations* Descartes insists that his "extensive doubt" is not an end itself but a means to an end and thus useful. "Its greatest benefit lies in freeing us from all our preconceived opinions [*praejudiciis*], and providing the easiest route by which the mind can be led away from the senses [*viamque facillimam sternat ad mentem a sensibus abducendam*]" (CSM II 9; AT VII 12).[1] Integral to Cartesian method, the practice of doubt marks out the "path to be followed" away from the senses. Doubt has the function of disentangling the mind from its engagement with the sensory world and turning it toward itself and, more generally, to "metaphysical matters" (CSM II 94; AT VII 131). At this point, it should come as no surprise that Descartes terms this turn of the mind toward itself a "conversion." In the "Preface to the Reader," he writes: "The human mind, when directed towards itself [*mens humana in se conversa*], does not perceive itself to be anything other than a thinking thing" (CSM II 7; AT VII 7–8). Moreover, when the mind turns toward itself and separates itself from the sensory world, it perceives something beyond itself. Or in the words of Descartes' meditator: "When I turn my mind's eye upon myself [*in meipsum mentis aciem converto*], I understand that I am a thing which is incomplete and dependent on another" (CSM II 35; AT VII 51). Thus, the ultimate destination of Descartes' conversive turn is a clear and distinct cognition of God: "And certainly, so long as I think only of God, and turn my whole attention to him [*totusque in eum me converto*], I can find no cause of error or falsity. But when I turn back to myself [*ad me reversus*], I know by experience that I am prone to countless errors" (CSM II 38; AT VII 54). At the beginning of the Fourth Meditation Descartes' meditator reviews the path that they have taken:

During these past few days I have accustomed myself to leading my mind away from the senses; and I have taken careful note [*animadverti*] of the fact that there is very little about corporeal things that is truly perceived, whereas much more is known about the human mind, and still more about God. The result is that I now have no difficulty in turning my mind away from imaginable things and toward things which are objects of the intellect alone and are totally separate from matter [*ulla difficultate cogitationem a rebus imaginabilibus ad intelligibiles tantum, atque ab omni materia secretas, convertam*]. (CSM II 37; AT VII 52–53)

The meditator's itinerary from initial doubt about the reliability of the senses to the final illumination in the *contemplatio Dei* at the end of the Third Meditation is made up of a series of turns. Once Descartes' meditator has achieved the clear and distinct cognition of God, laying the foundation for reliable philosophical and scientific inquiry, they can safely turn their mental gaze, *acies mentis*, back toward the sensory world. Armed with the *cogito* as the standard of clear and distinct cognition and the certain knowledge of a benevolent God who guarantees the principal reliability of sensory cognition, this return to the world is no longer figured only as a *reversio* (see CSM II 38; AT VII 54) but as a *conversio* as well. Not only Descartes' (first) philosophy is informed by *conversio* but also the subsequent scientific inquiry into the world. As I demonstrate later in this and the following chapters, the *Meditations* enacts a series of coordinated turns that together articulate a Cartesian "art of turning." Patterned on a meditative ascent, Descartes' meditator first follows the *via purgativa* and then the *via illuminativa* to arrive at the *via unitiva*. After the *contemplatio Dei* at the end of the Third Meditation the meditator turns back toward the world. Put more simply, by purging their mind of all confused and obscure ideas, they arrive at the clear and distinct cognition of the *cogito* and of God in the light of the *lumen naturale*, which serves as the foundation for the inquiry into the sensory world.

Meditating and Painting

Descartes' meditator begins the "general demolition" of their opinions with the observation that "whatever I have up till now accepted as most true I have acquired either from the senses or through the senses" (CSM II 17; AT VII 18). The question is, how can that which appears as "most true" in the scenario provided for the meditator—"I am here, sitting by the fire, wearing a winter dressing-gown, holding this piece of paper in my hands"— be thrown into doubt? After rejecting madness as a self-refuting basis for doubting sensory perception *tout court*, the meditator turns to dreaming,[2] and in this context they introduce an extended comparison of thinking and painting:

Suppose then that I am dreaming, and that these particulars—that my eyes are open, that I am moving my head and stretching out my hands—are not true. Perhaps, indeed, I do not even have such hands or such a body at all. Nonetheless, it must surely be admitted that the visions which come in sleep are like paintings [*pictas imagines*], which must have been fashioned in the likeness of things that are real [*ad similitudinem rerum verarum fingi potuerunt*], and hence that at least these general kinds of things—eyes, head, hands, and the body as a whole—are things which are not imaginary but real and exist. For even when painters [*pictores*] try to create [*formis fingere*] sirens and satyrs with the most extraordinary bodies, they cannot give them natures which are new in all respects; they simply jumble up the limbs from different animals. (CSM II 13; AT VII 19–20)

To illustrate how the mind could be dreaming when it is thinking, Descartes' meditator turns to the analogy of painting. Mental representations or ideas are "like paintings," with the mind simultaneously their creator and beholder. The mind forgets that its ideas are like paintings, fashioned (or, better, feigned, derived from the Latin verb *fingere*) by its own agency, manifesting their fictitiousness—in an echo of Horace's famous comparison with painting at the beginning of the *Ars poetica*[3]—only when composed arbitrarily of heterogeneous elements. As long as the mind practices an aesthetics of realism (aesthetics in the double sense of the Aristotelian *aisthesis*, that is, the faculty of perception, and the modern notion of aesthetics as concerned with artifacts), it believes that its mental representations reflect reality and are the "things themselves."

Scholars have tended to limit the comparison with painting to sensation and imagination, to those cogitations concerned with corporeal things, in pursuit of the argument that in the *Meditations* Descartes abandoned his earlier conceptualization of the imagination.[4] The analogy between thinking and painting, however, pervades the text and remains even after the discovery of the *cogito* and the proof of God, that is, the recognition of innate ideas, or ideas belonging solely to the intellect. Indeed, Descartes' meditator defines ideas by their "imagistic" quality: "Some of my thoughts are as it were the images of things [*rerum imagines*], and it is only in these cases that the term 'idea' is strictly appropriate—for example, when I think of a man, a chimera, or the sky, or an angel, or God [*ut cum hominem, vel Chimaerum, vel Coelum, vel Angelum, vel Deum cogito*]" (CSM II 25; AT VII 37). Significantly, not only thoughts of things of the corporeal world are "images" but also thoughts of angels and God. Nor is this the only time, as we see when Descartes' meditator discusses how to "imagine" the idea of God: "There are many ways in which I understand that this idea is not something fictitious which is dependent on my thought, but is an image of a true and immutable nature [*imaginem verae & immutabilis naturae*]" (CSM II 47; AT VII 68).

In Descartes' most elaborate articulation of this analogy between painting and thinking in the sense of the making of ideas, all mental faculties are conceived as producers of images or ideas. It appears in the dialogue *The Search for Truth by the Natural Light,* hailing from around the same time, and follows a pedagogical strategy and trajectory similar to those of the *Meditations*. In an extended simile, Epistemon, the representative of Scholasticism, likens

> the imagination of a child to a *tabula rasa* on which our ideas are to be traced, these ideas being like portraits drawn from nature. Our senses, inclinations, teachers and intellect [*l'entendement*] are the different artists who may work at this task, and among them the least competent are the first to take part, namely our imperfect senses, blind instincts and foolish nurses. The most competent is the intellect, which comes last; and it must serve an apprenticeship of many years, following the example of its masters for a long time before daring to correct any of their errors. In my opinion, this is one of the chief causes of the difficulties we have in acquiring knowledge. For our senses see nothing beyond the more coarse and ordinary things and our natural inclinations are entirely corrupt; and as to our teachers, although undoubtedly you might find very perfect ones among them, they cannot force our judgement to accept their reasonings until our intellect has done the work (which only it can do) of examining it. But the intellect is like an excellent painter who is called upon to put the finishing touches to a bad picture sketched out by a young apprentice. (CSM II 405–6 ; AT X 507–8)

It is not surprising that a Scholastic philosopher like Epistemon—for whom the Aristotelian commonplace, *nihil est in intellectu, nisi prius fuerit in sensu* (nothing is in the intellect that has not been in the senses before), appears as a truth—to draw this comparison. Yet Eudoxus, Descartes' alter ego in the dialogue, finds himself in rare but fundamental agreement with Epistemon,[5] an issue we return to later in this chapter. The *tabula* of the mind is the canvas on which external as well as internal artists are actively tracing lines and applying colors. The dilemma is that the first ones to mark the infantile tabula rasa, "namely our imperfect senses, blind instincts and foolish nurses," are the "least competent," and that the "most competent," the intellect, or understanding, comes last. At issue here is not the medium of painting but the idea that the intellect, while a better painter, even the best painter, is a painter nonetheless.

Conceiving thinking as painting or, more properly, as the manipulation of mental images has a long tradition back through the Scholastics to Aristotle's *De anima*,[6] which is a tradition Descartes was famously trying to overcome. At the time of its appearance, however, a text titled *Meditations* in which thinking is conceived as painting would have evoked a different yet related tradition, the production of mental images in monastic meditation,[7] as well as its early modern heir, the *Spiritual Exercises* of Ignatius of Loyola. The visualization of the *historia* of Christ's life and suffering is the red thread running through the entire regime of exercises,[8] and it is intimately intertwined with the making of an election, which is the purpose of undergoing Ignatius's spiritual *cursus*. Beginning with the contemplation of the fall and one's own sinfulness (during the first week) and continuing with the contemplation of Christ's life from annunciation to crucifixion (in the second and third week), it ends with the contemplation of his resurrection and ascension, so the exercitant moves from purgation in the first to illumination in the subsequent weeks. The exercitant is directed to meditate their own election just as they are visualizing Christ's baptism, the external act by which the self turns toward God.[9]

In the *Spiritual Exercises*, visualization or, more generally, sensualization, is the most important of the techniques the exercitant has to appropriate and assimilate the *historia* of Christ's life and suffering, to make it into a vivid *exemplum* that compels the self to its own *imitatio Christi*. It is not enough to remember the story of Christ's life and suffering. In the second annotation prefacing the *Spiritual Exercises* Ignatius calls for more than that:

For if a person begins contemplating with a true historical foundation, and then goes over the historical narrative and reflects on it personally, one may by oneself come upon things that throw more light on the history or better bring home its meaning.... For it is not so much knowledge that fills and satisfies the soul, but rather the intimate feeling and savoring of things. (SE § 2, p. 283)

By amplifying and visualizing the historical narrative, the self "feels and savors things." More than just knowing them, in the process it makes them its own.

In classical rhetoric the capacity of a speech to generate clear and vivid mental images is designated by the term "evidence," and Ignatius's specific techniques of mental visualization do not conceal this rhetorical provenance.[10] The Latin term *evidentia* translated and conflated the Greek paronyms *enargeia*, denoting perspicuity, and *energeia*, denoting activity and force. Although Quintilian classifies *evidentia* as a *figura in mentis*, it is better seen as pertaining to the persuasive effect of a host of rhetorical figures and tropes, such as *illustratio, demonstratio, hypotyposis, ekphrasis, subiectio sub oculos,* and *repraesentatio,* all employed to the same end, to bring before the listener's or reader's eyes what the text describes. Yet what distinguishes *evidentia* (vivid illustration) from *perspicuitas* (mere clearness) is its visual force, "since the latter merely lets itself be seen [*patet*], whereas the former thrusts itself upon our notice [*se quodammodo ostendit*]."[11] Quintilian defines the "ostentatious thrust" of *evidentia* as follows: "From such impressions arises that *enargeia* which Cicero calls illumination and actuality, which makes us seem not so much to narrate as to exhibit the actual scene, while our emotions will be no less actively stirred than if we were present at the actual occurrence" (IO II 435). In his *Progymnasmata,* Nicolaos of Myra similarly contrasts "ekphrastic writing," which exhibits *enargeia,* to "mere reporting": "the latter namely contains only a bare representation of the object while the former tries to turn readers into spectators."[12] *Evidentia* refers to discourse that prompts recipients to experience the events described as if they were not textually mediated and thereby transforms them seemingly into eyewitnesses. In other words, evidentiary techniques enact a kind of *autopsia,* allowing listeners or readers to see the things themselves for themselves without the mediating words of others.

The Ignatian exercises deploy evidentiary techniques of classical rhetoric, among them similes, amplification, enumeration, and partition, to produce sensate testimony for an event that is in particular need of authentication and validation—in this instance, that God assumed a body in which he lived and suffered. The moment language reaches its limit and becomes image resembles the moment the Word becomes flesh. In this vein, the Christian theology of incarnation figures the Word's becoming flesh as an effect of the evidentiary discourse of the Holy Spirit. Ignatius's *Spiritual Exercises* stand very much in this tradition of using rhetorical means to mentally visualize the mystery of the incarnation and passion of Christ. By undergoing the Ignatian exercises, the exercitant becomes an eyewitness, like the apostles with their mission founded on their testimony to Christ's life and suffering.

The simulation of eyewitnessing implies that observer and observed inhabit the same space—at least virtually. Not coincidentally, Ignatius begins every individual spiritual exercise with the *compositio loci,* or "seeing the place": "Where the object is invisible, as is the case in the present instance dealing with sins" (SE § 47, p. 294), the imagination must first provide a body that can then be situated in space: "the composition will be to see with the gaze of the imagination and to consider that my soul is imprisoned in this body" (§ 47, p. 294). From this co-presence of meditative subject and object it is only a step to the subject imagining itself as part of its own mental image. In his directions for the contemplation of the nativity, Ignatius writes: "This is to see people, i.e., Our Lady, and Joseph, and the servant girl, and the child Jesus after his birth. Making myself into a poor and unworthy little servant, I watch them, and contemplate them, and serve them in their needs as if I were present, with all possible submission and reverence" (§ 114, p. 306). As an eyewitness, one is so close as to literally become part of the observed events, and as part of the visualized scene the self becomes itself the object of its meditative gaze. Ignatian meditation involves a seeing of the self by the self—even though it assumes the role of another, in this case, the "unworthy little servant." In seeing oneself for oneself, Ignatian meditation is autopsy in yet another sense, in that this vision leads to actual self-reflection when, as Ignatius continues, "afterwards I reflect within myself to derive some profit" (§ 114, p. 306). In turning itself toward itself, the self can finally perceive itself as itself—and not as another. But Ignatian meditation is autoptic vision also in a third sense. As part of the imagined scene, it is not only the self that comes into focus but also its actions, which, not coincidentally, consist in seeing: "Making myself into a poor and unworthy little servant, I watch them, and contemplate them" (§ 114, p. 306). Whatever else meditative visualization may see, it always also sees itself seeing. In this tradition, meditation as an act of perception and cognition is intrinsically self-reflexive.

The structure and economy of the Ignatian technique of mental visualization, or as we termed it earlier, meditative matrix, is on display in many of the engravings of Antoine Sucquet's *Via vitae aeternae*, two of which we encountered in the first chapter. In Sucquet's chapter "On the Method of Meditating, by Which the Mind Ascends from Terrestrial Things to God," he defines meditation as mental picturing: "To meditate is to consider in one's mind, and as it were, to paint in one's heart the mystery or some doctrine of the Life of Christ, or even the perfection of God, by [representing] the circumstances: people, actions, words, place, and time."[13] The plate accompanying this chapter, *imago* 11 in the edition of 1620 (see Fig. 5),

FIGURE 5. Imago 11, engraved by Boëtius à Bolswert, in Antoine Sucquet, *Via vitae aeternae. Iconibus illustrata per Boëtium A Bolswert* (Antwerp: Typis Martini Nutij, 1620), 358v. Courtesy of the University of Chicago Library's Hanna Holborn Gray Special Collections Research Center.

emblematizes meditative practice in the figure of a painter who paints the mystery of the nativity on the canvas of his heart.

The *pictor in corde* (painter in the heart) parses the scene before him by applying the classical rhetorical *loci communes*: *Quis? Quid? Quomodo? Ubi? Quando? Cur?* (Who? What? How? Where? When? Why?). But given that the scene before the *pictor in corde* is "painted" or, more precisely, imagined by meditating, it is the rhetorical technique of amplification that generates the meditative image in the first place; it is these very questions that produce as their answers the images on the cardiac canvas. Thus, we get to see the precise mechanism of the evidentiary generation of images in meditation. The artist with his back turned at his easel stands in for the engraving's beholder. Both are directing their gaze at the scene of nativity unfolding before them. While the painter of the heart sees only the scene before him, the engraving's beholder also sees the painter seeing and picturing that very scene. As Walter Melion observes, "We are to see ourselves in the likeness of this man himself manipulating meditative images."[14]

The frontispiece to Jan David's *Orbita probitatis ad Christi imitationem* (Disk of righteousness for the imitation of Christ), the short treatise appended to his *Veridicus Christianus*,[15] similarly parallels painting and meditating—albeit with an important twist (see Fig. 6).

At the center of this engraving by Cornelis Galle stands Christ carrying his cross on the mound of Golgotha. This moment of Christ's passion is feeding the pictorial imagination of the ten painters at their easels surrounding him. But only the painter at the center and in the line of sight with the viewer represents the scene that presents itself to him accurately. He exemplifies the ideal meditative life that, as Walter Melion observed, "involves visualizing Christ as if He were vividly present to our eyes, and ultimately transforming the soul by indelibly fixing this image upon it, so that it becomes an imitation of Christ *ad vivum*, virtually indistinguishable from its source."[16] In contrast, the other nine deviate from this ideal of faithfully painting (and imitating) Christ. Whereas most painters, the three at top on the right and the three on the left closest to their subject, are inspired to envision other moments of Christ's life, from the adoration of the Magi to the entry into Jerusalem, the last three portray Judas with a bag of silver coins, Satan, and a woman with two beasts. Their inner vision has been corrupted by sin, prompting them to superimpose their own desires on to the *imago Dei*.

FIGURE 6. Title page to the appendix "Orbita probitatis ad Christi imitationem veridico Christiano subserviens," in Joannes David, *Veridicus Christianus* (Antwerp: Ex officina Plantiniana, 1601), 351. Courtesy of the Getty Research Institute.

Cartesian Doubt and the Discernment of Spirits

The three painters in David's frontispiece whose canvases do not show Christ carrying the cross are looking at the same subject as all the other painters, but somehow the translation of that aspect into a mental image is interrupted and what they paint and behold on their *tabula* fails to correspond to "reality." Their misrepresentations raise two distinct but related issues bearing on the discretion called for in meditating and thinking with images. The first is epistemological and most patently of consequence to Descartes: How can the mind distinguish true from false mental representations? The second is spiritual and ultimately soteriological: How can the self discern the origin of a mental image in the sense of its sender, that is, God, Satan, or oneself? For a Jesuit such as David the first is a function of the second. Satan, in Greek the *diabol*, sabotages the successful meditative symbolization of the savior. At first glance, Descartes seems to be concerned only with the veracity of mental representations. Yet, by introducing the *genius malignus* (and later claiming that God is responsible for clear and distinct cognition), that is, in linking veracity to provenance, he betrays his own Jesuit heritage.

The examination and evaluation of mental representations were integral to spiritual exercises going back to antiquity. Presumably, the prisoner in Plato's cave would have remained turned toward the shadows on the wall had he been entirely satisfied with their appearance, while later, after beholding the world in the light of the sun, he possesses an absolute criterion to evaluate the appearances back in the cave. The self's search for truth and acquisition of wisdom depends on its ability to examine and discern appearances and, by extension, mental representations. While Plato never fully developed such a practice, ancient Stoicism made the *chrēsis tōn phantasiōn*—the "use of appearances," or as *phantasiai* has also been translated, the "use of (mental) (re)presentations"—the centerpiece of its philosophical practice.[17] According to Epictetus the purpose of the *hegemonikon*, or "leading principle" of the soul and what we would call reason, is "to test the impressions and discriminate between, and apply none that has not been tested" (*Discourses* 1.20.7–8).[18] This is "the first and greatest task of the philosopher," which means that the self-reflexivity and autonomy of philosophical thought and practice hinge on the soul's "use of presentations." For reason "contemplates itself and everything else" (1.1.4), as it examines its presentations. Ideally, it should act like a sentry at the border between the self and the external world: "We ought not to accept a sense-impression unsubjected to examination, but should say: 'Wait, allow me to see who you are and whence you come' (just as the night-watch say, 'Show me your tokens [*synthēmata*]'). 'Do you have your token from nature [*tēs phusias symbolon*], the one which every sense-impression which is to be accepted must have?'" (3.12.15–16). Like a real messenger the sense impression has to show a *symbolon*, half of a broken clay coin, to authenticate itself and be granted entry. The soul has no control over who or what approaches the gates of its senses, but it has control over whom it lets enter. In epistemological terms, granting entry to a presentation is acknowledging it or, to use the Stoics' technical term, assenting to it. Epictetus recommends a welcoming protocol very similar to the sentry's procedure for all incoming sense impressions, lest they overpower the self: "If you confront your external impression with such thoughts, you will overcome it, and not be carried away by it. But, to begin with, be not swept off your feet, I beseech you, by the vividness of the impression, but say, 'Wait for me a little, O impression; allow me to see who you are, and what you are an impression of; allow me to put you to the test'" (2.18.23–25). The primary purpose of examining mental presentations is thus pragmatic, exercising self-control. But it also has an epistemological dimension in that the ability to maintain control over mental presentations is in part a function of determining their epistemological status: "to see who you are, and what you are an impression of." If we use presentations properly, "we shall never give our assent to anything but that of which we get a convincing sense-impression [*phantasia kataleptikē*]" (3.8.4), as Epictetus emphasizes.

Phantasia kataleptikē, or "apprehensive presentation,"[19] is a technical term in Stoic epistemology used in reference to the kind of impression that, "being plain and striking, all but grabs us by the hair, and draws us into assent, needing nothing else to strike us in this way or to suggest its difference to others."[20] A kataleptic presentation is kataleptic not only in the sense that the mind grasps the object of cognition almost by hand, as the famous comparison by Cicero illustrates, but it grabs the mind in such a way that the mind cannot but assent. The criterion for the reality and veracity of a sense perception is its *enargeia*, the force by which it appears and imposes itself on the mind, so kataleptic presentations distinguish themselves from a-kataleptic ones by their impressiveness. Kataleptic presentations are so distinct and clear that they not only reveal the (re)presented object in all its detail but also evidence its reality, as only real objects can have such an impact on the sensory self. Paradoxically, kataleptic presentations effect this immediacy by foregrounding their own mediality, in the sense that what demonstrates the reality of the represented is the quality of the presentation. The Stoic Chrysippus captures this aspect in another metaphor derived from the etymology of *phantasia*: "An impression is an affection occurring in the soul, which reveals itself and its cause. . . . The word *phantasia* is derived from *phos* [light]; just as *phos* reveals itself and whatever else it includes in its range, so *phantasia* reveals itself and its cause."[21] A kataleptic *phantasia* presents its cause by presenting itself and thereby provides its own conditions of intelligibility and visibility. In a way, kataleptic presentations are the mental equivalent of the rhetorical autopsy effected by the figure of *enargeia* or *evidentia*. Epictetus encapsulates the "use of presentations" in the image of the testing of coinage:

> Now just as it is the nature of every soul to assent to the true, dissent from the false, and to withhold judgement in a matter of uncertainty, so it is its nature to be moved with desire toward the good with aversion toward the evil, and feel neutral toward what is neither evil nor good. For just as neither the banker nor the greengrocer may legally refuse the coinage of Caesar, but if you present it, whether he will or not, he must turn over to you what you are purchasing with it, so it is also with the soul. (*Discourses* 3.3.2–4)

A clear sense impression of the good is like a coin bearing the image of Caesar, with the clear imprint of the sovereign's likeness authenticating its epistemological and spiritual validity and rendering it true and good. Significantly, the imprint does not represent the referent but the author, or better, the guarantor of the coin's value. In other words, the representational value of an impression is not only a function of its clearness and distinctness, which evidence its referentiality, but of its origin—which will prove relevant for the retooling of the testing of mental representations by early Christianity.

The Stoic *chrēsis tōn phantasiōn* was channeled into Christian tradition by Paul as the "discernment of spirits" (in Greek, *diakrisis pneumaton*; and in Latin, *discretio spirituum*) when he included it among the nine charismatic gifts bestowed by the Holy Spirit (I Cor 12:10).[22] The gift of discernment pertained to a variety of spiritual phenomena such as prophecies, glossolalia, revelations, visions, dreams, apparitions, miracles, but also thoughts and perceptions. Particularly the early desert monks—who we recall retreat from the world to devote their whole existence to the *mnēmē theou* (remembrance of God)—had been beset by distracting thoughts (*ponēroi logismoi*) and delusions (*phantasiai*),[23] leaving them in need of a spiritual technique to distinguish thoughts that advanced their spiritual progress and ascent from thoughts that could precipitate a relapse. Saint Antony, who by way of the *Vita Antonii* by Athanasius was formative for Christian monasticism, stressed the point that the constancy of one's conversion was subject to testing by the *phantasiai* sent by the evil spirit. Consequently, the *Vita* not only treats the discernment of spirits more extensively than any other patristic text but also makes it the centerpiece of his spiritual practice.[24] Only after thirty-five years of ascetic practice in the desert was Antony ready to share his technique laid out in a series of staged conversations, in which he emphasizes his belief that God aided him directly in his discernment of the demons tempting him in his pursuit of a pious life. In other words, discernment was for him dependent as much on ascetic discipline as on divine grace.

It was John Cassian who mediated the spirituality of Eastern monasticism to the Latin West. His *Conferences* (*Conlationes*) stage the encounter and interchange with several *abbas* in the Egyptian desert and synthesize their ideal of monastic life. Taking up the bulk of the first two *Conferences*, discernment clearly grounds monastic life and practice.[25] Its subject are not so much demons but "spirits that rise up in the monk himself [*ascendetium in sese spirituum*]" (*Conferences* 2.1.4).[26] The final end (*telos* or *finis*) of monastic existence is the kingdom of heaven and the concomitant *visio beatifica*, the vision of God, but the immediate goal (*scopos*) of the monk's daily practice, in order to attain this ultimate end, is the *puritas cordis* or purity of heart (1.4.3). The constant contemplation of the *scopos*, purity of heart or divine "love" and "holiness," as John Cassian calls it too, is imperiled by the self's inescapable fallenness, as the inconstancy of the mind is a function of the inconstancy of the self's "perishable flesh" (1.13.1). Just as the body is subject to desires and passions, the mind cannot fix its attention constantly on a single thought but is unsettled by superfluous thoughts and distractions. While it is "impossible for the mind not be troubled by thoughts," the self's free will does enable it to resist succumbing to the distractions and overcoming its mental inconstancy: "It is true that their origin does not in every respect depend on us, but it is equally true that their refusal or acceptance does depend on us" (1.17.1).

Similar to the Stoic sage, the monk cannot control the occurrence of such thoughts, but he can give or withhold his acceptance. Thus, the Stoic *chrēsis tōn phantasiōn* is put in the service of keeping the monk on track toward his *scopos*, the purity of heart, and the ultimate *telos*, the unceasing contemplation of God. By distinguishing between "holy and spiritual thoughts" and "earthly and carnal ones" (*Conferences* 1.17.2), the mind purifies itself and stays turned toward God. Discretion lends staying power to pious practice.[27] Discretion for Cassian, as a consequence, is not only the "first of the virtues" (1.23.3) but "is in some way the source and root of all the virtues" (2.9.1). It is the "eye and light of the Gospel" as "it sees and casts light on all a person's thoughts and actions and discerns everything that must be done" (2.2.5). Discretion is instrumental to the project of spiritual edification because without it neither can "our interior dwelling be built nor spiritual riches be gathered" (2.4.2). Correspondingly, discretion facilitates spiritual orientation and navigation as it "lead[s] the fearless monk on a steady ascent to God and always preserves the aforesaid virtues undamaged; as that with which the heights of perfection could be scaled with little weariness; and as that without which many of those who labor even with a good will would be unable to arrive at the summit. For discretion is the begetter, guardian, and moderator of all virtues" (2.4.3).

In contrast to the Stoic "use of presentations" monastic discretion is not so much concerned with the veracity of thoughts but with their origin or, more concretely, their sender. According to Cassian the self's thoughts have three sources: "They come from God, from the devil, and from ourselves" (*Conferences* 1.19.1). This concern with a thought's author manifests itself also in Cassian's adaption and reconfiguration of the image of the money changer. The focus of the money changer is twofold. He has to determine "whether something is gold of the purest sort" (1.20.1) and to authenticate the author or, more precisely, the minter or issuer whose image is stamped on the coin, aiming to identify counterfeits. In contrast to the Stoic *typosis en psychē*, which is molded by the object represented, Cassian's cognitive coinage always also bears the image of its author—whatever else it may represent.

Antony, Cassian, and a number of other "theoreticians" of early monasticism made discernment the centerpiece of ascetic practice and spiritual life.

Although they extended it to other medial and material manifestations of good and evil spirits, they shaped it into a meta-cognitional method that enabled the self to examine its thoughts and emotions. Discernment thus became essential for the formation of the interiority and spiritual life of Western monasticism. According to Gregory the Great, *The Rule of Saint Benedict*, one of the founding documents of monasticism, is distinguished by its *discretio*.[28] Echoing Cassian, Benedict calls *discretio* the "mother of all virtues."[29] Particularly, the abbot of a monastic community needs to be able to exercise *discretio* in his ordering of the spiritual and social life of its members. It thus is no longer concerned only with the discernment of spirits but informs all decision-making, lying at the heart of temperance and prudence. It is in this latter sense that *discretio* gets taken up by Thomas Aquinas.[30]

Toward the late Middle Ages the rise of millennial fears and hopes and the emergence of various religious movements were accompanied by a crisis of salvational media and communication.[31] The appearance of prophets and terrestrial and celestial signs (*monstra*) foretelling the last days of man and his impending judgment lent renewed urgency to the injunction from 1 John 4.1: "Do not believe every spirit, but test the spirits to see whether they are from God, because many false prophets have gone out into the world." The discernment of spirits was, accordingly, retooled to confront and manage this proliferation of religious media.[32] Susan Schreiner reminds us that "the problem of discernment crossed all confessional boundaries."[33] The specific techniques may have differed, but theologians and polemicists across the confessions equally felt the urgency to articulate methods and tools to face the outpouring of the spirit.

Jean Gerson, the most important theologian of the discernment of spirits in the late Middle Ages,[34] opens his first treatment of the subject, "On Distinguishing True from False Revelations" (1402), with an image that we know well from John Cassian of "the genuine coin of divine revelation, which can be distinguished from the counterfeit coin of diabolical trickery."[35] The metaphor of money changing structures the rest of the treatise and is extended into an allegory of discernment: "This coin of spiritual revelation, like gold, is to be examined mainly on five points: weight, flexibility or malleability, durability, conformability, and color. This can be done in accord with the five virtues from which the evidence is taken to legitimate spiritual coin. Humility provides weight; discretion malleability; patience durability; truth conformability; charity provides color" (*On Distinguishing* 338). The recourse to this ancient, venerable—and purportedly biblical—image, alongside the fine reticulation Gerson gives to it, suggests a much higher degree of confidence in the efficacy and reliability of this spiritual technique than Gerson actually possessed. For shortly thereafter, when subjecting John the Baptist's prophecy to discernment, he states categorically:

> We can also say that there is for human beings no general rule or method that can be given always and infallibly to distinguish between revelations that are true and those that are false and deceptive. If this were possible, we would not have to have only faith in our prophets, and consequently in our religion, for we would have the certitude of what was evident. (335)

Since prophecies and, more generally, religion are predicated on divinely instituted faith and a "general rule or method" of discernment would result in certain knowledge, thus obviating faith, discernment cannot be infallible without violating the principles of this religious epistemology. Thus, instead of making it subject to a "general method," Gerson views discernment more as "a matter of experience, dependent on a number of individual conditions, which are infinite, than a question of some technique" (351).

Given the historical as well as contemporary importance of dream visions as media of revelation, it may not be surprising that Gerson adduces them to test the efficacy of discernment, but it is surprising that the subsequent discussion is concerned not with the sender of those dream visions but with the distinction between dream and waking itself. In other words, Gerson's interest is in an epistemological question rather than the spiritual and soteriological one that is actually at the heart of the treatise. According to Gerson, the visions that one has in dreams are in many ways indistinguishable from their waking counterparts. They can be rational. Or, as exemplified by Descartes' dreams, they can "reflect upon their own content." Dreams can be so vivid that "a person even though awake and considering his state of being will ask himself whether he was then truly asleep." Furthermore, all actions characteristic of the waking state, "such as walking, speaking, and the like," also occur in dreams (*On Distinguishing* 351). Gerson concludes that there are no reliable criteria, no general method for distinguishing dreaming from waking; "only experience enables one to distinguish between the two states" (351). Yet, when he repeatedly presses a fictitious person "who is awake how he knows whether he is awake" (351), he is ultimately forced to admit that he cannot ascertain reliably that he is not being deceived, let alone explain how he knows that he is awake. He has only "experiential knowledge" through which "he does not so much have an opinion but knows and understands that he is awake" (352): it is the knowledge of being awake rather than the propositional knowledge of being able to state and explain the features of the state of wakefulness. For Gerson, this "experiential knowledge" is analogous, possibly even homologous, to the metaphorical awaking "when the good God rouses [man] from the sleep of sin" (352). Thus, the experiential knowledge of waking has the same kind of evidentiary certainty as conversion. When God or, more precisely, the Holy Spirit, intercedes directly, discernment occurs with utter certainty; when he does not, discernment lacks the reliability to ground religious life.

The most prominent articulation of the spiritual practice of discernment was undoubtedly the one from Ignatius of Loyola.[36] In contrast to Gerson's notion of discernment, which is primarily designed and deployed to evaluate spirits working in other selves, Ignatius's technique is directed inward. Similar to Cassian's, which is aimed at the "spirits that rise up in the monk himself" (*Conferences* 2.1.4), distracting him from his permanent *mnēmē theou*, Ignatius's discernment is a psychotechnique for examining one's thoughts and affects. Like Cassian's vision of monastic life, in which *discretio* is essential to the monk's pursuit of his *scopos* and *telos*, Ignatian discernment is always also a technique of spiritual orientation and navigation. Unlike Gerson, Ignatius displays considerable hermeneutical and epistemological optimism regarding the efficacy of discernment. Nonetheless, he is ultimately unable to provide a foolproof and reliable criterion for discerning spirits and evaluating one's thoughts and emotions; and this epistemological deficiency, I contend, informs the discernment that Descartes' meditator performs in the First Meditation.

Ignatius operationalizes the discernment of spirits to realize the *scopos* of the *Spiritual Exercises*, as we have seen, to make an election. The matters requiring an election to be made can involve an "unchangeable choice," such as entering the Societas Jesu, priesthood, marriage, and so forth, or a "changeable choice" (SE § 171, p. 317), such as taking an office, accepting or declining benefices, or acquiring or renouncing wealth. When making an election, the exercitant must have the ultimate *telos* in view: "The eye of our intention must be simple, looking only at what I have been created for, viz.

the praise of God Our Lord and the salvation of my soul, and therefore whatever I choose must help me towards the end for which I have been created, and I must not make the end fit the means, but subordinate the means to the end" (§ 169, p. 316). Put differently, the election must be made in conformity with God's will regarding the choice at hand so that the immediate objective of making an election is discovering that very will.

As described in Chapter 1, Ignatius distinguishes three forms in which elections are made, or as he calls them, "times of election" (SE § 175, p. 317). The first refers to what would be commonly called a conversion, "when God Our Lord so moves and attracts the will that without doubting or being able to doubt, such a dedicated soul follows what is shown" (§ 175, p. 317). As examples, in both the *Spiritual Exercises* and the *Official Directory of 1599*, Ignatius cites the vocations of Matthew and Paul, in which the direct intervention from God is "quite out of the ordinary and is not subject to any rule," so it is beyond human control and cannot be operationalized. In the *Spiritual Exercises* it forms the ideal limit case whose clarity and self-evidence the other forms of election can approximate but never achieve. The second-best time for making an election is "when sufficient light and knowledge [are] received through experience of consolations and desolations, and through experience of the discernment of different spirits" (§ 176, p. 317), making this spiritual technique the second-best way of making election, and preferable to the third, which Ignatius calls "the tranquil time," because "the soul is not disturbed by different spirits and can use her natural powers freely and calmly" (§ 177, pp. 317–18). Consequently, the third time should apply only to "changeable choices." It relies exclusively on human reason to discover the divine will because the exercitant has no movements in their soul to decipher. The *Official Directory* counsels: "Provided the movement comes directly from God, there is no doubt that the higher and more excellent way is when it is the will which, under God's illumination takes the lead and draws the intellect after it" (*Directory* § 190, p. 330).[37]

Ignatian discernment consists in following "rules by which to perceive and understand to some extent various movements produced in the soul" (SE § 313, p. 348), with the goal that is similar to that of the Stoics: "The good that they may be accepted and the bad that they may be rejected" (§ 313, p. 348). Like his patristic predecessors, Ignatius distinguishes "three sorts of thought processes in me, one sort which are properly mine and arise simply from my free will and choice, and two other sorts which come from outside, one from the good spirit and the other from the bad" (§ 32, p. 291). While the self's own thoughts are by and large characterized by tranquility, the thoughts induced by the good and bad spirits manifest themselves in moving the soul. The movements caused by the good spirit are called "consolations." They denote "any interior movement produced in the soul that leads her to become inflamed with love of her Creator and Lord, and, as a consequence there is no created thing on the face of the earth that we can love in itself, but we love it only in the Creator of all things" (§ 316, pp. 348–49).[38] More generally, Ignatius calls consolation "all interior happiness that calls and attracts a person towards heavenly things and to the soul's salvation" (§ 316, p. 349). "Desolation is the name" Ignatius gives to the contrary of what he defines in Rule 3 as consolation, for example, "darkness and disturbance in the soul, attraction towards what is low and of the earth" (§ 317, p. 349). Consolations and desolations are thus quite literally *regulae*, or "rules," governing how spirits direct the self in its spiritual journey: "Just as in consolation it is more the good spirit who guides and counsels us, so in desolation it is the bad spirit, and by following his counsels we can never find the right way" (§ 318, p. 349). If consolation is a movement, it is a movement (or turn away) from creation and toward the creator, from the world toward God. In other words, it is also a kind of conversion, only lacking the self-evidence and force of conversion in the first time. Also in contrast to the movement of the will in the first time, it is a movement toward God that is open to interpretation, which meant the possibility of misinterpretation or, worse, it could turn out to be a perversion in disguise. Quoting Paul and following patristic precedent, Ignatius warns that "it is characteristic of the bad angel to assume the form of 'an angel of light'" and draw "the soul into his hidden snares and his perverted purposes" (§ 332, p. 352).

Complications arise because the appearance of spirits, instead of being uniform, depends on the exercitant's spiritual and moral state. The spirit's mode of manifestation can either conform to or controvert the exercitant's state: "With people who go from one mortal sin to another it is the usual practice of the enemy to hold out to them apparent pleasures; so he makes them imagine sensual satisfactions and gratifications, in order to retain and reenforce them in their vices and sins. With people of this kind, the good spirit uses the opposite procedure, causing pricks of conscience and feelings of remorse" (SE § 314, p. 348). "In the case of people who are making serious progress in the purification of sins . . . the opposite to Rule 1 takes place, because then it is typical of the bad spirit to harass, sadden and obstruct . . . while the distinctive trait of the good spirit is to give courage and strength, consolations" (§ 315, p. 348). So it isn't as simple as the good spirit sending consolations, and the evil spirit, desolations. God may even induce desolations "to test our quality and to show how far we will go in God's service and praise, even without generous recompense in the form of consolations and overflowing graces" (§ 322, p. 350). And God deploys desolation to prevent the exercitant from becoming too arrogant and ascribing consolation to themself—so to speak as his own "good work." If the self believes to be the cause of its own consolation, then it commits the first and greatest sin: *superbia*, or pride. Desolation can thus indirectly evidence God's grace, which usually manifests itself more directly as consolation. And in this way the ability or inability to distinguish between one's own and alien thoughts becomes essential to salvation.

Even though God can appear *sub specie diaboli* as his adversary, the opposite scenario is more unsettling for Ignatius because the evil spirit's skill and power of dissimulation are more subtle and systematic. For the evil spirit enters the soul as "an angel of light" and "proposes good and holy thoughts well adapted to such a just soul, and then little by little succeeds in getting what he wants" (SE § 332, p. 352). The spiritual or moral value of a thought as such is, therefore, an insufficient criterion of its origin, because it is relative to the thoughts preceding and succeeding it. If the preceding thought is better than the succeeding thought, which is quite good in itself, then the latter can have come from the evil spirit. If the preceding thought is inferior, then the concluding better thought most probably stems from the good spirit. To be in the position to evaluate the relative merit of a thought, the self needs to be able to look simultaneously at the beginning, middle, and end of a chain of thoughts; and the longer the sequence, the more difficult it is to keep them present before the mind's eye—as Descartes observes regarding the difficulty of judging the evidence of long geometric proofs. Whether a sequence of mental events has been initiated or manipulated by the evil spirit can be determined only by its ultimate end.

In another series of rules recommended for the second week of exercises, Ignatius seems to be introducing a mode of discerning manifestations of the good spirit that is immune to error. While consolation is in itself already relatively good evidence that a movement of the soul stems from the good spirit, consolation "without cause" (SE § 330, p. 351) can come only from God, since it is an expression of the divine power of creation. In a manner of speaking, only God can create out of nothing. Or to put it soteriologically, consolation without cause is the purest expression of divine grace, because it gives itself seemingly randomly and autonomously. In contrast, the evil spirit, although powerful, has to use existing thoughts to achieve its ends: "When there is a cause, consolation can be given by the good or the bad angel . . . for opposite purposes" (§ 331, p. 352). By cause, Ignatius understands other thoughts or movements, so a consolation without cause is a thought that is not brought about by another mental event. Ignatius stipulates: "I mean without any previous perception or understanding of some object due to which consolation could come about through the mediation of the person's acts of understanding and will" (§ 330, p. 351). In contrast to a normal consolation that is mediated by other mental movements or thoughts, the consolation without cause appears unmediated; and precisely the fact that it is directly sent by God lends it its self-evidence and certainty.[39] No intermediaries can have contaminated or altered it, thereby opening it up to interpretation. Like rhetorical evidence, the Cartesian *cogito*, the consolation without cause appears as an instance of autopsy: God manifests himself for the self to be experienced directly.

Of course, although the consolation without cause is conceived to be immune to error, it does not escape contamination by ambiguity and doubt. Since mental events never occur alone but as part of a sequence, the solution has only shifted the problem: Even if the consolation without cause is a foolproof indicator of the workings of the good spirit, how can the consolation with cause and the consolation without a cause be distinguished from one another with matching certainty? How can the consolation without cause as a mental event be separated out from all other mental events so that it appears "uncaused" and unconnected? The problem is further exacerbated because the evil spirit is adept at hopping trains of thought steered by God and using divine consolations to cast evil thoughts in a holy light. The evil spirit bathes the thoughts it sends in the afterglow of the consolation induced by the good spirit. Thus, "the spiritual person to whom God gives this consolation must scrutinize the experience carefully and attentively, so as to distinguish the exact time of the actual consolation from the period following it, during which the soul is still aglow and favoured with the after-effects of the consolation now passed. For during this second period it often happens, owing either to thinking based on conclusions drawn from the relations between our own concepts and judgements, or to the agency of the good or bad spirit, that we form various plans and opinions that are not directly given to us by God Our Lord" (SE § 336, p. 353). Only by isolating individual mental events from each other, clearly distinguishing the present idea from the preceding and succeeding ones, can the self discern the genuinely divine origin of a thought. But that doesn't solve the problem either, because the workings of the good and evil spirits can be inferred only from a whole sequence of mental events and representations. Despite Ignatius's considerable hermeneutical and epistemological optimism regarding the discernment of spirits, a general method, as Gerson put it, which would ensure its certainty and reliability, remained elusive.

The meditative matrix, reaching back to the Stoics and the desert fathers, has always involved a critical examination of the images and mental representations it generates. Appearing uncalled before the mental gaze, they all need to be tested for their veracity and origin before the mind can accept and make them its own. Similarly, the analogy between thinking and painting used by Descartes' meditator prompts them to examine and critique systematically the structure and makeup of mental representations. Painters, we recall, don't create their "sirens and satyrs" ex nihilo (CSM II 13; AT VII 20), and even if they do invent something so new that it bears no resemblance to anything real, then at least the media employed, the colors and lines, have real referents. In the realm of thought, these "simpler and more universal things" such as color and line include corporeality in general, shape, quantity, size, number, location, and time. These are the building blocks of thought, and while their combination may be feigned, they themselves have to be real. By dissecting thoughts into medial constituents, echoing Stoic decomposition, Descartes' meditator seems to have arrived at an indubitable foundation. And it is at this point that the meditator introduces the notion of an omnipotent God capable of creating an entire world of mere illusion that deceives the thinking self even in regard to the "simplest and most general things" (CSM II 14; AT VII 20), such as "true colors" or two and three adding up to five. Even assuming God's benevolence, the possibility cannot be ruled out that the self is "so imperfect as to be deceived all the time" (CSM II 14; AT VII 21), given the inescapable fallibility of the thinking self.

Descartes's meditator, by shifting their focus from the verity or falsity of mental representations to God as both author and subject of these very thoughts, is able to universalize and radicalize their doubt. Then, albeit for primarily pragmatic reasons, they introduce the "malicious demon," or *genius malignus*: "It is not enough merely to have noticed [*advertisse*]" the falsity of all mental representations. Because of the persistence of old habits and the persuasiveness of the sensory world, the self easily relapses and relents in its "distrustful attitude" (CSM II 15; AT VII 22). Granting the demon "the utmost power and cunning" and supposing that he "has employed all his energies in order to deceive" (CSM II 15; AT VII 22) allows Descartes' meditator, much like Ignatius in the *Spiritual Exercises*, to "counter-balance" these "reverting" forces and "resolutely guard against assenting to any falsehoods" (CSM II 15; AT VII 23). With the introduction of the malicious demon, even if only for pragmatic reasons, the assent to falsehoods becomes soteriologically fraught. Believing in the reality of the sensory world isn't just an epistemological error but a sin, or given the conversive terminology running through the *Meditations*, a perversion. In hindsight from the end of the First Meditation, Descartes' practice of doubt thus appears in this new and different light.

The methodical doubt of the First Meditation has commonly been placed in the tradition of skepticism, whether in specific terms of, say, Pyrrhonian skepticism or in the more general vein of Michel Montaigne or Francisco Sanches.[40] However, when Descartes introduces the *genius malignus* as a way to invalidate all mental representations, his methodical doubt suddenly looks more like a blend of the Stoic *chrēsis tōn phantasiōn* and the Christian *discretio spirituum*. To be sure, like the Stoics, Descartes' primary focus is on the verity and falsity of mental representations and is thus more epistemological than spiritual. But his simultaneous concern with the origin of representations or, as in the case of clear and distinct cognition, their author, God, invokes the discernment of spirits and renders the *genius malignus* a not-too-distant descendant of the evil demons that tempted the desert fathers with alluring *phantasiai*. In short, Descartes borrows ancient and Christian techniques for the testing and analysis of mental representations for what could be called a Cartesian discernment.[41]

Descartes was well acquainted with discerning spirits and practiced it adroitly during his discovery of the "foundations of a marvelous science" in that stove-heated room on the banks of the Danube. After "ridding himself of his prejudices" and "stripping himself of himself," "it was enough that his imagination presented his mind to himself entirely naked, to make him believe that he had really stripped it bare. Nothing was left but the love of Truth, the pursuit of which was to be his sole occupation for the rest of his life."[42] But "reconstruction" proved itself more difficult than "destruction," as total doubt was easier than the differentiated critique necessary for evaluating individual mental representations. It was then that the search for the "ways" and "means" of pursuing truth "agitated his mind violently" and "so exhausted him that his brain took fire" (Cole 33; AT X 181). This transport of "enthusiasm" made him susceptible to "impressions of dreams and visions . . . from on high" (Cole 33; AT X 181), which he subjected to discernment. In the first dream, Descartes decodes the winds blowing him over and about as spirits, and in particular, the wind pushing him toward the chapel as the evil spirit clothed as the angel of light. However, despite his evident hermeneutical skill he finds neither refuge nor firm footing. He awakens terrified and prays to God for protection "from the evil effects of his dream" (Cole 34; AT X 182). His prayers are answered by the thunderclap of the second dream, which he recognizes as having being sent by God. Waking this time "he noticed many sparks of fire scattered around the room" (Cole 34–35; AT X 182), reassuring himself that it was actually his eyes that "sparkled enough that he could make out the objects closest to him" (Cole 35; AT X 182). Later he understands the fear marking the second dream as "his synderesis" (Cole 38; AT X 186), and the sparks as the inextinguishable *scintilla animae*—thereby covering all three possible origins of thoughts postulated by Cassian and Ignatius. In the third dream, not only does Descartes epistemologize the spiritual binaries of the first two dreams, in interpreting the Pythagorean "Yes and No" from the second poem by Ausonius as the "truth and falsehood in human understanding and the profane sciences" (Cole 37; AT X 185), but he effortlessly distinguishes sleeping and dreaming from waking and rational thought by self-consciously beginning with the interpretation of his dream before it is over. At the same time, he realizes that discernment is not learned from books but resides in the self, in the *scintilla animae* implanted by God at birth, which Descartes will reconfigure as the *lumen naturale* of reason.

If the *Meditations* is the operationalization of Descartes' conversion experience, it is only logical that the discernment of spirits, which played such an important role in his conversion, would reappear—albeit in retooled form—in its later philosophical working through. Descartes' meditator stages the breakdown of discernment to deconstruct an epistemology predicated on sensory perception. The need to wipe the mental *tabula* completely *rasa* arises only when the meditator introduces an epistemologically omnipotent evil spirit, whose projections cannot be distinguished from true mental representations. If discernment were infallible, then there would be no need to wipe the tabula rasa. But because there is no reliable criterion to discern true and false, good and evil spirits, Descartes' meditator turns inward and toward the self, where they discover not only the *cogito* but also God. Significantly, the discovery of these irrefutable foundations does not cause Descartes' meditator to abandon the practice of discernment. In fact, with the discovery of the *cogito*, the experience of clear and distinct cognition, and the proof of God (the idea of which grants and guarantees access to the sensory world), the meditator reinstitutes their own "method" of discernment. Sure enough, the discernment at the end of the *Meditations* is a truncated version, lacking the evil spirit as the author of perceptions and cognitions but retaining God as the author of all clear and distinct cognitions: "This is because every clear and distinct perception is undoubtedly something, and hence cannot come from nothing, but must necessarily have God for its author" (CSM II 43; AT VII 62). Correspondingly, even after proving the existence of God, and thereby rendering the construct of the *genius malignus* obsolete, Descartes' meditator retains what we could call the theory of "immission" (derived from the Latin verb *immittere* denoting "to send in, to insert, to introduce"), on which the discernment of spirits is predicated, the notion that thoughts and images are projected or sent into the mind by extramental sources as well as the self.

At the beginning of the Second Meditation, firm in their resolution to withhold assent to all mental representations and essentially denying the existence of an outside world, Descartes' meditator considers only two possible senders for these immissions: "Is there not a God, or whatever I may call him, who puts in me the thoughts [*ipsas cogitationes immittit*] I am now having? But why do I think this, since I myself may perhaps be the author of these thoughts?" (CSM II 16; AT VII 24). In the Third Meditation, following the formulation of the *cogito* but before the proof of God, the meditator reexamines the apparent evidence of the sensory world and again comes to the conclusion "that it is not reliable judgement but merely some blind impulse that has made me believe up till now that there exist things distinct from myself which transmit to me [*mihi immittant*] ideas or images of themselves [*ideas sive imagines suas*] through the sense organs or in some other way" (CSM II 27; AT VII 40).[43]

The meditator thus retains the trifold distinction of the origin of thoughts that we encountered in Cassian and Ignatius, even while slightly altering the possible authors:

Among my ideas, some appear to be innate, some to be foreign to me and come from outside,[44] and others to [have] been invented by me. My understanding of what a thing is, what truth is, and what a thought is, seems to derive simply from my own nature. But hearing a noise, as I do now, or seeing the sun, or feeling the fire, comes from things which are located outside me, or so I have hitherto judged. Lastly, sirens, hippogriffs and the like are my own invention. But perhaps all my ideas may be thought of as coming from outside [*adventitias*], or they may all be innate, or all made up; for as yet I have not clearly perceived their true origin. (CSM II 26; AT VII 37–38)

To perceive clearly the true origin of each idea is the objective of the Cartesian practice of discernment; and as the meditator indicates in the last sentence, at this point early in the Third Meditation, they have not sufficiently developed and refined their technique. They are neither able to account for the difference between invented and innate ideas, which both seem to originate in the self, or differentiate between adventitious and innate ideas, which both come from the outside. These skills in the art of discernment are what the meditator refines in the course of the remaining meditations.

Not surprisingly, the concept of immission, arguably the lynchpin of any theory and practice of discernment, plays a central role in Descartes' metaphysics as a whole. He conceives the reference and significance of ideas, that is, their representationality, in terms of their origin and authorship. The images immitted into the mind by the sensory things in turn represent the latter. Indeed, it is this causal relationship that ensures the general, although not the particular, reliability of sensory representations. Similarly, the idea of God has been immitted or, more precisely, implanted by him in the mind. Chapter 5 shows that immission is at the center of Descartes' distinction between the objective and formal reality of ideas, which in turn serves as the basis for his first proof of God. The fact that the mind contains an idea for whose existence it cannot account, and that therefore must come from elsewhere—or more concretely, from a supreme being—is predicated on the meditative matrix at the heart of discernment. After proving the existence of God, Descartes' meditator installs discernment as a method of cognition able to distinguish between clear and distinction impressions innate to the self and the dark and confused ones issued by the sensory world. The discernment of mental representations originating in the mind, as opposed to those originating in corporeal faculties such as perception and imagination, goes hand in hand with the distinction between soul and body, which the *Meditations* seeks to demonstrate to make evident the immortality of the soul. Thus, the two objectives of the *Meditations* stated in the subtitle—demonstrating "the existence of God and the distinction between the human soul and the body"—hinge on Descartes' revised art of discernment.

After staging the breakdown of discernment in the First Meditation, Descartes' meditator retools it as a new rational mode of thinking. The primary focus of the new art of discernment in the natural light of reason, at least in the *Meditations*, is to identify the ideas implanted innately in the self's mind by God, which is the project of Descartes' "first philosophy."[45] Only once when the innate ideas have been discerned, and with that the foundations of a first philosophy laid, is the mind equipped to turn back to the sensory world and the matter of discerning its representations. Starting with the Fourth Meditation, Descartes' meditator delineates the conditions and pitfalls of discerning confused and obscured ideas. The Fourth Meditation, devoted to the distinction between "truth and falsity" and the "cause of error," articulates the Cartesian art of discernment along the lines of the Stoic *chrēsis tōn phantasiōn*. Error originates not in the cognition itself, which cognizes what it cognizes, be it clearly and distinctly or obscurely and confusedly, but in the judgment that is based on it. In the case of sensory representations, for instance, the will might mistakenly conclude that the thing represented actually exists in the world. As in Stoic epistemology, the cause of error resides in the will assenting to or rejecting the contents of cognition or perception. Descartes' meditator concludes that the solution is to

restrain my will so that it extends to what the intellect clearly and distinctly reveals, and no further.... For I shall unquestionably reach the truth, if only I give sufficient attention to all the things which I perfectly understand, and separate these from all the other cases where apprehension is more confused and obscure. And this is just what I shall take good care to do from now on. (CSM II 43; AT VII 62)

The mind is called on to distinguish confused and obscure ideas from clear and distinct ones, and the will is to withhold judgment from the former and apply it only to the latter. To reach truth, the mind must turn toward and devote itself only to those things that it "perfectly understands." As Descartes' meditator admits, reining in the will is not as easy as it sounds:

I am aware of a certain weakness in me, in that I am unable to keep my attention fixed on one and the same item of knowledge at all times [*non possim semper uni & eidem cognitioni defixus inhaerere*]; but by attentive and repeated meditation [*attentâ & saepius iteratâ meditatione*] I am nevertheless able to make myself remember it as often as the need arises, and thus to get into the habit of avoiding error. (CSM II 43; AT VII 62)

Like its spiritual forebears, the Cartesian art of discernment is predicated on the self's fallenness. Although the *genius malignus*, Descartes' version of the *diabol*, is no longer in the picture, it remains the faculty responsible for epistemological error. It is not cognition, despite its finitude, that is responsible for fallacious cognition but the "will or freedom of choice" that overreaches and goes wrong by judging a mental representation to be true, that is, to correspond to reality. In other words, it is the faculty in us—in virtue of which, as Descartes' meditator observes, "I understand myself to bear in some way the image and likeness of God" (CSM II 40; AT VII 57)—that lets itself be tempted and deceived. Not coincidentally, the meditator invokes the language of sin and perversion to characterize the source of our mistaken cognition: "The scope of the will is wider than that of the intellect; but instead of restricting it within the same limits, I extend its use to matters which I do not understand. Since the will is indifferent in such cases, it easily turns from what is true and good [*a vero & bono deflectit*], and this the source of my error and sin [*fallor & pecco*]" (CSM II 40–41; AT VII 58). Instead of withholding judgment the mind turns away from those things it can perceive clearly and distinctly, the innate ideas implanted by God, and turns toward its confused and obscure perceptions of the sensory world.

At the end, in the last section of the Sixth Meditation, Descartes' meditator applies their newly won technique of rational discernment to the predicament with which everything started, my inability to distinguish between being asleep and being awake. For I now notice that there is a vast difference between the two, in that dreams are never linked by memory with all the other actions of life as waking experiences are. If, while I am awake, anyone were suddenly to appear to me and then disappear immediately, as happens in sleep, so that I could not see where he had come from [*unde venisset*] or where he had gone to [*abiret*], it would not be unreasonable for me to judge that he was a ghost [*spectrum*], or vision [*phantasma*] created in my brain, rather than a real man. But when I distinctly see where things come from and where and when they come to me [*adveniant*], and when I can connect my perceptions of them with the whole of the rest of my life without a break, then I am quite certain that when I encounter these things I am not asleep but awake. (CSM II 61–62; AT VII 89–90)

Descartes' experience recognizing apparitions and visions informs his discernment of dreams. When a mental representation appears in the way a ghost or phantasm comes into view, that is, sudden, unexpected, random, and disconnected from the rest of one's (waking) experience, then it must be a dream. The issue is not that oneiric representations come from somewhere else. Like sensory perceptions and unlike innate and fabricated ideas, they are "adventitious"; they are not under the mind's control but seem to come from the outside. Instead, their epiphanic character is a function of the mode of their advent. When they come into view, the mind cannot discern whence they came and where they are going. Oneiric representations cannot be discerned in the usual way, insofar as their origin; the criterion of the traditional discernment of spirits as well as its Cartesian variant, remains obscure; and unlike innate ideas, which appear clearly and distinctly to the mind's gaze, there is nothing about their appearance that sets them apart from perceptions of the real world.[46] And when they represent the sensory world, like all perceptions they appear confused and obscure. Descartes' meditator therefore discerns oneiric presentations because they appear ex nihilo, or more precisely, *ex nusquam*, and are thus not part of the fabric of our experience. Or, to put it succinctly, dreams can be discerned because they cannot be discerned like other mental representations. By transforming this failure of traditional discernment into the basis for a new mode of discernment, much as in the *Meditations* as a whole, Descartes succeeds where Jean Gerson failed in articulating a general method for distinguishing dreaming from waking and thus extending his new art of discernment to the "principal reason for doubt."

Nonetheless the question remains: Given this general method of discernment, how can it be that the self still goes wrong? The answer that Descartes' meditator gives in the final sentence of the *Meditations* is as simple as it is obvious. The world moves too fast for the mind to have time to examine all mental representations, so errors in human cognition are owed to man's finitude: "But since the pressure of things [*rerum agendarum necessitas*] does not always allow us the delay of such a meticulous examination [*accurati examinis*],[47] it must be admitted that in this human life we are often liable to make mistakes about particular things, and we must acknowledge the weakness of our nature [*naturae nostrae infirmitas*]" (CSM II 62; AT VII 90).

Meditation's *Cogito*

To arrive at this new Cartesian discernment, however, Descartes' meditator has a few more steps to take. Unable to detect the deception of the *genius malignus* and discern true and false ideas, the meditator resorts to a radical measure: resolving to "think that the sky, the air, the earth, colours, shapes, sounds, and all external things are merely the delusions of dreams which he [the malicious demon] has devised to ensnare our judgement" (CSM II 15; AT VII 22), and further vowing to "resolutely guard against assenting to any falsehoods" (CSM II 15; AT VII 23). Eudoxus, Descartes' alter ego in the dialogue *Search for Truth by the Natural Light*, arrives at the radicalization of doubt by a more direct path. After his interlocutor Epistemon has developed the extensive parallelization of thinking and painting, Eudoxus responds:

Your comparison nicely illustrates the first obstacle facing us; but you do not describe the means we must use if we wish to avoid it. Now it seems to me that your painter would do far better to make a fresh start on the picture; rather than wasting time in correcting all the lines he finds on the canvas, he should wipe them of it with a sponge. Similarly, as soon as a man reaches what we call the age of discretion [*connoissance*] he should resolve once and for all to remove from his imagination all traces of the imperfect ideas which have been engraved there up till that time. Then he should begin in earnest to form new ideas, applying all the strength of his intellect so effectively that if he does not bring these ideas to perfection, at least he will not be able to blame the weakness of the senses or the irregularities of nature. (CSM II 406; AT X 508–9)

In keeping with the analogy of thinking, imagining, and so forth, as painting, Eudoxus figures the radical critique and rejection of all mental representations as wiping the mental *tabula* completely *rasa*. Erasing all ideas in one fell swoop addresses the problem posed by Epistemon's conception of the mind essentially as a palimpsest of many successive paintings or impressions overlaying each other. Epistemon's objection derives from the medial specificity of impressed images:

> That would be an excellent remedy if it were easy to apply. But you are not ignorant of the fact that the opinions first received in our imagination remain so deeply imprinted there that our will cannot erase them on its own, but can do so only by calling on the assistance of powerful reasons. (CSM II 406; AT X 509)

"Deeply imprinted" ideas are not easily erased by the self's will alone. They require reasons as powerful as ones from "some malicious demon of the utmost power and cunning" (CSM II 15; AT VII 22), which are made lasting by repeated meditation and exercise.

At the beginning of the Second Meditation, Descartes' meditator faces the question of what remains after the breakdown of discernment and the denial of assent to all mental representations of the sensory world. Where can the meditator find the epistemological equivalent of Archimedes' "firm and immovable point" on which to build an edifice of knowledge? To understand how the solution is conditioned by the structure of the meditative matrix, I turn once again to a meditative image that stages the total erasure of the mental *tabula* proposed by Eudoxus in the *Search for Truth* and enacted in the First Meditation. The image is an emblem titled "Nothing but Jesus" (*Nichts als Jesus*), conceived by the German Protestant poet Catharina Regina von Greiffenberg.[48] Prefacing the first of Greiffenberg's twelve *Meditations on the Passion* (*Passionsbetrachtungen*), it may be read as a programmatic self-reflection of the meditative matrix (see Fig. 7).[49]

In its *pictura* we see a female figure posing as a painter in front of a canvas mounted on an easel, designated as *Tafel der Gedanken*, "table of thoughts." Instead of a brush she is holding a formless object that the subscription identifies as a "Gall- und Essig-Schwamm," the vinegar sponge of Christ's passion. Her gaze is fixed on the top half of the canvas, dominated by the figure of Christ on the cross. The epiphanic character of his appearance is underscored by the dramatic parting of the clouds. The bottom half is vacant or, more precisely, almost vacant, as it is still possible to discern a number of

Erklärung des Tittel-Kupfers.

LEsch aus/ die ganze Welt. Die Tafel der Gedanken
rein werd gewischet ab. Nichts bleib/ als JEsus Christ.
Nichts will ich dulten sonst. Es soll nichts in den schranken
der Angedächtnis seyn / als der / der Alles ist.
Es mag die wiß-begier viel schönes wesen reitzen:
mich labt mein JESUS nur / vor tausend-wissenschaft.
Die Welt mag / wie nach Geld / nach Kunst und Weißheit geitzen:
ich will und weiß sonst nichts / als seine Creutzeskraft.
Der Gall- und Essig-Schwamm lesch' aus all' Eitelkeiten:
nur der Gekreutzigte bleib stehn in meinem Sinn.
Wie weit / wann sie allein / die Allheit sich ausbreiten
und alles wenden kan/das siht man klar hierinn.
Die Allheit ich allein will im Gedächtnis haben:
so hab ich alls / und sie gekreutzigt noch darzu.
Nur unerreichlicher sind ihre Gnaden-Gaben /
je mehr sie angehäfft. In ihm / ist meine Ruh.

FIGURE 7. Title page emblem and accompanying text, in Catharina Regina von Greiffenberg, *Des Allerheiligst- und Allerheilsamsten Leidens und Sterbens Jesu Christi Zwölf andächtige Betrachtungen* (Neustadt an der Aysch: Drechsler, 1683), 1v and 2v. Digitized by the Sächsische Landes- und Universitätsbibliothek Dresden.

vague and blurred figures that the sponge has not yet wiped away. The first lines of the subscription articulate this aspect as a triple injunction to the reader/beholder: "Blot out the whole world. The table of thoughts ought to be wiped clean completely. Nothing should remain but Jesus Christ."

The female figure belongs to the same guild of painters as those depicted in David's and Sucquet's engravings. As it does for her colleagues, meditating has the effect of painting pictures on the "table of thoughts." Like theirs, her meditating is highly self-reflexive, as it is split and doubled. Not only is she represented twice, first as the allegorical female figure and then on the canvas so that she beholds herself when she meditates, but the act of meditating is conceived both as painting and beholding mental images. Greiffenberg's emblem offers a twist to this type of meta-image, however, as it foregrounds the erasure of the *tabula* as the necessary condition for the image of Christ to appear. Given that no other utensils of painting are depicted, the question of how it gets there remains unanswered. We return to the most likely interpretation in Chapter 5, which is that the *imago Dei* was always there and needed only to be noticed. Another possibility would be that the sponge doubles as an instrument of erasure and painting, that Greiffenberg figures meditation as a kind of "negative painting."

The emblem's primary concern is with the eventual appearance of Christ once the images of the world are wiped away, but I want to focus on the fleeting intermediary moment when the images are gone but Christ has not fully appeared. In that moment the table of thoughts itself comes into view. As long as it represents something else, be it the "whole world" or "nothing but Jesus," the meditational medium remains invisible. Only emptied out does it become visible as the medium of thought. And the answer to the meditator's question, what remains after all mental representations have been erased, is simple, albeit frustratingly elusive: the *tabula* itself. This is precisely the conclusion at which Descartes' meditator arrives, attempting to determine by way of the imagination what the ego of the self-evident and certain *ego sum, ego existo* might be:

> The fact that it is I who am doubting and understanding and willing is so evident that I see no way of making it any clearer. But it is also the case that the "I" who imagines is the same "I." For even if, as I have supposed, none of the objects of imagination are real, the power of imagination is something which really exists and is part of my thinking. Lastly, it is also the same "I" who has sensory perceptions, or is aware of bodily things as it were through the senses. (CSM II 19; AT VII 29)

The meditative generation of images can, therefore, be considered the matrix of the Cartesian *cogito*. When all meditative images have become dubious, nothing remains but the meditative subject, which is always also reflecting on itself in the meditative vision. As in all of these representations of meditative imaging in which meditators function both as painter and beholder, Descartes' meditator functions both as the author, or sender, and the recipient of mental representations. Even if the persuasive speech of the evil spirit is false and deceptive, sender and receiver cannot not exist. For even if they had not existed before the persuasive address, they would have to come into being as its addressor and addressee. What becomes visible when the images become precarious in this internal theater of meditation is the process of their generation or, more technically, the moment of presentation within every representation. Thus, the self-reflexive structure of the meditative matrix is precisely the condition of possibility for this (self-) presentation of (re)presentation. The Cartesian *cogito* is nothing but the bringing to mind of representational force, in short, pure evidence.

As only this mediative maneuver makes the *cogito* evident, Descartes cannot be interested in disposing of the deceptive setup of the meditative matrix. Descartes' meditator dramatically stages as much in the Third Meditation: "Yet when I turn to the things themselves which I think I perceive very clearly, I am so convinced by them that I spontaneously declare: let whoever can do so deceive me, he will never bring it about that I am nothing, so long as I continue to think I am something" (CSM II 25; AT VII 36). That "the things themselves" seem to appear and not their mental representations characterizes the *virtus illocutionis* of *evidentia*, demonstrating once again how evidence is generated. If "things" appeared to the self as representations pointing to their own status as representations, they would be much less self-evident, since, due to their apparent artificiality, the self would always remain conscious of their possible falsehood. The persuasive force of the "things themselves," their evidence, thus consists in their sensory and cognitive mediation remaining concealed. The evidentiary persuasion of the "things themselves" immediately evokes an utterance from the self assuring itself of itself or, more precisely, through which the self ascertains itself as the subject and/or object of this *persuasio*—be it a deception or not. Therefore, the deceptive schema and the ensuing doubt provoke and evoke the *cogito*. Otherwise, the self would be deceived by the persuasive reality of the "things themselves." With the proof of God Descartes' meditator does not dispose of the deceptive setup; they merely ensure that there is no evil demon inducing mental representations with no external referent. In effect, the meditator substitutes the evil deceiver with a benevolent projectionist, but the entry point and thus the structural possibility of deception continue to exist. Concomitantly, the need for discernment never ceases; its terms simply change.

That the presentation or self-presentation of representation is immune to error holds true not only for the *cogito* but for all mental acts and representations. To the question "But what was it about [external things] that I perceived clearly?," Descartes' meditator answers: "Just that the ideas, or thoughts, of such things appeared before my mind" (CSM II 24; AT VII 35). The evidence of ideas consists therefore in nothing else but the moment of "appearing before the mind" with sufficient insistence. As Descartes' meditator remarks, "Now as far as ideas are concerned, provided that they are considered solely in themselves and I do not refer them to anything else, they cannot strictly speaking be false; for whether it is a goat or a chimera that I am imagining, it is just as true that I imagine the former as the latter" (CSM II 26; AT VII 37). Irrespective of its object and content, imagining qua imagining or, put more generally, thinking qua thinking, is nothing but a simple and pure act; and as such it is immune to error. Neither true nor false, it simply is. This becomes even clearer when we turn to the example of volitions and emotions. In the case of willing, it is quite possible to want something bad, but it isn't false that one is wanting something when one is actually wanting it. The performance of volition validates itself, since willing is not a mental representation but a mental act. Ideas as pure presentations assert nothing (about the facticity of the outside world). Asserting is the domain of judgment that Descartes' meditator consequently pinpoints as the source of error:

> And the chief and most common mistake which is to be found here consists in my judging that the ideas which are in me resemble, or conform to, things located outside of me. Of course, if I considered just the ideas themselves simply as modes of my thought, without referring them to anything else, they could scarcely give me any material for error. (CSM II 26; AT VII 37)

Only once reference is established can error creep into thinking, because only then can an idea fail to correspond to its referential object. Even sensory perceptions and objects of the imagination, which Descartes' meditator considers most prone to error, are not false as "modes of thinking" (CSM II 24; AT VII 34) as pure acts or, more precisely, pure presentations. The possibility of error arises when the mind assumes it is perceiving the things themselves.

What the meditative gaze reveals is that referentiality isn't a primary moment of mental representations but the result of the secondary operation of judgment. Even the data of sensory perception, commonly taken to be simple and unmediated, turn out to be the result of a mental operation. The suspension of referentiality, effected by the meditative gaze, thus brings into focus the ubiquitous involvement of the mind in all mental acts, even in the supposedly lower ones such as sense perception or imagination. Descartes' meditative analysis exposes the double orientation of mental representations. While the "re-" points to the things to which they refer, the "presentation" belongs to the mind's very own fabric. In meditation these two aspects interact in a way exactly opposite to normal perception, and therein lies the former's heuristic and critical value. Whatever representation represents, it always also presents itself. In order for normal perception and cognition to function smoothly, the moment of presentation has to recede into the background. Representation as a mental act must not become the focus of attention, which instead must remain directed toward the represented. Only if the self-suspension or, more precisely, self-concealment is successful can representation of another thing occur. Referentiality thus is an effect of such a self-suspension.

Of course, this is also an integral moment of *evidentia*. As we have seen in the case of the Ignatian exercises, *evidentia* reveals itself as a figure of self-suspension whose effect depends on how successfully it manages to conceal its own textuality or, more generally, mediality in the spectacle it stages linguistically. The production of eyewitnessing intended by evidentiary discourse comes about only when the recipient is no longer conscious of the act of mediation and believes to see the mediated events for themself. Like Descartes' meditator of the First Meditation the Ignatian exercitant thinks to perceive "the things themselves." If this medial self-suspension is not successful, then representation no longer points beyond itself toward the represented and the dimension of presentation comes to the fore. Thus, representation ceases to be transparent, which is exactly what meditation makes possible, when under its "long gaze," as Aleida Assmann coined in a different context,[50] the perception of everyday things becomes opaque in order to impart them with a new spiritual significance. Descartes' meditations seek to stage exactly this moment of opacity when the old mental images have ceased and the new ones have not yet appeared. For only in the moment of its clouding does the mind become transparent to itself.

4

Cartesian Ceroplastics:
Meditating the Mediality of the Mind

Waxing Philosophically

The meditation on a piece of wax at the end of the Second Meditation has always puzzled readers. It seems to contribute little to what is stated in the subtitle as its agenda: to demonstrate "the nature of the human mind, and how it is better known than the body." Descartes's meditator had already established the latter in the articulation of the *cogito* at the beginning of the Second Meditation. Whereas the mind can be sure of "absolutely nothing in the world, no sky, no earth, no minds, no bodies," it can be certain of its own existence. But here Descartes' meditator claims to achieve more: not only to demonstrate the existence of the mind but its specific nature.[1] As Descartes emphasizes in his reply to Pierre Gassendi's Objections, the wax meditation does exactly that: "I am surprised that you should say here that all my considerations about the wax demonstrate that I distinctly know that I exist, but not that I know what I am or what my nature is; for one thing cannot be demonstrated without the other" (CSM II 248; AT VII 359). Descartes, in effect, is saying here that the certainty of the *cogito* depends on having a clear and distinct understanding of the nature of the mind as a thinking thing.[2] It is in the process of the meditation on the piece of wax that the meditator achieves that very understanding, and reading the Second Meditation in this context sheds light on this puzzling passage.

To know the nature of the mind, the discovery of the *cogito* alone is not enough, because at that point the self doesn't know the extent of the thinking thing it has recognized itself to be. Indeed, only a few lines after articulating the *cogito,* Descartes' meditator pauses to caution: "But I do not yet have a sufficient understanding what this 'I' is, that now necessarily exists. So I must be on my guard against carelessly taking something else to be this 'I,' and so making a mistake in the very item of knowledge that I maintain is the most certain and evident of all" (CSM II 17; AT VII 25). As long as the mind does not know its nature, it runs the immediate risk of confusing itself with psychic faculties that properly belong to the body. As Descartes writes in his Second Reply,

> All our ideas of what belongs to the mind have up till now been very confused and mixed up with the ideas of things that can be perceived by the senses. This is the first and most important reason for our inability to understand with sufficient clarity the customary assertions about the soul and God. So I thought I would be doing something worthwhile if I explained how the properties or qualities of the mind are to be distinguished from the qualities of the body. Admittedly, many people had previously said that in order to understand metaphysical matters the mind must be drawn away from the senses; but no one, so far as I know, had shown how this could be done. The correct, and in my view unique, method of achieving this is contained in my Second Meditation. But the nature of the method is such that scrutinizing it just once is not enough. Protracted and repeated study is required to eradicate the lifelong habit of confusing things related to the intellect with corporeal things, and to replace it with the opposite habit of distinguishing the two; this will take at least a few days to acquire. (CSM II 94; AT VII 131)

Descartes considered achieving the clear and distinct cognition of the mind's nature, which in turn affects its distinction from the body, his major contribution to metaphysics, and what he presents with the *Meditations* is essentially a program of how "to understand with sufficient clarity the customary assertions about the soul and God." Precondition for any understanding of "metaphysical matters" is quite literally a conversion, as "the mind must be" turned and "drawn away from the senses." Descartes stresses that "many people" stated this necessary precondition but that he is alone in showing a "method" of how to achieve this meditative turn. In other words, Descartes' originality lies in the pragmatic or performative dimension of this operation. The Second Meditation contains a training manual for making this distinction and slowly, but irrevocably "eradicating the lifelong habit of confusing" mind and matter. It would be a mistake to discount this pragmatic dimension as extrinsic to Descartes' philosophical argument. For, as having a clear and distinct idea of the mind as a thinking thing depends on its differentiation from psychic acts and faculties originating in the body, it is inversely the case that a clear and distinct cognition of itself necessarily entails its differentiation from corporeal acts involved in cognition. It is exactly this distinction or, shall we say, discernment, that Descartes' meditative analysis on the piece of wax is designed to achieve to make the nature of the mind as a thinking thing evident, or to conceive clearly and distinctly the ability to conceive clearly and distinctly. Even more succinctly, the mind as the medium of evidence must make itself evident to itself. As in the First Meditation, Descartes' meditator must work to dispel the instinctive fetishistic love of "things themselves" that characterizes postlapsarian humans and makes them equally evident.

Gassendi stands in for many subsequent readers in claiming that Descartes' meditative analysis on a piece of wax fails to achieve what it is designed to do just because it fails to make the mind's nature as a thinking thing evident.[3] My claim is that the critics are looking in the wrong place or, rather, in the wrong way. Maybe the wax poses a question not as much of the "that" as of the "how," less about the logical argument and more about mental practice. Constatively, Descartes tells us very little about the "nature of the mind": it is a thing defined by thinking, suggesting that the goal of the passage may instead be to provide a demonstration by doing, a doing that, as Descartes' title indicates, consists in meditating. In the Second Reply Descartes insists that the clear and distinct cognition of soul and God, which is both cause and effect of the self's separation from the overwhelming evidentiary quality of the senses, must be carefully enacted and practiced by the meditator. Here the pragmatic dimension of Descartes' mode of thinking in the *Meditations* becomes particularly apparent. The mind needs to be formed—just like the piece of wax. In fact, as Descartes' meditator molds and forms the piece of wax with their fingers, their mind is being molded and formed by what they are perceiving and thinking at the very same moment. Therefore, the question becomes unavoidable: What does Descartes' meditation on the piece of wax reveal about the nature of the mind, if we take its generic designation seriously and read it as a meditation? And if meditating is in some sense a molding of the mind, the related question poses itself: What can the meditation on a piece of wax tell us about the mind as thinking thing?

Descartes' Occasional Meditation and the Vanity of Things

The subgenre of occasional meditation, the model for Descartes' analytic meditation on a piece of wax, has a long history reaching back to the spiritual exercises of antiquity and early Christianity and had regained popularity at the end of the sixteenth century and blossomed in the seventeenth.[4] Just as the wider genre of meditational literature and devotional poetry was transdenominational, the subgenre of occasional meditation was popular with authors of all confessions. In its broadest sense, occasional meditation involves meditating on a naturally occurring, quotidian occasion or on mundane things of everyday life, whether a cloud, a spider, or children playing. "The Scrubbing Brush," a short poem written by the Dutch politician and poet Constantjin Huygens, who corresponded with Descartes for many years, may serve as an example:

> I've seen a stinking animal wear those bristles
> But, seeing they serve my purpose, why should I care?
> Though the man in the pulpit there attacks my failings
> With pepper and vinegar, he too is the world's guest,
> As human as I am, surely no less full of faults
> Than him his tongue lashes. Should I then not bear him
> Scouring my foulness? He's a swine? That's his affair.
> But he brushes sharp and clean, that's my concern.[5]

Huygens's publication of a collection of "epigrams of things," titled *Koren-Bloemen*, a few years after Descartes' death is evidence of the presence of this genre in the philosopher's intellectual environs during his work on the *Meditations*. Another example, by Jan Luyken, a Dutch engraver and poet, takes the equally quotidian object of a balloon as an occasion to meditate on the vanity of life and the world:

> *No matter, earthly child,* how hard you blow
> What is this world for those who understand?
> Nothing but a bladder full of wind.
> Let the unknowing infant play with it
> But not the wiser, greyer wit;
> Let him not hold such rubbish in his hand
> Or join in children's games. Away with it![6]

Probably the most famous collection of occasional meditations was published by Bishop Joseph Hall in 1630 and almost immediately translated into Latin, French, and German,[7] gaining widespread influence in Protestant circles across Europe. Judging by the many subsequent editions and translations, his *Art of Divine Meditation* (1601) was even more popular. There he distinguishes between two kinds of meditation, extemporal and deliberate:

> Our divine meditation is nothing else but a bending of discourse of the mind upon some spiritual object, through divers forms of discourse, until our thoughts come to an issue; and this must needs be either extemporal and occasioned by outward occurrences offered to the mind; or deliberate and wrought out of our own heart; which again is either in matter of knowledge, for the finding out of some hidden truth ... of reason, or in matter of affection for the enkindling of our love of God.[8]

The meditation Hall describes facilitates a turning or conversion. This "bending of the discourse of the mind upon some spiritual object" redirects the mind from the material to the spiritual world. While this redirection either can be prompted by "outward occurrences" (thus "extemporal") or is "wrought out of our own heart" (thus "deliberate"), *The Art of Divine Meditation* is concerned with "meditation deliberate," so "meditation extemporal" is defined only in passing, as "there may be much use" but "no rule,"

> forasmuch as our conceits herein vary according to the infinite multitude of objects and their divers manner of proffering themselves to the mind, as also for the suddenness of this act. Man is placed in this stage of the world to view the several natures and actions of the creatures; to view them, not idly, without his use, as they do him. God made all these for man and man for His own sake; both these purposes were lost if man should let the creatures pass carelessly by him, only seen, not thought upon.[9]

In occasional meditations, the mind is directed by external stewards, whose stewardship is contingent and capricious. It is driven by the things the mind encounters in the world—in contrast to "meditation deliberate," which, due to the uniformity of the mind, is more homogeneous and consistent. In fact, the laconic remark that meditations extemporal know "much use" and "no rule" suggests that they resist systematic treatment but must be practiced instead. It cannot be taught by delineating abstract rules but only in the performance and emulation of concrete and individual meditations.

If meditation deliberate is about the spiritual formation of the mind, meditation extemporal is about making spiritual use of the world of things.

By not merely seeing "the creatures" (and once again being absorbed by the world's visual allure) but also thinking upon them and thereby redirecting its thoughts toward the creator of them, the self avoids a fetishistic clinging to worldly things and their mere materiality. Through meditation the subject transforms mere things into spiritual objects, revealing meditation extemporal to constitute an intimate conjunction of seeing and thinking. Rather than limit its encounter with the outside world to simple sensory perception, meditation extemporal infuses seeing with thought. In not being bound to any specific or predetermined spatio-temporal setting the way "regular" meditation was, occasional mediations were vital to the profound spiritualization of world and life that took place over the course of the late Middle Ages and the early modern period.

Much as in Hall's meditations extemporal, Descartes' meditation on a piece of wax springs from his resolve to let his mind wander freely and be guided by sensory objects: "But I see what it is: my mind enjoys wandering off and will not yet submit to being restrained within the bounds of truth. Very well then; just this once let us give it a completely free rein, so that after a while, when it is time to tighten the reins, it may more readily submit to being curbed" (CSM II 20; AT VII 29–30). In part, the wax meditation thus has the function of training the mind. Like a horse, and the *gentil homme* Descartes very deliberately deploys equestrian metaphorology here, the mind will be more effectively harnessed having first been given free rein and made accustomed indirectly to tighter control. This pragmatic motivation should guide our reading of the wax meditation, because if the mind is being fully unleashed, the "bounds of truth" holding together the logical argument must necessarily be looser too.

In giving itself over to the sensory world, the meditator's mind becomes subject to its aleatory economy. And, indeed, what becomes the object of their meditation is the first thing the meditator comes across. Descartes ostentatiously stages its random particularity: "Let us take, for example, this piece of wax," says the meditator (CSM II 20; AT VII 30)—not wax in general, but *hanc ceram*, this particular piece of wax. Descartes likewise foregrounds the concrete situatedness. In the here and now of the ceroplastic meditation, he prompts his readers to place themselves imaginatively before a fire with the piece of wax in hand. In this case, however, its exemplarity serves to heighten the sensory particularity of the wax rather than subsume it under a general category. The meditator calls on a meditative technique with which Descartes would have been acquainted from his education at the Jesuit College of La Flèche. While the *applicatio sensuum*, application of the senses, was very common in early modern meditation in all denominations, Ignatius installed them as a standard feature of Jesuit spirituality by including them in his *Spiritual Exercises*.[10] Ignatius's meditation on hell, in the first week of the *Spiritual Exercises*, is perhaps the most spectacular and drastic of such an application of the senses. Its purpose is to generate "an interior sense of the suffering which the damned endure" to instill in exercitants fear of eternal punishment and purge them from their sins. Ignatius provides instructions for becoming a virtual witness by playing on all five sensorial registers:

> POINT 1 This will be to look with the eyes of the imagination at the great fires and at the souls appearing to be in burning bodies.
> POINT 2 To hear with one's ears the wailings, howls, cries, blasphemies against Christ Our Lord and against all the saints.
> POINT 3 To smell with the sense of smell the smoke, the burning sulphur, the cesspit and the rotting matter.
> POINT 4 To taste with the sense of taste bitter things, such as tears, sadness and the pangs of conscience.
> POINT 5 To feel with the sense of touch, i.e. how those in hell are licked around and burned by the fires.[11]

Like Ignatius, Descartes' meditator systematically employs all five senses, systematically enumerating the sensual qualities of the wax to render it as concrete and distinct as possible: "It has just been taken from the honeycomb; it has not yet quite lost the taste of honey; it retains some of the scent of the flowers from which it was gathered; its color, shape and size are plain to see; it is hard, cold, and can be handled without difficulty; if you rap it with your knuckles it makes a sound" (CSM II 20; AT VII 30). True to the generic law of "meditation extemporal" the outside world intrudes in unpredictable ways on the meditative analysis: "But even as I speak, I put the wax by the fire, and look: the residual taste is eliminated, the smell goes away, the color changes, the shape is lost, the size increases; it becomes liquid and hot; you can hardly touch it, and if you strike it, it no longer makes a sound" (CSM II 20; AT VII 30). While the initial description evoked the wax as a self-identical object that could be cognized clearly and distinctly with the senses, the fire transforms it, putting it at odds with itself. Suddenly, within the span of a sentence, two (or more) contradictory predicates apply to the very same object. Paradoxically, it is the light of the fire that enables the distinct sensory perception of the wax, even as the fire is simultaneously sabotaging it. The fire all but literally brings to light the wax's intrinsic mutability and variability.

By acting as a catalyst for the wax's mutability, the fire also activates its symbolic potential. Like many other transient things, such as smoke, ash, roses, arrows, ruins, bubbles, and echoes, wax belongs to the literary and pictorial iconography of vanity. The Psalms, a reservoir of Judeo-Christian imagery, repeatedly deploy wax as a figure for human frailty and impotence: "As smoke is driven away, so drive them away: as wax melteth before the fire, so let the wicked perish at the presence of God" (Ps 68:1–2). And on the pagan side, Marcus Aurelius cites wax in his *Meditations* to illustrate the vanity of the world in which even timeless virtues and values are subject to the relentless working of time:

In no time at all ashes or bare bones, a mere name or not even a name: and if a name, only sound and echo.... So what is there left to keep us here, if the objects of sense are ever changeable and unstable, if our senses themselves are blurred and easily smudged like wax, if our very soul is a mere exhalation of blood, if success in such a world is vacuous? (*Meditations* 5.33)[12]

By invoking the topos regarding the vanity of life and the world, Descartes is borrowing from the generic economy of vanitas discourse and using it for his own occasional meditation on the conditions of cognition.

The semiotic economy of vanitas discourse is predicated on the passing of time. Things signify the past or future states in their "life" history, mostly their past bloom or their future decay. Similarly, Descartes' piece of wax is never simply a thing but always already an indexical sign pointing to its origins: its scent points to the flowers from which the pollen was collected, its taste to the honeycomb from which it was taken. Its past is inscribed in its present perception. By bringing it closer to the fire, Descartes' meditator accelerates the passing of time, staging the wax's inconstancy and transience. Before our eyes it becomes discolored and formless, its taste disappears, and its smell evaporates. More abstractly, the truth of the wax, that it is something "flexible and changeable," is also a function of its temporality. The passing of time, artificially accelerated by the fire's heat, puts the wax at odds with itself and introduces an internal difference into a seemingly self-identical object. *Sub specie vanitatis* things are never what they seem. A rose may be brimming with health and beauty, but under its thin veneer lurk death and decay. Temporality puts a thing's appearance at odds with its truth, its *Erscheinung* or, better, *Schein* with its *Sein*. All the world is nothing but *Schein*, since in reality it is nothing. Thus, time's passage lends worldly things their characteristic allegoreality, for, as Walter Benjamin reminds us, "allegory signifies something other than it is. In fact, it signifies exactly the nonexistence of what it represents."[13] But this only prepares for the dialectical reversal of baroque allegory that opens the perspective upon the divine. Allegory, thus, negates the thing as it spiritually charges it.

Similarly, under Descartes' long meditative gaze a quotidian object such as a piece of wax loses its matter-of-factness and takes on a completely new meaning. Due to its exceptional mutability its present state is continually destroyed and negated so that, true to allegory's etymology, it points to itself as something else. In a sense, wax could be considered the matter or medium of allegory par excellence, particularly of baroque allegory. And as in baroque allegory, the wax's perceptual opacity, effected by Descartes' meditative gaze, is compensated by its new intellectual transparency. Since the gist of Descartes' ceroplastic meditation is not the world's nothingness but the unreliability of the senses, it seems to break with traditional meditations on vanity. However, as we saw in the passage from Marcus Aurelius, the conjunction of inconstancy and sensory perception is also a topos of vanity. The most influential locus for this link in the Christian tradition is surely Paul's Second Epistle to the Corinthians in which he declares "the things which are seen are temporal; but the things which are not seen are eternal" (2 Cor 4:18). Consequently, the self is urged to turn away from the material and, thus, temporal world toward the divine—not unlike Descartes' meditator.

Of course, Descartes epistemologizes the morally-theologically motivated meditation on vanity. And we should not overlook the differences in atmosphere, tone, outlook, and message that separate Descartes' treatment of the wax from conventional meditation on the vanity of the world. Nevertheless, I contend that it functions as the matrix of his meditative analysis, determining not as much its content as its movement. Instead of simply investing the wax with a spiritual meaning, as in a conventional meditation on vanity, Descartes' ceroplastic meditation demonstrates that the truth of the piece of wax resides not in its perceptual appearance but elsewhere, in the mind of the meditator. Taken structurally, Descartes' meditative gaze makes us see the epistemological allegoreality of things, that their sense is not sensorial or, more conventionally, that things are not as they appear.[14] The insight that being has an allegorical structure due to its fundamental transitoriness is, of course, a commonplace of baroque thought and culture. Similarly, the turn toward self and God that Descartes' meditator performs in the face of the world's transitoriness has precedents in both ancient Stoicism and its early modern resuscitation by Justus Lipsius.[15] Given allegory's conventional nature, the next question that we must pose is, What motivates the meditator's turn from the piece of wax to their mind?

Philosophical Wax Figures

The mind's turn toward itself and the resulting *inspectio mentis*, taken both as a *genitivus subjectivus* and *objectivus*, is motivated not only by the argument but also by the cultural and historical semantics of the wax itself. It cannot be a coincidence, in a text so carefully crafted, that the only thing actually at hand happened to be a piece of wax, in particular, as wax is symbolically so overdetermined. Although rarely noticed by readers of Descartes but well-known otherwise, wax has functioned as a metaphor of the soul since the beginnings of philosophical discourse. The *sensus allegoricus* of the wax is quite simply the soul or the various "parts" thereof. Had Descartes wanted to avoid the association between wax and mind, he could easily enough have chosen another object. That he did choose it, however, makes it fruitful to examine how wax and its historical semantics condition Descartes' exploration of the nature of the mind.

One of the earliest texts to refer to wax in explaining a faculty or feature of the mind is Plato's *Theaetetus*. To account for the possibility of false judgment, Socrates has his interlocutor assume

> that we have in our souls a block of wax, larger in one person, smaller in another, and of purer wax in one case, dirtier in another; in some men rather hard, in others rather soft, while in some it is of the proper consistency.... We may look upon it, then, as a gift of Memory, the mother of the Muses. We make impressions upon this of everything we wish to remember among the things we have seen or heard or thought of ourselves; we hold the wax under our perceptions and thoughts and

take a stamp from them, in the way in which we take the imprints of signet rings. Whatever is impressed upon the wax we remember and know so long as the image remains in the wax; whatever is obliterated or cannot be impressed, we forget and do not know. (*Theaetetus* 191 c/d)[16]

Socrates figures wax as the mind's medium for storing information. Whatever needs to be retained, whether from exogenous perceptions or endogenous thoughts, is impressed in the malleable wax like "the imprints of signet rings." What is not impressed is not retained. Implicit in this simile is the visual nature of all information stored in the ceroplastic memory. All perceptions (visual, auditory, tactile, olfactory, etc.) are converted into a representation conceived as an impressed form to be seen in the mind's eye. The accuracy and durability of the stored information are a function of the quality of the ceroplastic storage medium. "In some men," says Socrates, "the wax in the soul is deep and abundant, smooth and worked to the proper consistency," so that

when the things that come through the senses are imprinted upon this "heart" of the soul . . . the signs that are made in it are lasting, because they are clear and have sufficient depth. Men with such souls learn easily and remember what they learn; they do not get the signs out of line with the perceptions, but judge truly. As the signs are distinct and there is plenty of room for them, they quickly assign each thing to its own impress in the wax.

But

persons in whom the wax is soft are quick to learn but quick to forget; when the wax is hard, the opposite happens. Those in whom it is "shaggy" and rugged, a stony thing with earth or filth mixed all through it, have indistinct impressions. So too if the wax is hard, for then the impressions have no depth; similarly they are indistinct if the wax is soft, because they quickly run together and are blurred. If, in addition to all this, the impresses in the wax are crowded upon each other for lack of space, because it is only some little scrap of a soul, they are even more indistinct. All such people are liable to false judgement. (*Theaetetus* 194c–195a)

The quality of the information, which is grounded in the quality of the storage medium, accounts, in turn, for success or failure of the mind's judgment, which Socrates conceives as the process of matching a perception with the representation stored in memory. Remarkably, the quality of the perception plays no role in accounting for the veracity and accuracy of judgment. The sole variable is how distinctly the mnemonic impressions are defined.

If indistinct, either because they are crowded or because the ceroplastic medium is not of optimal consistency, sensory perceptions are mismatched and, consequently, incorrectly recognized. That Plato's model of ceroplastic memory grounds correct judgment in clear and distinct mental representations may have been part of its appeal to Descartes, given their importance in his own epistemology.

Plato is only the beginning of a long discursive tradition using wax to illustrate the soul's ability to retain and reproduce information. Aristotle, who invokes Plato's ceroplastic model to differentiate levels of mnemonic retention, sees retention as a function of age, as the mnemonic medium loses its retentive capability with excess moisture or dryness.[17] For other classical authors, rather than the wax block, it's the wax tablet, a quotidian stationery device in antiquity still being used in Descartes' day, that allows them to figure memorialization as an act of writing. Cicero construes the relationship of memory to writing by claiming that the former "is in a manner a twin sister of written speech and is completely similar to it, [though] in a dissimilar medium. For just as script consists of marks indicating letters and of the material on which those marks are imprinted, so the structure of memory, like a wax tablet, employs places [*loci*] and in these gathers together images like letters" (*Partitiones oratoriae* 26).[18] In providing a substrate for the placement of letters, the wax tablet merges with the storehouse, which holds images in their specific *loci*, as a model for rhetorical memory.[19] Cicero recounts that Metrodorus of Scepsis, who he says had "superhuman powers of memory," "wrote down things he wanted to remember in certain 'localities' in his possession by means of images, just as if he were inscribing letters on wax" (*De Oratore* II.360).[20] The extraordinary authority of Plato, Aristotle, and Cicero ensured the discursive resonance of the ceroplastic model of memory.[21] The monastic *mnēmē theou* was informed by the same typographic logic. Basil of Caesarea conceived the "holy thought of God" as being "stamped into our soul like an ineradicable seal by means of a distinct and continual remembrance."[22] In their commentaries on Aristotle's *On Memory and Recollection*, Albertus Magnus and Thomas Aquinas enshrined the cultural force of the ceroplastic model of memory for Scholasticism.[23] Due to the inestimable cultural currency of memory in premodern societies wax came to stand metonymically for the entire soul. Therefore, Plato called for the careful regulation of the stories (*logoi*) that are told to young children by their mothers and nurses because of how they shape their soft, wax-like souls.[24]

Only because perception and cognition follow this same typographic logic is the in-formation of the ceroplastic memory by mental representations possible. In a seminal passage in his *De anima*, Aristotle draws on the functioning of sealing wax to explain perception:

> Sense is that which is receptive of the form of sensible objects without the matter, just as the wax receives the impression [*sēmeion*] of the signet-ring without the iron or the gold, and receives the impression [*sēmeion*] of the gold or bronze, but not as gold or bronze; so in every case sense is affected by that which has colour, or flavour, or sound, but by it, not *qua* having certain quality, and in virtue of its formula. (*On the Soul* 424a)[25]

We see wax functioning here as a metaphor for sense perception's mediality, corresponding on the side of the sensory subject to the *metaxu*, "space in between," which transmits the sensory data from the sensory object (see *On the Soul* 2.7). Aristotle uses the metaphor of the signet ring impressing sealing wax to make it clear that the senses receive the object's form free of matter, which puts Aristotle's theory of sensory perception in dialogue with Plato, who contends that judgment requires matching sensory impressions to their respective mnemonic forms—which in Plato always also relate to the forms in the intelligible world. For Aristotle, that is, forms are immanent rather than transcendent. For him sensory impressions come already formed, as they derive their form from the (fully formed) material world. Thus, the ceroplastic sensory apparatus receives the form while simultaneously abstracting form from matter, and in this way Descartes' meditative abstraction, in stripping the wax of its material qualities, mirrors in a way the normal process of sensory perception.

Stoic epistemology expands the typographic logic to cover all kinds of mental representations, with Diogenes Laertius defining them as "impressions on the soul [*typosis en psychē*], the name having been appropriately borrowed from the imprints made by the seal in wax" (*Lives* 7.45).[26] Resulting from the impact that perceptual objects have on the soul, the more persistent the impression made on the sense is, the more distinctive and pronounced will be the resulting perception and cognition. We recall here the *phantasia kataleptikē*, "apprehensive presentation," referring to a perception that "comes from a real object, agrees with that object, and has been stamped, imprinted, and pressed seal-fashion on the soul, as would not be the case if it came from an unreal object" (7.50). Kataleptic presentations distinguish themselves from a-kataleptic presentations, at least in the minds of the Stoics, literally by their impressiveness.[27] They are so distinct and clear that they not only reveal the (re)presented object in all its detail but also attest to its reality, as only real objects can leave such an impressive imprint, which is to say, be so powerfully possessed of *enargeia*, "evidence" (see *Lives* 7.46 and discussion in Chapter 3). *Typosis*, as an epistemological term, represents the counterpart to *enargeia*. While the latter highlights the moment of expressiveness, the former denotes the impression, from which the expression, in all its vividness, springs.[28]

Typosis, the impressed image, constitutes a unique type of representation, which accounts for its widespread cultural usage and valence before the advent of mechanical reproduction.[29] Not only do impressed images presuppose direct contact, but the process of impression is quasi-mechanical and involves unspecialized craft or artistry. Because impressor and impression, original and copy must have occupied the same place and time in which the contact and in-formation occurred, typosis confers value and authenticity on the copy, as seals attest to the presence and identity of a signatory or stamps transform a piece of metal into currency. Along with its form, the original imparts to the copy some of its aura.[30] Particularly in religious contexts, impressed images derive their power from this form of (re)production. Christian cult images, modeled on the sweat cloth, *sudarium*, on which Christ's face was imprinted, are a prominent example. These icons, which were the result of typosis, were also termed *acheiropoeitai* (made without human hands) and were of two kinds: "Either they are images believed to have been made by hands other than those of ordinary mortals or else they are claimed to be mechanical, though miraculous, impressions of the original."[31] As Katherine Park has demonstrated, typosis was believed to be the way by which divinity and sanctity were communicated to the temporal and material world.[32] Or more generally, "impressed images were the way in which body spoke to soul ... and soul spoke to body."[33] Typosis, that is, was a preferred mode of mediating incommensurable spheres or substances.

And wax was the preferred medium for typosis. Somewhat counterintuitively, wax as a figure was associated less with matter and body and more with form and soul. Why this was the case is the subject of the final section of this chapter, while for now it's enough to note that this association between wax and soul remained alive and well in early modern Europe. As Christine

FIGURE 8. *Soul in Purgatory (anima purgata)*, wax figure by unknown Lombardian artist. © Veneranda Biblioteca Ambrosiana/Mondadori Portfolio.

Göttler has persuasively shown, wax, due to its peculiar materiality, was the artistic medium of choice to actually represent the soul's immateriality and invisibility in a drastic and veristic manner.[34] Rather than cite examples from early modern philosophical discourse in support of the claim, I close with a pictorial example from the sphere of religious devotion (see Figs. 8 and 9).

The generic invention of the *animae separatae* in the so-called Four

176 Cartesian Ceroplastics

FIGURE 9. *Soul in Heaven* (*anima beata*), wax figure by unknown Lombardian artist. © Veneranda Biblioteca Ambrosiana/Mondadori Portfolio

Last Things, the separated souls in heaven, hell, and purgatory, is attributed to the Neapolitan painter and ceroplastic sculptor Giovanni Bernardino Azzolino at the beginning of the seventeenth century, over the course of which they became a popular item in Counter-Reformation art and piety. When Descartes' meditator, in their early modern Catholic media environment, picked up a piece of wax, the figures of such corporealized souls would have been easily evoked in their mind.

More important, Descartes himself resorted frequently to ceroplasticity to explain the functioning of four principal faculties of the mind: sense perception, memory, imagination, and intellect. It appears for the first time in his earliest text, the unpublished *Rules for the Direction of the Mind*. In Rule Twelve, although he uses "figure" in place of "form," the Cartesian theory of sensation sounds unmistakably Aristotelian:[35]

> First, insofar as our external senses are all parts of the body, sense-perception, strictly speaking, is merely passive.... [It] occurs in the same way in which wax takes on an impression [*figuram*] from a seal. It should not be thought that I have a mere analogy in mind here: we must think of the external shape [*figuram externam*] of the sentient body as being really changed by the object in exactly the same way as the shape on the surface of the wax is altered by the seal. This is the case, we must admit, not only when we feel some body as having a shape [*figuratam*], as being hard or rough to the touch etc., but also when we have tactile perception of heat or cold and the like. The same is true of the other senses. (CSM I 40; AT X 412–13)

Notable is the stress Descartes puts on the literality of the comparison. In effect, the wax here is no longer a figure, as the *figurae* are literally impressions in the opaque ceroplastic membranes of the senses. Descartes goes even a step further, as this sealing also applies to nonfigural sense perceptions such as temperature, smells, and flavors. The "first membrane which is impervious to the passage of the object" (CSM I 40; AT X 413) in the respective sense takes on the *figura* of the particular sensorial quality.[36]

Thus, the different sensorial qualities are all converted into *figurae* that are then processed by the individual psychic faculties. Given that Descartes conceives the event of perception as "merely passive" (CSM I 40; AT X 412), it forms the beginning of a typographic chain of *figurae*. All the *figurae* generated by the ceroplastic membranes of the different sense organs are then routed to a central processor: "When an external sense organ is stimulated by an object, the figure which it receives is conveyed at one and the same moment to another part of the body known as the 'common sense,' without any entity really passing from the one to the other" (CSM I 41; AT X 414). The common sense, which a few years later in his *Treatise on Man* Descartes will locate in the pineal gland (CSM I 106; AT XI 177), traces back to Aristotle and remained a staple of early modern psychology.[37] The reception of *figurae* by the primary and the common sense is perfectly coordinated and simultaneous:

> In exactly the same way I understand that while I am writing, at the very moment when individual letters are traced on the paper [*singuli characteres in charta exprimuntur*], not only does the point of the pen move, but the slightest motion of this part cannot but be transmitted to the whole pen. All these various motions are traced out in the air by the tip of the quill, even though I do not conceive of anything real passing from one end to the other. (CSM I 41; AT X 414)

Descartes imagines the perception as a typographic inscription that is perfectly coordinated—by the stroke of a pen—with a parallel inscription in the common sense. The inscription of the sensorial *figurae* in the common sense forms the beginning of a typographic chain of replication, functioning "like a seal [*sigilli*], fashioning in the phantasy or imagination, as if in wax [*in cera formandas*], the same figures or ideas [*figuras vel ideas*] which come, pure and without body, from the external senses" (CSM I 41; AT X 414). The *figurae* deriving from the objects of the sensory world are processed by primary and common sensation, imagination, and memory, resulting in an unbroken typographic chain. Mental faculties transmit *figurae* by creating impressions like a seal in the ceroplastic surface of the receiving faculty, so that thinking, in a way, consists in the transmission or, more generally, processing of *figurae*.

Since this processing of *figurae* is performed by faculties that belong to the body rather than the mind, it might be objected that this "thinking" is really only corporeal and should not be called thinking in the Cartesian sense. And to be sure, for Descartes the intellect that is "the power through which we know things in the strict sense is purely spiritual" (CSM I 42; AT X 415). But this does not exclude the intellect from becoming part of the typographic chain:

> It is one single power, whether it receives figures [*figuras*] from the "common" sense at the same time as does the corporeal imagination, or applies itself to those which are preserved in memory, or forms [*format*] new ones which so preoccupy the imagination.... In all these functions the cognitive power is sometimes passive, sometimes active; sometimes resembling the seal [*sigillum*], sometimes the wax [*ceram*]. (CSM I 42; AT X 415)

Descartes cautions that the reference to wax and seal should be taken only *per analogiam*, but the intellect is able to act nonetheless as the latter and impress its ideas on the imagination and memory. In turn, it is also capable of receiving *figurae* from the other mental faculties, even if its ceroplasticity is of a different nature. Descartes scholars commonly argue that this corporeal conception of thought, and thus its comparison with ceroplastic formation, is restricted to his early years. However, as late as 1644, two years after the publication of the *Meditations*, in a letter to Father Mesland Descartes again compares the soul with a piece of wax, writing that he sees "the difference between the soul and its ideas as the same as that between a piece of wax and the various shapes it can take" (CSM III 232; AT IV 113). Compared to the Twelfth Rule for the Direction of the Mind, Descartes' position here has not changed much in using ceroplasticity to explain the "difference" or, better, unity of the "soul and its ideas." For no matter how much the soul shifts shape, it remains fundamentally the same.[38] Change has to do essentially with the in-formation of the soul by ideas, which are nothing other than forms of thought.

In Chapter 3 we saw that Descartes' meditator, in reflecting on ideas and images, insisted that "it is only in these cases [when their thoughts are images of things] that the term 'idea' is strictly appropriate" (CSM II 25; AT VII 37). Already at that point, they had described ideas as images "formed in my thought [*imagines cogitationes formantur*]" (CSM II 20; AT VII 29),[39] making it clear that ideas are a specific kind of image, that is, impressed images.[40] Thomas Aquinas, along with medieval philosophers generally, translated the Greek *idea* as *forma*,[41] writing in his *Summa Theologiae*: "For the Greek word *idea* is in Latin *forma*. Hence by ideas are understood the forms of things, existing apart from the things themselves" (ST I, q. 15).[42] And Descartes, in the Second Set of Replies to Mersenne's Objections, seems to be following suit:

I understand this term [*idea*] to mean the form of any given thought, immediate perception of which makes me aware of the thought. Hence whenever I express something in words, and understand what I am saying, this very fact makes it certain that there is within me an idea of what is signified by the words in question. Thus it is not only the images depicted in the imagination which I call "ideas." Indeed, in so far as these images are in the corporeal imagination, that is, are depicted in some part of the brain, I do not call them "ideas" at all; I call them "ideas" only in so far as they give form to the mind itself, when it is directed towards that part of the brain. (CSM II 113; AT VII 160)

Ideas are both the forms of thought and their perception or, more precisely, intuition by the mind.[43] These cognitive forms are called images when they are impressed on the mind by the "corporeal imagination," so the forms impressed in the corporeal imagination are strictly speaking not ideas qua images but only as forms. Like the intellect (*ingenium*) as described in the *Regulae*, the mind is capable of receiving as well as imparting impressions.[44] Aside from stressing the unity of mind and body, Descartes provides little argumentative substance for how we are to understand the in-formation of and by the mind. Expressions such as "ideas are forms [*formae*] of a kind, and are not composed of any matter" (CSM II 163; AT VII 232) suggest that Descartes had Aristotle's notion of "form without matter" in mind. Relations between the material body and the immaterial mind involve no exchange of matter but merely a reciprocal communication of forms. That is, mind and body have the capacity to impress each other. As Descartes makes clear in the Third Set of Replies (to Hobbes's Objections), the semantic heritage of "idea" as a transmission of form between mind and matter was one of the reasons he chose the term in the first place: "I used the word 'idea' because it was the standard philosophical term used to refer to the forms of perception belonging to the divine mind, even though we recognize that God does not possess any corporeal imagination. And besides, there was not any more appropriate term at my disposal" (CSM II 127; AT VII 181). Descartes is referring here to the Scholastic notion that "ideas are either the forms in God's mind according to which he makes things, or the exemplars in artificers' minds when they make their objects."[45] Creation, whether divine or artistic, is thus nothing else but the in-formation of matter with the ideas that the creator has in mind. In both cases, it is the process of in-formation that bridges the boundary between mind and matter. And not surprisingly, this notion of ideas as forms in the divine mind is most readily legible in Descartes' theory of innate ideas. For instance, "mathematical truths" are "all inborn in our minds just as a king would imprint his laws on the hearts of his subjects if he had the power to do so" (CSM III 23; AT I 145). Innate ideas are, thus, impressed into the human mind in such a way that they are part of its very fabric.[46] In in-forming, that is, imparting shape to the mind, innate ideas are inseparable from it. "It is no surprise," says the meditator,

> that God, in creating me, should have placed this idea in me to be, as it were, the mark of the craftsman [*nota artificis*] stamped [*impressa*] on his work—not that the mark [*nota*] need be anything distinct from the work itself. But the mere fact that God created me is a very strong basis for believing that I am somehow made

in his image and likeness, and that I perceive that likeness, which includes the idea of God, by the same faculty which enables me to perceive myself. (CSM II 35; AT VII 51)

The meditator's deiformity consists in nothing else but the idea of God impressed in their mind, and in turn this idea is nothing more than the specific form or shape of that very mind. God has in-formed their mind at birth, and its form thus resembles him. It is literally deiform, and therefore it is the medium for knowing God. By turning toward itself, the mind simultaneously turns toward its creator.

Given that Descartes never abandons wax as a figure of the mind, the question persists concerning what specifically it is about wax, beyond its philosophical heritage, that lends it such evidentiary force for his inquiry into the nature of the mind. Descartes' meditator, at the end of their ceroplastic meditation, claims to be able "to consider [the wax] naked," as it were, distinguished from its outward forms or stripped of its clothes (CSM II 22; AT VII 32). The rest of this chapter seeks to understand what the naked wax tells Descartes' meditator about the mediality of the mind. To do so, it will be necessary to heed Georges Didi-Huberman's advice and "go beyond the metaphorical uses of wax—without losing sight of the theoretical and conceptual foundations of wax—so that we may study more thoroughly the problem of plasticity by giving a voice not to just philosophers of matter, but also to technicians of matter."[47]

The Mediality of the Mind

What has defined the wax's materiality from antiquity to its more recent replacement by various human-made materials is its extreme versatility and multifunctionality.[48] As Pliny notes, "Wax . . . serves a thousand practical purposes" (*Natural History* 11.11).[49] In medicine it was used as an ingredient for dressings and salves, in cosmetics for making ointments. Wax candles were omnipresent in a myriad of different contexts. It was used as an adhesive and for sealing all sorts of documents. In painting and textile dyeing wax helped provide color. Particularly manifold were its ceroplastic uses: in funeral rites to fashion death masks, in religious ritual and devotion for reliquaries and votive objects, in anatomy to represent body parts, or in sculpture for casting bronze. Due to its moldable and protean character wax was imputed to have magical properties that could be harnessed and released in candles, amulets, and, particularly, votive offerings. And it is often forgotten that well into the early modern period wax tablets were an essential medium of literacy. As Mary and Richard Rouse point out, "Wax was the medium in which all children formed their first letters and then learned to write," and "the wax tablet was the place where most ancient and medieval texts first took shape."[50] Due to its extreme mutability and multifunctionality its defining character seems almost to be its lack of character or, as Didi-Huberman succinctly puts it: "Wax emerges therefore as a material that is insensitive to the contradictions of its material qualities."[51] Precisely this material mutability seems to have been responsible for what troubled Descartes, to quote Didi-Huberman once again, the "paradox of consistency, linked . . . to the fact that wax—whether liquid, pasty, solid, or even brittle—remains wax. No one can ever decide which is its 'primary' or 'principal' state."[52]

Wax's plasticity and malleability is the condition for its mimetic qualities that allowed artists to fashion particularly hyperrealistic, uncannily lifelike representations. Already Pliny emphasizes wax's aptitude to transmit the *similitudo mortalium* (*Natural History* 21.85), and, likewise, Vasari finds it particularly suited to represent the absent and the dead.[53] Wax's ceroplastic mediality was so proverbial that it became synonymous with illusion and deception.

Diogenes Laertius tells the following anecdote about the Stoic philosopher Sphaerus visiting Ptolemy Philopator at Alexandria:

One day a conversation took place on whether the wise man would opine, and Sphaerus said that he would not. Wishing to refute him, the king ordered wax pomegranates to be placed before him. Sphaerus was deceived and the king cried out that he had given his assent to a false impression. Sphaerus gave him a shrewd answer, saying that his assent was not [to the impression] that they were pomegranates but [to the impression] that it was reasonable that they were pomegranates. He pointed out that the cataleptic impression is different from the reasonable one. . . . The former is incapable of deceiving, but the reasonable impression can turn out otherwise.[54]

Although this passage contains much that is relevant to the present discussion, the logic of assent to mental impressions, I will have to restrict myself to a few brief observations pertaining to the use of wax here. By short-circuiting the level of the represented (the ceroplastic pomegranates) and the level of representation (the mental impression as a stamp in wax), the anecdote paves the way for Descartes' own deconstruction of the evidence of the perception of the piece of wax. Like Sphaerus, Descartes wants to dispel the notion that we see the "things themselves" when actually only cognizing mental representations, mental representations that are so verisimilar because they are as formable as the wax from which the pomegranates are made.

Wax's plasticity, its susceptibility to being endlessly in- and re-formed, made it the medium par excellence so that it was continually evoked in discussions of the mediality of other media. So what is its specific mediality, and how does it interact with the forms it adopts? Drawing on the Gestalt psychologist Fritz Heider, Niklas Luhmann proposed replacing the traditional distinction between substance and accident and the "object-oriented ontological concept of matter" with the distinction between medium and form.[55] A medium consists of loosely coupled elements, resulting in an "open-ended multiplicity of possible connections that are still compatible with the unity of an element" (*Art as Social System* 104). Forms, in contrast, "are generated in a medium via a tight coupling of its elements" (104). Medium and form, in consisting of the same elements, thus do not differ in substance but only in arrangement and structure or, put differently, form results from a rigidization of the medium and, inversely, medium from a loosening of form. In short, medium and form are inseparable. As the shapes taken by the piece of wax cannot be separated from the wax, it—qua medium—cannot be totally formless.

As important as its retentive qualities is the way a medium can take on new forms and, thereby, give up its old shape. Put differently, wax qua medium is characterized as much by its retentiveness as its forgetfulness. If it eternally retained any given information, its storage capacity would be quickly exhausted. But rather than being consumed, a medium is regenerated by being (re)formed, with the somewhat paradoxical consequence, according to Luhmann, that "the form's resilience is paid for with instability," while, in contrast, "the medium is more stable . . . , because it requires only loose couplings" (*Art as Social System* 106). However, the number of possibilities for coupling has to be large enough to allow for alternative forms, for otherwise they lose their distinctive character, in effect becoming identical with the medium and thus invisible. Media can only ever only be observed via their forms, never as such, an insight, as Luhmann notes, that "corresponds to the old doctrine that matter as such, as sheer chaos, is inaccessible to consciousness" (104). Only formed does the medium become visible and intelligible—however, not as medium. In order to function properly and let the form come into view, the medium itself has to be invisible. Physical media "spend themselves . . . in the process of mediation," observes Fritz Heider, "so that we believe that we hear the ticking directly. . . . The mediation of light waves is of the same nature. We do not perceive light waves as things that touch our eyes and refer to something else. We seem to see the mediated object directly."[56] Thus, the medium resists fixation and determination. All that can be perceived are the concrete forms, the process of articulation and dearticulation, suggesting what Dieter Mersch has termed "a constitutive blindness or negativity" that inheres the dialectics of mediality.[57]

Returning to the dilemma that confronts Descartes' meditator in the Second Meditation when they set out to investigate the "nature of the human mind," it now gains clearer contours. If, as it does for wax, the nature of the mind consists in its mediality, then all that can be apprehended are its forms, that is, ideas, fantasies, memories, and perceptions, and the mediality of the mind as a thinking thing remains elusive. The mind may be closer to itself than sensory perceptions and its objects, but as soon as it tries to grasp itself, it withdraws. But the meditator's dilemma can be also formulated less systems-theoretically. If the evidence of a clear and distinct idea or perception is predicated on the eclipse of its mediality, how then can the mind's role as medium of ideation and perception come into focus; or, put more generally, how can media itself become evident? This dilemma is exacerbated by the fact that, as Descartes makes clear in conjunction with the *cogito*, thinking needs to become evident to itself in action. In fact, before Descartes proves the existence of a benevolent God, past thoughts, mediated by memory, remain always potentially deceptive.

We are now also in a better position to understand why sensory perception and its objects appear as so much more evident than the mind itself. The impression that we perceive of the "things themselves" is the result of the suspension of mediality: in Descartes' case not so much of the light waves but of the act of judgment that our mental representations correspond to external objects; or more generally and abstractly, of the act of thinking as the medium of all perception and cognition. And because of this invisibility of judgment, sensory perception and its objects appear so much more evident to the mind than the mind itself, although the mind is structurally closer. In one last twist to the meditator's dilemma: Even if thinking could somehow get a glimpse of its own mediality, it still cannot cognize itself unformed, since thinking is nothing other, following the ceroplastic metaphorics, than a medium being in-formed by ideas.

To address and counter this dilemma that arises when thinking needs to become evident to itself, Descartes' meditator pursues a two-pronged strategy, First, because the mediality of the mind can be cognized only indirectly, they take an allegorical detour via the material medium and metaphor of wax. As a rhetorical trope, allegory has traditionally served to visualize and materialize something invisible and immaterial, giving concrete, sensual form to an abstract entity and lending it evidence in the process; and from his earliest writings, Descartes invokes wax as an example to illustrate the mediality of the mind and its associated psychic faculties. Yet, as the meditator also makes clear in the Second Meditation, the truth of the wax, that is, its mediality, lies beyond the realm of the figural, for otherwise it could be readily pictured by the imagination. In their meditation on ceroplasticity, they show that since the imagination is incapable of conceiving all possible forms the wax is capable of adopting, it cannot conceive its mediality as such. But, as Walter Benjamin reminds us, sensualization is only one moment of the movement of allegory. Signifying "exactly the nonexistence of what it represents," allegory entails the dialectical self-suspension of the signifier; and its evidence is owed as much to this moment of defiguration as to its figurality.

Second, it is precisely this defiguration that the meditator sees being literally and physically effected by the fire. Melting under the heat, the piece of wax loses all form: color, shape, taste, smell, and even sound. And what emerges in this meditation by fire—stripped naked of its clothes—is the wax's mediality. To understand its own nature, the mind must—quite literally—unform itself. It does so, in line with meditative practice, by reversing the course of normal perception, as Aristotle understood it. Instead of divesting a sense object of its matter and receiving only its form, Descartes' ceroplastic meditation performs the opposite operation, divesting it of its form and maintaining only its materiality or, more precisely, mediality. Under Descartes' long meditative gaze, the piece of wax loses its familiarity and becomes uncanny. Formless, it doesn't simply cease to function as a figure (of the mind); in its infinite plasticity it negates or, more precisely, transcends figurality and thus figures as a figure of the suspension of figurality—even while the paradigmatic mediality of its infinite and inexhaustible plasticity makes it the very figure of figurability. In losing form, the wax is not reduced to pure matter, which is the other side of the Aristotelian binary. In having many forms, the many different material qualities of the wax contradict and negate each other so that it simultaneously transcends its materiality—leaving it suspended in an uncanny state between form and matter. An immaterial material and a formed formlessness, the wax represents the essence of mediality—ideal for figuring the mind as a thinking thing. So when staging the wax's denudation by pyrotechnically de- and unforming it, what Descartes' meditator beholds is not only the naked wax but also and more important, the mind stripped of all forms or ideas, just as it was for Descartes in the overheated chamber on that fateful November night in 1619 when, having "stripped" himself of himself, he was able to apprehend his mind "naked."

5

Adversio, Animadversio, and *Attentio*:
Turning toward God

Thrice Over

Descartes' so-called proofs of God's existence have been among the least palatable portions of the *Meditations*. Indeed, in his Replies to readers' Objections and in letters he voiced his own misgivings about the length and the difficulty of the first proof in particular. His case is not strengthened by the fact that the first proof is immediately followed by a second, and in the Fifth Meditation, by a third, as if the first proof were not "doing the work" it needed to do. If the proof was valid, shouldn't it have worked once and for all? Why does it need backup? Descartes was aware of these issues from the start, as he indicates explicitly in his dedication to the Faculty of the Sorbonne. It was not his intent, he writes,

to collect here all the different arguments that could be put forward to establish the same results, for this does not seem worthwhile except in cases where no single argument is regarded as sufficiently reliable. What I have done is to take merely the principal and most important arguments and develop them in such a way that I would now venture to put them forward as very certain and evident demonstrations. (CSM II 4; AT VII 4)

Proving the same claim thrice over seems like a throwback to an older culture of knowledge, one that Cartesian philosophy set out to reform and overcome. Yet, if Descartes' assessment is to be taken at face value, he believed that his demonstrations were "very certain and evident," suggesting that the multiplication of proofs not only does not diminish their evidence but is entirely necessary for them to be effective. Thus, each proof must play a specific role in the order of reasons that structure the *Meditations*. Their purpose must be functional and pragmatic rather than purely logical, conditioned more by the limitations and needs of the meditating mind than logic of the argumentation.

The question raised in this chapter is therefore that of the meditative function of the three proofs. How do they guide the meditator first to clear and distinct cognition and, at the end of the Third Meditation, even to a contemplation of God? And why must the guidance be followed not just once but repeatedly? We saw in Chapter 2 that many of the mental operations Descartes detailed in the *Meditations* require practice to become habitualized and perfected. The meditator, in being directed to apply their doubt to ever-new sensory impressions and prejudices, reenacts it again and again. Similarly, as discussed in Chapter 3, discernment must be incessantly exercised if the normalization of doubt is to be achieved. Not even clear and distinct cognition just happens but takes effort and practice. Repetition is thus part of the answer. But to understand precisely how it works, we have to know which mental operation is being practiced and how it is effected in being practiced.

Descartes' Proofs

The Third Meditation unfolds the first two proofs of God's existence and, in doing so, follows the rhythm of traditional religious meditative practice. It begins by reiterating the *a-* and *conversio* of the First and Second Meditations, that is, the turn away from the sensory world and toward the self. However, much as in Augustine claiming in *De vera religione* that "the truth dwells within the inner man" (*in interiore homine habitat veritas*),[1] Descartes' *conversio ad ipsum* is in reality a *conversio ad Deum*. As early as in the *Regulae* Descartes claims to demonstrate that the thinking of the self (both as a *genitivus subjectivus* and *objectivus*) is intrinsically conjoined to the thinking of God. "I am, therefore God exists" (*sum, ergo Deus est*) (CSM I 46; AT X 422), as he concisely puts it. Also in the tradition of religious meditation, it is the recognition of the self as inherently and profoundly sinful that prompts the turn toward God. Augustine, in a famous passage from Book Eight of the *Confessions*, needs first to be shown his sinfulness before he is capable of hearing and heeding God's call. Similarly, in the first week of Ignatius's *Spiritual Exercises*, the exercitant meditates on their sins and possible infernal punishments before they can turn toward the contemplation of Christ's incarnation and sacrifice as the redemption of those very sins. Before this religious background, Descartes' exploration of the epistemological fallibility of the self in the first two meditations takes on new significance. As Lawrence Nolan observes, for Descartes "the idea of oneself naturally recalls the idea of God," which seems to confirm the meditative logic underlying the move from the *cogito* to the *cognitio*, and ultimately *contemplatio Dei*: "The idea of myself as finite, imperfect, and dependent triggers the idea of something infinite, perfect, and independent."[2]

The discovery of God in the self, in the sense in which that constitutes proof of God's existence, hinges on the meditator's examination—or discernment—of thoughts and ideas, which leads them to the conclusion "that it is not reliable judgement but merely some blind impulse that has made me believe up till now that there exist things distinct from myself which transmit to me ideas and images of themselves through the sense organs or in some other way" (CSM II 27; AT VII 40). They learn, in short, that traditional discernment is fallible, and Descartes' meditator is sent searching for "another way of investigating whether some of the things of which I possess ideas exist outside me" (CSM II 27; AT VII 40). The other way they find is predicated on the theory of ideas as in-formation that we encountered in the previous chapter. Descartes' meditator distinguishes two aspects that pertain to all ideas: their "objective reality" that denotes their representational content; and their "formal reality," referring to ideas as "modes of thought" (CSM II 27; AT VII 40) or, quite literally, as forms of thought. When the forms are images, they represent objects, which constitute their objective reality. Objects that are represented by ideas have themselves form, which is their formal reality.

We have seen that, for Descartes, the discernment of spirits rests on the premise that ideas occur in the mind according to the laws of causality. As he writes in the First Set of Replies, every idea "needs a cause enabling it to be conceived" (CSM II 75; AT VII 103). In other words, ideas are caused by something else to which they refer. Causality comes into play insofar as the objects trans- or, better, immit their form into the mind, which is thereby in-formed. This logic of in-formation is also at work when ideas engender another, and it explains why the attribute "formal" switches its place in some of Descartes' other explanations of the same issue. For instance, in his reply to Arnauld: "Since ideas are forms [*formae*] of a kind, and are not composed of any matter, when we think of them as representing something we are taking them not materially but formally. If, however, we were considering them not as representing this or that but simply as operations of the intellect, then it could be said that we were taking them materially, but in that case they would have no reference to truth or falsity of their objects" (CSM II 163; AT VII 232). When the mind considers ideas materially, it is considering cognition pragmatically as an operation, not representationally. Considering ideas formally keys on their ability to represent objects by virtue of their in-formation. L. J. Beck formulates the point concisely: "The formal reality is the cause, the objective reality, the effect."[3]

In his first proof Descartes exploits this logic of in-formation. Following the principle *ex nihilo nihil fit*, that nothing can be created out of nothing, he deduces that the objective reality of an idea cannot be greater than its formal reality, for otherwise it would be created out of nothing. He guides his meditator to reason further that if the idea of God contains infinite objective reality, which it does, and the mind possesses only finite formal reality, which is likewise true, then the self cannot be the cause of the objective reality of the idea of God. As God alone possesses infinite formal reality, only God can in-form the mind of the idea of himself. Yet, no sooner does Descartes' meditator conclude the first proof, than they become aware of a problem concerned not with the logic of their thinking but with practical considerations:

> If one concentrates carefully [*diligenter attendenti*], all this is quite evident [*manifestum*] by the natural light. But when I relax my concentration [*minus attendo*], and my mental vision [*mentis aciem*] is blinded by the images of things perceived by the senses, it is not so easy for me to remember why the idea of a being more perfect than myself must necessarily proceed from some being which is in reality more perfect. I should therefore like to go further and inquire whether I myself, who have this idea, could exist if no such being existed. (CSM II 32–33; AT VII 47–48)

The self-evidence of the first proof of God's existence becomes manifest only given diligent attention, for when the meditator's "mental vision" is absorbed by the sensory world and when the proof is no longer the exclusive object of the mind's attentive gaze, the proof loses its force. Now the mind has the challenge of remembering all the complicated considerations pertaining to "why the idea of a being more perfect than myself must necessarily proceed from some being which is in reality more perfect." It is the difficulty involved in remembering the long complicated first proof of God's existence that causes Descartes' meditator to want to "go further," resulting in their presentation of the second proof, which ties the self's existence, that is, *ego existo*, directly to the existence of God.

There has been much debate whether the second proof is really distinct from the first or whether it is merely an extension or variation.[4] In fact, Descartes himself often lumped both together. For instance, in a letter to Mesland on May 2, 1644, he writes: "It does not make much difference whether my second proof, the one based on our own existence, is regarded as different from the first proof, or merely as an explanation of it. Just as it is an effect of God to have created me, so it is an effect of him to have put the idea of himself in me; and there is no effect coming from him from which one cannot prove his existence" (CSM III 232; AT IV 122). Instead of beginning with the idea of God in the mind of the meditator, the second proof takes as its starting point the *ego sum*, the idea of the meditator as a thinking thing or, put differently, the *cogito*, because the meditator has not yet proven anything beyond their own mind. The meditator first distinguishes between two possible causes of the idea of the self: it is either due to itself or something else that the ego exists. The former is easy to rule out, but before settling on the latter, the meditator considers the possibility that the ego has always existed and therefore required no external cause, in which case the idea of the self would be innate and thus coeval with the self thinking it. The meditator wards off the objection of an uncreated self through recourse to the doctrine of the *creatio continua*, which, as we have seen, requires a cause not only for a thing's creation but for its continuation as well. Translating this argument into the language of ideas, we see the parallel to Descartes' conceptualization of innate ideas, which are authored not by the self but by God. The rest of the proof rehearses the argumentation of the first: The cause of a thinking thing with the idea of a perfect God must itself possess this perfection. In other words, I exist and have the idea of God, and because I am not perfect, God must exist.[5] *Sum, ergo Deus est*. It is the common grounding of the proofs in the principle of *ex nihilo nihil fit* that allows the two proofs to be collapsed into each other. In the first proof the idea of God in the meditator's mind, and in the second the meditator's existence, cannot have been caused by the meditator themself, who is finite, because it must have a cause that is infinite. Given this grounding of both proofs on the same principle, the second adds little to either the logic or the argument, suggesting its purpose must lie elsewhere. In being only half as long as the first, for example, it requires less concentrated attention, leaving the "mental vision" less likely to be "blinded by the images of things perceived by the senses."

The third demonstration of God's existence in the Fifth Meditation, the so-called ontological proof, is similar to the first in that its starting point is the idea of God in the meditator's mind.[6] Similar to both earlier proofs, the final one is presented in the context of the meditator's examination of their own mental representations. Here they consider the ideas they have of things in the material world, "in so far as they exist in my thought," so they can "see which of them are distinct, and which confused" (CSM II 44; AT VII 63). The meditator notices right away that they can distinctly cognize the quantitative or quantifiable aspects of things, "shape, number, motion and so on" (CSM II 44; AT VII 63). These features, it seems, don't adhere to the things outside the mind but are in the mind itself. Regarding the meditator's geometrical knowledge, for instance, they know that a triangle's "three angles equal two right angles" or "that its greatest side subtends its greatest angle" (CSM II 45; AT VII 64). And they would know it even if no triangles existed in the real world, because their "immutable and eternal" nature is real and "not invented by me or dependent on my mind" (CSM II 45; AT VII 64). If they are neither adventitious, that is, coming from outside, nor invented, they have to have been always already in the mind. They have to be part of the mind itself, or in brief, they are innate.

Descartes' meditator concludes that only innate ideas are both clear and distinct and necessarily true: "I cannot but assent to these things, at least as long as I clearly perceive them" (CSM II 45; AT VII 65). The meditator needs but turn their attention toward these features to find the "truth of these matters . . . so open and so much in harmony with my nature, that on first discovering them it seems that I am not so much learning something new as remembering [*reminisci*] what I knew before; or it seems like noticing for the first time things [*ad ea primum advertere*] which were long present within me although I had never turned my mental gaze on them before [*non prius in illa obtutum mentis convertissem*]" (CSM II 44; AT VII 63–64).

At this point it is no surprise that this turning of attention, this *adversio*, toward these "things which were long present within me" is figured in the *Meditations* as a turn or conversion of the mental gaze, a turn inward toward the mind's very fabric. The meditator's turn toward their innate ideas is pivotal for the turn toward God and final demonstration of his existence:

> But if the mere fact that I can produce from my thought the idea of something entails that everything which I clearly and distinctly perceive to belong to that thing really does belong to it, is not this a possible basis for another argument to prove the existence of God? Certainly, the idea of God, or a supremely perfect being, is one which I find within me just as surely as the idea of any shape or number. And my understanding that it belongs to his nature that he always exists is no less clear and distinct than is the case when I prove of any shape or number that some property belongs to its nature. (CSM II 45; AT VII 65–66)

The proof in its entirety is essentially contained in the last sentence, and the parallel to the *cogito* is so apparent it could be reformulated, *cogito Deum, ergo Deus est*. All that is left now for Descartes' meditator to do is sharpen their "understanding":

> At first sight, however, this is not transparently clear, but has some appearance of a sophism. Since I have been accustomed to distinguish between existence and essence in everything else, I find it easy to persuade myself that existence can also be separated from the essence of God, and hence that God can be thought of as not existing. But when I concentrate more carefully [*diligentius attendenti*], it is quite evident that existence can no more be separated from the essence of God than the fact that its three angles equal two right angles can be separated from the essence of the triangle, or than the idea of the mountain can be separated from the idea of the valley. Hence it is just as much a contradiction to think of God [*cogitare Deum*] (that is, a supremely perfect being) lacking existence (that is, lacking a perfection), as it is to think of a mountain without a valley. (CSM II 45–46; AT VII 66)

The meditator achieves this sharpening of understanding by attending more diligently to the idea of the essence of God. With their mental gaze focused on the idea of God in their mind, the meditator finds it "quite evident that existence can [not] be separated from the essence of God."

With that, the third is without doubt the shortest of the three proofs. Indeed, it is so short it cannot properly called a "proof" at all, understanding "proof" to entail a number of interdependent argumentative steps along the line of what Descartes called a deduction in the *Regulae*. Here the conclusion is immediately evident and thus more like an object of what in the *Regulae* he termed intuition. It consists solely in the cognition of the necessary relation between essence and existence in the idea of God, which is the cognition that God's essence necessarily includes his actual existence.[7] After putting to rest a number of possible objections to their reasoning, Descartes' meditator now reflects on the pragmatics of their proofs:

> But whatever method of proof I use, I am always brought back to the fact that it is only what I clearly and distinctly perceive that completely convinces [*persuadeant*] me. Some of the things I clearly and distinctly perceive are obvious to everyone, while others are discovered only by those who look more closely and investigate more carefully [*inspiciunt & diligenter investigant*]; but once they have been discovered, the latter are judged to be just as certain as the former. In the case of a right-angled triangle, for example, the fact that the square on the hypotenuse is equal to the square on the other two sides is not so readily apparent as the fact that the hypotenuse subtends the largest angle; but once one has seen it, one believes it just as strongly. (CSM II 47–48; AT VII 69)

All three proofs, in being equally clear and distinct, are certain, as clarity and distinctness amount to the universal criteria of innate ideas in general. But innate ideas are not all alike. Some are obvious; others require more diligent scrutiny. The cognition of the idea of God is particularly difficult to achieve because sensory impressions and preconceived opinions are in that case particularly distracting, and indeed the authorized French translation of the *Meditations* reads "ma pensée ne se trouvast point divertie par la presence continuelle des images des choses sensibles" (AT IX 54), pointing directly at the problem of diversion. In contrast to more apparent ideas, the cognition of God's existence (from its essence) requires particularly "close attention." But sensory overload is only one problem because the meditator's internal focus is also unstable:

> Admittedly my nature is such that so long as I perceive something very clearly and distinctly I cannot but believe it to be true. But my nature is also such that I cannot fix my mental vision [*obtutum mentis*] continually on the same thing, so as to keep perceiving it clearly [*non possim obtutum mentis in eandem rem semper defigere ad illam clare percipiendam*]; and often the memory of a previously made judgement may come back, when I am no longer attending to the arguments [*non amplius attendo ad rationes*] which led me to make it. And so other arguments can now occur to me which might easily undermine my opinion. (CSM II 48; AT VII 69–70)

Clear and distinct cognition is tied to present perception or, put differently, is a function of attention. Only those things toward which the mind directs its attention, and only while it is doing so, can be cognized clearly and distinctly, which is to say, appear completely self-evident to the mental gaze. The problem is that once one's attention has moved on to other things, the judgment that was made in the past is no longer based on clear and distinct cognition, as the mind is no longer attending to the arguments leading to the judgment in question. The memory of a clear and distinct cognition, in other words, is not itself clear and distinct. The memory is no longer compelling, and suddenly a cognition that once stood out in its incontrovertible self-evidence is no different from other arguments.

For example, when I consider the nature of a triangle, it appears most evident to me, steeped as I am in the principles of geometry, that its three angles are equal to two right angles; and so long as I attend to the proof [*quamdiu ad ejus demonstrationem attendo*], I cannot but believe this to be true. But as soon as I turn my mind's eye away from the proof [*mentis aciem ab illa deflexi*], then in spite of still remembering that I perceived it very clearly, I can easily fall into doubt about its truth, if I am unaware of God [*Deum ignorem*]. (CSM II 48; AT VII 69–70)

With all of the arguments equally compelling, knowledge becomes a matter of mere "shifting and changeable opinions."[8]

As Descartes makes clear in the Second Set of Replies, the case is otherwise with "simple intuitions":

When I said that we can know nothing for certain until we are aware that God exists, I expressly declared that I was speaking only of knowledge of those conclusions which can be recalled when we are no longer attending to the arguments by means of which we deduced them. . . . And when we become aware that we are thinking things, this is a primary notion which is not derived by means of any syllogism. When someone says "I am thinking, therefore I am, or I exist," he does not deduce existence from thought by means of a syllogism, but recognizes it as something self-evident by a simple intuition of the mind. (CSM II 100; AT VII 140)

Intuitions are certain regardless of whether the thinker in question has knowledge of God, but as we explore in Chapter 6, not without the existence of God, as he is the source of the natural light that makes them self-evident. They are the object of a single mental glance, because they don't exceed a person's capacity to pay attention, and their self-evidence can be renewed effortlessly by simply returning attention to them.

Syllogisms, on the contrary, exceed the capacity of the attention and therefore require the knowledge of God, for he is the guarantor of the certainty of their conclusions even though the finite mind is no longer attending to the arguments which led to them:

> There are other truths which are perceived very clearly by our intellect so long as we attend to the arguments on which our knowledge of them depends; and we are therefore incapable of doubting them during this time. But we may forget the arguments in question and later remember simply the conclusions which were deduced from them. The question will now arise as to whether we possess the same firm and immutable conviction concerning these conclusions, when we simply recollect that they were previously deduced from quite evident principles (our ability to call them "conclusions" presupposes such a recollection). My reply is that the required certainty is indeed possessed by those whose knowledge of God enables them to understand that the intellectual faculty which he gave them cannot but tend towards the truth; but the required certainty is not possessed by others. (CSM II 104–5; AT VII 146)

The demonstration of the existence of an omnipotent and benevolent God that is not a deceiver prevents this degradation of clear and distinct cognition into mere opinion.[9] The knowledge of God ensures that clear and distinct cognitions are not invalidated by slipping into memory, that storage and recall are sufficiently reliable so that clear and distinct cognitions do not lose their privileged epistemological status.

What is not entirely clear at this point is how the demonstration of the existence of God solves this problem. To be noted first is that the proofs of God are designed to exclude the possibility of a deceiving *genius malignus* rearing its ugly head in the very moment he is about to be banished. For by slipping from attention, or in Descartes' conceptual metaphorics, by dropping out of sight, a clear and distinct cognition becomes vulnerable to manipulation and thus subject to doubt. With the demonstration of an omnipotent and benevolent God the memory of clear and distinct conclusions is guaranteed as certain, even though their clarity and distinctness no longer constitute a *praesens evidentia*. Thus, Descartes' meditator can summarize:

> Now, however, I have perceived that God exists, and at the same time I have understood that everything else depends on him, and that he is no deceiver; and I have drawn the conclusion that everything which I clearly and distinctly perceive is

of necessity true. Accordingly, even if I am no longer attending to the arguments [*etiamsi non attendam amplius ad rationes*] which led me to judge that this is true, as long as I remember that I clearly and distinctly perceived it, there are no counterarguments which can be adduced to make me doubt it, but on the contrary I have true and certain knowledge of it. And I have knowledge not just of this matter, but of all matters which I remember ever having demonstrated, in geometry and so on. (CSM II 48; AT VII 70)

Having knowledge of an omnipotent and benevolent God is essential as it compensates for the limited capacity of attention and guarantees the memory of clear and distinct cognitions.

Yet a new dilemma immediately arises. How can Descartes' meditator demonstrate the existence of God without assuming the conclusion in advance? Or put differently, how can it be that Descartes' proofs of God are not also afflicted by the meditator's limited attention span?[10] In this mnemonic version of the Cartesian circle, the knowledge of God, brought about by the demonstration of his existence, guarantees the reliability of memory. Yet the first two proofs are so long that they rely for their successful functioning on memory that at that point has not been guaranteed. Descartes points to this dilemma in the dedicatory letter to the Faculty of the Sorbonne by drawing a parallel with geometrical proofs:

But although I regard the proofs as quite certain and evident, I cannot therefore persuade myself that they are suitable to be grasped by everyone. In geometry there are many writings left by Archimedes, Apollonius, Pappus and others which are accepted by everyone as evident and certain because they contain absolutely nothing that is not very easy to understand when considered on its own, and each step fits in precisely with what has gone before; yet because they are somewhat long, and demand a very attentive reader, it is only comparatively few people who understand them. In the same way, although the proofs I employ here are in my view as certain and evident as the proofs of geometry, if not more so, it will, I fear, be impossible for many people to achieve an adequate perception of them, both because they are rather long and some depend on others, and also, above all, because they require a mind which is completely free of preconceived opinions and which can easily detach itself from involvement with the senses. (CSM II 5; AT VII 4)

Like the "demonstrations of Apollonius," as he writes in a letter to Huygens on July 31, 1640 (CSM III 150–60; AT III 751–52), his metaphysical meditations elude the understanding of most readers. Each individual argumentative step, "considered separately," may be perfectly evident and certain, but the extraordinary length of each step undermines the reader's experience of evidence. For one, a step's evidence and certainty wane as soon as it is no longer the focus of the mind's attention and slips into memory. Furthermore, the proofs' extraordinary length puts a great demand on the memory of the reader, since they have to remember a large number of individual steps in the correct order without leaving any out, for otherwise the proof fails because its evidence is lost. If only a few possessed the necessary attention and memory to maintain focus and therefore certainty, then the soundness of the proofs would de facto depend on them. And this would mean that evidence and certainty paradoxically hinge on an old model of truth, that is, truth by authority, leading to the consequence that the proofs will merely be believed by the masses instead of understood. Descartes, of course, was all too aware of this dilemma, and his letter to the Sorbonne pointed to some possible remedies. Here as elsewhere he emphasizes that these proofs, like the *Meditations* as a whole, "demand a very attentive reader" and "require a mind which is completely free of preconceived opinions and which can easily detach itself from involvement with the senses." Withdrawal from the social world and the exercise of doubt free the meditator from the distractions of the sensory world and, thereby, ensures that their attention remains focused. In other words, the faculty of attention can be exercised, its capacity can be expanded, and its direction improved. Not surprisingly, to find techniques for practicing attention, the meditator turns to the tradition of spiritual exercises.

The Practice of Attention in Spiritual Exercises

As Pierre Hadot has shown, attention, *prosochē*, was integral to philosophical practice in antiquity. For the Stoic sage, in particular, attention involved "a continuous vigilance and presence of the mind, self consciousness which never sleeps, and a constant tension of the spirit. Thanks to this attitude, the philosopher is fully aware of what he does at each instant, and he *wills* his actions fully."[11] In the *Discourse* 4.12, which is exclusively devoted to attention, Epictetus writes about the application of the *kanōn*, the fundamental rule of life, requiring constant attention and vigilance: "We ought to have these principles at command [*echein procheira*], and to do nothing apart from them, but keep the soul intent upon this mark [*ton skopon*]; we must pursue none of the things external, none of the things which are not our own, but as He that is mighty has ordained; pursuing without any hesitation the things that lie within the sphere of the moral purpose, and all other things as they have been given to us" (*Discourses* 4.12.15).[12] At every moment, with each new situation the self needs to ask itself whether a given thing or action is under its control and serves its moral purpose, or whether it is extrinsic to it and belongs to the outside world so should be left alone. Since time never stops, the question arises ever anew and is never settled. In the ideal case the self's vigilance and alertness in applying the canon to the flow of life never cease.

The rule to allow oneself to become invested only in what is under one's control demands focusing the attention on the present moment, as it is only the present that the self can control. Particularly Marcus Aurelius stresses this point in his attempt to discredit the quest for glory and fame: "Jettison everything else, then, and lay hold of these things only, few as they are; and remember withal that it is only this present, a moment of time, that a man lives; all the rest either has been lived or may never be" (*Marcus Aurelius* 3.10).[13] By focusing on the present, the self is able to keep its passions at bay and realize the Stoic ideal of *apatheia*. In *De beneficiis*, Seneca describes the ideal as follows: "Such a man rejoices in the present, and puts no faith in the future; for he who leans upon uncertainties can have no sure support. Free, therefore, from the great anxieties that rack the mind, there is nothing which he hopes for or covets, and, content with what he has, he does not plunge into what is doubtful" (7.2.4).[14] To an extent, *prosochē* can be understood as mindfulness or self-consciousness. Stoic sages are always aware of who they are, what they do, and what their place is in the world, as they must be constantly mindful to align their thought, will, and action with eternal reason and the order of the universe.

The biggest threat for Stoics to the maintenance of mindfulness and to attending to the self and universal reason, not surprisingly, is the onslaught of sensory impressions. Therefore, the *chrēsis tōn phantasiōn* is in particular need of unceasing attention, so the self is ever alert to incoming sensory impressions so as to examine and test them and avoid getting absorbed and distracted. Epictetus devotes a whole discourse to these questions: "In how many ways do the external impressions arise, and what aids should we have ready at hand [*procheira*] to deal with them?" (*Discourses* 1.27). Attention was crucial to the philosophical *paideia* of antiquity, required along with vigilance for philosophy to be put into practice, to make otherwise abstract theoretical precepts one's own and to enact them: not just to have knowledge and wisdom but to act wisely. Otherwise, philosophy remains abstract and divorced from life. Moreover, attention is not required only to practice philosophy but is itself in need of practice. Seneca, Epictetus, and Marcus Aurelius all offer tricks, as it were, for how to "keep thine axioms ready for the diagnosis of things human and divine, and for the performing of every act," "just as physicians always keep their lancets and instruments ready to their hands [*procheira echousi*] for emergency operations" (*Marcus Aurelius* 3.13). For practicing attention eventually renders it habitual, making προσοχή something like the condition of possibility for *constantia*, for making the conversion of the self toward the self permanent. It keeps the mind turned toward itself, attentive to its own self-scrutiny, instead of being captivated by the sensory world and carried away by passions and desires.

Given that the remembrance of God was already part of ancient philosophical practice, it comes as no surprise that early Christian thinkers readily adopted and retooled the pagan exercises of attention for their own purposes.[15] Accordingly, *prosochē* plays a pivotal role in the seminal conversion of Saint Antony, the founding father of monasticism. As we have seen in many examples, Antony received a divine call: he enters a church twice, and twice he hears a verse from the Gospel that spoke directly to him. He sells the last of his possessions and gives his sister over to the care of "respected and trusted virgins," and only then does he "give heed to himself and patiently train himself," finally realizing his conversion. From Athanasius, author of *Vita Antonii*, we learn that Antony responds by following the example of those who "wishing to give attention to [their] life" left their villages so that he can discipline "himself in isolation" (*Vita Antonii* 3).[16] Athanasius thus conceives the monk's conversive turn toward himself and God as an act of attending, making monastic life and practice the operationalization of spiritual attention and vigilance. Free from the distractions of worldly and social life the monk can pay attention to his self as it attends exclusively to God or, as Antony advises, "Live as though dying daily, paying heed to yourselves" (91).

Basil of Caesarea, considered (together with Pachomius) one of the fathers of Eastern monasticism and via Benedict of Nursia and Rufinus of

Aquileia a significant influence on the emergence of Western monasticism, examines the monastic practice of *prosochē* in a sermon devoted to Deuteronomy 15:9: "Pay attention to yourself, lest a hidden word come to be in your heart."[17] "On this basis," as Hadot notes, Basilius "develops an entire theory of *prosochē*, strongly influenced by Stoic and Platonic traditions."[18] For him the practice means turning "the gaze of your soul toward self-scrutiny" (Give Heed 439). For the "scrupulous attention to yourself will be of itself sufficient to guide you to the knowledge of God" (443–44). As already suggested in the sermon's underlying verse, attending is crucial for discernment, not only for discerning the hidden word or thought sneaking into one's heart but more fundamentally for discerning the two natures of which man is composed: "'Give heed to thyself,' that is, to your soul. Adorn it, care for it, to the end that, by careful attention, every defilement incurred as a result of sin may be removed and every shameful vice expelled, and that it may be embellished and made bright with every ornament of virtue. Examine closely what sort of being you are. Know your nature—that your body is mortal, but your soul, immortal; that our life has two denotations, so to speak: one relating to the flesh, and this life is quickly over, the other referring to the soul, life without limit" (435). Attentive self-scrutiny allows the self "to know how to make a suitable allotment to each of the two sides of [its] nature" (435) and "to distinguish between the injurious and the salutary" (433–34). In other words, via discernment attention turns out to be instrumental for the soul's salvation.

John Cassian, one of the most important theologians of discernment, was equally seminal for the theorization of the role of attention in monastic life. Cassian treats attention in the last two conferences of the first part of the *Conferences* that are devoted to prayer,[19] which Abbe Isaac, Cassian's revered interlocutor, describes as follows:

The end of every monk and the perfection of the heart direct him to constant and uninterrupted perseverance in prayer; and, as much as human frailty allows, it strives after an unchanging and continual tranquillity of mind and perpetual purity.... For, as the structure of all the virtues tends to the perfection of prayer, so, unless all things have been joined together and cemented under this capstone, in no way will they be able to remain firm and stable. (*Conferences* 9.2.1)[20]

Prayer is the ultimate telos of the monk's endeavors, as its perfection gives him a foretaste of the "heavenly way of life and glory in this vessel" (10.7.3).

Only if unceasing prayer is the capstone of the edifice of the monk's self can the foundational purity of the heart become manifest in his virtues. One cannot endure without the other. Cassian thus conjoins edification and ascent—much like Descartes does later in a more philosophical and scientific vein. Prayer functions as a *machina mentis* with which the self raises itself up to God: "Every mind is upbuilt and formed in its prayer according to the degree of its purity" (10.6.1).

It is particularly the "small and insignificant" things that "do not permit a monk, for whom even a brief separation from that highest good must be believed to be immediate death and utter ruin, to lay aside earthly impurity and to long for God, upon whom his attention should be ever fixed" (*Conferences* 9.6.4). Because "whatever our soul was thinking about before the time of prayer inevitably occurs to us when we pray as a result of the operation of the memory" (9.3.3), the self needs to cleanse and purge itself before entering into prayer: from other thoughts and memories, its emotions and passions, from anything that distracts it from praying to God. Thus, attention is the psychic operation at the heart of continual prayer, to avoid the mind's "dangerous wandering and straying," which it must avoid "to be elevated to the contemplation of God and to spiritual vision" (9.3.2). Here as elsewhere, the problem manifests itself as distraction, the causes and occasions of which are many. Yet, "when the mind has been established in tranquillity and has been freed from the bonds of every fleshly passion, and the heart's attention is unwaveringly fastened upon the one and highest good, it will fulfill the apostolic words: 'Pray without ceasing'" (9.6.5). Attention is the psychic enactment of the conversive turn, the mind's turning toward God, of thinking of God; and *mnēmē theou*, which we first encountered in the context of meditation, was the phrase used to denote this turn of the mind.[21]

In response to Abbe Isaac's articulation of the ideal of perfect prayer, Cassian's more simple-minded companion Germanus raises a set of concerns he will voice twice more in the tenth conference, indicating their urgency and gravity:

If only we were able to enjoy uninterruptedly these spiritual thoughts in the same way and with the same ease that we usually conceive their beginnings. For when they have been conceived in our heart through the recollection of Scripture or through recalling some spiritual deeds or, even more, through a glimpse of the heavenly mysteries, they immediately vanish, having as it were imperceptibly taken flight. And when our mind finds further occasions for spiritual thoughts, others creep back in and those that had been laid hold of slip rapidly away. Thus the mind has no constancy of its own, nor does it possess of its own power any immutability with regard to holy thoughts even when it seems somehow or other to hold on to them, and it can be believed that it has conceived them by chance and not by its own effort. (*Conferences* 9.7.1)

For the monk, the problem is not the initial turn of one's attention toward God, that is, conceiving a "spiritual thought" in the first place. The problem is keeping one's attention fixed on it, persisting in a thought once conceived. The issue here is again *constantia*, staying turned (mentally) toward God, rather than *conversio*, which is the initial turn. Somewhat surprisingly, Germanus is concerned less with the mind getting distracted or perverted by impious thoughts than by other pious ones that intrude, framing the issue as distraction as such. Fallen and subject to temporality, the mind "has no constancy of its own." It cannot hold on to a single thought for long, with every one, however pious, being prematurely replaced by the next one—and so on. Due to this congenital inconstancy, the mind experiences its own activity of thinking as highly contingent and volatile, with thoughts coming and going seemingly of their own volition, making attention in a sense the measure of the mind's control over its own actions. The mind's distractibility, aside from raising the specter of thoughts not being one's own mental acts at all, is what makes discernment necessary. Were the mind able to control its thoughts and attend to them at will, it could minimize the occurrence of unwanted and unauthored thoughts. Conversely, perfect attention makes discernment obsolete. If the mind can control its thoughts in such a way that it thinks nothing but God and other holy thoughts, the thoughts must be good and must have the Holy Spirit as their author. *In extremis*, the monk would be able to think of nothing but God, to think no other thoughts. His *mnēmē theou* would be unending, ultimately culminating in a heavenly *visio beatifica*, and thus death and afterlife.

Of course, perfect and perpetual attention is not of this world, so when Germanus speaks again, it is to demand that Isaac provide his listeners with "this most sublime discipline [*sublimissimae disciplinae*], which teaches to cling constantly to God" (*Conferences* 10.8.3). Given that his mind is "ever wandering to and fro, tossed about by different things as if it were drunk" (10.8.5), Germanus's chief concern is not the initial lapse of its attention, which is unavoidable, but, much like the philosopher without the Cartesian method, the unnecessary delays and detours that impede its return to its original thought:

> For it happens that when we have strayed from spiritual theoria and then come back to ourselves [*convertimur*], as if we are awakened from out of a deadly sleep, and seek that by which we may be able to revive the spiritual awareness [*spiritalem memoriam*] that had disappeared, we are held back by the delay of searching [*inquisitionis mora*]. Before we find it we lose sight of our goal once again, and before any spiritual vision is brought forth, our heart's attentiveness [*cordis intentio*], already conceived, vanishes. (10.8.4–5)

Because of the mind's inherent flight of ideas, it always runs the danger of being distracted and diverted again so that it fails to return by the direct route and is destined to eternal errancy. What the mind needs is a point of orientation or landmark on which it can keep its gaze fixed and that can, thereby, guide its movement.

> This confusion certainly besets us because we do not keep something special fixed before our eyes as a kind of formula [*formulam*] to which the errant mind [*vagus animus*] can be recalled after numerous detours and divagations [*anfractus ac discursus*] and into which it can enter, as into a safe harbor, after repeated shipwrecks. (10.8.4–5)

With a such a formula the mind can stay on course, even when it has been detoured. Abbe Isaac assures his listeners that it is "not without reason" that the passage from Psalms, known subsequently as *Deus in adiutorium*, has been "selected from out of the whole body of Scripture" (10.10.3). Its brevity makes it easily memorable and recitable so it can always be kept ready at hand. It is universally applicable, as "it adjusts itself to every condition and every attack" (10.10.3–4). This universal applicability concerns not only one's circumstances but also the self. By continually meditating and reciting such verses, the monk makes them entirely his own, "not as if they were composed by the prophet but as if they were his own utterances and his own prayer" (10.11.4).

Most important, and somewhat paradoxically, Abbe Isaac insists, that Psalm 70:1 is also effective against distraction. Unlike other scriptural verses and prayers, Psalm 70:1 is not subject to distraction, and it is this immunity that makes it such an effective formula for keeping the mind's attention fixed on God.

If I am boiling over with a multitude of different distractions of soul and with a fickle heart and am unable to control my wandering thoughts, and if I cannot even pour out my prayer without interruption and without imagining foolish phantasies and recalling words and deeds, and if I feel myself constricted by such dry barrenness that I feel I am not begetting any spiritual thoughts at all, then, in order that I may deserve to be freed from this foulness of mind, from which I am unable to extricate myself with many groans and sighs, I will cry out in my need: "O God, incline [*intende*] unto my aid; O Lord, make haste to help me."

On the other hand, if

I feel that, thanks to the Holy Spirit's visitation, I have attained a direction of soul, steadfastness of thought, and joy of heart, along with an unspeakable gladness and ecstasy of mind, and if with an abundance of spiritual thoughts I have, due to a sudden illumination from the Lord, perceived an overflow of very holy ideas which had been completely hidden from me before, then, in order that I might deserve to abide longer in these, I should frequently and anxiously cry: "O God, incline [*intende*] unto my aid; O Lord, make haste to help me." (*Conferences* 10.10.11–12)

Psalm 70:1 is a prayer against distraction in prayer. Its invocation (performatively) frees the monk from intruding thoughts, and its recitation (again performatively) allows him to persist in his "very holy ideas." But how can this Psalm be immune from distraction? How does it differ from most other "holy ideas," which are subject to the same postlapsarian inconstancy of thought as the unholy ones? The exact wording in the Vulgate is revealing: "Deus in adiutorium meum intende; Domine ad adiuvandum me festina." Immediately striking about this invocation is that it calls on God to turn his attention (in Latin *intende*) to the *meum*, the speaker's self.[22] Evidently, the self's attention is aided by God's attention to the self. By calling on God's attention, the self admits to its "own frailty" and, simultaneously, communicates its "confidence in a protection that is always present and at hand [*praesentis semper adstantisque*]" (*Conferences* 10.10.3). Unlike one's inconstant self, God "is always looking upon our struggles" (10.10.4). As Augustine, to whom we will return shortly, lays things out in the *De civitate Dei*, God's attention is perfect. For "his knowledge is not like ours, which has three tenses: present, past, and future. God's knowledge has not change or variation. 'With him there is no alternation, or shadow of movement.' Nor does his attention pass from one thought to another; all things which he knows are present at the same time to his incorporeal vision. He knows events in time without any temporal acts of knowledge, just as he moves events in time, without any temporal motions in himself" (11.21).[23] God's attention never wanes and his turn toward the human self never lapses, making his help always available.

Always there, God's help must nevertheless be called upon. Psalm 70:1 "warns those of us who are enjoying spiritual successes and are glad of heart that we must never be exalted or puffed up because of our good fortune, which it testifies cannot be maintained without the protection of God, for it begs him to come to our aid not only at all times but also quickly" (*Conferences* 10.10.5). The admission of the human frailty of distraction, in other words, activates God's attention and assistance, making the invocation of Psalm 70:1 strangely performative. Paradoxically, the success of Psalm 70:1 springs from its failure. The unceasing invocation necessarily fails because human attention is inconstant. But because it cannot but fail, God attends to the self and is always on standby for when the mind's attention wanes, when it is reinvigorated and refocused in answer to the call for assistance. The formula of Psalm 70:1 thus works exactly as Germanus imagines. While not completely preventing the divagations of the erring mind, it does provide a fixed point that never drops out of mind entirely to which its mental gaze can return the instant it lapses. Abbe Isaac concludes confidently that following the formula and "continually meditating on this verse" will "keep the mind's whole and entire attention fixed on God" (10.14.3).

It falls to Augustine to combine the devotional utilization of attention with its philosophical conceptionalization. In *De Trinitate*, the account he gives of the different processes of human perception and cognition, as might be expected, is patterned on the trinity.[24] Vision, corporeal and mental, combines three different but interrelated processes: "(i) The form of the body that is seen, (ii) its image impressed [*imago eius impressa*] on the sense, which is vision, or the sense informed [*sensus formatus*], and (iii) the will of the soul [*voluntas animi*] which directs [*admovet*] the sense to the sensible thing and keeps the vision itself fixed [*tenet*] upon it" (*On the Trinity* 11.2.5).[25] The fixation of the mental vision on the impression Augustine calls "the attention of the mind [*animi intentio*]" (11.2.2). Whereas objects belong to the outer world, vision (as in-formed sense) to both the outer and inner world, the attention is "proper to the mind alone" (11.2.2). The attention draws object and vision together in such a way that the former can in-form the latter, making perception both passive and active. While the sense's in-formation is largely passive, the direction and fixation of the sense on the object are active. By defining attention as an act of will, its management becomes morally and soteriologically inflected so that this rather technical account of perception and cognition also offers a glimpse of attention's role in facilitating the soul's journey toward salvation.

Cognition is analogously trinitarian in its structure. In thought, the forms considered by the mental vision are not received directly from the senses but supplied by memory. To these forms "the will may again turn its gaze in order to be formed by it from within," in which case the trinity is formed by "memory, inner vision, and the will, which unites both. And when these three are drawn together [*coguntur*] into unity, then from that combination [*coactu*] itself, they are called thought [*cogitatio*]" (*On the Trinity* 11.3.6). This inner trinity looks very different. The external object is replaced by the mnemonic form, corporeal vision by its mental counterpart, and only the *voluntas animi* stays the same. In a way, then, the willful attention directs and organizes the self's entire mental life. It should thus not be surprising that this rather technical account of perception and cognition also offers a brief glimpse of attention's role in facilitating the soul's journey toward salvation. Attention's immediate end is the event of sensual in-formation that is vision, be it corporeal or intellectual. But given that the ultimate end of the will is happiness, the immediate end is only a "passing act" that refers beyond itself to higher ends and, ultimately, to the final *visio beatifica*, or vision of God himself.

> Therefore, the series of good wills that are joined together is a kind of road [*iter*] on which there are, as it were, certain steps for those ascending to happiness [*ascendentium ad beatitudinem*]; . . . we speak of the will at rest as an end, when it is still referred to something further, in the same way we speak of a foot at rest in walking, when it is placed whence another may tread in order to follow a man's steps. But if something so pleases us that the will rests and finds some delight in it, yet this is not yet the end for which it is striving; but this, too, is referred to something further, so that it may be regarded not as his native land, but the resting place or even the lodging of a traveler. (11.6.10)

Augustine thus inscribes attention into a kind of meditative ascent. When attention is absorbed by the visual allure of the outer world and finds fulfillment in the enjoyment (*frui*) of the visible and temporal, instead of using (*uti*) it to turn toward the inner light and ascend to the invisible things, it is caught up in sinful idolatry.[26] Attention must not become overly attached to the objects of vision insofar as all objects of corporeal vision and nearly all mental visions are not ends in themselves but waystations to the ultimate beatific vision of God. Of course, as a permanent vision of God is not attainable in this life, the *intentio* must go back to wandering even after realizing its goal, however briefly.

Not coincidentally, attention plays a pivotal role at key moments of the journey that Augustine narrates in his *Confessions*. Particularly in Book Eight, Augustine associates attention and its cognates with his complicated conversion. Ponticianus, he writes, "turned my attention back to myself [*eius retorquebas me ad me ipsum*]" when "I did not wish to observe myself [*nollem me adtendere*] ... twisted and filthy, covered in sores and ulcers. And I looked and was appalled, but there was no way of escaping from myself" (*Confessions* 8.7.16).[27] The turn to the self and the recognition of one's own iniquity is the first step in its turn toward God. The ultimate shift in attention for Augustine occurs in conjunction with the famous *tolle, lege*, for which attention is crucial to his discerning it as a divine command rather than a random and thus ultimately meaningless children's chant. This recognition is also a recognition of God's turn toward him that ultimately prompts him to complete his own turn toward God. Similar to Psalm 70:1 in Cassian's *Conferences*, in Augustine's conversion human and divine attention condition each other.

Given attention's importance in Augustine's biographical narrative, its inclusion in the theory of conversion that the last three books unfold is not surprising. His most extensive discussion of attention—along with distraction or, as he calls it, distension[28]—occurs in Book Eleven, where he describes how attention is integral to the human experience of time.

> What is by now evident and clear is that neither future nor past exists, and it is inexact language to speak of three times—past, present, and future. Perhaps it would be exact to say: there are three times, a present of things past, a present of things present, a present of things to come. In the soul there are these three aspects of time, and I do not see them anywhere else. The present considering the past is the memory, the present considering the present is immediate awareness [*contuitus*], the present considering the future is expectation. (*Confessions* 11.20.26)

Chadwick's translation of *contuitus* as "immediate awareness" points to Augustine's belief, which he shared with the Stoics, that the present is experienced through intuition, which is to say, attention (to the present moment). The tense of attention is the present, and the present is experienced as the present by being attended to. Yet by conceiving all tenses as a function of the present, Augustine runs into the difficulty of accounting for our experience "that time is some kind of extension [*distensionem*]" (11.23.30). For "how do we measure present time when it has no extension [*spatium*]?" (11.21.27). The difficulty arises because of Augustine's initial conflation of two fundamentally different manifestations of time, objective and subjective, or in Andrea Nightingale's vocabulary, earthly and psychic.[29] When time manifests itself as a spatial movement, for instance, in the sun's daily trajectory, it has no *spatium* because each interval within the solar course can be divided ad infinitum. But when the mind turns toward its own experience of time, it experiences it as extended, with some intervals longer than others. Somehow the mind measures time without taking recourse to the material and external world. It is this intuitive extension of time Augustine calls distension or *distensio*.

The question then becomes: "Of what is it a distension?" (*Confessions* 11.26.33). Augustine's answer is as simple as it is profound: "I do not know, but it would be surprising if it is not that of the mind itself" (11.26.33). Again Augustine's examination becomes performative as he exhorts himself:[30] "Stand firm, my mind [*anime meus*], concentrate with resolution [*adtende fortiter*]" (11.27.34). His mind standing firm, he arrives at the answer to his question:

> So it is in you, my mind, that I measure periods of time. Do not distract [*obstrepere*] me; that is, do not allow yourself to be distracted by the hubbub of impressions being made upon you. In you, I affirm, I measure periods of time. The impression which passing events make upon you abides when they are gone. That present consciousness is what I am measuring, not the stream of past events which have caused it. When I measure periods of time, that is what I am actually measuring. (11.27.36)

That the mind has to overcome the distraction "by the hubbub of impressions,"[31] as a condition of fully comprehending how it measures time, brings to the fore the role of attention. Put succinctly, the mind measures time with the span of its attention, the *praesens intentio* that "transfers the future into the past" (11.27.36). "For the mind expects and attends [*adtendit*] and remembers, so that what it expects passes through what has its attention [*quod adtendit*] to what it remembers" (11.28.37). But it cannot be simply the span of the present with which the mind measures time, because "none can deny that present time lacks an extension [*carere spatio*] since it passes in a flash. Yet attention is continuous [*perdurat attentio*], and it is through this that what will be present progresses towards being absent" (11.28.37). Attention stretches out just enough to expect something that isn't yet present and to remember something that is no longer, binding the three tenses together. Distension is the movement of attention from one thought to another, or shifting the perspective, the movement of thoughts before the mind's gaze from future to past. Paradoxically this means that attention measures time by being distracted, by moving from one thought to the next or, to use the terminology of conversion, by turning from the (passing) present thought to the future, next thought. This means that attention is always distension, necessarily distracted by the temporality of the human mind, or more generally, human existence.

Even more paradoxically, distension is a blessing in disguise, for only it propels the self onward and prevents it from attending to and enjoying the temporal world. Were man's attention more stable, he would not be propelled on, would not be always restless and longing for a state in which attention is eternal:

So "I might apprehend him in whom also I am apprehended" (Phil. 3.12–14), and leaving behind the old days I might be gathered to follow the One, "forgetting the past" and moving not towards those future things which are transitory but to "the things which are before" me, not stretched out in distraction [*non distentus*], but extended in reach [*extentus*], not by being pulled apart [*distentionem*] but by concentration [*intentionem*]. So I "pursue the prize of high calling" where I "may hear the voice of high praise" and "contemplate your delight" (Ps. 25.7; 26.4) which neither comes nor goes. (*Confessions* 11.29.39)

Distension both distracts the self and advances it toward the contemplation of divine delight, "which neither comes nor goes," when the mind's attention is extended and thereby capable, like God, of perceiving past, present, and future simultaneously so that there is no longer anything distending or distracting it.

Meditation's ascent toward the *visio beatifica* is fueled by the interplay between distension and attention. The latter keeps it on track and its goal in sight, and the former ensures that the mind doesn't rest along the way and forget its destination. In practical terms, attention is more important for meditation because it must be operationalized, as opposed to distraction, distension's unproductive other. Medieval manuals warned monks of the dangers of distraction and *curiositas* to their daily meditative prayers. Many of the mental tools, the *machina mentis* that Mary Carruthers details in her study on medieval monastic meditation, are designed to aid and improve the monk's attention.[32] In fact, so close was the relation of meditation and attention that the latter became virtually identified with the former, in meditation being understood as concentrated and attentive thought. Descartes was not only heir to his amalgamation; as we see in this chapter's final section, he operationalized attention for all aspects of his philosophical project of cultivating the mind.

Descartes' Art of Attention

From very early on Descartes was finely attuned to the workings of the attention.[33] We remember that the enthusiasm, which made him susceptible to dreams and visions, was brought about by his mind's rigid attentiveness in its search for truth so that he could find "diversion neither in walking nor in human company."[34] Only in his dreams does he find the diversion that his waking mind cannot achieve. Thus, it should not surprise us that attention stands at the center of the treatise he began composing shortly after his conversion. If, as the *Oxford English Dictionary* defines it, attention is "the earnest direction of the mind," then Descartes' *Regulae ad directionem ingenii* has to be read as an ensemble of rules to regulate and manage the attention in the mind's pursuit of truth. The *Meditations* is similarly concerned with the management and practice of attention, Descartes stating that he "would have nothing to do with anyone who was not willing to join me in meditating and giving the subject attentive consideration" (CSM II 112; AT VII 157). Like the *Regulae*, the *Meditations* is designed "to steer my readers' minds away from [opinions] which they have never properly examined—opinions which they have acquired not on the basis of any firm reasoning but from the senses alone" (CSM II 112; AT VII 158), so that ultimately for Descartes meditating and giving something "careful attention" are nearly synonymous (see also CSM II 97; AT VII 135). In this light, Descartes is not overly optimistic that there are many readers who are able to follow his direction: "For I expect that hardly any of my readers will be prepared to give such careful attention to everything I have written that they will remember all the contents by the time they come to an end. Those who do not remember everything may easily fall prey to certain doubts" (CSM II 109; AT VII 154–55). Thus, the *Meditations* as a whole is affected by the same limitations to attention as individual proofs. Before I turn to attention's significance for the various mental techniques employed in the *Meditations*, I examine more closely its role for the one particular mental operation on which the first two proofs of God hinges: deduction.

The two basic operations considered in the *Regulae*, intuition and deduction, "on which we must . . . exclusively rely in our acquisition of knowledge" (CSM I 33; AT X 400), depend on the operation of attention.[35] Indeed, given how Descartes defines it, intuition in particular seems little more than the operation of attention.[36] It is

> the indubitable conception of a clear and attentive mind [*mentis purae & attentae*] which proceeds solely from the light of reason. . . . Thus everyone can mentally intuit that he exists, that he is thinking, that a triangle is bounded by just three lines, and a sphere by a single surface, and the like. Perceptions such as these are more numerous than most people realize [*animadvertunt*]. (CSM I 14; AT X 368)

Cleansed of the contaminating sensations, fantasies, and thoughts that threaten to distract attention, intuition allows the mind to arrive at a distinct cognition. Yet the clear and distinct cognition of innate ideas such as the *cogito* is not easily noticed (*animadvertunt*), as most disdain "to turn their minds [*mentem convertere*] to such simple matters" (CSM I 14; AT X 368). We will come back to these two different forms of turning one's attention. To be noted here is that the *animadversio* of noticing hinges on the mind's *conversio* toward itself and the innate ideas it contains. Rule Nine, devoted to how "we must concentrate [*convertere*] our mind's eye totally upon the most insignificant and easiest of matters," registers the possibility of training "perspicacity in the distinct intuition of particular things" (CSM I 33; AT X 400). For example,

> craftsmen who engage in delicate operations, and are used to fixing their eyes [*oculorum aciem*] on a single point, acquire through practice the ability to make perfect distinctions between things, however minute and delicate. The same is true of those who never let their thinking be distracted [*distrahunt*] by many different objects at the same time, but always devote their whole attention to the simplest and easiest of matters: they become perspicacious. (CSM I 33; AT X 400–401)

The comparison of intuition with corporeal vision goes back as far as Plato (if not farther), exemplified by his allegory of the cave in Book Seven of the *Republic*. Via Plotinus (specifically *Ennead* I.6), it gets transmitted to Augustine for whom the notion of the *acies mentis*, the gaze of the mind, becomes pivotal in his notion of the *exercitatio animae*. His *On the Trinity*, in particular, presents such a training of the mind, instructing readers that the *acies mentis* requires purification to equip it to cognize God *per speculum et in aenigmate* (through a glass darkly) in this life and *facie ad faciem* (face-to-face) in the next (see 15.11.21–14.23). From there *acies mentis* becomes a common conceptual trope in medieval piety and philosophy.[37]

Much more could be said about the parallels between Augustine and Descartes in regard to their understanding of mental vision, to which we return in Chapter 6. Before moving on to the role of attention in deduction, we should note two aspects. First, the parallelization of mental vision and attention implies that the former can be trained like the eye of Descartes' craftsman.[38] The clarity and distinctness of intuition are achieved by fixing the mind's attention on a single thought and blocking out others, just as the craftsman can practice keeping his eyes fixed on a single object and making ever-finer distinctions. Second, Rule Eleven takes up intuition once again and introduces a new aspect by focusing on its temporality: "Two things are required for mental intuition: first, the proposition intuited must be clear and distinct; second, the whole proposition must be understood all at once, and not bit by bit" (CSM I 37; AT X 407). Like attention in ancient philosophy, intuition operates in the present tense and requires concentration on the present moment. In other words, its *praesens evidentia* doesn't last.

In the performance of a deduction, which entails "inferring one thing from another" (CSM I 37; AT X 407) and thus happens in time, attention's role is more complicated. Insofar as each individual and isolated deductive step is "performed by means of intuition" (CSM I 37; AT X 407), the links in the deductive chain are forged by individual acts of attention. Preempting doubts about the rationale for introducing a "second mode of knowing," Descartes observes early on in the *Regulae* that

this distinction had to be made, since very many facts which are not self-evident [*evidentes*] are known with certainty, provided they are inferred from true and known principles through a continuous and uninterrupted movement of thought [*per continuum et nullibi interruptum cogitationis motum*] in which each individual proposition is clearly intuited. This is similar to the way in which we know that the last link in a long chain is connected to the first: even if we cannot take in at one glance all the intermediate links on which the connection depends, we can have knowledge of the connection provided we survey the links one after the other, and keep in mind that each link from first to last is attached to its neighbor. Hence we are distinguishing mental intuition from certain deduction on the grounds that we are aware of a movement or a sort of sequence [*motus sive successio*] in the latter but not in the former, and also because immediate self-evidence [*praesens evidentia*] is not required for deduction, as it is for intuition; deduction in a sense gets its certainty from memory. It follows that those propositions which are immediately inferred from first principles can be said to be known in one respect through intuition, and in another respect through deduction. But the first principles themselves are known only through intuition, and the remote conclusions only through deduction. (CSM I 15; AT X 369–70)

In contrast to intuitions, which are self-evident, deductions can be certain only if they are directly inferred from clear and distinct intuitions. How it is precisely that self-evidence is downgraded to mere certainty is a matter of the limited capacity of attention, or mental vision. We recall that a clear and distinct intuition depends on attention being undivided and trained on a single thought, because once the mind's attention is divided and it must choose on what to focus, the previously focused thought is displaced, no longer present but absent and thus the object of memory rather than intuition; and memory is "fallible [*labilis*]," as Descartes remarks in Rule Sixteen (CSM I 67; AT X 454). At best it lends certainty, but no *praesens evidentia*. Thus, the farther the mind moves on from its original intuition anchoring the deductive chain, or the greater the number of propositions or thoughts that must be committed to memory, the more certainty is degraded.

As Julie Klein has astutely observed, "Descartes's position is that memory both enables and compromises deduction."[39] Descartes' frequent references to the "lapses of memory [*memoriae lapsum*]" (CSM I 43; AT X 417) and its characterization as "fallible [*labilis*]" suggest that he attributed its failings and limitations to man's postlapsarian condition. But whether we attribute the shortcomings of memory to its fallen, corporeal basis, as Klein does, is secondary to its close association with an intellectual and scientific culture that privileged authority and tradition over independent thinking.[40] As I demonstrated in Chapter 2, the overreliance on memory allowed the mind to absolve itself from thinking independently and grounding all knowledge in the self-evidence of autopsy. Descartes' response to this *aporia* is not to improve memory by developing his own *ars memoria*, as so many of his contemporaries did.[41] He chose instead to cultivate attention, thereby expanding the scope of the self's mental gaze and the range of self-evident cognition. After explicating "the main secret of my method" in Rules Five and Six, dealing with the "ordering and arranging of the objects on which we must concentrate our mind's eye [*ad quae mentis acies est convertenda*]" (CSM I 20; AT X 379), Descartes reveals in Rule Seven how to minimize the role of memory in deductions and, correspondingly, maximize attention:

> Truths which ... are not deduced immediately from first and self-evident principles ... sometimes require such a long chain of inferences that when we arrive at such a truth it is not easy to recall the entire route which led us to it. That is why we say that a continuous movement of thought is needed to make good any weakness of memory. If, for example, by way of separate operations, I have come to know first what the relation between the magnitudes A and B is, and then between B and C, and between C and D, and finally between D and E, that does not entail my seeing what the relation is between A and E; and I cannot grasp what the relation is just from those I already know, unless I recall all of them. (CSM I 25; AT X 387–88)

Descartes' starting point is a problem we have encountered before, both in the *Regulae* and the *Meditations*: While the individual relations between A and E can all be separately intuited, the deduction as a whole exceeds the scope of the mental gaze so that parts have to be committed to memory and recalled. The solution he proposes is somewhat counterintuitive:

> I shall run through them several times in a continuous movement of the imagination, simultaneously intuiting one relation and passing on the next, until I have learnt to pass from the first to the last so swiftly that memory is left with practically no role to play, and I seem to intuit the whole thing at once. In this way our memory is relieved [*subvenitur*], the sluggishness [*tarditas*] of our intelligence redressed, and its capacity in some way enlarged. (CSM I 25; AT X 388)

By running through the individual steps over and over and faster and faster, more and more of them fit into the scope of attention until finally the whole deduction can be intuited in a single and unified glance—and "memory is left with practically no role to play."[42] Repeatedly practicing a deduction permanently expands the capacity of the attention, enabling it to hold a greater number of elements without being divided and confused. The movement of the mind thus eliminates itself, resulting in an intuition in which all individual relations are present simultaneously. At the same time, the paradoxical consequence of training the mind's attention is that it renders deduction, the mental operation central to building the edifice of knowledge, increasingly obsolete—akin to the sublation of textual mediation in rhetorical *evidentia*. By expanding the attention, all steps become subject of *praesens evidentia* and object of the mind's autopsy.

In Rule Fifteen Descartes suggests that symbolic notation can help ameliorate the limitations of attention: "It is generally helpful if we draw these figures and display them before our external senses. In this way it will be easier for us to keep our mind alert [*attenta*]" (CSM I 65; AT X 453). Bringing the thoughts represented by the figures before one's physical eyes takes little mental effort, as they remain fixed by their material inscription and are no longer subject to the mind's inexorable flight of thought. Furthermore, the physical *tabula* is more capacious than the *tabula* of thoughts we encountered in Chapter 3, so the mind can intuit more thoughts in a single gaze. Rule Sixteen details how graphic and symbolic representation keeps ready at hand, the equivalent of the Stoic *procheira echein*, those thoughts that slip from the mind's attention and would have to be committed to memory: "As for the things which do not require the immediate attention of the mind [*praesentem mentis attentionem*], however necessary they may be for the conclusion, it is better to represent them by very concise symbols rather than by complete figures. It will thus be impossible for our memory to go wrong, and our mind will not be distracted [*distrahetur*] by having to retain these while it is taken up with deducing other matters" (CSM I 66; AT X 454). Symbolic notation economizes thought in ways that can be exploited to solve the problem with deductive reasoning, as we discussed earlier, using "very concise symbols" to move through the steps in the reasoning "with the swiftest sweep of thought and intuit as many as possible at the same time" (CSM I 67; AT X 455).[43] By displaying the individual steps on a *tabula* that can be taken in one glance, symbolic notation achieves the same *evidentia* as an intuition:[44] "With this device we shall not just be economizing with words but, and this is the important point, we shall also be displaying the terms of the problem in such a pure and naked light that, while nothing useful will be omitted, nothing superfluous will be included" (CSM I 67; AT X 455). Using symbolic notation in this way to facilitate deduction is not an option for Descartes' meditator in the *Meditations*. They don't prove the existence of their body and the outside world until the Sixth Meditation, and here in the Third the meditator is still firm in their resolve to doubt all sensory perceptions. Belonging to the sensory and corporeal world, writing simply doesn't yet exist for them. So what does Descartes' meditator do to escape the vicious circle? In contrast to Descartes' suggestion in the *Regulae*, the meditator doesn't go over the first proof again and again in ever-faster movements of thought until it can be taken in *tota simul*. It was probably too long, complicated, and technical for that or, in short, unintuitive, which may have been Descartes' takeaway from the *Regulae*. Moreover, the intuition of innate ideas had turned out to be not as straightforward and foolproof as he imagined then. With the exception of the *cogito*, which we have seen him cite as an example of an intuition already in the *Regulae*, the other innate ideas are not totally immune to doubt. As Descartes' meditator demonstrates in the First Meditation, like sensory perceptions and deductions, the other innate ideas need to be grounded even though their validation is accomplished differently—needless to say, through the clear and distinct cognition of an omnipotent and benevolent God.

Instead, Descartes' meditator chooses a parallel path. Rather than try to compress the long first proof, which would probably have remained beyond the capacity of the attention anyway, the meditator replaces it with progressively shorter ones until arriving at the third, which no longer counts as a deduction but as an intuition, because the entire ontological argument can be taken in *tota simul*, which is to say, simply intuited.[45] Each succeeding proof not only relies less and less on memory but also benefits from the way each builds on the other, with succeeding proofs taking up elements of the preceding ones and incorporating them in abbreviated form.[46] Not coincidentally, the final and shortest proof occurs when Descartes' meditator turns back toward the sensory world and runs the greatest risk of being distracted. In the face of distracting sensory impressions they cannot afford to run through the whole first or second proof every time they want to assure themself of the reliability of their memory. Instead, they simply bring to mind the intuition of God's necessary existence before turning toward the sensory world again.

Yet this is not the whole story. The function of the deductive demonstration of God in the *Meditations* is not the same as the more "secular" deductions of the *Regulae*. The flavor of the latter is scientific, its conversive origin notwithstanding. The goal is the formulation of a *mathesis universalis*, and the rules' deployment of attention is thus more or less technical. In contrast, attention in the *Meditations* is more meditative and psychagogic, in line with the book's spiritual pedigree and character, and closer to John Cassian's and Augustine's usage. The *Regulae* prescribes starting from a generic intuition and from there constructing a deductive chain that reaches as far as possible, into infinity if possible. The movement of thought is centrifugal; it goes outward, with attention focused on the solidity of the individual (though generic) connective links, not on a particular destination. In contrast, the meditative movement of the mind in the *Meditations* has a quite specific beginning and end. It begins by turning away from the sensory world toward the self and a very particular intuition—the *cogito*—and from there ascends to God. Only once God has been intuited can the movement be reversed and the mind turn back toward the world, at which point the *Meditations* comes to a close. In this sense, the *Meditations* is the prequel to the *Regulae* or, of course, to Descartes' physics. Inversely, the *Regulae* starts where the *Meditations* ends. Attention thus also has the function of keeping the mind steadily on track during its meditative journey inward. The focus is not on sensory or adventitious ideas, and also not on the fictitious ideas of the imagination, but on the ideas that are innate to the mind. Correspondingly, attention is the *voluntas*, to invoke Augustine's terminology in *De trinitate*, that directs thought, as opposed to perception or the imagination. In short, in the *Meditations* attention is not only endogenous but also endoteleological.

To deepen this understanding, let us retrace, once again, the path of Descartes' meditator, this time guided by Descartes' treatment of attention. They withdraw from the social world so that their concentration will be unencumbered. Their radicalization and universalization of doubt has a similar function, as it turns their attention away from the sensory world and its distractions. By habituating doubt, itself contingent on constant vigilance, the mind is able to resist being distracted by the constant flow of sensory impressions. Attention plays a similarly important role in the performance of the *cogito*. The "*I am, I exist*," writes Descartes, "is necessarily true whenever [*quoties*] it is put forward by me or conceived in my mind" (CSM II 17; AT VII 25). The *cogito* becomes true and self-evident "whenever" the mind attends to its act of thinking. And concomitantly, the *ego sum, ego existo* "is certain ... for as long as [*nempe quandiu*] I am thinking" (CSM II 18; AT VII 27).⁴⁷ The *praesens evidentia* of the *cogito*, in other words, is coextensive with the mind's attention span, and attention in the sense of concentration on the present moment is responsible for the *praesens evidentia* of the *cogito*. Descartes' meditator even goes on to claim, "Were I totally to cease from thinking, I should totally cease to exist." And in modulated form Descartes repeats the claim in the Sixth Set of Replies by making the *cogito* a function of attention: "The inner awareness of one's thought and existence is so innate in all men that, although we may pretend [*fingere*] that we do not have it if we are overwhelmed by preconceived opinions and pay more attention [*attenti*] to words than to their meanings, we cannot in fact fail to have it. Thus when anyone notices [*advertit*] that he is thinking and that it follows from this that he exists, even though he may never before have asked what thought is or what existence is, he still cannot fail to have sufficient knowledge of them both to satisfy himself in this regard" (CSM II 285; AT VII 422). Because the "inner awareness of one's thought" is innate, attention makes everyone capable of the *cogito*. It only has to be actualized by turning the mind's attention away from sensory impressions and preconceived opinions toward its own activity of thinking.

Descartes' sophisticated and differentiated vocabulary to describe the workings of attention comes to light in this passage. *Attendere* and *attentus*, which together appear more than twenty times in the *Meditations*,⁴⁸ capture acts of attention that are more deliberate, controlled, and sustained, as it were, "intentional."⁴⁹ *Advertere*, which occurs seventeen times, denotes the act of noticing, of taking note, that is, the initial turning of and coming to the mind's attention. *Adversio* is thus more fortuitous or, to use a Cartesian term, adventitious. The mind's attention is directed toward its object rather than actively directs it. Put succinctly and more technically, *adversio* is more exogenous and *attentio* more endogenous.⁵⁰ Descartes frequently (also twenty-four times) employs a third term, *animadvertere*, that functions similarly to *advertere* to refer to acts of noticing or realizing. Interestingly, *animadversio*, in contrast to *adversio*, often entails the realization of a falsehood: that something is not as it seemed. The most striking and significant instance of such a "turning of the soul" toward and recognition of falsehood is the *animadverti* with which the First Meditation begins: "Some years ago I was struck [*Animadverti jam ante aliquot annos*] by the large number of falsehoods that I had accepted as true in my childhood, and by the highly doubtful nature of the whole edifice that I had subsequently based on them" (CSM II 12; AT VII 17).[51] Thus, the meditator's *aversio* from the sensory world, enacted by the radical doubt, is launched by an act of (coming to) attention—bringing us to the final term employed by Descartes to designate the working of attention: *convertere*. As we saw in Chapter 3, Descartes, like John Cassian and Augustine, figures the attention's turn toward the self and concomitantly toward God as a conversion—and vice versa. Attending to the self requires a conversion of the mental gaze (CSM II 35; AT VII 51), and thinking of God is turning the "whole attention to him" (CSM II 38; AT VII 54). The following passage from the beginning of the third proof shows the complicated interplay of the different forms of attending:

> Not only are all these things [ideas of material things] very well known and transparent to me when regarded in this general way, but in addition there are countless particular features regarding shape, number, motion, and so on, which I perceive when I give them my attention [*attendendo percipio*]. And the truth of these matters is so open and so much in harmony with my nature, that on first discovering them [*primùm detego*] it seems that I am not so much learning something new as remembering what I knew before; or it seems like noticing for the first time [*ad ea primùm advertere*] things which were long present within me although I had never turned my mental gaze [*in alla obtutum mentis convertissem*] on them before. (CSM II 44; AT VII 63–64)

The geometrical features of material of things become intelligible when the mind attends to them, for they are part of the very fabric of the mind, which is the reason that detecting them seems to Descartes' meditator less like acquiring new knowledge and more akin to Platonic *anamnesis*.[52] The invocation of Plato here is, of course, no coincidence, as Descartes figures this remembering "what I knew before" as his ancient predecessor did as a turning of the mental gaze, or *conversio obtutus mentis*.

Significantly, Descartes does not often speak of remembering in this regard; instead, he employs variations on attention to describe how the mind accesses its innate ideas.[53] "I consider my opinions to be the oldest opinions of all, since they are the truest," he writes in the Seventh Set of Replies. "My principal aim has always been to draw attention [*animadvertendis*] to certain simple truths which are innate in our minds, so that as soon as they are pointed to others, they will consider that they have always known them" (CSM II 312; AT VII 464). Thus, the *Meditations* seeks to direct readers' attention toward their innate ideas, which they have latently always already known yet never noticed.⁵⁴ Descartes' role is merely to point them out to his readers, thereby preserving their self-reliance and autonomy so that they can exercise their own powers of thought (see CSM II 97; AT VII 136). In paragraph 75 of the *Principia philosophiae* Descartes summarizes the "rules to be observed in order to philosophize correctly." After laying aside all preconceived opinions, "we must give our attention [*attendendum*] in an orderly way to the notions that we have within us, and we must judge to be true all and only those whose truth we clearly and distinctly recognize when we attend [*attendendo*] to them in this way" (CSM I 221; AT VIIIA 38). Put succinctly, it is an act of attention that gives the mind access to its innate ideas and that enables the mind to do metaphysics.

But as paragraph 75 indicates, attention's role in metaphysical inquiry does not end there. To arrive at a clear and distinct cognition of the innate ideas that have been noticed, the ideas need to be sufficiently distinguished and separated from preconceived opinions and sensory impressions. Only then will we "acquire the habit of forming clear and distinct concepts of all the things that can be known" (CSM I 221; AT VIIIA 38). As we have seen, Descartes had contended since the *Regulae* that the clear and distinct cognition of an idea hinges on the full commitment of the mind's attention. Paragraph 45 of the *Principia* provides a summary of the criteria: "I call a perception 'clear' when it is present and accessible to the attentive mind [*menti attendenti*]—just as we say that we see something clearly when it is present to the eye's gaze [*oculo intuenti*] and stimulates it with a sufficient degree of strength and accessibility." A cognition is distinct, if in addition to being clear, "it is so sharply separated from all other perceptions that it contains within itself only what is clear" (CSM I 207–8; AT VIIIA 22). Only with the mind's undistracted attention does an idea show itself with its full evidence in the natural light of reason. The cultivation of the mind that Descartes' philosophy champions and endeavors to bring about consists essentially in "attending to the light of nature [*ad naturae lumen attendere*]" (CSM II 77; AT VII 107): the natural light that Descartes noticed, in the sense of the Latin *ad-* and *animadvertere*, when he woke up from his second dream and found his room filled with sparks; the visible manifestations of the *scintilla animae*; the spark of the divine that is buried deep in the human soul and that Cartesian method seeks to uncover and fan.

6

"To Gaze with Wonder and Adoration": *Contemplatio Dei* and Meditative Ascent

Meditation's Final Turn

After bringing to a conclusion the second proof of the existence of God at the end of the Third Meditation, Descartes' meditator interrupts their reasoning, stating a desire "to pause here and spend some time in the contemplation of God [*in ipsius Dei contemplatione*]." The meditator has just established that God "cannot be a deceiver, since it is manifest by the natural light that all fraud and deception depend on some defect" (CSM II 35; AT VII 52), and now the Fourth Meditation will be devoted to deliberating on the conditions of truth and falsity, laying the groundwork for the meditator's reengagement with the sensory world by the end of the Sixth Meditation. The end of the Third thus represents and enacts the culmination of the mind's turn toward itself, before Descartes' meditator returns to the world that they averred in the First Meditation. Now that the meditator has proven God's existence, they want

> to reflect on his attributes, and to gaze with wonder and adoration [*intueri, admirari, adorare*] on the beauty of this immense light [*immensi hujus luminis pulchritudinem*], so far as the eye of my darkened intellect [*caligantis ingenii mei acies*] can bear it. For just as we believe through faith that the supreme happiness [*summam foelicitatem*] of the next life consists solely in the contemplation of the divine majesty [*divinae majestatis contemplatione*], so experience tells us that this same contemplation, albeit much less perfect, enables us to know the greatest joy of which we are capable in this life. (CSM II 35–36; AT VII 52)

This passage is very different in tone and mood from the complex deductive chain immediately preceding it. In contrast to the somber tone of the first two proofs, the text here is not only personal but also exuberant, almost ecstatic, as the enacted contemplation offers a foretaste of the happiness to be experienced by the blessed in heaven.

Readers like the fictional friend of Gabriel Daniel, who was impelled by the *Meditations*' title and dedicatory letter to the Faculty of the Sorbonne to borrow "this spiritual book" for "his Devotions during Passion Week," may have felt the passage met their expectations, but for professional readers it has been more confounding perhaps than any other.[1] As a result, the passage is usually passed over in silence, although a few have noted its climactic function and central place in Descartes' oeuvre, pointing to how it echoes the contemplative tradition from Plato through Augustine and Bonaventure and beyond.[2] Very few have subjected the text to serious interpretation and analysis,[3] so it is my goal in the following pages to read it more closely and in the process contextualize Descartes' *contemplatio Dei* within the meditative tradition outlined in the preceding chapters.

The meditator's contemplation of God is immediately preceded by the discovery that the idea of him is "stamped" in their mind like the "mark of the craftsman" (CSM II 35; AT VII 51). Given the analytic order (see Chapter 2) of the *Meditations*, the contemplation of God is made possible by the prior recognition that God has impressed his image into the self, which need only turn toward itself to turn toward God and know him. Put succinctly, it is this discovery that effects the shift from meditation to contemplation, the telos and climax of the preceding proof of God.

In the *Meditations* Descartes employs the noun *contemplatio* three times and the verb *contemplari* once, suggesting with the term's parsimonious and deliberate use how significant contemplation was for him. All three occurrences of the noun are connected to the *contemplatio Dei* at the end of the Third Meditation. Descartes' meditator uses it twice as they enact their contemplation and again at the beginning of the Fourth Meditation (CSM II 37; AT VII 53), referring back to the event closing the Third. In contrast, the meditator uses the verb *contemplari* in the Second Meditation in a less specific and technical way, which is nonetheless illuminating, when they define imagining (*imaginari*) as "simply contemplating the shape or image of a corporeal thing" (CSM II 19; AT VII 28). Thus, *contemplari* refers to the activity of observing with the mind's eye the idea of a corporeal thing, so that contemplating is a form of intuiting, an act of intellectual vision undertaken by the mental gaze, the *acies ingenii*. And indeed, *intueri* is one of the synonyms Descartes' meditator uses in spelling out what the *contemplatio Dei* entails: "to weigh his attributes, to intuit [*intueri*], to admire, and to adore the beauty of his immense light."[4]

At this climactic moment at the end of the Third Meditation contemplation has, however, a more expansive meaning, encompassing a range of intellectual and spiritual operations. In particular, the term seems to combine two distinct, yet related components, involving different activities and different focal points. The first consists in weighing or considering God's attributes, and the second, in relating in different ways to God as light. The question for the meditator is whether the "immense light" is an attribute of God so that in attending to it, they will be able to engage in its intuition, admiration, and adoration. These three intellectual or, better, spiritual operations seem to follow a progression: first, intuition, the intellectual perception of the divine light by means of the *acies ingenii*; then, admiration, which is a more intellectual emotion involving wonder in the face of the immensity and beauty of the light;[5] and finally, adoration, the more or less religious affect of love and respect that the creature has for its creator and that shades over into veneration and worship.

Descartes' meditator has already noted and examined a number of divine attributes over the course of the Third Meditation. Yet here God appears to their contemplative gaze not as an idea but in the form of an "immense light," and indeed a light with the primary attribute of being so beautiful that it cannot but evoke wonder and adoration. In other words, contemplation is as much an intellectual act of knowing as it is an aesthetic and spiritual experience. Given that the intentional object of this cognitive and aesthetic experience is the light of God, contemplation literally involves an intellectual illumination of some kind. However, the illumination is constrained by the mind's limited optical tolerance, for its regard, its *acies ingenii,* is clouded. And, indeed, as the meditator concedes at the end of the Third Meditation, their contemplation of God will extend only "so far as the eye of my darkened intellect [*caligantis ingenii mei acies*] can bear it" (the Latin verb *caligare* derives from noun *caligo*, which signifies "vapor, fog, darkness" and, figuratively, "inability to see corporeally or mentally"). By comparing the contemplation of which the "darkened intellect" is capable with the contemplation of God in the "next life," Descartes' meditator suggests that the clouding of their mental vision is ultimately attributable to their fallen state. The contemplation of God in the next life, in contrast, is not of his light but of his "majesty," which will be "perfect" and confer "supreme happiness" on its beholder. In this life the mind has only indirect access to this kind of vision of God through faith, which is classically defined as the "evidence of things not seen" (Hebr 11:1) or, as the Vulgate translates, an *argumentum non apparentium*.

The way Descartes' meditator characterizes the "contemplation of the divine majesty" in the next life evokes, I would claim, the theological concept of the *visio beatifica*, the beatific vision experienced by the blessed in heaven.[6] In fact, Descartes' meditator claims that the *contemplatio Dei* they enact is a less perfect version of the "same contemplation" in which the blessed engage in the next life. And Descartes' frequent conjoining of contemplation with happiness elsewhere is further indication that the *visio beatifica* is the foil and telos of all temporal contemplation. As early as in the First Rule of the *Regulae*, Descartes states that contemplating truth is "the only happiness in this life that is complete and untroubled by any pain" (CSM I 10; AT X 361). Later, in the preface to the French edition of *Principles of Philosophy*, Descartes promises that the attainment of wisdom brings "perfection and felicity in life" (CSM I 190; AT IXB 20). We see in more detail later in this chapter that the precise nature and scope of the beatific vision were topics of passionate debate among theologians and philosophers from Augustine to Malebranche. Of more immediate concern here is the precision of Descartes' usage of the term "contemplation" in this context, which raises a host of questions: What does he mean by contemplation? How does it relate to intellectual operations such as meditation, deduction, and intuition? And what is the provenance of the concept and practice of contemplation? How does the tradition of spiritual exercises Descartes draws on elsewhere in the *Meditations* influence his understanding of contemplation? What is the role of contemplation in the historical practice of meditation? What is the relation of contemplation to beatific vision? More specifically, how does the Cartesian *contemplatio Dei* relate to the concept of *visio beatifica* from Augustine to Thomas Aquinas? Is there any precedent for light as the object of the contemplative gaze? How does the vision of the divine light relate to other instances of illumination in Descartes? What is the relation to the *lumen naturale*, so important in the *Regulae* and reappearing here in the Third Meditation? And finally, given this soteriological and eschatological dimension of the *contemplatio Dei*, what are its place and role in the Cartesian art of turning?

A Brief History of Contemplation

Originally, *contemplatio* was a technical term referring to the observation of Roman augurs, which is derived from "to mark out a space for observation" (*com* + *templum*).[7] In classical Latin it takes on a wider meaning in denoting the act of looking, of gazing attentively at something. It was Cicero who chose *contemplatio* to translate the Greek philosophical term *theoria*, paving the way for its adoption for describing the concentrated consideration of intellectual or spiritual matters. Andrea Nightingale has shown that the Greek term *theoria*, so central to Platonic and Aristotelian philosophy, has a similar origin:

> In the effort to conceptualize and legitimize theoretical philosophy, the fourth-century thinkers invoked a specific civic institution: that which the ancients called "*theoria*." In the traditional practice of *theoria*, an individual (called the *theoros*) made a journey or pilgrimage abroad for the purpose of witnessing certain events and spectacles. In the classical period, *theoria* took the form of pilgrimages to oracles and religious festivals.... At its center was the act of seeing, generally focused on a sacred object or spectacle.... This sacralized mode of spectating was a central element of traditional *theoria*, and offered a powerful model for the philosophic notion of "seeing" divine truths.[8]

Books Five to Seven of the *Republic* offer Plato's most detailed account of *theoria*, with the allegory of the cave in particular articulating a paradigm for philosophical *theoria*.[9] Socrates is well aware of the originality of this new paradigm of philosophy, as he is of its roots being modeled on the notion and practice of religious and civic *theoria*. Although the word pertains to the concluding climactic vision of the truth and the good, *theoria* encompasses the whole journey to this telos. Philosophical *theoria* in the allegory of the cave is clearly modeled on the traditional practice composed of a departure from one's community, a journey upward, and the eventual return home. In more ways than one, then, the theoretical journey in which philosophy engages involves a turning around and reorientation or, as I have called it earlier, a conversion.

Theoria is what the Platonic "art of turning around" (*Republic* 518d) aims to achieve. However, given that *theoria* is standing *pars pro toto* for the journey of ascent as a whole, it becomes coextensive with the art of turning or conversion. Plato's model of *theoria* in the allegory of the cave hinges on the analogy, even homology, between corporeal and intellectual vision, a physical and a figural inward light. Wisdom takes the form of "seeing" truth, making philosophers *theoroi* and "lovers of the sight of truth" (475d). The ultimate telos of the metaphysical quest of philosophical *theoria* is "to see and delight in the nature of beauty itself" (476b; translation modified), that is, the idea of good (517c) as it manifests itself in the register of intellectual vision. Autopsy, seeing the Good itself for oneself, is an integral part of *theoria* and responsible for the (self-)evidence of the envisioned truth, so the philosophical pursuit of wisdom culminates in an act of intellectual eyewitnessing.[10] For this goal to be achieved, the "eye of the soul" (*Republic* 519b; my translation), which is naturally turned downward toward the material and temporal world, has to be "turned around toward the true things" (519b). The Platonic "art of turning," thus, consists first and foremost in the redirection of *theoria*, in the training of intellectual vision and its training on the intelligible realm of ideas.

Aristotle adopted Plato's concept of a philosophical *theoria*, stripped of its narrative frame and metaphorical embellishments. Regarding *theoria* as an exclusively intellectual, "theoretical" activity (*Nicomachean Ethics* 1139a),[11] he divorces it almost completely from social and political life. Deemed useless in the practical sphere, *theoria* becomes an end itself to be engaged in for its own sake (1177a). Aristotle here is opening up the opposition between practical and theoretical knowledge and the corresponding modes of life in which they are pursued, that is, the famous choice between the *vita activa* and *vita contemplativa*. Of course, a social dimension comes in through the back door in that the latter presupposes a life of leisure, open only to the aristocracy or the wealthy.[12] The lack of utility is not to be understood as a deficiency but, to the contrary, its finality, that is, that it cannot be subservient to the attainment of some other telos marks its exalted position in the Aristotelian economy of ends and means. For Aristotle, *theoria* is the ultimate telos and, consequently, to be set apart from other activities and virtues on account of its purity, stability, and above all, its self-sufficiency. "The wise person can contemplate even when he is by himself, the more so the wiser he is," writes Aristotle (1177a). His eudaemonistic ethics equips *theoria* with another trait that continues to be associated with contemplation all the way through Descartes. As the exercise of the highest virtue it confers supreme happiness. By engaging in *theoria* we exercise the "divine element" in us, that is, the intellect, and take on "immortality as much as possible" (1177b). In fact, it is in contemplation that we become most like the gods and share in their blessedness (1178b). *Theoria* characterizes the wisest man and the happiest life.

Plotinus, the founder of Neoplatonism, was reputed to have actually achieved the telos of the philosophical art of turning.[13] According to his biographer Porphyry, "to Plotinus 'the goal ever near was shown': for his telos was to be united to, to approach the God who is over all things. Four times while I was with him he attained that goal, in an unspeakable actuality and not in potency only."[14] What Plato described in poetic images, Plotinus supposedly achieved in real life, and in doing so he adopted the salient features of Platonic *theoria*. The Plotinian soul, like Plato's cave dweller, needs to turn away from the sensory world, inward and toward the intelligible realm, where it will ascend to contemplate the "blessed sight" (*Ennead* 1.6.7) of the "absolute beauty which exists pure by itself, uncontaminated by flesh or body, not in earth or heaven, that it may keep its purity" (1.6.7). "Wisdom is an intellectual activity which turns away [*apostrophē*] from the things below and leads the soul to those above" (1.6.6). The self must "strip off what [it] put on in [its] descent" (1.6.7) and train itself to contemplate the beautiful, first in the physical world, then in the spiritual world, and finally in the metaphysical realm where the Good and One reside. In Plotinus, then, the concept of contemplation is radically expanded, we might even say universalized. It is no longer solely an intellectual operation of the individual mind but an ontological principle and cosmic relation. On the one hand, contemplation denotes the emanation from the One, and on the other, it is the way that individual beings relate to their ultimate origin. In short, Plotinian contemplation is not merely "theoretical" but instead participatory, transformational, and unitive.

Augustine's innovation regarding the conceptualization of contemplation has been succinctly summarized in a recent book by John Peter Kenney:

Augustine's "articulation of the soul's access to 'being' commingled Platonic and Christian elements in [a] way that transformed both, but which was reducible to neither," for the object of Augustinian contemplation is "both the intelligible 'being' of Platonism and the personal 'being' of the Pauline God."[15] If *theoria* was ancient philosophy's favored mode of access to the intelligible world and its truths, the intellectual and spiritual journey that Augustine recounts in the *Confessions* can likewise be understood as a search for a reliable mode of contemplation. It begins with his encounter with Cicero's *Hortensius*, "an exhortation to study philosophy," which prompted him to long "for the immortality of wisdom with an incredible ardour" (*Confessions* 3.4.7),[16] and it culminates in the so-called vision at Ostia, where he joined his mother, Monica, in a preview of the vision that the blessed experienced in the afterlife. Similar to that of Plato's cave dweller, Augustine's long and laborious journey from the "region of unlikeness" (7.10.16) back to his creator, his turn from the sensory and temporal to the intelligible and eternal world—beginning at the latest with his discovery of philosophy and culminating in the divine call in the garden outside Milan—is as much contemplative as it is conversive.

Concomitant with his search for the right *theoria*, Augustine confronted the question of how the object of contemplation, the intelligible world and its transcendence, was to be correctly understood. It was his discovery of the "books of the Platonists" (*Confessions* 7.9.13) that had catalyzed his dissatisfaction with and divorce from the materialism of Manichaeism, and Platonism offered Augustine a conceptualization of the intelligible world and *theoria* as a mode of accessing it. His early dialogues document his adoption and adaptation of philosophical contemplation. In the early text *On the Immortality of the Soul*, Augustine defines reason as "the contemplation itself of the true" (6.10),[17] that is, without the mediation of the created, material world. In another early text, *On the Teacher*, he similarly conceives of contemplation as the mind's mode of accessing the intelligible world:

> When we deal with things that we perceive by the mind, namely by the intellect and reason, we're speaking of things that we look upon immediately in the inner light of Truth, in virtue of which the so-called inner man is illuminated and rejoices [*illustratur et fruitur*]. Under these conditions our listener, if he likewise sees these things with his inward and undivided eye, knows what I'm saying from his own contemplation, not from my words. . . . He's taught not by my words but by the things themselves made manifest within when God discloses them. (12.40)[18]

In *On the Trinity*, a much later text, Augustine continues to operate with this philosophical notion of contemplation, defining wisdom as the contemplation of eternal and intelligible things (see 12.14.22 and 12.15.25).[19] The ultimate telos is the contemplation of God, "the supreme reward of the saints" (12.14.22). However, the *Confessions* also makes clear that Augustine eventually realized that the philosophical *theoria* of Platonism provided insufficient and unsatisfactory access to the intelligible world. Augustine compresses the realization into a dramatic conversion in the *Confessions*. But the work, in fact, is the result of his articulation of nearly a decade of genuine Christian contemplation. The Platonist roots remain readily discernible, but they have undergone crucial modifications in the light of his new understanding of God's salvational work.

The second contemplative vision of God that Augustine recounts in Book Seven of the *Confessions* illustrates the limitations of philosophical, specifically Platonic, *theoria*:

> I found the unchangeable and authentic eternity of truth to transcend my mutable mind. And so step by step I ascended from bodies to the soul which perceives through the body, and from there to its inward force, to which bodily senses report external sensations, this being as high as the beasts go. From there again I ascended to the power of reasoning to which is to be attributed the power of judging the deliverances of the bodily senses. This power, which in myself I found to be mutable, raised itself to the level of its own intelligence, and led my thinking out of the ruts of habit. It withdrew itself from the contradictory swarms of imaginative fantasies, so as to discover the light by which it was flooded. At that point it had no hesitation in declaring that the unchangeable is preferable to the changeable, and that on this ground it can know the unchangeable, since, unless it could somehow know this, there would be no certainty in preferring it to the mutable. So in the flash of a trembling glance it attained to that which is. At that moment I saw your "invisible nature understood through the things which are made" (Rom 1:20). (7.17.23)

Augustine's vision has all the hallmarks of Platonic *theoria*. It transpires as the result of a meditative ascent that turns inward, away from the sensory world: first to the soul and the imagination; then to the "power of reasoning"; and onward to "its own intelligence [*intelligentia sua*]." The ascent is a movement from the physical and mutable to the intelligible and immutable. It culminates in a contemplative vision of God, who in the first vision (*Confessions* 7.10.16) revealed himself as Being itself, by reciting the famous "I am who I am" from Exodus 3:14. However, this vision of immutable

Being is inherently unstable and, therefore, cannot last: "I did not possess the strength to keep my vision fixed. My weakness reasserted itself, and I returned to my customary condition." The self, due to the "weakness" of its "customary condition," lacks control over its vision, a realization Augustine paradoxically comes to in the moment he achieves a "perfect" philosophical *theoria*. Not only does it demonstrate to Augustine his fallen state, but it also shows that he lacks the power to overcome his weakness and secure stable access to the divine. As Kenney observes, "If contemplation is to be salvific and an enduring vision of God, then it must be catalyzed by divine grace."[20] To be sure, the self must do everything to train and to cleanse itself of its attachment to the physical and sensory world (*exercitatio animae*), but it cannot do so successfully without the salvational work of Christ—which is the point of the beatific vision of Ostia, in which Augustine under the guidance of his philosophically uneducated mother, Monica, is provided a foretaste of heaven. This tension between human agency and divine grace remains unresolved or, better, unresolvable in Augustine, functioning as the engine for the numerous spiritual ascents staged in his later writings.[21] And his extraordinary spiritual authority ensured that this tension at the heart of the Christian notion of contemplation would be bequeathed to the Latin West.

Jean Leclercq has called the twelfth century the "highpoint of the Middle Ages from the point of view of spirituality."[22] It saw a widespread and intense spiritual awakening, characterized by "an inward-looking and affective piety based on a doctrine of contemplation stressing personal will, liberty, and experience."[23] The main protagonists were Cistercians such as Bernard of Clairvaux, the so-called Victorines Hugh and Richard of Saint Victor, and Franciscans such as Saint Bonaventure.[24] In contrast to their classical and early Christian predecessors, these spiritual writers designed and developed a theory as well as practice of contemplation. In ancient philosophy and to a lesser extent among Christian "theoreticians," the practice of contemplation remained largely unthematized and implicit, leaving it to the spiritual masters of the twelfth century to devise and systematize the mental methods and techniques of *theoria*. The Cistercians' adoption of a methodological approach necessarily foregrounded the self's agency in reaching the ultimate telos of contemplation—an intellectual vision of the divine—shifting somewhat the mature Augustine's emphasis on grace, yet the systematic synthesis of contemplative theory and practice became formative for the resurgence of personal piety in the late Middle Ages and the Renaissance.

Bernard of Clairvaux (1090–1153) epitomized the spirituality of Cistercian monasticism in his blend of spiritual practice and scriptural exegesis, providing a powerful model of the contemplative life that reverberated far beyond the order. In *De consideratione* (*On Consideration*), his proposal to Pope Eugene III for reforming the church, he distinguishes contemplation from consideration (which is "thought searching for truth") by defining the former as "true and sure intuition of the mind concerning something, or the apprehension of truth without doubt" (2.5).[25] In the final section of the final book, devoted to the question of how we can possess God, Bernard unfolds a graded system of four types of contemplation, each a step on the way to the ultimate telos, the "expectation of what has been promised, and . . . the meditation on eternity" (5.32).

Hugh (1096–1141) was the leading thinker of the first generation of Victorines, responsible for founding the spiritual tradition and defining its unique culture and practice. The abbey of Saint Victor was founded to renew the cloistered religious life under the aegis of the Rule of Saint Augustine and became the most important spiritual center of the time. In addition to its focus on spiritual renewal, the abbey fostered an intellectual environment that was open to the new theological developments at the University of Paris, with Hugh and Richard of Saint Victor the towering representatives of the Victorine "school," and their spiritual writings among the "best selling books" in the Middle Ages. In a number of texts Hugh devises a fine-grained classification of mental operations distinguishing between meditation and contemplation, a distinction that prefigures Descartes' usage. In the *Didascalicon*, for instance, Hugh enumerates four ways by which the life of the just man is "raised, as it were by certain steps, to its future perfection—namely, study or instruction [*doctrina*], meditation [*meditatio*], prayer [*oratio*], and performance [*operatio*]. Then follows a fifth, contemplation [*contemplatio*], in which as by a sort of fruit of the preceding steps, one has a foretaste, even in this life, of what the future reward of good work is" (5.2).[26] The first of these steps, study, is for beginners; the last and highest, contemplation, for those who have reached perfection and in doing so restored the divine likeness in man—to the extent possible in this life. In his unfinished *Commentary on Ecclesiastes* Hugh devises a slightly different classification, conceiving thinking, meditating, and contemplating as "the rational soul's three ways of seeing."[27] Thinking "occurs when the mind becomes aware of things passing through it"; meditation "is the concentrated and judicious reconsideration of thought"; and contemplation is "the piercing and spontaneous intuition of the soul."[28] For Hugh, in a way that helps us understand the use of these mental operations in Descartes, meditation has "to do with things that are obscure to our intelligence, whereas contemplation is concerned with things that are clear, either of their nature or in relation to our intellectual capacity." Whereas meditation has to work for its insights, contemplation "grasps [them] clearly with entire comprehension. Thus in some ways contemplation possesses that for which meditation seeks."[29] Subsequently, Hugh introduces an intermediary step between meditation and contemplation, which we recognize from Descartes' *contemplatio Dei*: admiration. It mediates between a mode of cognition that is still enmeshed in the messiness of the material world and a mode of cognition in which the soul is "rapt in spirit above all transient and perishable things":[30] "In meditation, the inopportune disturbance that arises from the fleshly passions clouds the mind that a loving devotion has enkindled. In admiration, the novelty of the unwonted vision lifts up the soul in wonder. In contemplation, the taste of a wondrous sweetness changes everything to joy and gladness. In meditation, therefore, there is care, in admiration wonder, in contemplation sweetness."[31]

Richard of Saint Victor (1110–73), the spiritual heir to Hugh, took the systematization of contemplation (and meditation) even farther.[32] The first to offer a systematic account of contemplation as a spiritual technique, he also intended the work to be useful for instruction in the practice. He was deemed, as it were, the modern master of contemplation, on a par with the ancient fathers such as Augustine and Pseudo-Dionysius; and Dante considered him "in contemplation . . . more than man."[33] Richard wrote two treatises that were primarily devoted to contemplation, the *Benjamin minor* and the *Benjamin major* (titled in medieval manuscripts *The Twelve Patriarchs* and *The Mystical Ark*, respectively). Adapting Hugh's differentiation among thinking (*cogitatio*), meditation, and contemplation in a way that remains resonant in Descartes' early modern usage, Richard saw contemplation as differing from thinking and meditation not in its objects but solely in its mode. Describing the three modes, he employs the familiar itinerant metaphorics of motion. Thinking, "by means of inconstant and slow feet . . . wanders here and there in all directions without any regard for arriving" (*Benjamin maior* 1.3).³⁴ In contrast, meditation has method. It is a purposeful and determined movement oriented toward a single goal. Contemplation, in combining thinking and meditation, transcends them both. Unifying multiplicity, it is the "penetrating and free gaze of a soul extended everywhere in perceiving things" (1.4). Each mode is associated with a mental faculty: "Thinking is from imagination; meditation from reason; contemplation from understanding [*intelligentia*]" (1.3). All three modes are, however, "a kind of sight of the soul" (1.4).³⁵

Richard recommends the meditative path taken by Plato and Augustine. The ascent to God leads through the self, which needs to turn inward and cleanse itself as the condition for knowing God. In its contemplative ascent the soul passes through six stages, enacting the corresponding mode of contemplation. The first two involve the imagination and focus on the material and sensory world. The third and fourth modes of contemplation involve reason; they ascend from the "similitude of visible things" to the "speculation of invisible things (*Benjamin maior* 1.6), arriving ultimately at rational self-knowledge. The last two stages transcend reason, the first in being "above but not beyond reason" and the last in being "above and beyond reason" (4.3). As opposed to the first four modes and their concern with the created world, modes five and six involve the understanding and focus on "uncreated and divine things" (1.7). "Exercised in ecstasy of the mind" (4.22), they depend on divine grace. Achieving the telos of the contemplative ascent is, thus, the result of a "joint effort" of the human soul and divine intervention. Like Hugh, Richard conceives the soul's ascent and culmination in the wonder of beholding God as an interplay of meditation and contemplation; and like Descartes, he lets meditation do the hard work of preparing the soul for turning away from and transcending the sensory world.

Richard's model of contemplation is plainly adopted by Bonaventure (1221–74) in his codification of the Franciscan meditative and contemplative practice.³⁶ And in his twin roles as eminent theologian at the University of Paris and minister general of the Franciscans, Bonaventure shaped the spirituality of the Latin West in the high and late Middle Ages. Modeled on Saint Francis's visionary experience on Mount Alverno, Bonaventure's slender treatise *Itinerarum mentis in Deum* (*The Journey of the Mind to God*) is conceived as a guide for the soul in its ascent toward its own vision of God. The final contemplative vision is brought about by "penetrating meditation, holy living, and devout prayer" (*Itinerarium* 1.8).[37] Bonaventure uses the six wings of the seraph seen by Francis in his vision as the structuring principle of his contemplative ascent. Similar to the six steps in Richard's *Benjamin maior*, the wings represent the six "progressive steps of enlightenment" by which the soul arrives at the "quiet of contemplation" it seeks (1.5). The steps correspond to the six powers of the soul, "the senses, imagination, reason, understanding, intelligence, and the summit of the mind or the spark of synderesis" (1.6), the same *synderesis* that Descartes beholds and recognizes in the second dream of his conversion.

As Richard's guide followed predecessors, so does Bonaventure roughly follow the path delineated by Richard. First comes contemplation of God's vestiges in the visible world, then the turn inward to the contemplation of the "image of the most Blessed Trinity" (*Itinerarium* 3.1), the first principle residing in the mind. In the last two steps the mind contemplates God above us, first his "essential attributes" and then the "proper attributes of the three Persons" (5.1). The final step of the contemplative ascent is "the perfect illumination of our mind, when, as it were, on the sixth day it sees man made to the image of God" (6.7). Reaching this ultimate contemplation, resembling Saint Francis's vision on the mountaintop, the mind transcends "not only this visible world, but even itself. In this passing over, Christ is the way and door" (7.1). For Bonaventure the "passing over" is a mystical experience: in it "all intellectual activities ought to be relinquished and the loftiest affection transported to God, and transformed into Him. This, however, is mystical and most secret, which no one knows except him who receives it, and no one receives except him who desires it, and no one desires it except he who is penetrated to the marrow by the fire of the Holy Spirit" (7.4). Needless to say, the last stages of contemplation, in particular the final one, are contingent on divine grace and cannot be engineered by the mind itself. Such visions are granted only to the elect few, such as Saint Paul or Francis.

As Giles Constable has shown, some of the most prominent spiritual authors of the late Middle Ages and the Renaissance looked to the piety of the twelfth century for models in their articulations of the contemplative life.[38] Jean Gerson (1363–1429), who was very much indebted to both Hugh and Richard, channeled the contemplative tradition being sketched out here for a lay audience. Directed "more to women than to men," his *Mountain of Contemplation* is for that reason written in "French rather than in Latin."[39] The *devotio moderna* (modern devotion), a movement of religious reform that emerged at the time in the Low Countries and Northern Germany, expanded the dissemination of the Victorine practice of contemplation among the laity.[40] It was via the *devotio moderna* and its Spanish adaptor Garcia de Cisneros that the spiritual tradition of the twelfth century came to inform Ignatius of Loyola's use of contemplation in the *Spiritual Exercises* as well as in his autobiography. He includes contemplation among the mental and spiritual operations that comprise "spiritual exercises" (SE §1, p. 281),[41] using "meditation" and "contemplation" interchangeably, often conjoining them with "or." The *Spiritual Exercises*, while graded, thus do not lead up to a climactic contemplative vision, even though the Ignatian technique of mental visualization, of imagining Gospel scenes in a place marked out by the *compositio loci* (seeing the place) is nothing other than the enactment of the etymological root of *contemplatio*. Ignatius thus absorbs meditation as mental visualization into contemplation. However, other Jesuit writers were more conventional, adopting the notion of contemplation articulated in the twelfth century. Louis Richeome, for instance, elevates it above meditation in his *Pilgrim of Loreto*:

So that contemplation is more than meditation, and as it were the end thereof, and it groweth and springeth vpon it many tymes, as the branch doth vpon the body of the tree, or the flowre vpon the branch.... For meditation is lesse cleere, lesse sweet, and more painefull than contemplation: it is as the reading of a booke, which must be done sentence after sentence; but contemplation is like casting the eyes upon a picture, discerning all at once.[42]

The other great French spiritual writer of the seventeenth century, Francis de Sales, likewise draws on the conceptual tools of the Victorines in distinguishing between contemplation and meditation. In his *Treatise on the Love of God* contemplation occupies the apex of the meditative ascent, so we "raise us above ourselves and range us with the angels" (6.6).[43] Contemplation is the end of all spiritual exercises, bringing the soul, having "found God and his holy love" (6.6), supreme delight. Whereas "meditation considers in detail, as it were piece by piece ... contemplation takes a very simple and collected view of the object it loves" (6.5). By defining contemplation as "being attentive to and occupied in seeing [God's] beauty" (6.6), Francis evinces its roots in the Platonic *theoria*.

The spiritual writers of the medieval and early modern Latin West took over the "theoretical" matrix underlying Plato's and Augustine's contemplative ascents and operationalized it for their students and readers to enable them to enact it on their own. This particular operationalization was premised on the assumption that the self has considerable control in regard to making the ascent and achieving the ultimate goal of a contemplative *visio Dei*. To be sure, the self's culminating vision depended on an act of grace. Moreover, there were many grades of such a vision. Only the rarest minds were granted a vision like the one Saint Francis experienced. Yet, as evidenced by Augustine's *Confessions*, "lesser" visions were not out of the ordinary and thus achievable. Part of the operationalization is the demarcation of what is in the control of the self and what is beyond it. The spiritual masters of the twelfth century captured much of spiritual and mental labor that the self performed under the term "meditation." It involves method as the path to be followed, the turn away from the sensory world, the work of cleansing the mind of sensory representations and passions, the direction of the mind's attention, and constitutes, thus, a pivotal part of the art of turning. Contemplation, the fruit of meditation, then gives the self access to the intelligible world, whether to its immortal soul or God, and thereby completes the conversive turn.

Descartes shares this understanding and usage of *contemplation* as the goal and fruit of the meditative work of following his *methodos*. This means drawing a sharp distinction between contemplation and meditation—much as the spiritual masters of the twelfth century did. Unlike them, however, Descartes' meditative labor does not end with the contemplative vision at the end of the Third Meditation but continues with the reengagement of the sensory world. Moreover, Descartes' meditative *methodos* does not exhibit the noticeable incline of earlier notions. To be sure, the Cartesian art of turning involves the familiar turn away from the sensory world, inward, first toward the self and finally toward the innate ideas impressed by God, including the idea of God himself. But this turn is not portrayed as an upward movement, although in his earlier and earliest works there is sufficient evidence that Descartes understood the search for truth as an ascent and his method as a technique for elevating the mind. In *Olympia*, his earliest notebook, he proposes that we "philosophize in a more exalted way, and develop the knowledge to raise our minds to lofty heights" (CSM I 4; AT X 217). Rule Three in the *Discourse on the Method* makes clear that the "path to be followed" ascends. Method directs one's "thoughts in an orderly manner, by beginning with the simplest and most easily known objects in order to ascend little by little, step by step, to knowledge of the most complex" (CSM I 120; AT VI 18).

Nevertheless, Descartes' meditative method for arriving at the climactic contemplation differs from traditional ascents in the techniques and tools employed. Descartes' meditator does not resort to prayer and scriptural interpretation. And they make little use of the traditional *machina mentis* described by Mary Carruthers in her magisterial study noted earlier.[44] In previous chapters we have seen that Descartes' meditator by and large relies on a set of techniques not usually found in traditional meditative ascents. In addition to intuition, which is at the heart of contemplation, the meditator employs discursive reasoning, that is, arguments and proofs, to proceed along their meditative path and arrive at their contemplative vision. Thus, their way of proceeding is more akin to the method of ascent found in the *Proslogion* by Anselm of Canterbury.[45]

That Anselm's ontological proof of the existence of God is one of the models on which Descartes built and improved his own version is well-known. Similar to his early modern descendant, Anselm conceived his ontological proof as a tool of conversion. For the "argument" in the *Proslogion* is aimed at unbelievers. It is designed to persuade "the fool," the person who "said in his heart, 'There is no God' (Ps 14:1, 53:1)."[46] The ontological proof itself, contained in chapters 2 through 4 of the book, is treated by most scholars in isolation, removed from the context of the work as a whole. This approach ignores the important detail that in conceiving and writing down his proof, Anselm adopted "the role of someone trying to raise his mind to the contemplation of God and seeking to understand what he believes."[47] The proof is a vehicle for the ascent of Anselm's meditator; or to use a different metaphor, it constitutes the initial stage of her ascent, which culminates in a *contemplatio Dei*. The climactic vision of God achieved by Anselm's meditator at the end of the *Proslogion* is thus not incompatible with the rationality of the proof. In fact, Anselm's second purpose is for the meditator to understand what they already believe. By transforming faith into understanding, the meditations have the capacity to make the unbeliever understand rather than merely believe. Analogously, contemplating and understanding of God are coterminous, inextricably linked and both reachable by a path that ascends.

Contemplatio Dei and the Visio Beatifica

Descartes' meditator follows in the footsteps of Augustine, Thomas Aquinas, and others by explicitly setting their *contemplatio Dei* apart from the *visio beatifica*.[48] Vision remains nevertheless an essential moment in the notion of contemplation described in this chapter, leaving theorists of the time with the question of what the mind sees when it contemplates God. Does the contemplative mind see God the way the patriarchs did in Genesis or Moses in Exodus, or what Paul sees when he is lifted into the third heaven (2 Cor 2:12)? Is the contemplative vision similar to or even identical with the *visio beatifica*, the vision of God that the blessed are granted in heaven? Or was seeing God reserved for distinguished saints and the chosen in the afterlife and thus not realistically within reach of anyone in this life, even the most perfectly contemplative? Augustine took up these questions in a number of texts that became formative for the medieval debates. One of the two most elaborate treatments occurs in Letter 147, known later under the title *De videndo Deo* (*On Seeing God*), written in 413 to Paulinus of Nola.[49] *De videndo Deo* sets out to answer the question "whether the invisible God can be seen by bodily eyes" (DvD 1.1).[50] Quickly rejecting the position that God can been seen by the eyes of the body as well as the eyes of the mind, Augustine still has to contend with contradictory statements in scripture. In Exodus 33:20, God tells Moses: "You cannot see my face, for no one will see me and live." But in Genesis 32:20, Jacob says, after wrestling with God: "I saw God face to face, and my soul was saved." The New Testament is no less equivocal. The prologue of the Gospel of John states categorically that "no one has ever seen God" (Jn 1:18). But only a little later it quotes Christ saying, "He who sees me sees the Father" (Jn 14:9); and Matthew promises: "Blessed are the pure of heart because they will see God" (Mt 5:8).

In his effort to reconcile the contradictory statements, Augustine turns to the *Commentary on the Gospel of Luke* by his mentor, Ambrose, who insists on the fundamental difference between seeing God and seeing sensible objects. While the latter are by nature visible, the former is not. God can be seen only if and when he wills it; and it depends on his will in which form he is seen:

> God was, therefore, in that form in which he had willed to appear, but he did not appear in his own nature, which Moses longed to see. That vision is, of course, promised to the saints in the next life. Hence, the reply given to Moses is true, that no one can see the face of God and live (Ex 33:20), that is, no one can, while living in this life, see him as he is. (DvD 8.20)

Seeing God in his true nature is thus reserved for the blessed in the afterlife, and Augustine is unequivocal about the *visio beatifica* not being granted to man in this life. He concedes, however, that the truly pious desire not "to gaze upon that form in which he appears when he wills, which is not himself, but to gaze upon that substance by which he is what he is" (8.20), and that it is to these that Matthew 5:8 ("blessed are the clean of heart because they will see God") applies. When these blessed ones (*beati*), like Moses or Paul, have a vision of God in his true nature in this life, they see God neither with the eyes of the body nor with the eyes of the mind but with the "eyes of the heart [*oculis cordis*]" (17.41).

Augustine's second extensive consideration of the *visio beatifica* appears in the twelfth and final book of his *Literal Meaning of Genesis*, where he elaborates the trifold categorization of vision from *De videndo Deo*. His question is how to understand the meaning and reference of "paradise" and "third heaven" in Paul's famous third-person account of his rapture:

> I know a man in Christ who fourteen years ago—whether in the body I do not know, or out of the body I do not know, God knows—such a one was caught up to the third heaven. And I know such a man—whether in the body or out of the body I do not know, God knows—that he was caught up in Paradise and heard secret words that man may not repeat. (2 Cor 12:2–4)

To understand what Paul saw during his rapture, Augustine distinguishes three kinds of vision: corporeal, spiritual (that is, by interior images), and intellectual. The first two cannot capture God in his true nature. Only intellectual vision, which belongs to the mind alone and "is on a higher plane" (*Literal Meaning* 12.10.21),[51] can access "the region of the intellectual and intelligible," where the brightness of the Lord is seen, not through a symbolic or corporeal vision, as it was seen on Mount Sinai, nor through a spiritual vision such as Isaiah saw and John in the Apocalypse, but through a direct vision and not through a dark image, as far as the human mind elevated by the grace of God can receive it. In such a vision God speaks face to face to him whom He has made worthy of this communion. And here we are speaking not of the face of the body but of that of the mind. (12.26.54)

However, such an intellectual vision "is granted only to him who in some way dies to this life, whether he quits the body entirely or is turned away and carried out of the bodily senses" (12.27.55)—like Paul, who could not tell whether he was in or outside his body when he was rapt to "third heaven." By "third heaven" and "paradise" Paul denotes not only the place of intellectual vision but also "the life that is to be ours forever after this life on earth" (12.28.56). While Augustine concedes the possibility of different grades of intellectual vision, the full vision granted to Paul (forming the basis of his apostolate) is exceedingly rare if not singular. The takeaway for medieval readers of Augustine was that a *visio beatifica* is (virtually) impossible in this life but that lesser forms of intellectual vision of God are possible, depending on one's level of purification and bestowal of grace. Of course, alternative views were expressed from both sides, some arguing that given a sufficiently purified heart, God could indeed be seen close to his true nature, others denying that God's essence could ever really be seen either in this life or in the one to come.

Thomas Aquinas gave the orthodox theology of beatific vision its canonical expression.[52] In his indebtedness to the Augustinian theology of heaven, he drew on the tools of Scholastic Aristotelianism to explain with greater precision why the human mind cannot know God's essence.[53] Like Augustine, Thomas quickly rules out the possibility of God being perceived by any of the sensory powers, including sight (ST I-I, q. 12, a. 3). His sensualist epistemology (according to which nothing can be in the intellect that has not been in the senses) would require "fitting" God's infinite essence into a species, the intelligible forms usually abstracted from sensory impressions; and it is immediately apparent that God cannot be known *per similitudinem* of such forms.

However, as man's "highest function," the intellect must be able to fulfill its ultimate purpose of achieving a beatific *theoria*. And what could be more beatific than seeing God? Yet, if the "created intellect" cannot "see the essence of God by its own natural power" (ST I-I, q. 12, a. 4), how could that possibly happen? Thomas gives an unsurprising answer, divine grace:

> Now this increase of the intellectual powers is called the illumination of the intellect, as we also call the intelligible object itself by the name of light of illumination. And this is the light spoken of in the Apocalypse (Rev 21:23): *The glory of God has enlightened it*—viz. the society of the blessed who see God. By this light the blessed are made *deiform*—i.e., like God, according to the saying: *When He shall appear we shall be like to Him, and we shall see Him as He is* (1 John 2:2). (ST I-I, q. 12, a. 5)

The *lumen gloriae* (light of glory) brings into being a different kind of similitude between the created intellect and its creator, such that in the divine light man can see and know God in his true nature.[54] Illumination by the *lumen gloriae* may be the default condition in the heavenly afterlife, but it is exceedingly rare in this life. Seeing God here—paradoxically—requires a separation from mortal life (see ST I-I, q. 12, a. 10), in short, a "rapture." To be "uplifted to the sublime vision of God's essence," the intellect must have withdrawn entirely from the senses and phantasms (ST IIa–IIae, q. 175, a. 5). Even if the rapt *visio Dei* is like the vision had by the blessed in respect to the "thing seen," it is not in respect to the "mode of seeing" and thus less perfect than the true *visio beatifica*, which remains a strictly otherworldly *theoria*. Despite his emphatic separation of the heavenly *visio beatifica* from intellectual vision in this life, Thomas Aquinas, like Augustine, allows for lesser forms of contemplating God, forms that resemble to a certain degree and, thereby, adumbrate the perfect vision of the blessed.

"The Beauty of This Immense Light"

So what is the "thing seen" in these more mundane modes of intellectual vision of God? What does the contemplative gaze of Descartes' meditator see when they see God? As in Thomas's intellectual illumination, they see an "immense light," befitting the etymological beginnings of *theoria* and contemplation, which both operate in an optical register. Truth, knowledge, and their opposites are coded as light and darkness.[55] The three similes of the sun, the line, and the cave in Plato's *Republic* most prominently and famously figure the Good as a kind of light.[56] In the first, Socrates maintains that as the idea of "the Good is in the intelligible region with respect to intelligence and what is intellected, so the sun is in the visible region with respect to sight and what is seen" (*Republic* 508b–c). The sun "provides what is seen with the power of being seen" (509b); and idea of the Good "provides the truth to the things known and gives the power to the one who knows" (508e). When the soul "fixes itself on that which is illumined by truth and that which is, it intellects, knows, and appears to possess intelligence" (508d). Corporeal and intellectual illumination are both possible because light and sight are "sunlike," and knowledge and truth are "Goodlike" (508d). The sun and the Good not only provide the conditions of visibility and intelligibility; they also are responsible for their being. The sun provides "generation, growth, and nourishment," and the Good "existence and being" (509b). Of course, the sun, however powerful it may be in the visible world, is always only a metaphor or a shadow of the true source of all illumination, the idea of the Good. For "in the visible it gave birth to light and its sovereign; in the intelligible, itself sovereign, it provided truth and intelligence" (517c). The allegory of the cave extends the analogy between the sun and the idea of the Good and between corporeal and mental vision and spins it into a story of *paideia* and enlightenment. In the subterranean world of the allegory it is the ultimate source of light, the sun in physical and the Good in the intelligible realm, that drives the soul's quest for illumination, which in turn fuels the narrative. To make the "journey up to the intelligible place" (517b), the soul must train its intellectual vision, slowly accustoming it to the brighter illumination until it finally has the ability to engage in "acts of divine contemplation" (517d) of "the sun itself by itself in its own region" (516b) without being "dazzled by the greater brilliance" (518b). In the *Symposion* and the *Phaedrus* Plato foregrounds beauty as the salient phenomenological quality of the Good, adding an aesthetic dimension to the contemplation of light.

With Plotinus Plato's photic epistemology is expanded and deepened into a metaphysics of light,[57] in which it serves as the model for the conceptualization of the One in its radical transcendence and simultaneous diffusion among all things. Due to its apparent immateriality, light gives itself to everything without exhausting itself. Everywhere and nowhere, the One is in everything itself—very much like the light of the sun. The entire universe is enlightened in proportion to its participation in the One, growing dimmer and dimmer until shading off into darkness, the almost total privation of light, which is matter. Conversely, the mind participates in this omnipresent light and strives to make its way back, by way of contemplative thought, to the One. As in Plato, for Plotinus light is the condition of possibility and telos of *theoria*.

The self's return to light, the source of all visibility and intelligibility, is also at the heart of the Augustinian contemplative ascent. In Book Seven of the *Confessions* Augustine tells how, guided "by the Platonic books,"

> I was admonished to return to myself. With you as a guide I entered my innermost citadel, and was given the power to do so because you had become my helper. I entered and with my soul's eye, such as it was, saw above that same eye of my soul the immutable light higher than my mind—not the light of every day, obvious to anyone, nor a larger version of the same kind which would, as it were, have given out a much brighter light and filled everything with its magnitude. It was not that light, but a different thing, utterly different from all our kinds of light. It transcended our mind, not in the way that oil floats on water, nor as heaven is above earth. It was superior, because it made me, and I was inferior because I was made by it. (7.10.16)

The light that Augustine reaches at the end of his ascent, however reminiscent it might be, is not the Platonic Good but God himself.[58] Particularly Augustine's earlier writings echo the Platonic phenomenology of the Good, for instance, in the *Soliloquies* where he joins beauty to the appearance of the divine light.[59] Augustine marries the Greek metaphysics of light with the Judeo-Christian theology of light—similarly here to the way he does it in his theory of contemplation.[60]

What sets Augustine's understanding of the divine light apart is its location within the self. Unlike Plato, whose allegories figure light as the telos of a physical journey (see *Republic* and *Phaedrus*), and unlike Paul, who encountered Christ as a blinding light on the road to Damascus, Augustine seeks the triune God by looking into the depth of his soul. A famous passage in *De vera religione* (*On True Religion*) declares introspection the salient feature of the Augustinian art of turning:

> Do not go abroad. Return within yourself [*In te ipsum redi*]. In the inward man dwells truth [*In interiore homine habitat veritas*]. If you find that you are by nature mutable, transcend yourself. But remember that in doing so it is the reasoning soul that is doing the transcending. Make for the place from where the light illuminates your reason. (39.72)[61]

God, "the true light which ... enlightens every man" (Jn 1:9), is to be found in the soul, providing the illumination required for knowing the self, truth, and, of course, God himself. Divine illumination comes in addition to intellectual vision and its objects as the third necessary ingredient for rational thought to operate (see also *Soliloquies* 1.6.12, 1.8.15).[62] Joining the notion of God as light to this theory of cognitive illumination, Augustine writes in *The Literal Meaning of Genesis* that the light by which the soul is illuminated lets it

> see and truly understand everything, either in itself or in the light. For the Light is God Himself, whereas the soul is a creature; yet since it is rational and intellectual, it is made in His image. And when it tries to behold the Light, it trembles in its weakness and finds itself unable to do so. Yet from this source comes all the understanding it is able to attain. (12.31.59)

Under normal conditions of cognition the divine light illuminating the objects of understanding remains itself imperceptible; on the one hand, because the mind is not ready yet to behold it directly, and on the other, because as medium it goes unnoticed when attention is being absorbed by the illuminated objects. However, in contemplation and rapture the light of God itself becomes the object of intellectual vision:

> When, therefore, [the soul] is thus carried off and, after being withdrawn from the senses of the body, is made present to this vision in a more perfect manner (not by spatial relation, but in a way proper to its being), it also sees above itself that Light in whose illumination it is enabled to see all the objects it sees and understands in itself. (*Literal Meaning* 12.31.59)

As we have seen earlier, only those who have cleansed themselves and are pure of heart are elevated to such a *contemplatio Dei*, and even so, beholding God dwell "in unapproachable light" can occur only as the result of an act of divine grace. Whether the illumination necessary for the operation of ordinary rational thought is contingent on direct divine intervention or on the more indirect endowment of a light of reason has been the subject of intense scholarly debate—in large part because Augustine is vague and equivocal about the precise workings of the divine light in normal cognition. Not surprisingly, the vagueness was in no small part responsible for the considerable influence that Augustine's theory of illumination exerted on later thinkers all the way to Descartes and Malebranche.

Richard of Saint Victor, for instance, describes in the *Benjamin minor* how to wipe the mirror of one's soul, which is "dirty from the dust of useless thoughts," so that

> a kind of splendor of divine light begins to shine in it and a great beam of unexpected vision appears in his eyes. This light illumined the light of him who said: "the light of your face has been sealed upon us, Lord; you have put joy in my heart" (Ps 4:7). Therefore, from the vision of this light that it wonders at within itself, the soul is kindled from above in a marvelous way and is animated to see the living light that is above it. (chap. 72)

In Bonaventure's *Itinerarium* the divine light comes into the focus as the self turns away from the visible world and returns within itself to discover in the three mental faculties—memory, intellect, and will—the image of the triune God:

> But since our mind itself is changeable, it could not see this truth shining forth in so changeless a manner were it not for some other light absolutely and unchangeably resplendent; nor can this light possibly be a created light subject to change. The intellect, therefore, knows in that light *that enlightens every man who comes into the world*, which is the *True Light* and *the Word in the beginning with God*. (III.3, p. 20)

Even Thomas Aquinas, whose theory of the agent intellect is thought to have put an end to the Augustinian theory of divine illumination, appears more of a holdout defender, shoring it up by placing it in an Aristotelian framework. For the echoes of Augustine are clearly audible in passages like the following from the *Summa Theologiae*:

> For the intellectual light itself which is in us, is nothing else than a participated likeness of the uncreated light, in which are contained the eternal types [*rationes aeternae*]. Whence it is written (Psalms 4:6f.), *Many say: Who showeth us good things?* which question the Psalmist answers, *The light of Thy countenance, O Lord, is signed upon us*, as though he were to say: By the seal of the Divine light in us, all things are made known to us. (ST Ia, q. 84, a. 5)

God, the ultimate telos of contemplation, thus manifests himself in the form of a resplendent light, so resplendent that it threatens to overwhelm the eyes of the mind, which are feeble due to man's fallenness. As I demonstrate in the concluding section of this chapter, a version of Augustine's theory of divine illumination was alive and well in Descartes' thought.

Descartes' *Contemplatio Dei* and the *Lumen Naturale*

By reserving the term "contemplation" for the vision of the divine light at the end of the Third Meditation, Descartes was clearly striving to set it apart from meditation or, given that this is also the climactic moment of the meditations, to conceive it as a meditative mode in its own right, clearly distinguishable from its more mundane counterpart. Descartes, in placing contemplation at the exact midpoint of the *Meditations*, marks contemplation as the telos of the performed meditative work and thus as the culmination of the turn away from the sensory world, both inward and upward toward the intelligible world. As the apex of the mind's meditative work, the contemplation of Descartes' meditator involves the vision of God by the *acies mentis* or *obtutus mentis*, Descartes' terms for the mind's gaze in the intuition of intellectual matters.[63] Like Plato, Plotinus, Augustine, and the other philosophers and theologians in the tradition we have outlined, Descartes regularly compares mental to corporeal vision. And like them, he believes that mental vision can be trained and cleansed in order to behold the self and God. Like the spiritual masters of the twelfth century, Descartes characterizes meditation in terms of movement, and he makes it part of the Cartesian *methodos*. By meditating, the meditator makes their way toward the ultimate end of contemplation, when and where the mind's movement comes to rest (even if only for a moment). Unlike meditation, which is extended, continuous, and repeatable, contemplation is punctiform, ephemeral, and rare. Accordingly, Descartes' meditator describes their *contemplatio Dei* as a deliberate indulgence, that is, as a pause before returning to the hard work of meditating. The meditator clearly identifies their *contemplatio Dei* as an intuition, in contrast to the meditation occurring elsewhere in the work, which includes both deductions and intuitions. Once they have moved from meditation to contemplation, they leave behind the doubt and uncertainty associated with the meditative mode. Or, putting it another way, contemplation is characterized by certitude of a different kind. Correspondingly, meditation and contemplation have different objects. Whereas the former is concerned with sensible as well as intelligible things, contemplation concerns itself only with the intelligible world. Or put differently, contemplation cognizes innate ideas exclusively, in contrast to meditation, which also takes adventitious and fictive ideas as its objects, which are immitted by the external world. In meditation the mind is cleansed and the self trained to be ready and worthy to contemplate God. It enacts both aversion and conversion, whereas contemplation represents the final step of conversion, fixing the mind's attention on itself and its deiformity.

By referencing beatific vision, Descartes' meditator raises the question of the nature of the object of their contemplation or, to put it less technically, the question of what they are contemplating and what they see when they see God in the form of a beautiful light. In the spring of 1648 Descartes provides an answer of a sort in elaborating his understanding of the extent of our knowledge of God both in this life and the next, in a little-known letter to Jean de Silhon, whose *L'immortalitaté de l'âme* (1634) prefigures a number of Cartesian positions. In response to Silhon's question "about the nature of our knowledge of God in the beatific vision" (CSM III 330; AT V 136), Descartes indicates Silhon had himself provided a partial answer in distinguishing it "from our present knowledge of God in virtue of it being intuitive" (CSM III 330–31; AT V 136). However, Descartes parts ways on the matter of whether "this intuitive knowledge of God will be similar to ours or different only in extent and not in the manner of knowledge" (CSM III 331; AT V 136).[64] He writes:

Intuitive knowledge is an illumination of the mind, by which it sees in the light of God whatever pleases him to show it by a direct impression of the divine clarity on our understanding, which in this is not considered as an agent but simply as a receiver of the rays of divinity. Whatever we can know of God in this life, short of a miracle, is the result of reasoning and discursive inquiry. It is deduced from the principles of faith, which is obscure, or it comes from the natural ideas and notions we have, which even at their clearest are only gross and confused on so sublime a topic. Consequently, whatever knowledge we have or acquire by way of reason is as dark as the principles from which it is derived, and is moreover infected with the uncertainty we find in all our reasonings. (CSM III 331; AT V 136–37)

In answer to Silhon's question, Descartes takes recourse to well-worn terminology he has employed as early as *Rules for the Direction of the Mind* and adapts it to conceptualize the knowledge of God in beatific vision and sublunary life. The knowledge of God in a *visio beatifica* is intuitive, and Descartes characterizes such an intuition very much like the one his meditator enacts in their *contemplatio Dei* at the end of the Third Meditation. Essentially, intuition is the illumination of the mind by the light of God by which he communicates his essence, to use the standard vocabulary. Descartes continues:

Now compare those two kinds of knowledge to see if there is any similarity between such a troubled and doubtful perception (which costs us much labour and which is enjoyed only momentarily once acquired) and a pure, constant, clear, certain, effortless and ever-present light.

Can you doubt that our mind, when it is detached from the body, or has a glorified body which will no longer hinder it, can receive such direct illumination and knowledge? Why, even in this body the senses give it such knowledge of corporeal and sensible things, and our soul has already some direct knowledge of the beneficence of its creator without which it would not be capable of reasoning. I agree that such knowledge is somewhat obscured by the soul's mingling with the body; but still it gives us a primary, unearned and certain awareness [*connaissance*] which we touch with our mind with more confidence than we give the testimony of the eyes. You will surely admit that you are less certain of the presence of the objects you see than the truth of the proposition "I am thinking, therefore I exist." Now this knowledge is not the work of your reasoning or information passed on to you by teachers; it is something that your mind sees, feels and handles; and although your imagination insistently mixes itself up with your thoughts and lessens the clarity of this knowledge by trying to clothe it with shapes, it is nevertheless a proof of the capacity of the soul for receiving intuitive knowledge from God. (CSM III 331; AT V 137–38)

Drawing on Thomas Aquinas's notion of spiritual cognition, Descartes conceives divine communication as a "direct impression of the divine clarity on our understanding." Once again simultaneously invoking and challenging a Scholastic position, he maintains that the illumination is not the doing of what Thomas Aquinas calls the "agent intellect"; on the contrary, the mind is the passive "receiver of the rays of divinity." God gives the mind something to be seen in the light he casts. In being "unearned," intuition is tantamount to a divine gift of grace. Again and again, Descartes stresses the directness and immediacy of such an intuitive knowledge. Whatever the mind sees in such an intuition, it sees because it has been directly impressed by God rather than by the objects in question. The series of attributes Descartes uses to characterize intuition, "pure, constant, clear, certain, effortless and ever-present," sets it apart from its counterpart, deduction. Deductive knowledge of God is necessarily indirect and mediated. It originates either in articles of faith, which by definition are not clear and distinct, or innate ideas, which while clear and distinct regarding all other things, are "gross and confused on so sublime a topic." And not only does discursive inquiry leading to knowledge of God begin in darkness and obscurity; its subsequent progress is "infected with the uncertainty we find in all our reasonings." Descartes suggests that a chain of deduction can end in a form of intuitive knowledge of God, an intuition, however, that in its "troubled," "doubtful," laborious, and ephemeral quality is the polar opposite of the direct illumination received by the mind in its "glorified body" during a beatific vision.

Nevertheless, Descartes states explicitly that even in this life the mind is capable of some forms of direct knowledge. Sensory perception is an unmediated form of knowledge, with intuition understood correspondingly as a kind of intellectual perception. The second form is the mind's "direct knowledge of the beneficence of its creator" by which it is "capable of reasoning." In other words, the direct knowledge that the mind has of God in this life is not of himself but of his beneficence, of the good he does. Note how beneficence, derived from the Latin verb *bene-ficere*, echoes *beatifica*, which is derived from *beati-ficere*. Beneficence is a lesser, mundane version of beatificence, the ultimate beatitude that the blessed receive in heaven, which while dimmed in the direct knowledge of the soul in union with the body, still gives the mind "a primary, unearned and certain awareness [*connaissance*]." As an example here Descartes cites the evidence of the *cogito,* which cannot be mediated either by external authority or deductive reasoning.[65] We saw in Chapter 2 that the mind needs to think and perform the *cogito* by and for itself; as an intuition the *cogito* "is something that your mind sees, feels, and handles" without mediation. However, this cannot be entirely correct, since the *cogito* is "proof of the capacity of the soul for receiving intuitive knowledge from God." In other words, the intuition of the *cogito* is enabled by God's beneficence.

So what form does this divine beneficence take? What is the role of God in the mind's intuitions? Descartes' answer is that it takes the form of the "immediate light cast by the Godhead on our mind." For this "direct illumination" is definitive of all "intuitive knowledge," not just the intuitive knowledge of God but every kind of intuition, no matter what its object. Whatever the mind sees in an intuition, it sees because God illuminates it with his light. Yet at the same time, it seems unlikely that the meaning here is that every intuition is the result of a miracle or direct intervention by God since Descartes distinguishes explicitly between any such miraculous illumination and the "normal" illumination, the *lumen naturale*, which is responsible for illuminating every intuition and, of course, for the self-evidence of the *cogito*. And in the Second Set of Replies, he defines the light of grace, the *lumen gratiae*, in contrast, as a "a certain inner light which comes from God, and when we are supernaturally illumined by it we are confident that what is put forward for us to believe has been revealed by God himself" (CSM 105; AT VII 148). The *lumen gratiae* lends "clarity and transparency" to matters of faith, which are constitutively obscure, and does so in a way that the mind recognizes God's direct intervention in real time. It is the natural light that Descartes' meditator intuits in their *contemplatio Dei* at the end of the Third Meditation—a claim I seek to demonstrate in the remaining pages of this chapter.[66]

Not coincidentally, the natural light makes its first appearance in the Third Meditation. The term *lumen naturale* occurs thirteen times in the *Meditations*, once in the Synopsis, which is not actually part of the meditative turn, once in the Sixth Meditation, twice in the Fourth Meditation, and nine times in the Third Meditation—ten times if one counts the "immense light" that Descartes' meditator contemplates in their beatific vision. The first mention of the "natural light" in the Third Meditation (CSM II 26–27; AT VII 38) occurs when Descartes' meditator contrasts their impulse to believe that their ideas have referents in the outside world, which they attribute to nature, with the natural light, which has revealed the *cogito* to them.[67] Thus, Descartes' meditator had already relied on the natural light when they discovered and enacted the *cogito*—however, without recognizing it as such. The task of recognizing the role of the natural light in the meditator's cognition of innate ideas, such as the *cogito* and the idea of God, and attending to its operation falls to the Third Meditation. The next time the natural light occurs is an instance of its use or operation. For it becomes "manifest" to Descartes' meditator "by the natural light that there must at least as much [reality] in the efficient and total cause as in the effect of that cause" (CSM II 28; AT VII 40). From then on the natural light plays a crucial role in the proof of God or, put differently, the discovery of the idea of God in the meditator's mind. In fact, the discovery of the innate idea of God and the gradual revelation of the natural light condition each other until they merge in the final *contemplatio Dei*. More broadly, the *Meditations* can be read as a way or *methodos* to unveil the indwelling *lumen naturale* that has been clouded by sensory perceptions and prejudices. By turning away from the sensory world and discerning their prejudices, Descartes' meditator cleanses their mental gaze, *acies mentis*, so that they can see clearly the innate ideas imprinted in their mind.

While the Cartesian meditator has to put in considerable effort discovering the *lumen naturale* in the course of their meditations, Descartes himself had been assigning the *lumen naturale* a pivotal role in a variety of contexts from very early on. Increasing the natural light of reason was essential to Descartes' agenda in the *Rules for the Direction of the Mind*, "not with a view to solving this or that scholastic problem, but in order that [the] intellect should show [the] will what decision it ought to make in each of life's contingencies" (CSM I 10; AT X 361). In the *Discourse on the Method* Descartes traverses the same trajectory in compressed and accelerated form when he writes, "I gradually freed myself from many errors which may obscure our natural light and make us less capable of heeding reason" (CSM I 116; AT VI 10). And in the preface to the French edition of the *Principles of Philosophy*, Descartes' attempt to produce an alternative to Scholastic textbooks, he defines the supreme good, "considered by the natural light without the light of faith," as "nothing other than the knowledge of the truth through its first causes, that is to say wisdom, of which philosophy is the study" (CSM I 181; AT IXB 4). The natural light, in short, is the medium in which the mind knows truth from first causes, which as a philosophical program is spelled out in the title of Descartes's attempt at philosophical dialogue, written roughly at the same time as the *Meditations*: *The Search for Truth by Means of the Natural Light*.[68] It is no surprise, then, that Descartes' work was so closely associated with light among contemporary readers that the frontispiece of his collected letters portrays him illuminated in the manner of Augustine, Luther, or Ignatius (see Fig. 10).

As Descartes observes in the *Discourse*, the natural light enables the mind "to distinguish truth from falsehood" (CSM I 124; AT VI 27). In a letter to Marin Mersenne, written only two years after the *Discourse*, Descartes goes a step further, claiming: "I have no criterion for [my truths] except the natural light" (III 139; AT II 598). He goes on to explain that while everyone knows what truth is, "no logical definition can be given which will help anyone discover its nature. I think the same of many other things which are very simple and are known naturally, such as shape, size, motion, place, time and so on: if you try to define these things you only

FIGURE 10. Frontispiece, in René Descartes, *Opera Philosophica* (Frankfurt: F. Knochius, 1692), 1v. Courtesy of the University of Chicago Library's Hanna Holborn Gray Special Collections Research Center.

obscure them and cause confusion" (CSM III 139; AT II 598). Cognition by the natural light, in other words, is irreducible. Just as the physical light is the condition of possibility for corporeal vision, the natural light is the medium for the intellectual vision of intuition. The physical light makes visible the objects of the material world; the natural light illuminates, thereby revealing, the objects of the intelligible world. The natural light is natural because it is innate and indwelling—in contrast to the physical light, which comes from outside and is thus adventitious. And aside from the natural light, there is no way to prove the truth of ideas. Indeed, cognition by the natural light is the foundation for all other reasoning. It is nothing other than intuition, which, as we remember from the *Regulae*, is the "indubitable conception of a clear and attentive mind" proceeding "solely from the light of reason" (CSM I 14; AT X 361).[69] Importantly, this description suggests that Descartes believed that cognition by the natural light is a kind of epistemic revelation in which the mind has little agency. In the *lumen naturale* truths appear *per se manifesta*, or self-evident. And as the medium of evidence, the natural light enables the autopsy on which Descartes' epistemology is predicated.

Descartes concedes, in the previously quoted letter to Mersenne, that, although everyone possesses "the same natural light," "hardly anyone makes good use of that light." Explaining why this is the case, Descartes frequently identifies two obstacles that stand in the way. First, the self's mental vision can be "blinded by the images of things perceived by the senses" (CSM II 32; AT VII 47). Because of the mind's union with the body, it is flooded, and consequently clouded, by sensory ideas as soon as it relaxes its attention. The second factor involves preconceived opinions or prejudices, that is, ideas judged to be true on the authority of others, which have the effect of eclipsing the mind's indwelling powers of insight (see, for instance, CSM II 97; AT VII 135). The chronic failure of people to employ reason or the power of understanding is thus for Descartes not a question of being insufficiently endowed but of the improper use or corruption of reason so that education appears as a double-edged sword. It can either further the obfuscation of the mind's natural light by informing it with knowledge that is literally preconceived by others or it can train the mind in the use of its own powers of reasoning, thereby clarifying its innate natural light. We recall from the intellectual *Bildungsgeschichte* Descartes provided in the *Discourse on the Method* how he "gradually freed [him]self from many errors which may obscure our natural light and make us less capable of heeding reason" (CSM I 116; AT VI 10), and that Cartesian method was conceived as a cleansing agent, to rid the mind of "such haphazard studies and obscure reflections" that "blur the natural light and blind our intelligence" (CSM I 16; AT X 371). In his later work the role of training and improving mental vision is taken over by meditative thought. Mersenne writes to his friend in the Second Set of Objections: "You have trained your mind by continual meditations for several years, so that what seems doubtful and very obscure to others is quite clear to you; indeed you may have a clear mental intuition of these matters and perceive them as the primary and principal objects of the natural light" (CSM II 87; AT VII 122).

In summary, while the mind is the passive recipient of illumination by the natural light, it has an active role to play in undoing the dimming or obstruction of the mind. The remaining question, then, is whether the natural light we have seen spanning Descartes' entire oeuvre is identical with the light that his meditator intuits, admires, and adores in their *contemplatio Dei* at the end of the Third Meditation. At first glance it seems unlikely that they are the same. Their vision of the "immense light" bears many of the trappings of a traditional vision of God. The prominent and exalted position of the vision in the text, the immensity of the light, and the admiration and even adoration it prompts are not usually associated with philosophical *theoria*. Descartes seems to have his meditator recalling visions from the Bible or the lives of saints in which God appears as a blinding light. At second glance, however, the reading is more complicated. Looking more closely, we cannot but notice that the object of the meditator's description is not the beauty of *his* light but the beauty of "this [*huius*] immense light." Descartes' meditator is careful not to identify the light directly with God, which means that the illumination they receive in their contemplation does not have the *lumen gloriae* as its source. To be sure, the *lumen naturale* also comes from God; the point is that the manner of its communication is different. The decisive difference between the *lumen gloriae* in a beatific vision and *lumen naturale* in this contemplation of God is that the former happens in real time, while the latter takes place at birth. The *lumen naturale*, in contrast to the *lumen gloriae*, is not immitted but implanted. By virtue of its innateness the natural light suffuses the human mind itself and hence requires no separate intervention.

Similarly, reinforcing a critical point discussed more extensively in Chapter 4, it is in being guided by deductive reasoning that the mind discovers the idea of God in itself. When Descartes' meditator finally intuits God as an idea in their mind, they recognize it as having been woven into the fabric of their mind like the mark of the craftsman is impressed into the work, which is to say that receiving the idea of God into the mind entails a profound modification of the mind. Belonging to the mind itself, it cannot adequately represent the true essence of God and thus subtend a *visio beatifica*. Following in the footsteps of Thomas Aquinas, Descartes has his meditator know their creator only through its creation, that is, their own mind. Thus, the intuition of the idea of God in their mind is unmediated and not the referent of this idea: God. However, because it is directly impressed by the craftsman God, as it were, no idea in the mind is as clear and distinct once it has been recognized as the idea of God. The recognition itself comes about through the perception of the light by which the meditator intuits the idea of God so utterly clearly and distinctly. The light is the *lumen naturale* that has been dwelling in their mind from birth, like the idea of God and other innate ideas. And, indeed, the idea of God and the light illuminating it by which it is revealed and perceived are concomitant. We have seen this already in a passage from the *Summa Theologiae* (ST Ia, q. 84, a. 5), where Thomas Aquinas cites the Psalmist's assurance that "the light of Thy countenance, O Lord, is signed upon us," figuring the mind's illumination as the imprinting of a seal. Descartes follows suit, in believing that the illumination of the mind by God is the same as God impressing the idea of himself in the mind. Deiformity is not simply a matter of form being stamped into the mind by God, so that the mind is formed like that of its creator, but extends to its inner and innate luminosity, to the light by which the mind intuits its deiformity.

Only now, with the mind's recognition of its deiformity, that it is informed by the idea of God it finds implanted in itself, does the mind become capable of perceiving the indwelling natural light. Prior to this, the mind's clarity has been obscured by its orientation toward the sensory world and its contamination with prejudices. Like the mediality of mind, which remains invisible in ordinary acts of thought, the "light of reason" goes unnoticed as it makes visible the objects of the mind's intuitions. As Bonaventure remarks on the mind's inability to see the medium of its own illumination, "Just as the eye, intent on the various differences of color, does not see the light through which it sees other things, . . . so our mind's eye, intent on particular and universal beings, does not notice that Being which is beyond all categories, even though it comes first to mind, and through it, all other things" (*Itinerarium* 5.4).[70]

For Descartes, the telos of the contemplative ascent is the *theoria* of the divine light illuminating everything, so his meditator's *contemplatio Dei* is not a beatific vision. It is the recognition and perception of the natural light in its full splendor, after being cleansed and having some of its prelapsarian shine restored. It is the seeing of the light itself as the medium and thus condition of possibility, of intellectual vision: in short, the illumination of illumination or the clear and distinct cognition of the medium of clear and distinct cognition. By intuiting the indwelling natural light implanted by God in their mind and proceeding into the *contemplatio Dei* at the end of the Third Meditation, the meditator reenacts the *synderesis*, the vision of the *scintilla animae* the youthful Descartes experienced in his conversion. The vision of the *lumen naturale* in the *contemplatio Dei*, in short, is the telos and culmination of Descartes' meditative turn.

Acknowledgments

Over fifteen years in the making, this book has benefited from many institutions, interlocutors, and personal friendships; and in the process I have accrued substantial intellectual debts. The Humanities Division at the University of Chicago provided me with vital sabbatical leave. Fellowships from the Kulturwissenschaftliches Kolleg at the Universität Konstanz and the Franke Institute for the Humanities at the University of Chicago afforded me not only with additional free time but also a stimulating ambience in which to develop my ideas. Two intensive workshops at Indiana University and the University of Chicago, co-organized with Hall Björnstad, helped me test my understanding of early modern conversion and Descartes' preoccupation with spiritual exercises. Students in my graduate seminars at the University of Chicago and UCLA and in compact seminars at the Universität Zürich were eager to put my ideas about spiritual exercises and the pragmatics of thinking to the test. Audiences at Harvard University; the University of California at Santa Barbara; the University of York; the Universities of Zürich, Konstanz, and Hildesheim; the Humboldt Universität and the Zentrum für Literaturforschung in Berlin; the Ludwig-Maximilians Universität München; and the Internationales Forschungszentrum Kulturwissenschaften in Vienna provided valuable feedback at various stages of the project. Timothy Harrison, Armando Maggi, Constantin Nakassis, Richard Neer, Mark Payne, Benjamin Saltzman, Eric Santner, Richard Strier, Anubav Vasudevan, and David Wellbery from the University of Chicago commented on different parts of the manuscript. Christopher Braider, Peter Erickson, Andrea Gadberry, Dalia Judovitz, Christian Kiening, Walter Melion, Dominik Perler, and Stephan Schmid asked probing questions and offered valuable insights. Hall Björnstad has been a thought partner on early modern religious thought and discourse for the last decade. Eric Downing, David Levin, and Andreas Schmidt have accompanied this seemingly interminable project from the beginning and are paradigms of intellectual friendship. The many conversations with Andreas Schmidt helped gestate and mature it. Eric Downing's mentorship has made much of the book better, including its title. And I could not imagine a more generous colleague and friend than David Levin. I cannot thank them enough. Deans John Boyer and Anne Robertson provided publication support as well as unflagging encouragement when it seemed impossible to combine a life of scholarship with the day-to-day demands of a university administrator. Don Reneau was an understanding and perspicacious first copyeditor who cut the original manuscript significantly and made my at times "Germanic" prose much more readable. I am grateful to the two anonymous readers from Stanford University Press for their suggestions on the manuscript and to Cynthia Lindlof for her extraordinary editorial care and exactitude. Most important, I want to thank my family. A project like this can at times be all-absorbing, and they bore my distraction with generosity and love. Finally, I want to thank Elizabeth, who cheered and carried this book across the finish line.

I thank the publishers for permission to draw on material from the following two essays, which allowed me to develop my understanding of conversion that permeates this book and to conceptualize what I call the Cartesian art of turning:

"*Techne tes periagogeis*: Conversion and the Art of Spiritual Navigation," in *Konversion als Medium der Selbstbeschreibung in Spätantike, Mittelalter und Früher Neuzeit*, ed. Werner Röcke, Ruth von Bernuth, and Julia Weitbrecht (Berlin: De Gruyter, 2015), 61–83.

"*Apertio Libri*: Codex and Conversion," in *Literary Studies and the Pursuits of Reading*, ed. Eric Downing, Richard Benson, and Jonathan Hess (Rochester, NY: Camden House, 2012), 17–39.

Notes

Introduction

1. See Dominik Perler, "Was ist ein frühneuzeitlicher philosophischer Text? Kritische Überlegungen zum Rationalismus/Empirismus-Schema," in *Zwischen den Disziplinen? Perspektiven der Frühneuzeitforschung*, ed. Helmut Puff and Christopher Wild (Göttingen: Wallstein, 2003), 58–65. See also John Cottingham, "The Desecularization of Descartes," in *The Persistence of the Sacred in Modern Thought*, ed. Nathan Jacobs and Chris Firestone (Notre Dame, IN: University of Notre Dame Press, 2012), 15–37.

2. On the following, see Pierre Hadot, *Philosophy as a Way of Life: Spiritual Exercises from Socrates to Foucault*, ed. Arnold Davidson, trans. Michael Chase (Oxford: Blackwell, 1995), 59, and more generally 59–65. Cited in the text as PWL followed by page number.

3. Michel Foucault, *The Hermeneutics of the Subject: Lectures at the Collège de France, 1981–82*, ed. Frédéric Gros, trans. Graham Burchell (New York: Palgrave Macmillan, 2005), 178. Cited in the text as HS followed by page number.

4. It seems important to note that the Jewish tradition, most notably Philo of Alexandria, had already adopted ancient philosophy.

5. See Jean Leclercq, "Pour l'histoire de l'expression 'philosophie chrétienne,'" *Mélanges de science religieuse* 9 (1952): 221–26.

6. He claims that "scholasticism was already an effort to remove the condition of spirituality laid down in all of ancient philosophy and all Christian thought (Saint Augustine and so forth)" (HS 191).

7. For the debate between these two historians of spiritual practice, see Pierre Hadot, "Un dialogue interrompu avec Michel Foucault. Convergences et divergences," in *Exercices spirituels et philosophie antique* (Paris: A. Michel, 2002), 305–11. Hadot discusses some other differences in a conversation with Arnold Davidson in Pierre Hadot, *The Present Alone Is Our Happiness: Conversations with Jeannie Carlier and Arnold I. Davidson* (Stanford, CA: Stanford University Press, 2011), 136.

8. This is not the place to sort out these seeming inconsistencies or contradictions in Foucault's account of Descartes. For that, see Edward F. McGushin, "Foucault's

Cartesian Meditations," *International Philosophical Quarterly* 45 (2005): 41–59; and his *Foucault's Askēsis: An Introduction to the Philosophical Life* (Evanston, IL: Northwestern University Press, 2007), 173–94. Not entirely convincingly, McGushin argues that Descartes resorts to the spiritual knowledge of the *epimeleia heautou* in order to overcome it and usher in philosophy as theoretical knowledge: The *Meditations* "are an *askesis* to end all *askesis*" (McGushin, "Foucault's Cartesian Meditations," 58).

9. Michel Foucault, "My Body, This Paper, This Fire," in *Aesthetics, Method, and Epistemology*, ed. James D. Faubion (New York: New Press, 1998), 405.

10. Throughout, "AT" refers to the standard edition of Descartes' works, in either its original Latin or French: René Descartes, *Oeuvres de Descartes*, ed. Charles Adam and Paul Tannery, 12 vols. (Paris: Vrin, 1964–76). "CSM" refers to the standard English translation: René Descartes, *The Philosophical Writings of Descartes*, ed. John Cottingham, Robert Stoothoff, Dugald Murdoch, and Anthony Kenny, 3 vols. (Cambridge: Cambridge University Press, 1984–91). I have modified the translations as needed. In his dedicatory letter to Elisabeth of Bohemia, Descartes writes similarly that "philosophy is nothing else but the study of wisdom" (CSM I 192; AT VIIIA 4).

11. As Hadot observes, "Genuinely creative philosophical activity would develop *outside* the university, in the persons of Descartes, Spinoza, Malebranche, and Leibniz" (PWL 270).

12. Plato, *The Republic of Plato*, trans. Allan Bloom (New York: Basic Books, 1991), 197 (518d).

13. For an elaboration of this media-theoretical framing of the Reformation, see Helmut Puff, Ulrike Strasser, and Christopher Wild, eds., *Cultures of Communication: Theologies of Media in Early Modern Europe and Beyond* (Toronto: University of Toronto Press, 2017).

14. See John Van Engel, *Sisters and Brothers of the Common Life: The Devotio Moderna and the World of the Later Middle Ages* (Philadelphia: University of Pennsylvania Press, 2008).

15. See Rachel Fulton Brown, "My Psalter, My Self; or How to Get a Grip on the Office according to Jan Mombaer (d.c. 1501): An Exercise in Training the Attention for Prayer," *Spiritus: A Journal of Christian Spirituality* 12 (2012): 75–105.

16. For the following discussion, see Martin Nicol, *Meditation bei Luther* (Göttingen: Vandenhoek and Ruprecht, 1984).

17. Martin Luther, "Preface to the Complete Edition of Luther's Latin Writings," in Martin Luther, *Selections from His Writings*, trans. John Dillenberger (Garden City, NY: Doubleday, 1961), 11.

18. For France, see L. W. B. Brockliss, *French Higher Education in the Seventeenth and Eighteenth Centuries: A Cultural History* (Oxford: Clarendon Press,

1987); A. Lynn Martin, *The Jesuit Mind: The Mentality of an Elite in Early Modern France* (Ithaca, NY: Cornell University Press, 1988).

19. A particularly telling example is one of the most famous Jesuit dramas, *Cenodoxus* by Jakob Bidermann, which portrays the fate of the vainglorious doctor of Paris whose name lends the play its title. His condemnation to hell prompts a group of followers to convert and found the Carthusian order, on which Ignatius modeled his own new order. In other words, *Cenodoxus* stages in a veiled form the founding of the Jesuit order and exhorts its actors and spectators to reenact the foundational conversion. Not surprisingly, legend has it that the play's first performance impelled the lead actor to enter the Jesuit order and thirteen of the Bavarian nobility in the audience to opt to undergo the Ignatian exercises. See Christopher Wild, "1609— The Munich Production of Jakob Bidermann's *Cenodoxus* Effects the Conversion of Fourteen Nobles from the Bavarian Court: Jesuit Theater and the Blindness of Self-Knowledge," in *A New History of German Literature*, ed. David Wellbery (Cambridge, MA: Harvard University Press, 2004), 270–75.

20. There is significant debate about this question. See Michel Hermans and Michel Klein, "Ces *Exercices spirituels* que Descartes aurait pratiqués," *Archives des philosophie* 59 (1996): 427–40.

21. See Anthony Levi, S.J., *French Moralists: The Theory of Passions 1585 to 1649* (Oxford: Clarendon Press, 1964), 136–41.

22. For Descartes' relation with Bérulle, see Adrien Baillet, *La vie de Monsieur Descartes* (Paris: Chez D. Horthemels, 1691), 160–66; Stephen Gaukroger, *Descartes: An Intellectual Biography* (Oxford: Clarendon Press, 1995), 183–85; Geneviève Rodis-Lewis, *Descartes: His Life and Thought*, trans. Jane Marie Todd (Ithaca, NY: Cornell University Press, 1998), 67–69; Richard Popkin, *The History of Scepticism: From Savonarola to Bayle* (Oxford: Oxford University Press, 2003), 145–47; Ben-Yami Hanoch, *Descartes' Philosophical Revolution: A Reassessment* (London: Palgrave Macmillan, 2015), 153–62.

23. See Peter Dear, *Mersenne and the Learning of the Schools* (Ithaca, NY: Cornell University Press, 1988).

24. See Günther Abel, *Stoizismus und Frühe Neuzeit. Zur Entstehungsgeschichte modernen Denkens im Felde von Ethik und Politik* (Berlin: De Gruyter, 1978); Gerhard Oestreich, *Neostoicism and the Early Modern State* (Cambridge: Cambridge University, 1982); Mark Morford, *Stoics and Neostoics: Rubens and the Circle of Lipsius* (Princeton, NJ: Princeton University Press, 1991); Adriana McCrea, *Constant Minds: Political Virtue and the Lipsian Paradigm in England, 1584–1650* (Toronto: University of Toronto Press, 1997).

25. One notable exception is John Sellars, "Justus Lipsius's *De constantia*: A Stoic Spiritual Exercise," *Poetics Today* 28 (2007): 339–62.

26. Christopher Brooke, *Philosophic Pride: Stoicism and Political Thought from Lipsius to Rousseau* (Princeton, NJ: Princeton University Press, 2012), 76.

27. Jan Papy, "Lipsius' (Neo-)Stoicism: Constancy between Christian Faith and Stoic Virtue," *Grotiana* 22/23 (2001–2): 47–72; John M. Cooper, "Justus Lipsius and the Revival of Stoicism in Late Sixteenth-Century Europe," in *New Essays on the History of Autonomy*, ed. Natalie Brender and Larry Krasnoff (Cambridge: Cambridge University Press, 2004), 7–29; Jacqueline Lagrée, "Constancy and Coherence," in *Stoicism: Traditions and Transformations*, ed. Steven K. Strange and Jack Zupko (Cambridge: Cambridge University Press, 2004), 148–76.

28. *De constantia* was published in more than eighty editions between the sixteenth and eighteenth centuries, over forty in the Latin original and the rest in vernacular translations.

29. See Levi, *French Moralists*, 74–94. Du Vair also published a short handbook, *De la sainte philosophie*, translated as *The Moral Philosophie of the Stoicks*, summarizing the main tenets of his philosophy.

30. See Levi, *French Moralists*, 95–111; Popkin, *The History of Scepticism*, 7–61; José R. Maia Neto, "Charron's Epoché and Descartes' Cogito: The Sceptical Base of Descartes' Refutation of Scepticism," in *The Return of Scepticism from Hobbes and Descartes to Bayle*, ed. Gianni Paganini (Dordrecht: Kluwer Academic Publishers, 2003), 81–113.

31. See Derk Pereboom, "Stoic Psychotherapy in Descartes and Spinoza," *Faith and Philosophy* 11 (1994): 592–625; John Marshall, *Descartes's Moral Theory* (Ithaca, NY: Cornell University Press, 1998); Edouard Mehl, "Les méditations stoïcennes de Descartes: Hypothèses sur l'influence du stoïcisme dans la constitution de la pensée cartésienne (1629–1637)," in *Le stoïcisme au XVIe et au XVIIe siècle*, ed. P.-F. Moreau (Paris: A. Michel, 1999), 251–80; Donald Rutherford, "On the Happy Life: Descartes vis-à-vis Seneca," in *Stoicism: Traditions and Transformations*, ed. Steven K. Strange and Jack Zupko (Cambridge: Cambridge University Press, 2004), 177–97; Donald Rutherford, "Reading Descartes as a Stoic: Appropriate Action, Virtue, and the Passions," *Philosophie antique* 14 (2014): 129–55.

32. Pierre Mesnard, "L'arbre de la sagesse," in *Descartes. Cahiers de Royaumont, Philosophie, no. 2* (Paris: Éditions de Minuit, 1957), 336–59. The discussion with Gueroult's position is on pp. 350–51.

33. See L. J. Beck, *The Metaphysics of Descartes: A Study of the* Meditations (Oxford: Clarendon Press, 1965), 31; Arthur Thomson, "Ignace de Loyola et Descartes. L'influence des exercises spirituels sur les oeuvres philosophiques de Descartes," *Archives de philosophie* 35 (1972): 61–81; Walter John Stohrer, "Descartes and Ignatius Loyola: La Flèche and Manresa Revisited," *Journal of the History of Philosophy* 17 (1979): 11–27; Zeno Vendler, "Descartes' Exercises," *Canadian Journal of Philosophy* 19 (1989): 193–224; Hermans and Klein, "Ces *Exercices spirituels* que Descartes aurait pratiqués," 427–40.

34. See Hermans and Klein, "Ces *Exercices spirituels* que Descartes aurait pratiqués," 436–37.

35. Gary Hatfield, "The Senses and the Fleshless Eye: The *Meditations* as Cognitive Exercises," in *Essays on Descartes' Meditations*, ed. Amélie Oskenberg Rorty (Berkeley: University of California Press, 1986), 45–76; Stephen Menn, *Descartes and Augustine* (Cambridge: Cambridge University Press, 1998).

36. Matt Hettche, "Descartes and the Augustinian Tradition of Devotional Meditation: Tracing a Minim Connection," *Journal of the History of Philosophy* 48 (2010): 283–311.

37. Dennis Sepper, "The Texture of Thought: Why Descartes' *Meditationes* Is Meditational, and Why It Matters," in *Descartes' Natural Philosophy*, ed. Stephen Gaukroger, John A. Schuster, and John Sutton (London: Routledge, 2000), 736–50. I will refrain here from summarizing the individual findings in more detail and instead note my intellectual debts to these studies when discussing Descartes' specific spiritual practices and cognitive techniques in the following chapters. Extensive summaries of the different positions can be found in the articles by Stohrer, "Descartes and Ignatius Loyola"; Bradley Rubidge, "Descartes's *Meditations* and Devotional Meditations," *Journal of the History of Ideas* 51 (1990): 27–49; and Matt Hettche, "Descartes and the Augustinian Tradition of Devotional Meditation: Tracing a Minim Connection," *Journal of the History of Philosophy* 48 (2010): 283–311.

38. See Brian Stock, *Augustine the Reader: Meditation, Self-Knowledge, and the Ethics of Interpretation* (Cambridge, MA: Harvard University Press, 1996); Brian Stock, *After Augustine: The Meditative Reader and the Text* (Philadelphia: University of Pennsylvania Press, 2001).

39. Theodor Kobusch, "Descartes' *Meditations*: Practical Metaphysics: The Father of Rationalism in the Tradition of Spiritual Exercises," in *Philosophy as a Way of Life: Ancients and Moderns: Essays in Honor of Pierre Hadot*, ed. Michael Chase, Stephen R. L. Clark, and Michael McGhee (Chichester, UK: Wiley, 2013), 167–83.

40. Matthew L. Jones, *The Good Life in the Scientific Revolution: Descartes, Pascal, Leibniz, and the Cultivation of Virtue* (Chicago: University of Chicago Press, 2006).

41. M. Jones, *The Good Life*, 15.

42. M. Jones, *The Good Life*, 272n15.

43. Harold Bloom, *The Anxiety of Influence: A Theory of Poetry* (New York: Oxford University Press, 1973).

44. See Hettche, "Descartes and the Augustinian Tradition," 286–87; M. Jones, *The Good Life*, 26.

45. See the letters to Mersenne, November 15, 1638 (CSM III 129; AT II 435), and December 1640 (CSM III 161; AT III 261); and the letter to Colvius, November 14, 1640 (CSM III 159; AT III 247–48). For the comparison of the Augustinian and Cartesian *cogito*, see Gareth Matthews, *Thought's Ego in Augustine and Descartes*

(Ithaca, NY: Cornell University Press, 1992); Christoph Horn, "Welche Bedeutung hat das augustinische Cogito? (Buch XI. 26)," in *Augustinus, De civitate dei*, ed. Christoph Horn (Berlin: De Gruyter, 1997), 109–29; Matthew Drever, *Image, Identity, and the Forming of the Augustinian Soul* (New York: Oxford University Press, 2013), 116–31.

46. For other variants, see *De trinitate* 10.10.14; *Enchiridion* 7.20; *De libero arbitrio* 2.3.7.

47. Mary Carruthers, *The Craft of Thought: Meditation, Rhetoric, and the Making of Images, 400–1200* (Cambridge: Cambridge University Press, 1998), 2, 4.

48. Carruthers, *The Craft of Thought*, 72.

49. In modern philosophy Hannah Arendt has raised such questions most pointedly and insistently in her late lectures *The Life of the Mind* (San Diego: Harcourt, 1978).

50. Even though this question might appear to be paradoxical, given that Descartes conceived the *res cogitans* as the very opposite of the *res extensa*, i.e., unextended, incorporeal, etc., he repeatedly resorts to various metaphors to describe the nature of thought.

Chapter 1

1. Anthony Grafton, *Traditions of Conversion: Descartes and His Demon* (Berkeley: University of California Press, 2000), 23.

2. Grafton, *Traditions of Conversion*, 22.

3. The contrast that I am drawing here is undercut to a certain extent by a number of details. That Descartes writes that he could find no diversion and that he was "fortunately" free of "cares and passions" suggests that his experience in the stove-heated room was more circumstantial. I owe this insight to my colleague Timothy Harrison. The circumstantiality of Descartes' conversion is discussed later in this chapter.

4. Alice Browne, "Descartes's Dreams," *Journal of the Warburg and Courtauld Institutes* 40 (1977): 271. See also Claus Zittel, "*Mirabilis scientiae fundamenta*. Die Philosophie des jungen Descartes (1619–1628)," in *Seelenmaschinen. Gattungstraditionen, Funktionen und Leistungsgrenzen der Mnemotechniken vom späten Mittelalter bis zum Beginn der Moderne*, ed. Jörg Jochen Berns and Wolfgang Neuber (Vienna: Böhlau, 2001), 320.

5. I am using the translation by John R. Cole, *The Olympian Dreams and Youthful Rebellion of René Descartes* (Urbana: University of Illinois Press, 1992), 33. The French original is found in AT X 181. Further references are to these two editions.

6. The most famous example is the reciprocal announcement of dream visions to Ananias and Paul in the course of the latter's conversion (Acts 9:5–18).

7. See Browne, "Descartes's Dreams," 267.

8. In fact, it became one of the pillars of a Jesuit's practical training. Novices were encouraged to undertake the pilgrimage to Loreto just as Descartes imagined—by foot and by begging their way to Loreto. See Karin Annalise Vélez, "Resolved to Fly: The Virgin of Loreto, the Jesuits, and the Miracle of Portable Catholicism in the Seventeenth-Century Atlantic World" (PhD diss., Princeton University, 2008), 128.

9. This question, in which form Descartes came into contact with the Ignatian exercises, is complicated and controversial. For more, see the discussion in the Introduction.

10. Leibniz, who was one of the few who got to look and read through Descartes' early notebook during a trip to Paris, reproduces this doubling in his various accounts of his predecessor's conversion. In one of his excerpts from the notebook he writes: "Descartes for a long time devoted himself to studies at the Jesuit college of La Flèche and, as a young man, formed the plan of emending philosophy after some dreams and long meditation on that passage of Ausonius: 'What path in life shall I follow?'" (Gottfried Wilhelm Leibniz, *Philosophische Schriften* [Berlin: Akademie Verlag, 1999], 2057; my translation). In a passage from the *Theodicy*, which I discuss in more detail later, Leibniz conflates Augustine's and Descartes' conversions, placing the latter among other examples of religious conversions.

11. This famous passage reads in its entirety: "Actors, taught not to let any embarrassment show on their faces, put on a mask. I will do the same. So far, I have been a spectator in this theatre which is the world, but I am now about to mount the stage, and I come forward masked" (CSM I 2; AT X 213).

12. Plato, *The Republic of Plato*, trans. Allan Bloom (New York: Basic Books, 1991), 197 (514a). Further references are to this edition.

13. See Werner Jaeger's chapter "Paideia as Conversion," in *Paideia: The Ideals of Greek Culture* (New York: Oxford University Press, 1943), 295. Not only does the *paideia* allegorized by Plato start with a conversion, but many of the biographies narrated by Diogenes Laertius also begin with a momentous experience through which the future philosopher breaks with his old life and turns toward philosophy. See Olof Gigon, "Antike Erzählungen über die Berufung zur Philosophie," *Museum Helveticum* 3 (1946): 1–21.

14. Michel Foucault, *The Hermeneutics of the Subject: Lectures at the Collège de France, 1981–82*, ed. Frédéric Gros, trans. Graham Burchell (New York: Palgrave Macmillan, 2005), 206–27.

15. See Pierre Hadot, *Philosophy as a Way of Life: Spiritual Exercises from Socrates to Foucault*, ed. Arnold Davidson, trans. Michael Chase (Oxford: Blackwell, 1995), 127.

16. Augustine, *Confessions*, trans. Henry Chadwick (Oxford: Oxford University Press, 1998), 38–39. Further references are to this edition.

17. See Fragments 1 and 2 in Aristotle, *The Complete Works of Aristotle: The Revised Oxford Translation*, ed. Jonathan Barnes (Princeton, NJ: Princeton University Press, 1984), 2:2389–90. See also Gigon, "Antike Erzählungen," 6.

18. Grafton, *Traditions of Conversion*, 1–6.

19. Ignatius of Loyola, *Personal Writings:* Reminiscences, Spiritual Diary, *Select Letters—including the Text of* The Spiritual Exercises, trans. Joseph A. Munitiz and Philip Endean (London: Penguin Books, 1996), 26–27. In the following I cite his autobiography and the *Spiritual Exercises* as *Acta* and SE, respectively, followed by paragraph and page numbers.

20. See Acts 9:1–20, 22:3–21. The third account in Acts 26:4–18 simplifies the complicated dramaturgy of Paul's conversion somewhat.

21. It is disconnected from a self's experiences. In that respect, conversion resembles dream apparitions that, as Descartes observes at the end of the Sixth Meditation, are not connected to the self's other experiences.

22. The oldest manuscript reads *domus divina* (house of God) instead of *domus vicina* (neighboring house), signaling the transcendent dimension of Augustine's conversion both in its spatial and religious sense.

23. For the following I am indebted to Albrecht Koschorke's work on narrative beginnings. See Albrecht Koschorke, "System. Die Ästhetik und das Anfangsproblem," in *Grenzwerte des Ästhetischen*, ed. Robert Stockhammer (Frankfurt: Suhrkamp, 2002), 146–63; see also Albrecht Koschorke, "Zur Logik kultureller Gründungserzählungen," *Zeitschrift für Ideengeschichte* I/2 (2007): 5–12.

24. To my knowledge Grafton, *Traditions of Conversion*, is the only scholar who reads the events of November 10, 1619, as a conversion. For different interpretations of Descartes' three dreams, cf. Heinrich Quiring, "Der Traum des Descartes. Eine Verschlüsselung seiner Kosmologie, seiner Methodik und der Grundlage seiner Philosophie," *Kant-Studien* 46 (1954–55): 135–56; Georges Poulet, *Studies in Human Time*, trans. Elliott Coleman (Baltimore: Johns Hopkins University Press, 1956), 50–73; Henri Gouhier, *Les premieres pensées de Descartes. Contribution a l'histoire de l'anti-Renaissance* (Paris: J. Vrin, 1958), 11–58; Wilhelm Kamlah, "Der Anfang der Vernunft bei Descartes—autobiographisch und historisch," *Archiv für Geschichte der Philosophie* 43 (1961): 70–84; W. T. Jones, "*Somnio Ergo Sum*: Descartes's Three Dreams," *Philosophy and Literature* 4 (1980): 145–66; Fernand Hallyn, "*Olympica*: Les songes du jeune Descartes," in *Le songe a la Renaissance*, ed. Françoise Charpentier (Saint-Etienne: Université de Saint-Etienne, 1987), 41–51; Françoise Meltzer, "Descartes' Dreams and Freud's Failure, or the Politics of Originality," in *The Trial(s) of Psychoanalysis*, ed. Françoise Meltzer (Chicago: University of Chicago Press, 1988), 81–102; Michael Keevak, "Descartes's Dreams and Their Address for Philosophy," *Journal of the History of Ideas* 53 (1992): 373–96; Jean-Pierre Cavaillé, "L'itinéraire onirique de Descartes: De l'âge des songes aux temps du rêve," in *Les* Olympiques *de Descartes: Études et textes*, ed. Fernand

Hallyn (Geneva: Libr. Droz, 1995), 73–90; Charles D. Minahan, "The Turbulent Dream-Vision of Descartes's 'Olympian' Experience," in *Dreams in French Literature: The Persistent Voice*, ed. Tom Conner (Amsterdam: Rodopi, 1995), 65–84; Michael H. Keefer, "The Dreamer's Path: Descartes and the Sixteenth Century," *Renaissance Quarterly* 49 (1996): 30–76; Alan Gabbey and Robert E. Hall, "The Melon and the Dictionary: Reflections on Descartes' Dreams," *Journal of the History of Ideas* 59 (1998): 651–68; Cesare Vasoli, "Le rapport entre les *Olympica* et la culture de la Renaissance," in *Descartes et la Renaissance*, ed. Emmanuel Faye (Paris: H. Champion, 1999), 187–208; Jean-Luc Marion, *Cartesian Questions: Method and Metaphysics* (Chicago: University of Chicago Press, 1999), 1–19.

25. For Ignatius's chivalric errancy, see Marjorie O'Rourke Boyle, *Loyola's Acts: The Rhetoric of Self* (Berkeley: University of California Press, 1997), 22–52. Ignatius's and Descartes' shared chivalric errancy is also indicated by their youthful infatuation with the *Amadis of Gaul*. For Descartes, see Richard Watson, *Cogito, Ergo Sum: The Life of René Descartes* (Boston: David R. Godine, 2002), 73.

26. See Poulet, *Studies in Human Time*, 53, who speaks of a "complete denudation of the mind."

27. Much recent work has begun to examine imagination's role in the young Descartes. Most important is still Dennis Sepper, *Descartes's Imagination: Proportion, Images, and the Activity of Thinking* (Berkeley: University of California Press, 1996).

28. See Zittel, *Mirabilis scientiae fundamenta*, 319, who observes that for the young Descartes the imagination is the locus for staging the dream visions.

29. Traditionally, the site for such foundational visions was the bed. For instance, both Boethius and Ignatius undergo their conversions in bed: the former when he was visited by Lady Philosophy and the latter when he was recovering from his injuries at Pamplona. Mary Carruthers has shown that bed and bedroom were among the classical places to which one retired for rhetorical and meditative composition: "In classical as in monastic rhetoric, withdrawal to one's chamber indicates a state of mind, the entry to the 'place' of meditative silence which was thought essential for invention" (*The Craft of Thought: Meditation, Rhetoric, and the Making of Images, 400–1200* [Cambridge: Cambridge University Press, 1998], 174). From his school days at La Flèche Descartes supposedly had the habit of spending his mornings in bed reading and thinking. See Geneviève Rodis-Lewis, *Descartes: His Life and Thought*, trans. Jane Marie Todd (Ithaca, NY: Cornell University Press, 1998), 12.

30. For this and some of the following, see Pierre Hadot, "Conversio," in *Historisches Wörterbuch der Philosophie*, ed. Joachim Ritter (Basel: Schwabe, 1971–2007), 1:1033–36; Pierre Hadot, *Exercises spirituels et philosophie antique* (Paris: A. Michel, 2002), 175–82.

31. See Gerhart Ladner, "Homo Viator: Mediaeval Ideas on Alienation and Order," in *Images and Ideas in the Middle Ages: Selected Studies in History and Art*,

by Gerhart Ladner (Rome: Edizioni di storia e letteratura, 1983), 942: "The topoi of *xeniteia* and *peregrinatio*, of pilgrimage, of homelessness, of strangeness in this world, are among the most widespread in early Christian ascetic literature, and not a few ascetics, monastic and otherwise, practiced it by voluntary and migratory exile from their fatherland."

32. See Heb 11:13–16, where the author speaks of the faithful as "strangers or passing travellers on earth" who are "longing for a better country—I mean, the heavenly one."

33. John C. Olin, "The Idea of Pilgrimage in the Experience of Ignatius Loyola," *Church History* 48 (1979): 392.

34. Olin, "The Idea of Pilgrimage," 392.

35. See Olin, "The Idea of Pilgrimage," 392.

36. As Olin, "The Idea of Pilgrimage," 396, points out, the *Constitutions* of the society list pilgrimaging as an educational tool: "In the training of candidates who seek to join the new order Ignatius specified 'six principal testing experiences,' one of which was to make a pilgrimage."

37. See Veléz, "Resolved to Fly," 132.

38. Ignatius of Loyola, *The Constitutions of the Society of Jesus*, trans. George E. Ganss, S.J. (St. Louis: Institute of Jesuit Studies, 1970), 104.

39. Olin, "Idea of Pilgrimage," 396. See the prefatory dedication of the *Meditations* to the Sorbonne, where Descartes conceives them as a missionary tool to convert unbelievers by rational means, as they prove the existence of God and the immortality of the soul. Usually this dedication is dismissed as a political maneuver to gain favor with the theological establishment.

40. See Jeffrey Chips Smith, *Sensuous Worship: Jesuits and the Art of the Early Catholic Reformation in Germany* (Princeton, NJ: Princeton University Press, 2002), 23–27.

41. Antoine Sucquet, *Via vitae aeternae. Iconibus illustrata per Boëtium A Bolswert* (Antwerp: Martini Nutij, 1620), 2.

42. Cole, *The Olympian Dreams*, 137, points out that "lateral right and perpendicular right" as well as "rectilinear right" are all connected.

43. See Cole, *The Olympian Dreams*, 134–35.

44. See Marjorie O'Rourke Boyle, *Senses of Touch: Human Dignity and Deformity from Michelangelo to Calvin* (Leiden, Netherlands: Brill, 1998).

45. Bernard of Clairvaux, *Sermones super Cantica canticorum* 4.149, cited in O'Rourke Boyle, *Loyola's Acts*, 43. For a more detailed account of Scholastic theology on lameness, see John Freccero, "The Firm Foot on a Journey without a Guide," in *Dante: The Poetics of Conversion* (Cambridge, MA: Harvard University Press, 1988), 29–54.

46. Rourke O'Boyle, *Loyola's Acts*, 42–43, makes this same point. See also See Peter Hays, *The Limping Hero: Grotesques in Literature* (New York: New York University Press, 1971), 24.

47. Minahan, "The Turbulent Dream-Vision," gives this spinning a very different interpretation.

48. See Aldo Scaglione, *Liberal Arts and the Jesuit College System* (Amsterdam: John Benjamins, 1986).

49. It is important to note that the interpretation of ghosts and wind as being the "work of some evil spirit" is Descartes' doing when awake. But the introduction of the evil spirit happens already at this early point and not only in the context of the all-encompassing interpretation following the final dream.

50. In explaining his oneiric self's leftward leaning and lack of uprightness, at least in part, physiologically, Descartes joins a number of medieval dream theorists who held that lower types of dreams sprung from somatic conditions. See Steven F. Kruger, *Dreaming in the Middle Ages* (Cambridge: Cambridge University Press, 2005), 70–73.

51. This is where John Cole's reading goes astray (*The Olympian Dreams*, 137–38), since he argues that what the first dream is staging is Descartes turning away from the study and practice of law, *le droit*.

52. Baillet noted in the margin: "I was driven to the Church by an evil spirit [*a malo spiritu ad templum propellebar*]" (Cole, *The Olympian Dreams*, 38; AT X 186).

53. Ignatius told the story of his life to the young Jesuit Luis Gonçalves de Câmara, who later wrote down what he had heard from memory. Ignatius's reminiscences are, thus, an autobiography, but one mediated by his young listener and his undoubtedly selective memory.

54. "And having received no small clarity from this reading, he began to think more in earnest about his past life, and about how much need he had to do penance for it" (*Acta* § 9, p. 16). See O'Rourke Boyle, *Loyola's Acts*, 38, who is more skeptical about the earnestness of Ignatius's desire for penance. While Ignatius undoubtedly still has a long way to go in his spiritual journey, it seems incontrovertible that the discernment of spirits is a huge step in the right direction.

55. One need to think only of Augustine, who is prompted to take the final step by being shown "how vile [he] was, how twisted and filthy, covered in sores and ulcers" (*Confessions* 8.7.16)—in the eyes of God.

56. See Michael B. Crowe, *The Changing Profile of the Natural Law* (The Hague: Nijhoff, 1977), 123–41; Timothy C. Potts, *Conscience in Medieval Philosophy* (Cambridge: Cambridge University Press, 1980); Robert A. Greene, "Synderesis, the Spark of Conscience, in the English Renaissance," *Journal of the History of Ideas* 52 (1991): 195–219; Robert A. Greene, "Instinct of Nature: Natural Law, Synderesis, and the Moral Sense," *Journal of the History of Ideas* 58 (1997): 173–98.

57. Most scholars agree that the appearance of *synderesis* in medieval manuscripts of Jerome's commentary is the result of a scribal error. Originally it probably read *syneidesis*, which is the common correlate in Greek patristic literature for the Latin *conscientia*. For a short summary of this reasoning, see Crowe, *The Changing Profile*, 125–27; for further references, see Uta Störmer-Caysa, *Gewissen und Buch. Über den Weg eines Begriffes in die deutsche Literatur des Mittelalters* (Berlin: De Gruyter, 1998), 58–60; Potts, *Conscience in Medieval Philosophy*, 79–80; Latin text in Jacques-Paul Migne, ed., *Patrologiae Cursus Completus, Series Latina* (Paris, 1844–90), 25.22.

58. Potts, *Conscience in Medieval Philosophy*, 128.

59. Potts, *Conscience in Medieval Philosophy*, 123.

60. "The light of Thy countenance, O Lord, is signed upon us."

61. Thomas Aquinas, *Summa Theologiae*, ed. John Mortenson and Enrique Alarcón, trans. Fr. Laurence Shapcote, O.P. (Lander, WY: Aquinas Institute, 2012), 205. Further references are to this edition, cited as ST. Authors of the English Renaissance still identified reason as the *scintilla divinae lucis*. For this, see Greene, "Synderesis," 213.

62. Bonaventure, *The Journey of the Mind to God*, ed. Stephen F. Brown, trans. Philotheus Boehner, O.F.M. (Indianapolis, IN: Hackett, 1993), 6–7.

63. See Störmer-Caysa, *Gewissen und Buch*, 132–33.

64. For a similar argument, see Greene, "Synderesis," 196.

65. I have made some minor changes to the English translation of CSM. An almost identical formulation in the synoptic interpretation of all three dreams indicates the importance of this "theory" of thought for the young Descartes. See Claus Zittel, *Theatrum philosophicum. Descartes und die Rolle ästhetischer Formen in der Wissenschaft* (Berlin: Akademie Verlag, 2009), who provides a comprehensive examination of Descartes' aesthetic modes of thought.

66. For the role of *machina mentis* in meditation, see Carruthers, *The Craft of Thought*, 22–24.

67. Seneca, *Epistles 93–124*, trans. Richard M. Gummere (Cambridge, MA: Harvard University Press, 2006), 383. See also Ep. 90.29: "Then she goes back to the beginnings of things, to the eternal Reason which was imparted to the whole, and to the force which inheres in all the seeds of things, giving them the power to fashion each thing according to its kind" (Seneca, *Epistles 66–92*, trans. Richard M. Gummere [Cambridge, MA: Harvard University Press, 2006], 417.) For the discursive history of these metaphorics, see Maryanne Cline Horowitz, *Seeds of Virtue and Knowledge* (Princeton, NJ: Princeton University Press, 1998); and for its Stoic roots, see Henry Dyson, *Prolepsis and Ennoia in the Early Stoa* (Berlin: Walter de Gruyter, 2009).

68. Cicero, *On the Republic—On the Laws*, trans. Clinton Walker Keyes (Cambridge, MA: Harvard University Press, 2006), 333.

69. Augustine, *Concerning the City of God against the Pagans*, trans. Henry Bettenson (London: Penguin Books, 1984), 1070.

70. Earlier Descartes had already employed the same metaphorics: "The human mind has something divine it, in which the first seeds of useful ways of things are sown" (CSM I 17; AT X 373).

71. As a matter of fact, Baillet speaks of *sa syndérèse* (AT X 186), i.e., "his synderesis" as if *synderesis* is something that belonged to a specific self.

72. Baillet writes: "d'avoir les yeux assez étincellans" (AT X 182).

73. Gottfried Wilhelm Leibniz, *Theodicy: Essays on the Goodness of God, the Freedom of Man, and the Origin of Evil*, ed. Austin Farrer, trans. E. M. Huggard (La Salle, IL: Open Court, 1985), 178–79. Further references in the text include paragraph and page number.

74. Leibniz was one of the few to leaf and read through Descartes' early notebook when he visited Paris in 1676. He made extensive excerpts from the manuscript titled "Cogitationes Privatae," which were among the manuscripts that remained "lost" in the archive of his manuscripts at the Royal Library of Hanover until they were discovered in 1859 by Count Alexandre Foucher de Careil and published in his *Oeuvres inédites de Descartes*.

75. For the use of sacred books in cledonomancy, the so-called *sortes*, see Pieter W. Van der Horst, "*Sortes*: Sacred Books as Instant Oracles in Late Antiquity," in *The Use of Sacred Books in the Ancient World*, ed. L. V. Rutgers, P. W. Van der Horst, H. W. Havelaar, and L. Teugels (Leuven, Belgium: Peeters, 1998), 143–74.

76. Homer, *Odyssey*, 20.98–120.

77. One of the most important models is the use of lots to determine who will succeed Judas as the twelfth apostle in Acts 1:26.

78. The following is a much shorter version of an argument I develop at length in Christopher J. Wild, "*Apertio Libri*: Codex and Conversion," in *Literary Studies and the Pursuits of Reading*, ed. Eric Downing, Richard Benson, and Jonathan Hess (Rochester, NY: Camden House, 2012), 17–39.

79. For the different modes of reading afforded by scroll and codex, see Peter Stallybrass, "Books and Scrolls: Navigating the Bible," in *Books and Readers in Early Modern England*, ed. Jennifer Andersen and Elizabeth Sauer (Philadelphia: University of Pennsylvania Press, 2002), 42–79.

80. For the codex's "capacity for random access," see Harry Y. Gamble, *Books and Readers in the Early Church: A History of Early Christian Texts* (New Haven, CT: Yale University Press, 1995), 63. See also Stallybrass, *Books and Scrolls*, 42.

81. Joannes David, *Veridicus Christianus* (Antwerp: Ex officina Plantinian, 1601). For the following, see Ludger Lieb, "Emblematische Experimente. Formen und Funktionen der frühen Jesuiten-Emblematik am Beispiel der Emblembücher Jan Davids," in *The Jesuits and the Emblem Tradition*, ed. John Manning and Marc van Vaeck (Turnhout, Belgium: Brepols, 1999), 307–21; Werner Waterschoot,

"*Veridicus Christianus* and *Christeliiken Waerseggher* by Joannes David," in *Emblemata Sacra: Rhétorique et herméneutique du discours sacré dans la littérature en image*, ed. Ralph Dekoninck and Agnès Guiderdoni-Bruslé (Turnhout, Belgium: Brepols, 2007), 527–34.

82. This device was part of the appendix titled "Orbita probitatis ad Christi imitationem Christiano subserviens," starting on p. 374.

83. See Watershoot, *Veridicus Christianus*, 528: "David also intended his work as a refutation if not the antidote of a very popular fortune-telling book, *'t Huys der Fortuynen* (The house of fortunes) by using the methods of the latter book against itself."

84. The full epigraph reads: *Tolle, lege; tolle, lege. . . . Arripui, aperui, legi in silentio capitulum, quo primum coniecti sunt oculi mei.*

85. Ralph Dekoninck, *Ad Imaginem. Statuts, fonctions et usages de l'image dans la littérature spirituelle jésuite du XVIIe siècle* (Geneva: Droz, 2005), 286.

86. The editions of Pierre des Brosses's *Corpus omnium veterum poetarum latinorum* that Descartes probably would have known were the ones published in 1603 in Lyon or 1611 in Geneva. In the first edition the poems are found on: 2:655 and 2:655–56; in the second edition, on 2:658–59 and 2:659. The verses to which Descartes alludes appear either on the same page (1603) or on facing pages (1611). This means that Descartes is much in the same situation as Augustine, who did not know which verse follows the one he chanced upon in Paul's Letter to the Romans.

87. For a different reading of the role of Ausonius' *Eclogues*, see Richard Kennington, "Descartes' 'Olympica,'" *Social Research* 28 (1961): 171–204.

88. *Ausonius*, trans. Hugh G. Evelyn-White (Cambridge, MA: Harvard University Press, 2014), 1:162–69, 170–73. Further references are to this edition.

89. Keefer, "The Dreamer's Path," 40, discusses this issue.

90. Carruthers, *The Craft of Thought*, 80.

91. Carruthers, *The Craft of Thought*, 77. Of course, due to the pivotal role of memory in rhetoric, ductus always already had a mental dimension.

92. Augustine, *On Christian Teaching*, trans. R. P. H. Green (Oxford: Oxford University Press, 1997), 33–35. See also Carruthers, *The Craft of Thought*, 80.

93. Keefer, "The Dreamer's Path," 42, also draws concrete connections between this "primal scene" and Descartes' mature thought.

Chapter 2

1. For echoes of Plato's allegory of the cave in Descartes, see *Regulae* (CSM I 16; AT X 371). See Stephen Buckle, "Descartes, Plato and the Cave," *Philosophy* 82 (2007): 301–37; John Cottingham, *Cartesian Reflections: Essays on Descartes's Philosophy* (Oxford: Oxford University Press, 2008), 292–318. See also Frederick Van Fleteren, "Ascent of the Soul," in *Augustine through the Ages: An Encyclopedia*, ed.

Allan Fitzgerald, O.S.A. (Grand Rapids, MI: William B. Eerdmans, 1999), 63–67. See Chapter 6 for Descartes' version of the meditative "ascent" and more on *theoria* and the contemplation of God.

2. Plato, *The Republic of Plato*, trans. Allan Bloom (New York: Basic Books, 1968), 197. Further references are to this edition.

3. See Irénée Hausherr, *The Name of Jesus*, trans. Charles Cummings, OCSO (Kalamazoo, MI: Cistercian, 1978), 158–65.

4. See Pierre Hadot, *Philosophy as a Way of Life: Spiritual Exercises from Socrates to Foucault*, ed. Arnold Davidson, trans. Michael Chase (Oxford: Blackwell, 1995), 264–76.

5. See Giorgio Agamben, *The Highest Poverty: Monastic Rules and Form-of-Life*, trans. Adam Kotsko (Stanford, CA: Stanford University Press, 2013).

6. See Dirko Thomsen, *"Techne" als Metapher und als Begriff der sittlichen Einsicht. Zum Verhältnis von Vernunft und Natur bei Platon und Aristoteles* (Freiburg: K. Alber, 1990); David Roochnik, *Of Art and Wisdom: Plato's Understanding of Techne* (University Park: Pennsylvania State University Press, 1996). For relating the ancient notion of *technē* to the concept of know-how, see Jaako Hintikka, "Plato on Knowing How, Knowing That, and Knowing What," in *Knowledge and the Known: Historical Perspectives on Epistemology* (Dordrecht: Reidel, 1974), 31–49.

7. Descartes' interest in medicine and diathetics is well documented by his correspondence with Princess Elisabeth of Bohemia. See, for instance, their letters from May to June 1645 in René Descartes, *The Correspondence between Princess Elisabeth of Bohemia and René Descartes*, ed. and trans. Lisa Shapiro (Chicago: University of Chicago Press, 2007), 85–95. See also Steven Shapin, "Descartes the Doctor: Rationalism and Its Therapies," *British Journal for the History of Science* 33 (2000): 131–54.

8. Again, the correspondence with Elisabeth is of interest in this regard, as they read Seneca's *De vita beata* together. See Descartes, *Correspondence*, 96–114. See also Adriaan Peperzak, "Life, Science, and Wisdom according to Descartes," *History of Philosophy Quarterly* 12 (1995): 133–53; John Cottingham, *Philosophy and the Good Life: Reason and the Passions in Greek, Cartesian and Psychoanalytic Ethics* (Cambridge: Cambridge University Press, 1998), 61–103; and Cottingham, *Cartesian Reflections*, 271–91.

9. In the *Discourse on the Method* Descartes writes that he fled Paris and moved to Amsterdam, where "amidst this great mass of busy people who are more concerned with their own affairs than curious about those of others, I have been able to lead a life as solitary and withdrawn as if I were in the most remote desert, while lacking none of the comforts found in the most populous cities" (CSM I 126; AT VI 31). See also Kevin Dunn, "'A Great City Is a Great Solitude': Descartes's Urban Pastoral," *Yale French Studies* 80 (1991): 93–107.

10. I borrow the term "conceptual metaphors" from George Lakoff and Mark Johnson, *Metaphors We Live By* (Chicago: University of Chicago Press, 1980).

11. This insistence on the reform's self-reliance also translates into a certain self-limitation. By refraining from rebuilding the whole body or, better, city of collective knowledge, Descartes must also refrain from rebuilding other houses: "My plan has never gone beyond trying to reform my own thoughts and construct them upon a foundation that is all my own.... The simple resolution to abandon all the opinions one has hitherto accepted is not an example that everyone ought to follow" (CSM I 118; AT VI 15).

12. Although Descartes' frequent and extensive architectural metaphorics has received considerable attention from historical scholarship, its debt to the meditational practice and discourse of Western Christianity has been overlooked. On the former, see most notably Claudia Brodsky Lacour, *Lines of Thought: Discourse, Architectonics, and the Origin of Modern Philosophy* (Durham, NC: Duke University Press, 1996). As her subtitle indicates, Brodsky takes architectonics of Descartes' thought as a site of its modernity. In contrast, I seek to show that edification connects him to an older tradition reaching back to the spiritual exercises of antiquity and monastic meditation. Other studies of Descartes' architectural metaphorics include Nathan Edelman, "The Mixed Metaphor in Descartes," *Romanic Review* 41 (1950): 167–78; Jeanette Bicknell, "Descartes's Rhetoric: Roads, Foundations, and Difficulties in Method," *Philosophy and Rhetoric* 36 (2003): 22–38.

13. This metaphor comes, of course, from Augustine's *Confessions* 10.8.12. For the following, see Mary Carruthers, *The Book of Memory: A Study of Memory in Medieval Culture* (Cambridge: Cambridge University Press, 1990), 71–74; and Mary Carruthers, *The Craft of Thought: Meditation, Rhetoric, and the Making of Images, 400–1200* (Cambridge: Cambridge University Press, 1998), 16–24, which builds on her earlier work and applies it to meditative practice.

14. *Ad Herennium*, trans. Harry Caplan (Cambridge, MA: Harvard University Press, 1954), 211. Further references are to this edition.

15. See Carruthers, *The Craft of Thought*, 16: "In ancient mnemotechnic, architecture was considered to provide the best source of familiar memory locations."

16. See Philipp Vielhauer, "*Oikodome*. Das Bild vom Bau in der christlichen Literatur vom Neuen Testament bis Clemens Alexandrinus," in *Aufsätze zum Neuen Testament*, by Philipp Vielhauer (Munich: C. Kaiser, 1979), 1–168; Gerhard Bauer, *Claustrum Animae. Untersuchungen zur Geschichte der Metapher vom Herzen als Kloster* (Munich: W. Fink, 1973), 32–42; John S. Coolidge, *The Pauline Renaissance in England: Puritanism and the Bible* (Oxford: Clarendon Press, 1970), 27–41.

17. What I have in view here is the tradition of meditation and, thus, the spiritual dimension of *aedificatio*. In contrast, Vielhauer stresses that Paul is focused on its communal aspect: the edification of the congregation and, more generally, the church through cult and piety.

18. To make the linguistic echoes between Descartes' and Paul's language evident, I have supplied the Latin equivalents from the Vulgate.

19. The preoccupation with the issue of foundation is not limited to Paul but can be found elsewhere in the New Testament. See Matthew 16:18, where Jesus says to Peter (which means "rock" in Greek), "upon this rock I will build my church, and all the powers of hell will not conquer it."

20. This, of course, differs somewhat from Descartes. Although the foundation conditions all subsequent *superaedificationes* in Descartes, the edifice of knowledge is dependent on the rest of the construction.

21. Carruthers, *The Craft of Thought*, 17.

22. This translation is already anticipated in the occasional usage of οἰκοδομεῖν and its cognates in Hellenistic philosophy. Representative is the following passage from Epictetus's *Discourses* 2.15.8: "Do you not wish to make your beginning and foundation firm, that is, to consider whether your decision is sound or unsound, and only after you have done that proceed to rear thereon the structure [*epoikodomein*] of your determination and your firm resolve? But if you lay a rotten and crumbling foundation, you cannot rear thereon [*oikodomēmation*] even a small building, but the bigger and the stronger your superstructure is the more quickly it will fall down." In Epictetus, *Discourses as Reported by Arrian: Books I–II*, trans. W. A. Oldfather (Cambridge, MA: Harvard University Press, 2000), 309.

23. *Spiritual Exercises* § 47, in Ignatius of Loyola, *Personal Writings:* Reminiscences, Spiritual Diary, *Select Letters—including the Text of* The Spiritual Exercises, trans. Joseph A. Munitiz and Philip Endean (London: Penguin Books, 1996), 294. Further references are to this edition, cited as SE followed by paragraph and page numbers.

24. Carruthers, *The Craft of Thought*, 60.

25. Carruthers, *The Craft of Thought*, 77.

26. See, for instance, Desmond M. Clarke, *Descartes' Philosophy of Science* (Manchester: Manchester University Press, 1982).

27. See, for instance, Daniel Garber, *Descartes Embodied: Reading Cartesian Philosophy through Cartesian Science* (Cambridge: Cambridge University Press, 2001), 33.

28. Matthew L. Jones, *The Good Life in the Scientific Revolution: Descartes, Pascal, Leibniz, and the Cultivation of Virtue* (Chicago: University of Chicago Press, 2006).

29. After the Greek compound *meta*, meaning "after, following," and *hodos*, the "path, way."

30. See, for instance, the *Discourse on the Method*, which Descartes famously begins by observing that "good sense is the best distributed thing in the world" and that "the power of judging well and of distinguishing the true from the false ... is naturally equal in all men." The diversity of opinions and difference in judgments are, thus, not a function of the quantity and quality of reason everyone possesses but of its use; more precisely, it depends, not surprisingly, on how "we direct

our thoughts along different paths and do not attend to the same things" (CSM I 111; AT VI 1–2).

31. There is more discussion on the verbs *advertere* and *animadvertere* that Descartes employs to denote intellectual discovery and the mind's attention in Chapters 3 and 5.

32. See CSM I 111 (AT VI 2), 112 (AT VI 3–4), 118 (AT VI 14–15), 119 (AT VI 16), and 123 (AT VI 24–25).

33. Jacques Derrida, "Le langue et le discourse de la méthode," *Recherches sur la philosophie et la langage* 3 (1983): 38.

34. These two mental operations are not as easily separable as my cursory sketch has made them appear, but because we will consider their pragmatic dimension more closely and, thus, complicate their interaction in Chapter 5, this will have to suffice for now.

35. See Frederick Van De Pitte, "Intuition and Judgement in Descartes' Theory of Truth," *Journal of the History of Philosophy* 26 (1988): 453–70; Stephen Gaukroger, *Descartes: An Intellectual Biography* (Oxford: Clarendon Press, 1997), 115–24; Thomas C. Vinci, *Cartesian Truth* (Oxford: Oxford University Press, 1998), 19–23; M. Jones, *The Good Life*, 27, 61.

36. Evert van Leeuwen, "Method, Discourse, and the Act of Knowing," in *Essays on the Philosophy and Science of René Descartes*, ed. Stephen Voss (Oxford: Oxford University Press, 1993), 232.

37. For the following discussion, see Neal W. Gilbert, *Renaissance Concepts of Method* (New York: Columbia University Press, 1963); Joachim Ritter, "Methode," in *Historisches Wörterbuch der Philosophie*, ed. Joachim Ritter, Karlfried Gründer, and Gottfried Gabriel (Basel: Schwabe, 1971–2007), 5.1304–13.

38. Gilbert, *Renaissance Concepts of Method*, 40.

39. See Ottfrid Becker, *Das Bild des Weges und verwandte Vorstellungen im frühgriechischen Denken* (Berlin: Weidmann, 1937), 2.

40. Gilbert, *Renaissance Concepts of Method*, 49.

41. Ritter, "Methode," 1307–8.

42. Gilbert, *Renaissance Concepts of Method*, 66.

43. Jacopo Zabarella, *On Methods*, ed. and trans. John P. McCaskey (Cambridge, MA: Harvard University Press, 2013), 3.

44. Zabarella, *On Methods*, 7.

45. Zabarella, *On Methods*, 7.

46. Another example for Descartes' practice regimen can be found in the *Discourse on the Method*: "Moreover, I continued practicing the method I had prescribed for myself. Besides taking care in general to conduct all my thoughts according to its rules, I set aside some hours now and again to apply it more particularly to mathematical problems" (CSM I 125; AT VII 29).

47. See Van Leeuwen, "Method, Discourse," 228.

48. For the need of practice and cultivating the intellect, see Garber, *Descartes Embodied*, 277–95.

49. In the *Discourse on the Method* Descartes writes: "But what pleased me most about this method was that by following it I was sure in every case to use my reason, if not perfectly, at least as well as was in my power" (CSM I 121; AT VI 21).

50. Descartes, *Correspondance*, 113.

51. See M. Jones, *The Good Life*, 32–38, 41–48, on Descartes' notion of habituation.

52. Hans von Arnim, ed., *Stoicorum veterum fragmenta* (Leipzig: B. G. Teubneri, 1903–24), vol. 1.20.30, 1.110.8.

53. Zabarella, *On Methods*, 7.

54. The term *Bahnung* is notoriously difficult to translate. Literally meaning "pathing" or "tracking," it is also often translated as "facilitation." Alan Bass was the first to translate it more felicitously as "breaching." See his translation of Jacques Derrida, "Différance," in *The Margins of Philosophy*, trans. Alan Bass (Chicago: University of Chicago Press, 1982), 3–27.

55. This is, of course, a false etymology, but that did not prevent medieval monastic authors from exploiting it readily.

56. For Descartes' mental technique of running through a chain of thoughts again and again, see Chapter 5.

57. Michel Foucault, *The Hermeneutics of the Subject: Lectures at the Collège de France, 1981–82*, ed. Frédéric Gros, trans. Graham Burchell (New York: Palgrave Macmillan, 2005), 84.

58. Per Rönnegård, "Melétē in Early Christian Ascetic Texts," in *Meditation in Judaism, Christianity and Islam: Cultural Histories*, ed. Halvor Eifring (London: Bloomsbury Academic, 2013), 87. See also Robert J. Newman, "*Cotidie meditare*: Theory and Practice of the *meditatio* in Imperial Stoicism," *Aufstieg und Niedergang der römischen Welt* 36 (1989): 1474–75.

59. Epictetus, *Discourses, Books III–IV: The Encheiridion*, trans. W. A. Oldfather (Cambridge, MA: Harvard University Press, 2000). Further references are to this edition.

60. Hausherr, *Name of Jesus*, 174. See also Newman, *Cotidie meditare*, for references to Seneca's usage of *meditari*.

61. *Meditari* and *meditatio* stand for the Hebrew *hagah*, "to moan, growl, mutter, speak, muse, meditate," of the Hebrew Old Testament, and *melétan* and *meléte* of the Greek Septuaginta. See Emmanuel von Severus, "Das Wort 'Meditari' im Sprachgebrauch der Heiligen Schrift," *Geist und Leben* 26 (1953): 365–75.

62. See Heinrich Bacht, "'Meditatio' in den ältesten Mönchsquellen," *Geist und Leben* 28 (1955): 360–73.

63. Hadot, *Philosophy as a Way of Life*, 82, calls Ignatius's spiritual exercises a "Christian version of Greco-Roman tradition." Cited in the text as PWL followed by page number.

64. Foucault, *Hermeneutics of the Subject*, 333.

65. See Newman, "*Cotidie meditare*," 147s, 148s.

66. See Foucault, *Hermeneutics of the Subject*, 468–73; Mireille Armisen-Marchetti, "Imagination and Meditation in Seneca: The Example of *Praemeditatio*," in *Seneca*, ed. John G. Fitch (Oxford: Oxford University Press, 2008), 102–13.

67. In the Third Meditation Descartes' meditator uses a slightly different terminology to make the same distinction. There they call the "formal reality" of an idea "considered simply as a mode of thought" (CSM II 27; AT VII 40), in contrast to its "objective reality" when it is considered as an "image which represents different things" (CSM II 28; AT VII 40). In the Fourth Set of Replies Descartes tweaks his terminology yet again: "Since ideas are forms of a kind, and are not composed of any matter, when we think of them as representing something we are taking them not materially but formally. If, however, we were considering them not as representing this or that but simply as operations of the intellect, then it could be said that we were taking them materially, but in that case they would have no reference to truth or falsity of their objects" (CSM II 163; AT VII 232). I address the apparent contradiction and tension in Descartes' terminology in Chapter 5.

68. Descartes' meditator employs this operation at several pivotal moments. See Chapters 3, 4, and 6.

69. Carruthers, *The Craft of Thought*, 1. She stresses that it is primarily "an art of *mneme*, 'memory,' rather than one of mimesis. This is not to say that the aesthetics of 'representation' were unknown to it, only that in it mimesis was less of an issue, less in the forefront of their conscious practice, than *mneme*. The questions raised about a work of *mneme* are different from those raised by mimesis. They stress cognitive uses and the instrumentality of art over questions of its 'realism'" (3).

70. Carruthers, *The Craft of Thought*, 4–5.

71. Carruthers, *The Craft of Thought*, 5. See also Paul F. Gehl, "*Competens Silentium*: Varieties of Monastic Silence in the Medieval West," *Viator* 18 (1987): 125–60. Historians of spirituality employ the term "orthopraxis" to describe this kind of practical knowledge rather than "orthodoxy," which is communicated by canonical texts, while orthopractical education relies on learning by imitation and continual practice. For the classical philosophical articulation of this issue, see Gilbert Ryle, "Knowing How and Knowing That," *Proceedings of the Aristotelian Society* 46 (1946): 14: "Learning-how differs from learning-that. We can be instructed in truths, we can only be disciplined in methods. Appropriate exercises (corrected by criticisms and inspired by examples and precepts) can inculcate second natures. But knowledge-how cannot be built up by accumulation of pieces of knowledge-that." For the current state of the discussion, see John Bengson and Marc A. Moffett, eds., *Knowing How: Essays on Knowledge, Mind and Action* (Oxford: Oxford University Press, 2011).

72. See Christiane Schildknecht, "Erleuchtung und Tarnung. Überlegungen zur literarischen Form bei René Descartes," in *Literarische Formen der Philosophie*, ed. Gottfried Gabriel and Christiane Schildknecht (Stuttgart: J. B. Meltzer, 1990), 103–4; see also Bicknell, "Descartes' Rhetoric."

73. See also M. Jones, *The Good Life*, 26–27.

74. The phrase is of course Harold Bloom's. See his *The Anxiety of Influence: A Theory of Poetry* (New York: Oxford University Press, 1973). In philosophy few have suffered as severely as Descartes from this intellectual "disorder."

75. I should note that Descartes became spiritual director to Elisabeth of Bohemia, but nonetheless their relationship was an essentially epistolary one. Of course, spiritual direction by the means of letters has a long tradition going back at least to Seneca.

76. See Bicknell, "Descartes's Rhetoric," 28–29; Garber, *Descartes Embodied*, 291–95.

77. See Amelie Oksenberg Rorty, "Experiments in Philosophic Genre: Descartes' *Meditations*," *Critical Inquiry* 9 (1983): 545–64. Christiane Schildknecht, "Erleuchtung und Tarnung," 93, argues for a functional relationship between philosophical method, content, and the literary form of presentation.

78. Rorty, "Experiments in Philosophic Genre," 538.

79. Jacques Derrida, "Is There a Philosophical Language?," in *Points . . . Interviews, 1974–1994*, ed. Elisabeth Weber, trans. Peggy Kamuf and others (Stanford, CA: Stanford University Press, 1995), 216–27.

80. See the introduction in the new edition/translation of René Descartes, *Regulae ad directionem ingenii—Cogitationes privatae. Lateinisch—Deutsch*, ed. and trans. Christian Wohlers (Hamburg: Felix Meiner Verlag, 2011), vii–lxxvii.

81. See his letter to Mersenne of April 15, 1630 (CSM III 20–23; AT I 135–147).

82. This is not entirely correct. As I show in Chapter 5, the act of intuition can be practiced and improved.

83. See Garber, *Descartes Embodied*, 33; John D. Lyons, "Subjectivity and Imitation in the *Discours de la méthode*," *Neophilologus* 66 (1982): 508–24.

84. For more on this issue, see Brodsky Lacour, *Lines of Thought*, 13–17.

85. See Brian Stock, *After Augustine: The Meditative Reader and the Text* (Philadelphia: University of Pennsylvania Press, 2001).

86. See also the "Preface of the Publisher," which was appended to the French translation of the *Meditations* and approved by Descartes (AT IX 3).

87. For Descartes' "order of reasoning," see Martial Gueroult, *Descartes's Philosophy Interpreted according to the Order of Reasons* (Minneapolis: University of Minnesota Press, 1984–85).

88. For discussions of this term, see Edwin Curley, "Spinoza as an Expositor of Descartes," in *Speculum Spinozanum*, ed. Siegfried Hessing (London: Routledge and Kegan Paul, 1977), 133–42; Edwin Curley, "Analysis in the *Meditations*: The

Quest for Clear and Distinct Ideas," in *Essays on Descartes'* Meditations, ed. Amélie Oskenberg Rorty (Berkeley: University of California Press, 1986), 153–76; Jaako Hintikka, "A Discourse on Descartes's Method," in *Descartes: Critical and Interpretive Essays*, ed. Michael Hooker (Baltimore: Johns Hopkins University Press, 1978), 74–88; Daniel Garber and Lesley Cohen, "A Point of Order: Analysis, Synthesis, and Descartes's Principles," *Archiv für Geschichte der Philosophie* 64 (1982): 135–47; Gueroult, *Order of Reasons*, 7–11, 257–60; Benoit Timmermans, "The Originality of Descartes's Conception of Analysis as Discovery," *Journal of the History of Ideas* 60 (1999): 433–47. Most helpful are Schildknecht, "Erleuchtung und Tarnung," 104–6; and Lawrence Nolan, "The Ontological Argument as an Exercise in Cartesian Therapy," *Canadian Journal of Philosophy* 35 (2005): 531–40.

89. For the sake of convenience and convention I refer to the intuition of the performance of thinking as the *cogito*. Needless to say, Descartes employed different linguistic expressions of this intuition. The *cogito* actually hails from the *Principia philosophiae*, where it is part of the famous phrase "cogito, ergo sum." As I will show shortly, Descartes actually tailored the particular expression to fit the generic form and pragmatic purpose of the text that contained it.

90. This may explain Descartes' dyspeptic reaction to Colvius's suggestion that his *cogito* is anticipated by Augustine. See CSM III 159; AT III 247–48.

91. The scholarship on the *cogito* is, of course, vast. I have found most useful Jaako Hintikka, "Cogito, Ergo Sum: Inference or Performance?," *Philosophical Review* 71 (1962): 3–32; Mark Glouberman, "Cogito: Inference and Certainty," *Modern Schoolman* 70 (1993): 81–98.

92. In regard to articulation of the *cogito* in the *Discourse on the Method*, Lyons, "Subjectivity and Imitation," 521, makes a similar point. As will become clear shortly, he does not take into account sufficiently the generic and textual differences of the "method of demonstration" that set the *Meditations* apart from the *Discourse*.

93. Lyons, "Subjectivity and Imitation," 521.

94. See Jean-Luc Nancy, "Larvatus pro Deo," *Glyph* 2 (1977): 14–36.

95. It has become customary to refer to the subject or ego of the *Meditations* as "meditator" or "Descartes' meditator." I adopt the latter to indicate the dual and ambiguous status of this persona as both belonging to Descartes and whoever reads the text.

96. In his very insightful essay John D. Lyons calls the subject of the *Meditations* a "methodic subject." See John D. Lyons, "The Cartesian Reader and the Methodic Subject," *L'esprit createur* 21 (1981): 37–47. He too observes that the text creates a "role for the reader in order to guide him through the steps of the discoveries *as if the reader were thinking for himself*" (43).

97. Emile Benveniste, "The Nature of Pronouns," in *Problems in General Linguistics*, trans. Mary Elizabeth Meek (Coral Gables, FL: University of Miami Press, 1971), 218. See also his "Subjectivity in Language" (223–30).

98. Hintikka, "Cogito, Ergo Sum," 13.

99. See Günter Butzer, *Soliloquium. Theorie und Geschichte des Selbstgesprächs in der europäischen Literatur* (Munich: Fink, 2008), 363–79.

100. Coined by Otto Jespersen in 1923, the term "shifter" was popularized by Roman Jacobson in his 1956 essay "Shifters, Verbal Categories, and the Russian Verb." See Roman Jacobson, *Selected Writings II: Word and Language* (The Hague: Mouton, 1971), 130–47.

101. Benveniste, "The Nature of Pronouns," 220.

102. Robert McMahon, *Understanding the Medieval Meditative Ascent: Augustine, Anselm, Boethius and Dante* (Washington, DC: Catholic University of America Press, 2006), 51.

103. See also Lyons, "The Cartesian Reader," 40–41.

104. In the Second Set of Replies Descartes even speaks of weeks and months: "Now the best way of achieving a firm knowledge of reality is first to accustom ourselves with doubting all things, especially corporeal things. . . . And I should like my readers not just to take the short time needed to go through it, but to devote several months, or at least weeks, to considering the topics dealt with, before going on to the rest of the book. If they do this they will undoubtedly be able to derive much greater benefit from what follows" (CSM II 94; AT VII 130). See also Schildknecht, "Erleuchtung und Tarnung," 97.

105. See Zeno Vendler, "Descartes' Exercises," *Canadian Journal of Philosophy* 19 (1989): 201; L. Aryeh Kosman, "The Naïve Narrator: Meditation in Descartes' *Meditations*," in *Essays on Descartes' Meditations*, ed. Amélie Oskenberg Rorty (Berkeley: University of California Press, 1986), 21–43.

106. See Curley, "Spinoza as an Expositor"; Garber and Cohen, "A Point of Order."

107. This explains the syllogistic form of the famous "cogito, ergo sum" in the *Principia*.

108. As indicated in the subtitle, "This light alone, without any help from religion or philosophy, determines what opinions a good man [*un honnête homme*] should hold on any matter that may occupy his thoughts, and penetrates into the secrets of the most recondite sciences" (CSM II 400; AT X 495). See also Alberto Guillermo Ranea, "A 'Science for *honnêtes hommes*': *La recherche de la vérité* and the Deconstruction of Experimental Knowledge," in *Descartes' Natural Philosophy*, ed. Stephen Gaukroger, John Schuster, and John Sutton (London: Routledge, 2000), 313–29.

Chapter 3

1. In a letter to Antoine Vatier, a French Jesuit, Descartes conceives skepticism as a way to "withdraw the mind from the senses [*ad abducendam mentem a sensibus*]" (CSM III 86; AT I 560–61).

2. Of course, much could be said about the implications of this maneuver and Descartes' privileging of oneiric delusions over their psychotic cousins. Jacques Derrida's critique of Michel Foucault's remarks in Michel Foucault, *Folie et déraison: Historie de la folie à l'âge classique* (Paris: Librairie Plon, 1961), set off a lengthy debate. For Derrida, see Jacques Derrida, "Cogito and the History of Madness," in *Writing and Difference*, trans. Alan Bass (Chicago: University of Chicago Press, 1978), 31–63.

3. "Imagine a painter who wanted to combine a horse's neck with a human head, and then clothe a miscellaneous collection of limbs with various kinds of feathers, so that what started out at the top as a beautiful woman ended in a hideously ugly fish. If you were invited, as friends, to the private view, could you help laughing? Let me tell you, my Piso friends, a book whose different features are made up at random like a sick man's dreams, with no unified form to have a head or a tail, is exactly like that picture." From D. A. Russell, and M. Winterbottom, eds. and trans., *Classical Literary Criticism* (Oxford: Oxford University Press, 1989), 98.

4. See Dennis L. Sepper, "Descartes and the Eclipse of the Imagination, 1618–1630," *Journal of the History of Philosophy* 27 (1989): 379–403. It is, of course, true that Descartes most commonly compares mental representations of sensory things to images. See, for instance, CSM II 27, AT VII 40; CSM II 24, AT VII 34; CSM II 27, AT VII 40; CSM II 47, AT VII 69. However, as I have shown earlier, the analogy is not restricted to those usages. See also John Carriero, "Painting and Dreaming in the First Meditation," in *Norms and Modes of Thinking in Descartes*, ed. Tuomo Aho and Mikko Yrjönsuuri (Helsinki: Societas Philosophica, 1999), 13–46.

5. On these peculiar role reversals, see Saskia Brown, "The Childhood of Reason: Pedagogical Strategies in Descartes's *La recherche de la vérité par la lumière naturelle*," *Romanic Review* 87 (1996): 465–80.

6. See Aristotle, *On the Soul/Parva Naturalia/On Breath*, trans. W. S. Hett (Cambridge, MA: Harvard University Press, 1986), III.7 (431a), III.8 (432a).

7. See Mary Carruthers, *The Craft of Thought: Meditation, Rhetoric, and the Making of Images, 400–1200* (Cambridge: Cambridge University Press, 1998), 116–70. Jerome coined the phrase *(de-)pingere in corde nostro* (to paint in our heart) for this mental image making in meditation (133).

8. For Ignatian technique of making mental images, see Roland Barthes, *Sade Fourier Loyola*, trans. Richard Miller (New York: Hill and Wang, 1976), 48–52, 62–68; Antonio T. de Nicolas, *Powers of Imagining: Ignatius de Loyola* (Albany: State University of New York Press, 1986); Pierre-Antoine Fabre, *Ignace de Loyola*,

Le lieu de l'image (Paris: Librairie Philosophique J. Vrin, 1992). For meditative image making in the early modern Catholic context, see Walter S. Melion, *The Meditative Art: Studies in the Northern Devotional Print, 1550–1625* (Philadelphia: St. Joseph's University Press, 2009).

9. Ignatius of Loyola, *Personal Writings:* Reminiscences, Spiritual Diary, *Select Letters—including the Text of* The Spiritual Exercises, trans. Joseph A. Munitiz and Philip Endean (London: Penguin Books, 1996), 175, 317. Further references to this edition, cited as SE.

10. For the following, see Christopher Wild, "'Weder mit worten und rutten': The Force of Gryphius' Examples," *Germanic Review* 76, no. 2 (2001): 99–118. For the role of evidentia in classical rhetoric, see Heinrich Lausberg, *Handbuch der literarischen Rhetorik. Eine Grundlegung der Literaturwissenschaft* (Munich: M. Heuber, 1960), 399–407; Fritz Graf, "Ekphrasis: Die Entstehung der Gattung in der Antike," in *Beschreibungskunst - Kunstbeschreibung. Ekphrasis von der Antike bis zur Gegenwart*, ed. Gottfried Boehm and Helmut Pfotenhauer (Munich: Brill, 1995), 143–55; Andreas Kemmann, "Evidentia, Evidenz," in *Historisches Wörterbuch der Rhetorik*, ed. Gert Ueding (Tübingen: Niemeyer, 1996), 3:33–47; Bernhard F. Scholz, "Ekphrasis and Enargeia in Quintilian's *Institutionis oratoriae libri XII*," in *Rhetorica movet: Studies in Historical and Modern Rhetoric in Honour of Heinrich F. Plett*, ed. Peter L. Oesterreich and Thomas O. Sloane (Leiden, Netherlands: Brill, 1999), 3–24; Rüdiger Campe, "Vor Augen Stellen. Über den Rahmen rhetorischer Bildgebung," in *Poststrukturalismus. Herausforderung an die Literaturwissenschaft*, ed. G. Neumann (Stuttgart: J. B. Metzler, 1997), 208–25.

11. Quintilian, *The Institutio Oratoria of Quintilian*, trans. H. E. Butler (Cambridge, MA: Harvard University Press, 1980), III 245, VIII.3.61. Further references are to this edition, cited as IO.

12. Nicolaos of Myra, *Progymnasmata*, 68. Quoted in Scholz, "Ekphrasis and Enargeia," 7.

13. Quoted after David Freedberg, *The Power of Images. Studies in the History and Theory of Response* (Chicago: University of Chicago Press, 1989), 184–85. For the Latin original, see Antoine Sucquet, *Via vitae aeternae: Iconibus illustrata per Boetius a Bolswert* (Antwerp: Typis Martini Nutij, 1620), 501.

14. Melion, *The Meditative Art*, 157.

15. This is the frontispiece of the appendix "Orbita probitatis ad Christi imitationem Christiano subserviens" in Joannes David, *Veridicus Christianus* (Antwerp: Ex officina Plantiniana, 1601).

16. Melion, *The Meditative Art*, 339. See also Freedberg, *The Power of Images*, 184–85; Jeffrey Chips Smith, *Sensuous Worship: Jesuits and the Art of the Early Catholic Reformation in Germany* (Princeton, NJ: Princeton University Press, 2002), 48–49; Ralph Dekoninck, *Ad Imaginem: Statuts, fonctions et usages de l'image dans la littérature spirituelle jésuite du XVIIe siècle* (Geneva: Droz, 2005), 194–95.

17. *Phantasia* is translated as "appearance, impression" as well as "(re)presentation." For the Stoic *chrēsis tōn phantasiōn*, see E. P. Arthur, "The Stoic Analysis of the Mind's Reactions to Presentations," *Hermes* 111 (1983): 69–78; Anthony A. Long, "Representation and the Self in Stoicism," in *Stoic Studies*, by Anthony A. Long (Berkeley: University of California Press, 2001), 264–85.

18. Epictetus, *Discourses, Books III–IV: The Encheiridion*, trans. W. A. Oldfather (Cambridge, MA: Harvard University Press, 2000). Further references are to this edition.

19. The term *kataléptikē* is notoriously difficult to translate. Often it is translated as "cognitive," yielding "cognitive impression" or "cognitive presentation." "Apprehensive" has the advantage of preserving the etymological root of *katalēpsis* as "grasping." For the following discussion, see F. H. Sandbach, "Phantasia Kataleptike," in *Problems in Stoicism*, ed. A. A. Long (London: Athlone Press, 1971), 9–21; Michael Frede, "Stoics and Sceptics on Clear and Distinct Impressions," in *Essays in Ancient Philosophy*, by Michael Frede (Oxford: Clarendon Press, 1987), 151–76; Julia Annas, "Stoic Epistemology," in *Epistemology: Companions to Ancient Thought I*, ed. Stephen Everson (Cambridge: Cambridge University Press, 1990), 184–203; Anna-Maria Ioppolo, "Presentation and Assent: A Physical and Cognitive Problem in Early Stoicism," *Classical Quarterly* 40 (1990): 423–49; Michael Frede, "Stoic Epistemology," in *The Cambridge History of Hellenistic Philosophy*, ed. Keimpe Algra, Jonathan Barnes, Jaap Mansfeld, and Malcolm Schofield (Cambridge: Cambridge University Press, 1999), 295–322.

20. Sextus Empiricus, *Against the Logicians*, trans. Richard Bett (Cambridge: Cambridge University Press, 2005), 52.

21. A. A. Long and D. N. Sedley, *The Hellenistic Philosophers* (Cambridge: Cambridge University Press, 1987), 237. See also Epictetus, *Discourses* 3.3.20: "The soul is something like a bowl of water, and the external impressions something like the ray of light that falls into the water."

22. Scholars usually trace the early Christian doctrine of the discernment of spirits to Jewish sources and neglect a possible Stoic connection. One exception is Michel Foucault, *The Hermeneutics of the Subject: Lectures at the Collège de France, 1981–82*, ed. Frédéric Gros, trans. Graham Burchell (New York: Palgrave Macmillan, 2005), 299–301.

23. See Joseph T. Lienhard, S.J., "On 'Discernment of Spirits' in the Early Church," *Theological Studies* 41 (1980): 505–29.

24. See Robert Penkett, "Discerning the Divine and the Demonic in the *Life of Antony*," *Reading Medieval Studies* 24 (1998): 79–94.

25. See Dr. Fr. Dingjan, O.S.B., *Discretio. Les origines patristiques et monastiques de la doctrine sur la prudence chez saint Thomas d'Aquin* (Assen, Netherlands: Van Gorcum, 1967), 14–76; Gerd Summa, *Geistliche Unterscheidung bei Johannes Cassian* (Würzburg: Echter, 1992); Antony D. Rich, *Discernment in the Desert Fathers:*

Διάκρισις in the *Life and Thought of Early Egyptian Monasticism* (Milton Keynes, UK: Pater Noster, 2007), 75–122.

26. John Cassian, *The Conferences*, trans. Boniface Ramsey, O.P. (New York: Paulist Press, 1997), 84. References in the text are to this edition.

27. Antony is quoted saying, "Although the works of the aforesaid virtues [fasting, vigils, prayer, etc.] abounded in them, the lack of discretion by itself did not permit those works to endure to the end" (Cassian, *Conferences*, 2.2.4).

28. Gregory the Great, *Dialogues*, trans. Odo John Zimmermann, O.S.B. (Washington, DC: Catholic University Press, 1959), II.36.

29. Benedict of Nursia, *The Rule of Saint Benedict*, ed. and trans. Bruce L. Venarde (Cambridge, MA: Harvard University Press, 2011), 208–9. On *discretio* in Benedictine religious culture, see D. Feuling, "Discretio," *Benediktinische Monatsschrift* 7 (1925): 241–58, 349–66; H. Walter, "Die benediktinische Discretio," in *Einsicht und Glaube*, ed. Josef Ratzinger and H. Fries (Freiburg: Herder, 1962), 209–15; Aquinata Böckmann, "Discretio im Sinn der Regel Benedikts und ihrer Tradition," *Erbe und Auftrag* 52 (1976): 362–73; A. M. Raabe, "Discernment of Spirits in the Prologue to the *Rule* of Benedict," *American Benedictine Review* 23 (1972): 397–423.

30. See Grazia Mangano Ragazzi, *Obeying the Truth: Discretion in the Spiritual Writings of Saint Catherine of Siena* (Oxford: Oxford University Press, 2014), 138–49. For an interesting take on *discretio* as a "paradigm of subjectivity" in the Middle Ages, see Niklaus Largier, "Rhetorik des Begehrens. Die 'Unterscheidung der Geister' als Paradigma mittelalterlicher Subjektivität," in *Inszenierungen von Subjektivität in der Literatur des Mittelalters*, ed. Martin Baisch, Jutta Eming, Hendrikje Haufe, and Andrea Sieber (Königstein: Helmer, 2005), 249–70.

31. For more, see the introduction to Helmut Puff, Ulrike Strasser, and Christopher Wild, eds., *Cultures of Communication: Theologies of Media in Early Modern Europe and Beyond* (Toronto: University of Toronto Press, 2017), 3–14.

32. See Nancy Caciola, *Discerning Spirits: Divine and Demonic Possession in the Middle Ages* (Ithaca, NY: Cornell University Press, 2002), 1–31; Moshe Sluhovsky, *Believe Not Every Spirit: Possession, Mysticism, and Discernment in Early Modern Catholicism* (Chicago: University of Chicago Press, 2007); Susan Schreiner, *Are You Alone Wise? The Search for Certainty in the Early Modern Era* (Oxford: Oxford University Press, 2012), 261–322.

33. Schreiner, *Are You Alone Wise?*, 285.

34. Gerson composed the treatise "On the Testing of Spirits" in 1415 at the Council of Constance, when the council revisited the canonization of Brigitta of Sweden from 1391. Gerson also attempted to vindicate Joan of Arc. See Dyan Elliott, "Seeing Double: John Gerson, the Discernment of Spirits, and Joan of Arc," *American Historical Review* 112 (2002): 26–54. For Gerson's theory of the discernment of spirits more generally, see Paschal Boland, O.S.B., *The Concept of Discretio Spirituum in John Gerson's "De Probatione Spirituum" and "De Distinctione Verarum Visionum a*

Falsis" (Washington, DC: Catholic University of America Press, 1959); Cornelius Roth, *Discretio spirituum. Kriterien geistlicher Unterscheidung bei Johannes Gerson* (Würzburg: Echter, 2001); Sluhovsky, *Believe Not Every Spirit*, 175–80; Schreiner, *Are You Alone Wise?*, 263–68.

35. Jean Gerson, "On Distinguishing True from False Revelations," in *Early Works*, trans. Brian Patrick McGuire (New York: Paulist Press, 1998), 334. Further references are to this edition.

36. On the discernment of spirits in Ignatius, see John Carroll Futrell, S.J., "Ignatian Discernment," *Studies in the Spirituality of the Jesuits* 2 (1970): 47–88; Michael Buckley, S.J., "Discernment of Spirits," *The Way*, Supplement 20 (1973): 19–37; Jules Toner, *A Commentary on St. Ignatius' Rules for Discernment of the Spirits* (St. Louis: Institute of Jesuit Sources, 1982); Marjorie O'Rourke Boyle, "Angels Black and White: Loyola's Spiritual Discernment in Historical Perspective, *Theological Studies* 44 (1983): 241–57; Norbert Bäumert, "Zur 'Unterscheidung der Geister,'" *Zeitschrift für katholische Theologie* 111 (1989): 183–95; Hugo Rahner, S.J., *Ignatius the Theologian*, trans. Michael Barry (London: Geoffrey Chapman, 1990), 136–80; Schreiner, *Are You Alone Wise?*, 270–85.

37. Martin E. Palmer, S.J., ed. and trans., *On Giving the Spiritual Exercises: The Early Jesuit Manuscript Directories and the Official Directory of 1599* (St. Louis, MO: Institute of Jesuit Sources, 1996).

38. Ignatius alludes here to the Augustine distinction between *frui*, "to enjoy for its own sake," and *uti*, "to use for the sake of another." Book One of *De doctrina christiana* is the most important text of Augustine on this pair of terms.

39. Schreiner, *Are You Alone Wise?*, 284, makes a similar point: "Immediacy guarantees, or brings with it, a subjective or experiential certainty. Any form of mediation, be it human or demonic, could lead the soul astray into deception."

40. For the argument regarding Descartes' debt to Pyrrhonian skepticism, see Richard Popkin, *The History of Scepticism: From Savonarola to Bayle* (Oxford: Oxford University Press, 2003), 143–73. For a more general skepticism, see J. L. Bermudez, "The Originality of Cartesian Scepticism: Did It Have Ancient or Medieval Antecedents?," *History of Philosophy Quarterly* 17 (2000): 333–60; Dominik Perler, "Was There a 'Pyrrhonian Crisis' in Early Modern Philosophy? A Critical Notice of Richard Popkin," *Archiv für Geschichte der Philosophie* 86 (2004): 215–19. Only recently has Descartes' allegiance to the skeptical tradition, be it Pyrrhonian or more diffuse, been questioned.

41. To my knowledge the connection between Descartes' critique of mental representations and the discernment of spirits has been overlooked. The only notable exception is the article by Anthony Ossa-Richardson, "Gijsbert Voet and *Discretio Spirituum* after Descartes," in *Angels of Light? Sanctity and the Discernment of Spirits in the Early Modern Period*, ed. Clare Copeland and Jan Machielsen (Leiden,

Netherlands: Brill, 2013), 235–53. Unfortunately, it only skirts Descartes, focusing primarily on Voetius.

42. John R. Cole, *The Olympian Dreams and Youthful Rebellion of René Descartes* (Urbana: University of Illinois Press, 1992), 32. For the original, see AT X 180–88. Further references are to these editions.

43. Shortly before, Descartes' meditator invokes the same model and comments: "And the most obvious judgement for me to make is that the thing in question transmits to me [*in me immittere*] its own likeness rather than something else" (CSM II 26; AT VII 38).

44. I translate *adventitiae* in line with the authorized French version and seventeenth-century usage as "arriving, coming from somewhere else" rather than "coincidental" (as CSM renders it).

45. It may be objected that, in contrast to the traditional discernment of spirits, which happens in real time, Descartes' is not a true discernment because it concerns thoughts that are implanted at birth. *Sub specie aeternitatis* this distinction might be irrelevant, as both moments, the moment of the self's birth and the present moment, are simultaneous and co-present in God's mind; and indeed, in a letter to Elisabeth of Bohemia Descartes conflates this eternal and present perspective: "It is true that faith alone teaches us what grace is, by which God elevates us to a supernatural true happiness. But philosophy alone is sufficient for knowing that the slightest thought could not enter into the mind of man unless God wants and has wanted from all eternity that thought to enter there" (AT IV 314; René Descartes, *The Correspondence between Princess Elisabeth of Bohemia and René Descartes*, ed. and trans. Lisa Shapiro [Chicago: University of Chicago Press, 2007], 120). From the perspective of predestination every thought entering the self's mind is supposed to be there according to God's will. Thus, the self discerns thoughts willed by God when it cognizes clearly and distinctly.

46. In fact, things are a little more complicated. As Descartes' meditator observes in the Fifth Meditation (CSM II 49; AT VII 71), clear and distinct cognition is indifferent and immune to its occurrence in dreams. That is, clear and distinct ideas are true whether the mind is awake or dreaming when thinking them. Descartes thus entertains the possibility that the mind can think clearly and distinctly even in dreams. Because of this indifference, clarity and distinctness cannot serve as marks of distinction.

47. The phrase *rerum agendarum necessitas* literally means "the necessity of things to be done."

48. The meditative matrix was by and large denominationally ambidextrous. Luther, for instance, used the psychological phenomenon that the word "Christum" invokes the mental image of a man on the cross to defend religious images against Andreas Karlstadt. See Martin Luther, *Werke. Kritische Gesamtausgabe* (Weimar: Herman Böhlau, 1883), 18:83. Thus, shifting the denominational context

from the Counter-Reformation saint Ignatius of Loyola to this Protestant poetess, whose oeuvre is profoundly meditational, is less problematic than appears at first glance. Although the Ignatian exercises were often viewed somewhat suspiciously by Protestant writers and readers, the meditational literature of all confessions draws on the same psychagogical techniques developed by classical rhetoric. Moreover, Ignatius and Greiffenberg share a decided Christocentrism resulting in a deep spiritual affinity.

49. Catharina Regina von Greiffenberg, *Des Allerheiligst- und Allerheilsamsten Leidens und Sterbens Jesu Christi Zwölf andächtige Betrachtungen* (Neustadt an der Aysch, Germany: Drechsler, 1683), title page.

50. Aleida Assmann, "Die Sprache der Dinge. Der lange Blick und die wilde Semiose," in *Materialität der Kommunikation*, ed. Hans Ulrich Gumbrecht and Karl Ludwig Pfeiffer (Frankfurt: Suhrkamp, 1995), 237–51.

Chapter 4

1. See John Carriero, "The Second Meditation and the Essence of the Mind," in *Essays on Descartes' Meditations*, ed. Amélie Oskenberg Rorty (Berkeley: University of California Press, 1986), 200.

2. Stephen I. Wagner, "Descartes' Wax: Discovering the Nature of Mind," *History of Philosophy Quarterly* 12 (1995): 171.

3. For other interpretations, see L. J. Beck, *The Metaphysics of Descartes: A Study of the Meditations* (Oxford: Clarendon Press, 1965), 99–107; Ben Mijuskovic, "Descartes's Bridge to the External World: The Piece of Wax," *Studi internazionali di filosofia* 3 (1971): 65–81; Donald Sievert, "The Importance of Descartes's Wax Example," *Ratio* 21 (1979): 73–85; Julian Pacho, "Über einige erkenntnistheoretische Schwierigkeiten des klassischen Rationalismus," *Zeitschrift für Philosophische Forschung* 38 (1984): 561–81; M. Glouberman, "Descartes's Wax and the Typology of Early Modern Philosophy," *Modern Schoolman* 74 (1997): 117–41; Amy Schmitter, "The Wax and I: Perceptibility and Modality in the Second Meditation," *Archiv für Geschichte der Philosophie* 82 (2000): 178–201.

4. The subgenre of occasional meditation has received much less scholarly attention than its "deliberate" (see discussion of Bishop Hall) cousin and has often appeared under other classifications, such as occasional poetry or emblems. Exceptions are Louis L. Martz, *The Poetry of Meditation: A Study in English Religious Literature of the Seventeenth Century* (New Haven, CT: Yale University Press, 1962), 331–48; Karel Portman, "Cats' Concept of the Emblem and the Role of Occasional Meditation," *Emblematica* 6 (1991): 65–82; Marie-Louise Coolahan, "Redeeming Parcels of Time: Aesthetics and Practice of Occasional Meditation," *Seventeenth Century* 22 (2007): 124–43; Raymond A. Anselment, "Robert Boyle and the Art of Occasional Meditation," *Renaissance and Reformation* 32 (2009): 73–92; Courtney

Weiss Smith, *Empiricist Devotions: Science, Religion, and Poetry in Early Eighteenth-Century England* (Charlottesville: University Virginia Press, 2016), 33–68.

5. *Light of the World: An Anthology of Seventeenth-Century Dutch Religious and Occasional Poetry*, trans. Christopher Levenson (Windsor, ON: Netherlandic Press, 1982), 39.

6. *Light of the World*, 41.

7. The Latin translation was probably made by his son Robert Hall, who was also the first editor of the *Occasional Meditations*, and published in 1635 as *Josephi Hall Exoniensis Episcopi vel Meditatiunculae Subitanae*. A French translation by Theodore Jacquemont appeared in 1632 in Geneva. The import into the German lands is somewhat more complicated, as several authors such as Georg Philipp Harsdörffer and Christian Scriver plundered Hall's collection before it was "properly" translated and published under Hall's name in 1673.

8. Frank Livingstone Huntley, ed., *Bishop Joseph Hall and Protestant Meditation in Seventeenth-Century England: A Study with the Texts of* The Art of Divine Meditation *(1606) and* Occasional Meditations *(1633)* (Binghampton, NY: Center for Medieval and Renaissance Studies, 1981), 72.

9. Huntley, *Bishop Joseph Hall*, 73.

10. For the Ignatian practice of the *applicatio sensuum*, see Hugo Rahner, S.J., "Die 'Anwendung der Sinne' in der Betrachtungsmethode des Hl. Ignatius von Loyola," in *Meditation in Religion und Psychotherapie*, ed. Wilhelm Bitter (Stuttgart: E. Klett, 1958), 58–83; James Walsh, "Application of the Senses," *The Way*, Supplement 27 (1976): 59–68; Philip Endean, "The Ignatian Prayer of the Senses," *Heythrop Journal* 31 (1990): 391–418. For an interesting perspective on the application of the senses in medieval mysticism, see Niklaus Largier, "Inner Senses—Outer Senses: The Practice of Emotions in Medieval Mysticism," in *Von Emotionen im Mittelalter / Emotions and Sensibilities in the Middle Ages*, ed. Stephen Jaeger and Ingrid Kasten (Berlin: De Gruyter, 2003), 3–15.

11. Ignatius of Loyola, *Personal Writings:* Reminiscences, Spiritual Diary, *Select Letters—including the Text of* The Spiritual Exercises, trans. Joseph A. Munitiz and Philip Endean (London: Penguin Books, 1996), § 65–70, pp. 298–99. Further references are to this edition, cited as SE.

12. Marcus Aurelius, *Meditations*, trans. Martin Hammond (London: Penguin, 2006), 44.

13. Walter Benjamin, *Gesammelte Schriften*, ed. Rolf Tiedemann and Hermann Schweppenhäuser (Frankfurt: Suhrkamp, 1991), 406 (my translation).

14. For an aesthetic reading, see Niklaus Largier, "Praying by Numbers: An Essay on Medieval Aesthetics," *Representations* 103 (2008): 73–91. Here he conceives the "aesthetic" (in the sense of the sensorial) work of such meditations as "an art of figuration that is meant to inform the workings of perception, to alienate sensation and emotions from their everydayness, and to immerse them in artificial

states that both negate and reveal the natural and historical face of the world" (88). He also touches on Ignatius's application of the senses (79).

15. See Justus Lipsius, *On Constancy*, ed. John Sellars, trans. Sir John Stradling (1594) (Exeter: Liverpool University Press, 2006). For reading Lipsius's treatise as a spiritual exercise, see John Sellars, "Justus Lipsius' *De constantia*: A Stoic Spiritual Exercise," *Poetics Today* 28 (2007): 339–62.

16. Plato, *The Theaetetus of Plato*, ed. Myles Burnyeat, trans. M. J. Levett (Indianapolis, IN: Hackett, 1990), 325. Further references are to this edition. There are many problems in Plato's arguments concerning the wax, which I will leave aside, as they are not germane to my reading of Descartes. For a discussion of some of these problems, see Raphael Woolf, "Shaggy Soul Story: How Not to Read the Wax Tablet Model in Plato's *Theatetus*," *Philosophy and Phenomenological Research* 69 (2004): 573–604.

17. See Aristotle, *On Memory and Recollection* 450a, in Aristotle, *On the Soul/ Parva Naturalia/On Breath*, trans. W. S. Hett (Cambridge, MA: Harvard University Press, 1986).

18. Cicero, *De Oratore III. De Fato. Paradoxa Stoicorum. De Partitione Oratoria*, trans. H. Rackham (Cambridge, MA: Harvard University Press, 1992), 331. Further references are to this edition.

19. The author of the *Rhetorica ad Herennium*, similarly, compares the backgrounds to wax tablets (*cerae*) or papyrus and the images placed on them to writing (3.18.31). For more on this model of memory, see Chapter 2.

20. Cicero, *De Oratore I–II*, trans. E. W. Sutton and H. Rackham (Cambridge, MA: Harvard University Press, 1988), 471.

21. For this history, see Mary Carruthers, *The Book of Memory: A Study of Memory in Medieval Culture* (Cambridge: Cambridge University Press, 1990), 16–32.

22. Basil of Caesarea, *Regula fusius tractata* 5.2, cited in Irénée Hausherr, *The Name of Jesus*, trans. Charles Cummings, OCSO (Kalamazoo, MI: Cistercian, 1978), 162.

23. See Mary Carruthers and Jan M. Ziolkowski, eds., *The Medieval Craft of Memory: An Anthology of Texts and Pictures* (Philadelphia: University of Pennsylvania Press, 2002), 132, 166.

24. See Plato, *The Republic of Plato*, trans. Allan Bloom (New York: Basic Books, 1991), 197 (377b).

25. Aristotle, *On the Soul/Parva Naturalia/On Breath*, 13.

26. Diogenes Laertius, *Lives of Eminent Philosophers, Books VI–X*, trans. R. D. Hicks (Cambridge, MA: Harvard University Press, 1931). Further references are to this edition.

27. The younger Stoics seemed to have retreated a bit from the literality of this conception, for Chrysippus said, according to Diogenes Laertius, that "we must not take 'impression' in the literal sense of the stamp of a seal, because it is impossible

to suppose that a number of such impressions should be in one and the same spot at one and the same time" (*Lives* VIII.50). Nonetheless, even Chrysippus thinks of presentation as a physical change of the materially conceived soul.

28. See Andreas Kemmann, "Evidentia, Evidenz," in *Historisches Wörterbuch der Rhetorik*, ed. Gert Ueding (Tübingen: Niemayer, 1996), 3:44.

29. See Verity Platt, "Making an Impression: Replication and the Ontology of the Graeco-Roman Seal Stone," *Art History* 29 (2006): 233–57; Verity Platt, "Burning Butterflies: Seals, Symbols, and the Soul in Antiquity," in *Pagans and Christians: From Antiquity to the Middle Ages*, ed. Lauren Gilmour (Oxford: Archeopress, 2007), 89–99.

30. See Platt, "Making an Impression," 243.

31. Ernst Kitzinger, "The Cult of Images in the Age before Iconoclasm," *Dumbarton Oaks Papers* 8 (1954): 113.

32. Katherine Park, "Impressed Images: Reproducing Wonders," in *Picturing Science, Producing Art*, ed. Caroline A. Jones and Peter Galison (New York: Routledge, 1998), 254–71.

33. Park, "Impressed Images," 264.

34. Christine Göttler, "Wachs und Interdisziplinarität: Giovanni Bernadino Azzolinos 'Vier Letzte Dinge,'" in *Zwischen den Disziplinen. Perspektiven der Frühneuzeitforschung*, ed. Helmut Puff and Christopher Wild (Göttingen: Wallstein, 2003), 113. See also Christine Göttler, "'Seelen in Wachs': Material, Mimesis und Memoria in der religiösen Kunst um 1600," in *Ebenbilder. Kopien von Körpern—Modelle des Menschen*, ed. Jan Gerchow (Ostfieldern-Ruit, Germany: Hatje Cantz, 2002), 83–96.

35. In fact, Descartes starts out by acknowledging that he should explain "what the human mind is, what the body is and how it is informed by the mind" (CSM I 40; AT X 411), thus consciously invoking Aristotle's hylomorphism. For continuities between Aristotle's and Descartes' psychologies, see Peter R. Anstey, "*De Anima* and Descartes: Making up Aristotle's Mind," *History of Philosophy Quarterly* 17 (2000): 237–60.

36. These Aristotelian echoes in Descartes' account of sensory perception were not youthful errors. In the Fourth Set of Replies to Antoine Arnauld, he invokes Aristotle to explain how bread and wine in the Eucharist are perceived by the senses. Citing *De anima* 3.13 ("all the other senses, too, perceive by means of touching" [CSM II 175; AT VII 251]), he states unequivocally that "nothing can have an effect on any of our senses except through contact." And through this contact the "form [*speciem*]" of the perceived object is transferred to the sense's ceroplastic membrane (CSM II 175; AT VII 252).

37. See Daniel Heller-Roazen, *The Inner Touch: Archaeology of a Sensation* (New York: Zone Books, 2007).

38. In his letter to Mersenne of October 16, 1639, he makes a similar argument about the unity of the soul: "He [Lord Herbert of Cherbury in his book *On Truth*] would have it that we have as many faculties as there are different objects of knowledge. This seems to me like saying that because some wax can take on an infinite number of shapes, it has an infinite number of faculties for taking them on. . . . I prefer to think that the wax, simply by its flexibility, takes on all sorts of shapes, and that the soul acquires all its knowledge by the reflection which it makes either on itself (in the case of intellectual matters) or (in the case of corporeal matters) on the various dispositions of the brain to which it is joined, which may result from the action of the senses or from other causes" (CSM III 140; AT II 598).

39. See also CSM II 24; AT VII 34.

40. See also Robert McRae, "'Idea' as a Philosophical Term in the Seventeenth Century," *Journal of the History of Ideas* 26 (1965): 175–90.

41. For the sources of Descartes' concept of idea, see Roger Ariew and Marjorie Grene, "Ideas, in and before Descartes," *Journal of the History of Ideas* 56 (1995): 87–106; Norman J. Wells, "Descartes' *Idea* and Its Sources," *American Catholic Philosophical Quarterly* 67 (1993): 513–35.

42. Thomas Aquinas, *Summa Theologiae*, ed. John Mortenson and Enrique Alarcón, trans. Fr. Laurence Shapcote, O.P. (Lander, WY: Aquinas Institute, 2012). See also Mark D. Jordan, "The Intelligibility of the World and the Divine Ideas in Aquinas," *Review of Metaphysics* 38 (1984): 17–32.

43. For the conjunction of form and its perception, see also Descartes' Third Set of Replies: "For by an 'idea' I mean whatever is the form [*forma*] of a given perception. Now everyone surely perceives that there are things he understands. Hence everyone has the form or idea of understanding; and by indefinitely extending this he can form the idea of God's understanding" (CSM II 132; AT VII 188).

44. See Descartes' letter to Hyperaspistes of August 1641: "The mind, though really distinct from the body, is none the less joined to it, and is affected by traces impressed on it, and is able to impress new traces on its own account" (CSM III 190; AT III 424).

45. Ariew and Grene, "Ideas," 92. Ariew and Grene document that this sense of "idea" had widespread currency in the seventeenth century.

46. Alan Nelson argues that innate ideas are "created as the thinker's initial structure." See Alan Nelson, "Cartesian Innateness," in *A Companion to Descartes*, ed. Janet Broughton and John Carriero (Oxford: Oxford University Press, 2007), 322.

47. Georges Didi-Huberman, "The Order of Material: Plasticities, *Malaises*, Survivals," in *Sculpture and Psychoanalysis*, ed. Brandon Tayler (Aldershot UK: Ashgate, 2006), 197.

48. For the following discussion, see Reinhard Bull, *Das grosse Buch vom Wachs. Geschichte, Kultur, Technik* (Munich: Callwey, 1977).

49. Pliny, *Natural History Books 8–11*, trans. H. Rackham (Cambridge, MA: Harvard University Press, 2006), 439. Further references are to this edition.

50. Richard Rouse and Mary Rouse, "Wax Tablets," *Language and Communication* 9 (1989): 175. See also Richard Rouse and Mary Rouse, "The Vocabulary of Wax Tablets," in *Vocabulaire du livre e de l'écriture au moyen age*, ed. Olga Weijers (Turnhout, Belgium: Brepols, 1989), 220–30.

51. Didi-Huberman, "The Order of Material," 199.

52. Didi-Huberman, "The Order of Material," 200.

53. See Georgio Vasari, *The Lives of the Artists*, trans. Julia Conaway Bondanella and Peter Bondanella (Oxford: Oxford University Press, 1998), 240.

54. Diogenes Laertius, *Lives of Philosophers* 7.177, cited in A. A. Long and D. N. Sedley, *The Hellenistic Philosophers* (Cambridge: Cambridge University Press, 1987), 1:243.

55. Niklas Luhmann, *Art as Social System* (Stanford, CA: Stanford University Press, 2000), 103. Further references are to this edition.

56. Fritz Heider, "Thing and Medium," *Psychological Issues* 1 (1959): 2.

57. Dieter Mersch, *Medientheorien* (Hamburg: Junius, 2006), 218.

Chapter 5

1. John Cottingham, *Cartesian Reflections: Essays on Descartes's Philosophy* (Oxford: Oxford University Press, 2008), 281, 292.

2. Lawrence Nolan, "The Third Meditation: Causal Arguments for God's Existence," in *The Cambridge Companion to Descartes' Meditations*, ed. David Cunning (Cambridge: Cambridge University Press, 2014), 132.

3. L. J. Beck, *The Metaphysics of Descartes: A Study of the* Meditations (Oxford: Clarendon Press, 1965), 159.

4. See Nolan, "Third Meditation," 140.

5. In Descartes' words, "The mere fact that I exist and have within me an idea of a most perfect thing, that is, God, provides a very clear proof that God indeed exists" (CSM II 35; AT VII 51).

6. The validity of this third proof depends on the earlier proofs. See Beck, *Metaphysics of Descartes*, 237.

7. Descartes admits as much in a letter to Mersenne in July 1641, writing that reflecting on God as a "supremely perfect being" is so close to "the knowledge of his existence that it is almost the same thing to conceive of God and to conceive that he exists" (CSM III 186; AT III 396).

8. In paragraph 73 of the *Principia philosophiae* Descartes explains how the limited capacity of attention leads to the formation of "preconceived opinions;" precisely those opinions that the radical doubt of the First Meditation was supposed to purge: "*The third cause of error is that we become tired if we have to attend to things*

which are not present to the senses; as a result, our judgements on these things are habitually based not on present perception but on preconceived opinion. What is more, our mind is unable to keep its attention on things without some degree of difficulty and fatigue; and it is hardest of all for it to attend to what is not present to the senses or even to the imagination. This may be due to the very nature that the mind has as a result of being joined to the body; or it may be because it was exclusively occupied with the objects of sense and imagination in its earliest years, and has thus acquired more practice and a greater aptitude for thinking about them than it has for thinking about other things" (CSM I 220; AT VIIIA 37).

9. The third proof of God prevents the meditator from falling back into the doubts of the First Meditation. See Beck, *Metaphysics of Descartes*, 233.

10. In paragraph 16 of the *Principia* Descartes acknowledges the relevance of attention to the cognition of God: "At times when we are not intent [*defixi*] on the contemplation of the supremely perfect being, a doubt may easily arise as to whether the idea of God is not one of those which we made up at will, or at least one of those which do not include existence in their essence" (CSM I 198; AT VIIIA 11).

11. Pierre Hadot, *Philosophy as a Way of Life: Spiritual Exercises from Socrates to Foucault*, ed. Arnold Davidson, trans. Michael Chase (Oxford: Blackwell, 1995), 84. See also Michel Foucault, *The Hermeneutics of the Subject: Lectures at the Collège de France, 1981–82*, ed. Frédéric Gros, trans. Graham Burchell (New York: Palgrave Macmillan, 2005), 336–51. See in particular David Marno, *Death Be Not Proud: The Art of Holy Attention* (Chicago: University of Chicago Press, 2016).

12. Epictetus, *Discourses Books III–IV: The Encheiridion*, trans. W. A. Oldfather (Cambridge, MA: Harvard University Press, 2000), 427. Further references are to this edition.

13. C. R. Haines, trans., *Marcus Aurelius* (Cambridge, MA: Harvard University Press, 2003), 59. Further references are to this edition. Other meditations by Marcus Aurelius exhorting to attend to the present are 2.14, 7.54, and 8.36.

14. Seneca, *Moral Essays*, trans. John W. Basore (Cambridge, MA: Harvard University Press, 1935), 461.

15. Pierre Hadot makes the point emphatically: "*Prosochē* or attention to oneself, the philosopher's fundamental attitude, became the fundamental attitude of the monk." In Hadot, *Way of Life*, 131.

16. Athanasius, *Select Works and Letters*, trans. Philip Schaff and Henry Wace (New York: Christian Literature, 1890). Further references are to this edition.

17. Basil of Caesarea, *Ascetical Works*, trans. Monica Wagner (Washington, DC: Catholic University of America Press, 1962), 431–46. Further references are to this edition, cited as Give Heed followed by page number. See also Basilius of Caesarea and Rufinus von Aquileia, *Nosce te ipsum . . . animum tuam . . . Deum. Predigt 3 des Basilius Caesariensis in der Übersetzung des Rufinus*, ed. and trans. Heinrich Marti (Berlin: De Gruyter, 2012), 1–90. The Septuaginta translates the Hebrew as

"πρόσεχε σεαυτῷ μή ποτε γένηται ῥῆμα κρυπτὸν ἐν τῇ καρδίᾳ σοθ ἀνόμημα"; and the Latin translation of Basilius's sermon by Rufinus also makes the association with attention explicit by rendering the verse as "Attende tibi, ne forte fiat in te sermo absconsus in corde tuo iniquitas."

18. Hadot, *Way of Life*, 130.

19. Since the *Conferences* was probably originally planned to consist only of these first ten conferences, these last two form the work's culmination and conclusion. Accordingly, their main subject, prayer, is the very end of monastic existence with which the first conference opens. For the following, see also Columba Stewart, "John Cassian on Unceasing Prayer," *Monastic Studies* 15 (1984): 159–77; Columba Stewart, *Cassian the Monk* (New York: Oxford University Press, 1988), 105–13.

20. John Cassian, *The Conferences*, trans. Boniface Ramsey, O.P. (New York: Paulist Press, 1997), 329. Further references are to this edition.

21. See Irénée Hausherr, *The Name of Jesus*, trans. Charles Cummings, OCSO (Kalamazoo, MI: Cistercian, 1978), 158–65.

22. *Intentio* and *attentio* are not only etymologically related but were used interchangeably to denote attention, as Augustine demonstrates.

23. Augustine, *Concerning the City of God against the Pagans*, trans. Henry Bettenson (London: Penguin Books, 1984), 452.

24. For the following, see also Deborah Brown, "Augustine and Descartes on the Function of Attention in Perceptual Awareness," in *Consciousness: From Perception to Reflection in the History of Philosophy*, ed. S. Heinämaa, V. Lähteenmäki, and P. Remes (Berlin: Springer, 2007), 153–75.

25. Augustine, *On the Trinity: Books 8–15*, trans. Gareth B. Matthews (Cambridge: Cambridge University Press, 2002), 65. Further references are to this edition.

26. See Augustine, *On Christian Teaching*, trans. R. P. H. Green (Oxford: Oxford University Press, 1997), 1.22.20, for the distinction and definition of *uti* and *frui*.

27. Augustine, *Confessions*, trans. Henry Chadwick (Oxford: Oxford University Press, 1998), 235. Further references are to this edition.

28. The scholarship on Augustine's notion of *distentio* is vast. I have particularly profited from Andrea Nightingale, *Once out of Nature: Augustine on Time and the Body* (Chicago: University of Chicago Press, 2011), 55–104. See also Burcht Pranger, *Eternity's Ennui: Temporality, Perseverance and Voice in Augustine and Western Literature* (Leiden, Netherlands: Brill, 2010), 295–328.

29. See Nightingale, *Once out of Nature*, 56.

30. Andrea Nightingale, *Once out of Nature*, 80, argues that "by using the first person and calling attention to his efforts to stay focused, he emphasizes that his attempt to construct a theory of temporality is carried out by a person who is mired in time."

31. See Nightingale, *Once out of Nature*, 85.

32. Mary Carruthers, *The Craft of Thought: Meditation, Rhetoric, and the Making of Images, 400–1200* (Cambridge: Cambridge University Press, 1998).

33. To my knowledge attention has been largely neglected by Descartes scholars. Deborah Brown's essay "Augustine and Descartes on the Function of Attention" focuses almost exclusively on the *Passions of the Soul* and construes Descartes' concept of attention as primarily exogenous. As the following makes clear, my account comes to a very different conclusion. Most useful is Deborah Boyle, *Descartes on Innate Ideas* (London: Continuum, 2009), 106–12; Theodor Kobusch, "Descartes' *Meditations*: Practical Metaphysics: The Father of Rationalism in the Tradition of Spiritual Exercises," in *Philosophy as a Way of Life: Ancients and Moderns: Essays in Honor of Pierre Hadot*, ed. Michael Chase, Stephen R. L. Clark, and Michael McGhee (Chichester, UK: Wiley, 2013), 167–83.

34. John R. Cole, *The Olympian Dreams and Youthful Rebellion of René Descartes* (Urbana: University of Illinois Press,1992), 32. The French original is found in AT X 181.

35. For the following discussion, see also Julie R. Klein, "Memory and the Extension of Thinking in Descartes's *Regulae*," *International Philosophical Quarterly* 42 (2002): 23–29.

36. Matthew L. Jones makes a similar point in *The Good Life in the Scientific Revolution: Descartes, Pascal, Leibniz, and the Cultivation of Virtue* (Chicago: University of Chicago Press, 2006), 61.

37. See Michelle Karnes, *Imagination, Meditation, and Cognition in the Middle Ages* (Chicago: University of Chicago Press, 2017).

38. See also M. Jones, *The Good Life*, 61–62.

39. Klein, "Memory and the Extension of Thinking," 25.

40. On Descartes' critical stance toward traditional mnemonic practice, see M. Jones, *The Good Life*, 25–26.

41. For example, Raimundus Lullus, whom he viewed critically. See his letter to Beeckman of April 29, 1629 (CSM III 4–5; AT X 164).

42. Klein, "Memory and the Extension of Thinking," 35, calls this "running through" a "subvention of memory."

43. For symbolic notation, see M. Jones, *The Good Life*, 33–34.

44. See also Rüdiger Campe, "Shapes and Figures: Geometry and Rhetoric in the Age of Evidence," *Monatshefte* 102 (2010): 285–99.

45. See Lawrence Nolan and Alan Nelson, "Proofs for the Existence of God," in *The Blackwell Guide to Descartes'* Meditations, ed. Stephen Gaukroger (Malden, MA: Blackwell, 2006), 112–13.

46. For instance, all three proofs take as their starting point the idea of God that Descartes' meditator encounters in their mind, an idea with a set of distinctive features that they progressively examine and explicate. The first two proofs depend on the causal principle of *ex nihilo nihil fit*, which Descartes' meditator recognizes as

innate to their mind. Whereas the first proof utilizes it rather counterintuitively and, thus, arrives at it in a somewhat circuitous way, the second can simply presuppose it and apply it in a much more straightforward manner. The same obtains to the idea of the self as a finite being compared to God's infinity. Again, the first proof brings this idea to bear in a somewhat complicated way. The second proof, in contrast, uses it as its starting point. The second and third proofs are linked together by the notion of existence. The idea of the self as a thinking thing does not entail existence (except as long as it thinks), in contrast to the idea of a perfect God that cannot be thought without existing. Furthermore, the implication of the infinite by the finite operates across proofs rather than within a single demonstration. By deploying certain elements as connective links, they are rehearsed and practiced so that the mind has them close at hand and can move through the whole demonstration more quickly.

47. In the preface to the French edition of the *Principia* Descartes puts it this way: "Who wishes to doubt everything cannot, for all that, doubt that he exists while he is doubting" (CSM I 184; AT IXB 9–10).

48. Twenty-four times, according to Katsuzo Murakami, Meguru Sasaki, and Tesuichi Nishimura, eds., *Concordance to Descartes' Meditationes de Prima Philosophia* (Hildesheim, Zürich: Olms-Weidmann, 1995).

49. It is interesting to note that Descartes does not employ *intentio* and its cognates a single time in the *Meditations*.

50. This distinction seems paradoxical in the case of Descartes' meditator, who denies the existence of an outside world. How can attention be exogenous if there is no outside? As I show shortly, both the latency of innate ideas and absorptive force of sensory impressions make this distinction pertinent.

51. For other examples of *animadversio* as a detection of falsehood, see CSM II 18, AT VII 27; CSM II 19, AT VII 28; CSM II 20, AT VII 29; CSM II 37, AT VII 52. It should be noted that Descartes also uses *animadversio* to describe the realization of positive knowledge, for instance, of the "immense power of God" (CSM II 39; AT VII 56) or of the certainty of all other things depending on the existence of God (CSM II 48; AT VII 69).

52. See also Descartes' Fifth Reply (CSM II 262; AT VII 382). John Morris also speaks of recognition. See his "Descartes' Natural Light," *Journal of the History of Philosophy* 11 (1973): 170.

53. Beck, *Metaphysics of Descartes*, 156, makes a similar point.

54. Descartes writes similarly in a letter to Hyperaspistes in August 1641: "None the less, [the mind] has in itself the ideas of God, of itself and of all such truths as are called self-evident, in the same way as adult human beings have these ideas when they are not attending to them; for it does not acquire these ideas later on, as it grows older" (CSM III 190; AT III 424).

Chapter 6

1. Gabriel Daniel, *A Voyage to the World of Cartesius: Written Originally in French, and Now Translated into English* (London: Thomas Bennet, 1692), 4–5. The French Jesuit relates this anecdote as a satirical endorsement of Marin Mersenne's defense of Descartes against atheism that "we shall find nothing more of a Christian Temper, and that inspires us more ravishingly with the Love of God than Descartes' Philosophy." For the opposite charge that Descartes was an enthusiast, see Michael Heyd, *"Be Sober and Reasonable": The Critique of Enthusiasm in the Seventeenth and Early Eighteenth Centuries* (Leiden, Netherlands: Brill, 1995) 109–43.

2. See John Cottingham, *Cartesian Reflections: Essays on Descartes's Philosophy* (Oxford: Oxford University Press, 2008), 281, 289–90, 306–7.

3. See Aza Goudriaan, *Philosophische Gotteserkenntnis bei Suárez und Descartes im Zusammenhang mi der niederländischen reformierten Theologie und Philosophie des 17. Jahrhundert* (Leiden, Netherlands: Brill, 1999), 227–30; Andreas Schmidt, *Göttliche Gedanken. Zur Metaphysik der Erkenntnis bei Descartes, Malebranche, Spinoza und Leibniz* (Frankfurt: Klostermann, 2009), 61–73.

4. My translation.

5. In the *Passions of the Soul* Descartes defines admiration as the only passion that has "no relation with the heart and blood . . . but only with the brain" (CSM I 353; AT XI 381). Its purpose is epistemological, as it "makes us learn and retain in our memory things of which we were previously ignorant" (CSM I 354; AT XI 383).

6. Goudriaan, *Philosophische Gotteserkenntnis*, as well as Schmidt, *Göttliche Gedanken*, identify the *contemplatio Dei* with a *visio beatifica*. As will become clear in the following discussion, I aim to advance a more nuanced reading.

7. Adolf Lumpe, "Kontemplation," in *Reallexikon für Antike und Christentum*, ed. Georg Schöllgen (Stuttgart: Hiersemann, 2006), 21:486.

8. Andrea Nightingale, *Spectacles of Truth in Classical Greek Philosophy: Theoria in Its Cultural Context* (Cambridge: Cambridge University Press, 2004), 3–4.

9. Further references in the text are to the following translation: Plato, *The Republic of Plato*, trans. Allan Bloom (New York: Basic Books, 1991).

10. Nightingale, *Spectacles of Truth*, 68, makes the same point.

11. Further references in the text are to the following translation: Aristotle, *Nicomachean Ethics*, trans. Roger Crisp (Cambridge: Cambridge University Press, 2014).

12. See Nightingale, *Spectacles of Truth*, 187–252.

13. For the following discussion, see Pierre Hadot, *Plotinus or the Simplicity of Vision*, trans. Michael Chase (Chicago: University of Chicago Press, 1998).

14. Porphyry, "The Life of Plotinus and the Order of His Books," in *Plotinus, Porphyry on Plotinus, Ennead I*, trans. A. H. Armstrong (Cambridge, MA: Harvard University Press, 1989), 71. Further references are to this edition.

15. John Peter Kenney, *Contemplation and Classical Christianity: A Study of Augustine* (Oxford: Oxford University Press, 2013), 61.

16. Further references in the text are to the following translation: Augustine, *Confessions*, trans. Henry Chadwick (Oxford: Oxford University Press, 1998).

17. Augustine, *The Immortality of the Soul. The Magnitude of the Soul. On Music. The Advantage of Believing. On Faith in Things Unseen*, trans. L. Schopp, J. J. McMahon, R. C. Taliaferro, L. Meagher, O.S.B., R. J. Deferrari, and M. F. McDonald, O.P. (Washington, DC: Catholic University of America Press, 1947), 27.

18. Augustine, *Against the Academicians/The Teacher*, trans. Peter King (Indianapolis, IN: Hackett, 1995), 140–41.

19. Augustine, *On the Trinity: Books 8–15*, trans. Gareth B. Matthews (Cambridge: Cambridge University Press, 2002), 98–99, 102.

20. Kenney, *Contemplation and Classical Christianity*, 74.

21. Representative examples are *On the Quantity of the Soul* 33.70–76; *On Free Will* 2.3.7–2.15.39; *Confessions* 7.10.16, 7.17.23, 7.20.26, 9.10.23–26, 10.17.26, 10.25.35–36; *On Christian Doctrine* 2.7.9–11.

22. Bernard of Clairvaux, *Selected Works*, ed. Gillian R. Evans (New York: Paulist Press, 1987), 13.

23. Giles Constable, "Twelfth-Century Spirituality and the Late Middle Ages," *Medieval and Renaissance Studies* 5 (1971): 32.

24. See Etienne Gilson's assessment: "Rightly seen the Cistercians gathered around St. Bernard, the Victorines around Hugh and Richard, the Franciscans around St. Bonaventure represent the affective life of the medieval West at its most intense and its most beautiful." In Etienne Gilson, *The Philosophy of St. Bonaventure* (Paterson, NJ: St. Anthony Guild Press, 1965), xii.

25. Bernard of Clairvaux, *Five Books on Consideration: Advice to a Pope*, trans. John Anderson and Elizabeth Kennan (Kalamazoo, MI: Cistercian Publication, 1976), 52. Further references are to this edition.

26. Hugh of Saint Victor, *The Didascalicon of Hugh of Saint Victor: A Medieval Guide to the Arts*, trans. Jerome Taylor (New York: Columbia University Press, 1961), 132. In his little treatise *De meditatione* Hugh describes the relation of meditation and contemplation in a similar manner: "Reading offers material to know the truth, meditation assimilates it, prayer lifts it up, action organizes it, and contemplation rejoices in it." See Christopher P. Evans, ed., *Writings on the Spiritual Life: A Selection of Works of Hugh, Adam, Achard, Richard, Walter and Godfrey of St. Victor* (Turnhout, Belgium: Brepols, 2013), 387.

27. Hugh of Saint Victor, *Selected Spiritual Writings* (London: Faber, 1962), 183. Latin original in MPL 175.116.

28. Hugh of Saint Victor, *Spiritual Writings*, 183.

29. Hugh of Saint Victor, *Spiritual Writings*, 183.

30. Hugh of Saint Victor, *Spiritual Writings*, 186.

31. Hugh of Saint Victor, *Spiritual Writings*, 185.

32. See Marc-Aeilko Aris, *Contemplatio: Philosophische Studien zum Traktat Benjamin Maior des Richard von St. Viktor. Mit einer verbesserten Edition des Textes* (Frankfurt: J. Knecht, 1996); Karl Baier, "Meditation and Contemplation in High and Late Medieval Europe," in *Yogic Perception, Meditation and Altered States of Consciousness*, ed. Eli Franco (Vienna: Austrian Academy of Sciences, 2009), 325–49.

33. *Paradiso* 11.132 in Dante Aleghieri, *The Divine Comedy*, trans. Charles S. Singleton (Princeton, NJ: Princeton University Press, 1975), III.1: *Paradiso*, 115.

34. Richard of St. Victor, *The Twelve Patriarchs, The Mystical Ark, and Book Three of the Trinity*, trans. Grover A. Zinn (New York: Paulist Press, 1979), 155. Further references are to this edition.

35. Richard's classification resonated beyond the monastic context among Scholastic philosophers. For instance, Thomas Aquinas cites Richard's distinction of cogitation (thinking), meditation, and contemplation (*Summa Theologiae* IIa–IIae, q. 180, a. 3) and even references his sixfold distinction of contemplation (*Summa Theologiae* IIa–IIae, q. 180, a. 4).

36. See Friedrich Andres, "Die Stufen der *Contemplatio* in Bonaventuras *Itinerarium mentis in Deum* und im *Beniamin maior* des Richard von St. Viktor," *Franziskanische Studien* 7 (1921): 189–200.

37. Bonaventure, *The Journey of the Mind to God*, ed. Stephen F. Brown, trans. Philotheus Boehner, O.F.M. (Indianapolis, IN: Hackett, 1993). Further references are to this edition.

38. Constable, "Twelfth-Century Spirituality," 257–95.

39. Jean Gerson, *Early Works*, trans. Brian Patrick McGuire (New York: Paulist Press, 1998), 75.

40. See Nikolaus Staubach, "L'influence victorine sur la dévotion moderne," in *L'école de Saint-Victor de Paris: Influence et rayonnement du moyen âge à l'époque moderne*, ed. Dominique Poirel (Turnhout, Belgium: Brepols, 2010), 583–99.

41. They denote "every way of examining one's conscience, of meditating, contemplating, praying vocally and mentally, and other spiritual activities." Ignatius of Loyola, *Personal Writings:* Reminiscences, Spiritual Diary, *Select Letters—including the Text of* The Spiritual Exercises, trans. Joseph A. Munitiz and Philip Endean (London: Penguin Books, 1996), § 1, p. 283.

42. Louis Richeome, *The Pilgrime of Loreto. Performing His Vow Made to the Glorious Virgin Mary Mother of God. Conteyning Divers Devout Meditations upon the Christian and Catholic Doctrine*, trans. E. W. (Paris: English College Press, 1630), 50. See also Louis Martz, *The Poetry of Meditation: A Study in English Religious Literature of the Seventeenth Century* (New Haven, CT: Yale University Press, 1962), 13–20.

43. Francis de Sales, *Treatise on the Love of God*, trans. Henry Benedict Mackey, O.S.B. (Grand Rapids, MI: Christian Classics Ethereal Library, 2000), 230. Further references are to this edition.

44. I am thinking here of rhetorical tropes and techniques such as metaphor, allegory, ekphrasis, ductus, or *memoria*. Of course, they are not absent and, indeed, at times are crucial for characterizing the cognitive operations in the *Meditations*, as I have shown in the preceding chapters. See Mary Carruthers, *The Craft of Thought: Meditation, Rhetoric, and the Making of Images, 400–1200* (Cambridge: Cambridge University Press, 1998), 1–10, 22–24, 92–94.

45. For the following, see Anselm Stolz, "Anselm's Theology in the *Proslogion*," in *The Many-Faced Argument: Recent Studies on the Ontological Argument for the Existence of God*, ed. John Hick and Arthur C. McGill (New York: Macmillan, 1967), 183–206; Robert McMahon, *Understanding the Medieval Meditative Ascent: Augustine, Anselm, Boethius, and Dante* (Washington, DC: Catholic University of America Press, 2006), 159–210.

46. Anselm of Canterbury, *Proslogion with the Replies of Gaunilo and Anselm*, trans. Thomas Williams (Indianapolis, IN: Hackett, 2001), 7.

47. Anselm of Canterbury, *Proslogion*, prologue, 2.

48. For the theological history of the beatific vision, see the compendious study of Christian Trottmann, *La vision béatifique: Des disputes scolastiques à sa définition par Benoît XII* (Rome: Ecole Française de Romer, 1995). Very helpful are also Bernard McGinn, "Visions and Visualizations in the Here and Hereafter," *Harvard Theological Review* 98 (2005): 227–46; and Bernard McGinn, "*Visio Dei*: Seeing God in Medieval Theology and Mysticism," in *Envisaging Heaven in the Middle Ages*, ed. Carolyn Muessig and Ad Putter (New York: Routledge, 2007), 15–33.

49. Other texts by Augustine in which he discusses this issue are Letters 92 (To Italica), 148 (To Fortunatian), and 162 (To Evodius); Sermon 277; the Twelfth Book of his *Commentary on the Literal Meaning of Genesis*; and *On the City of God* 22.29. In addition, he reports on his own visions of God in this life in *Confessions* 7.10.16, 7.17.23, and 9.10.23. In light of the significance of this issue in Augustine's thought, it is surprising that scholars have not given it commensurate attention. Exceptions are Margaret Miles, "Vision: The Eye of the Body and Eye of the Mind in Saint Augustine's *De Trinitate* and *Confessiones*," *Journal of Religion* 63 (1983): 125–42; Augustine, *Augustinus: Über Schau und Gegenwart des unsichtbaren Gottes*, trans. Erich Naab (Stuttgart-Bad Cannstatt: Frommann-Holzboog, 1998).

50. Augustine, *Letters 100–155 (Epistulae)*, ed. Boniface Ramsey, trans. Roland Teske (Hyde Park, NY: New City Press, 2003), 319–49. Further references are to this edition.

51. Augustine, *The Literal Meaning of Genesis*, trans. John Hammond Taylor, S.J. (New York: Newman Press, 1982), 190. Further references are to this edition.

52. See William Hoye, *Actualitas omnium actuum: Man's Beatific Vision of God as Apprehended by Thomas Aquinas* (Meisenheim: Hain, 1975); William Hoye, "Gotteserkenntnis per essentiam im 13. Jahrhundert," in *Die Auseinandersetzungen an der Pariser Universität im XIII. Jahrhundert*, ed. Albert Zimmermann (Berlin: De Gruyter, 1976), 269–84; Dominic J. O'Meara, "Eriugena and Aquinas on Beatific Vision," in *Eriugena redivivus: Zur Wirkungsgeschichte seines Denkens im Mittelalter und im Übergang zur Neuzeit*, ed. Werner Beierwaltes (Heidelberg: C. Winter, 1987), 224–36; Trottmann, *La vision béatifique*, 302–20; Philip L. Reynolds, "Spiritual Cognition in Thomas Aquinas," *The Thomist* 67 (2003): 505–38.

53. Like Augustine, Aquinas discusses the beatific vision frequently. Question 12 of the *Summa Theologiae,* which asks "how God is known by us," takes up the vision of God. Sections on prophecy (ST IIa–IIae, q. 172–74), rapture (ST IIa–IIae, q. 175), and contemplation (ST IIa–IIae, q. 179–82) also touch on the *visio beatifica*. See McGinn, *Visio Dei*, 3n41, for further loci.

54. It's a little more complicated, as Thomas differentiates the intellect's knowledge of God's essence in the beatific vision from God's knowledge of himself and his essence. See O'Meara, "Eriugena and Aquinas," 228–29.

55. See Hans Blumenberg, "Licht als Metapher der Wahrheit. Im Vorfeld der philosophischen Begriffsbildung," in *Ästhetische und metaphorische Schriften*, ed. Anselm Haverkamp (Frankfurt: Suhrkamp, 2001), 139–71.

56. For the role of light in the metaphysical thought of ancient Greece, see Werner Beierwaltes, "Lux intelligibilis: Untersuchung zur Lichtmetaphysik der Griechen" (PhD diss., Ludwig-Maximilians-Universität München, 1957). For Plato's deployment of light, see W. Luther, "Wahrheit, Licht, Sehen und Erkennen im Sonnengleichnis von Platons Politeia: Ein Ausschnitt aus der Lichtmetaphysik der Griechen," *Studium Generale* 18 (1963): 479–96; Nightingale, *Spectacles of Truth*, 113–18.

57. See Werner Beierwaltes, "Die Metaphysik des Lichtes in der Philosophie Plotins," *Zeitschrift für philosophische Forschung* 15 (1961): 334–62.

58. In the Psalms God is not only the source of light but light itself, either appearing with a radiating "countenance" (Ps 4:6, 89:15) or "covering" Himself "with light as with a cloak" (Ps 104:2). In the New Testament the Gospel of John contains the most fully developed theology of light. Jesus Christ is the "true light which, coming into the world, enlightens every man" (Jn 1:9). In the Word made flesh the divine light is dimmed just enough so that it does not dazzle and overwhelm humans. However, in his transfiguration Christ "shone like the sun, and His garments became as white as light" (Mt 17:2), approximating the full radiation of God the Father. Referring to this divine radiation, 1 Timothy 6:16, a passage frequently quoted by Augustine and others, states that God "lives in an unapproachable light, whom no one has seen or can see."

59. See the mnemonic ascent of Book Ten of the *Confessions* where Augustine adds beauty to his characterization of the divine light (*Confessions* 10.27.38). See also Johann Kreuzer, *Pulchritudo: Vom Erkennen Gottes bei Augustin. Bemerkungen zu den Büchern IX, X und XI der Confessiones* (Munich: W. Fink Verlag, 1995).

60. See also Ronald H. Nash, "Some Philosophic Sources of Augustine's Illumination Theory," *Augustinian Studies* 2 (1971): 47–66.

61. Augustine, *Earlier Writings*, trans. John H. S. Burleigh (Philadelphia: Westminster, 1953), 262. See also DvD 17.42.

62. For more on Augustine's doctrine of illumination, see Ronald H. Nash, *The Light of the Mind: St. Augustine's Theory of Knowledge* (Lexington: University Press of Kentucky, 1969); Etienne Gilson, *The Christian Philosophy of Saint Augustine* (New York: Octagon Books, 1988), 77–96; Gareth B. Matthews, "Knowledge and Illumination," in *The Cambridge Companion to Augustine*, ed. Eleonore Stump and Norman Kretzmann (Cambridge: Cambridge University Press, 2002), 171–85.

63. Descartes' meditator uses the term *acies mentis* six times and the corresponding *obtutus mentis* twice in the *Meditations*. It occurs the first time in the transition from the first to the second proof of God, when Descartes' meditator observes that their "mental vision is blinded by the images of things perceived by the senses" (CSM II 32; AT VII 47), as they relax their attention. The *acies mentis* is thus invoked to explain the difficulty of directing and holding the meditator's attention. The second occurrence happens at the end of the second proof when Descartes' meditator recognizes that their mind is made in God's image and likeness and that this likeness is perceived "by the same faculty which enables [them] to perceive [them]self" (CSM II 35; AT VII 51) by their mental gaze. It occurs a third time in the *contemplatio Dei* at the end of the Third Meditation when Descartes' meditator pauses "to gaze with wonder and adoration on the beauty on this immense light, as far as the eye of [their] darkened intellect can bear it" (CSM II 36; AT VII 52). The two occurrences of *obtutus mentis* CSM II 44 and 48; AT VII 64 and 69) and the fourth occurrence of *acies mentis* (CSM II 48; AT VII 70) are to be found in the Fifth Meditation, closely connected to the third proof of God. All three instances pertain to the direction and management of attention. The final occurrences of the *acies mentis* are in the Sixth Meditation (CSM II 50 and 51; AT VII 72) in the context of a discussion of the imagination.

64. See Vincent Carraud, "De la connaissance intuitive de dieu selon A.T., V, pp. 136–139," in *La biografia intellettuale di Rene Descartes attraverso la* Correspondance, ed. Jean-Robert Armogathe, Giulia Belgioioso, and Carlo Vinti (Napoli: Vivarium, 1999), 287–315; Andreas Schmidt, *Göttliche Gedanken*, 67–69.

65. As early as in the *Regulae* Descartes uses the *cogito*, or the mind's awareness of its own thinking, as an example of intuition. See CSM I 46; AT X 422.

66. Despite its crucial role in Cartesian epistemology, the *lumen naturale* has not received much attention by Descartes scholars. Nicholas Jolley's monograph *The*

Light of the Soul: Theories of Ideas in Leibniz, Malebranche, and Descartes (Oxford: Clarendon Press, 1998) seems the most germane but focuses instead on Descartes' theory of ideas. Most helpful is Deborah Boyle, *Descartes on Innate Ideas* (London: Continuum, 2009). See also John Morris, "Descartes' Natural Light," *Journal of the History of Philosophy* 11 (1973): 169–87; Stephen H. Daniel, "Descartes' Treatment of 'lumen naturale,'" *Studia Leibnitiana* 10 (1978): 92–100; Dale Jacquette, "Descartes' Lumen Naturale and the Cartesian Circle," *Philosophy and Theology* 9 (1996): 273–320; Jan Rothkamm, "Lichtmetaphorik bei Francis Bacon, Rene Descartes, Thomas Hobbes und Baruch de Spinoza," *Archiv für Begriffsgeschichte* 52 (2010): 73–92; Stephan Gregory, "Lumen naturale: Licht und Wahrheit bei Descartes," *Zeitschrift für Kulturphilosophie* 8 (2014): 261–78.

67. For the following discussion on the role of the natural light in the *Meditations*, see Boyle, *Descartes on Innate Ideas*, 111–15.

68. The natural light appears under yet other guises in Descartes' oeuvre, as he uses it interchangeably with a number of other terms or phrases, often yoked with a simple "or." Other terms for the "natural light of reason" (CSM I 10; AT X 361) are "light of the mind" (CSM I 18; AT X 376), "power of understanding [*vis intelligendi*]" (CSM II 42; AT VII 60), "faculty of knowledge [*facultas cognescendi*]" (CSM I 203; AT VIIIA 16), or even "mental vision [*intuitus mentis*]" (CSM III 140; AT II 599).

69. In the Third Set of Replies Descartes states plainly that "a 'light in the intellect' means transparent clarity of cognition" (CSM II 135; AT VII 192).

70. We recall from Chapter 4 Fritz Heider's observation that physical media "spend themselves, so to speak, in the process of mediation so that we believe that we hear the ticking directly. In this case we are ordinarily not aware that mediation exists. The mediation of light waves is of the same nature. We do not perceive light waves as things that touch our eyes and refer to something else. We seem to see the mediated object directly." Fritz Heider, "Thing and Medium," *Psychological Issues* 1 (1959): 2.

Bibliography

Abel, Günther. *Stoizismus und Frühe Neuzeit. Zur Entstehungsgeschichte modernen Denkens im Felde von Ethik und Politik*. Berlin: De Gruyter, 1978.
Ad Herennium. Translated by Harry Caplan. Cambridge, MA: Harvard University Press, 1954.
Agamben, Giorgio. *The Highest Poverty: Monastic Rules and Form-of-Life*. Translated by Adam Kotsko. Stanford, CA: Stanford University Press, 2013.
Andres, Friedrich. "Die Stufen der *Contemplatio* in Bonaventuras *Itinerarium mentis in Deum* und im *Beniamin maior* des Richard von St. Viktor." *Franziskanische Studien* 7 (1921): 189–200.
Annas, Julia. "Stoic Epistemology." In *Epistemology: Companions to Ancient Thought I*, edited by Stephen Everson, 184–203. Cambridge: Cambridge University Press, 1990.
Anselm of Canterbury. *Proslogion with the Replies of Gaunilo and Anselm*. Translated by Thomas Williams. Indianapolis, IN: Hackett, 2001.
Anselment, Raymond A. "Robert Boyle and the Art of Occasional Meditation." *Renaissance and Reformation* 32 (2009): 73–92.
Anstey, Peter R. "*De Anima* and Descartes: Making up Aristotle's Mind." *History of Philosophy Quarterly* 17 (2000): 237–60.
Arendt, Hannah. *The Life of the Mind*. San Diego: Harcourt, 1978.
Ariew, Roger, and Marjorie Grene. "Ideas, in and before Descartes." *Journal of the History of Ideas* 56 (1995): 87–106.
Aris, Marc-Aeilko. *Contemplatio: Philosophische Studien zum Traktat Benjamin Maior des Richard von St. Viktor. Mit einer verbesserten Edition des Textes*. Frankfurt: J. Knecht, 1996.
Aristotle. *The Complete Works of Aristotle: The Revised Oxford Translation*. Edited by Jonathan Barnes. 2 vols. Princeton, NJ: Princeton University Press 1984.
Aristotle. *Nicomachean Ethics*. Translated by Roger Crisp. Cambridge: Cambridge University Press, 2014.
Aristotle. *On the Soul/Parva Naturalia/On Breath*. Translated by W. S. Hett. Cambridge, MA: Harvard University Press, 1986.
Armisen-Marchetti, Mireille. "Imagination and Meditation in Seneca: The

Example of *Praemeditatio.*" In *Seneca*, edited by John G. Fitch, 102–13. Oxford: Oxford University Press, 2008.

Arthur, E. P. "The Stoic Analysis of the Mind's Reactions to Presentations." *Hermes* 111 (1983): 69–78.

Assmann, Aleida. "Die Sprache der Dinge. Der lange Blick und die wilde Semiose." In *Materialität der Kommunikation*, edited by Hans Ulrich Gumbrecht and Karl Ludwig Pfeiffer, 237–51. Frankfurt: Suhrkamp 1995.

Athanasius. *Select Works and Letters*. Translated by Philip Schaff and Henry Wace. New York: Christian Literature, 1890.

Augustine. *Against the Academicians/The Teacher*. Translated by Peter King. Indianapolis: Hackett, 1995.

Augustine. *Augustinus: Über Schau und Gegenwart des unsichtbaren Gottes*. Translated by Erich Naab. Stuttgart-Bad Cannstatt: Frommann-Holzboog, 1998.

Augustine. *Concerning the City of God against the Pagans*. Translated by Henry Bettenson. London: Penguin Books, 1984.

Augustine. *Confessions*. Translated by Henry Chadwick. Oxford: Oxford University Press, 1998.

Augustine. *Earlier Writings*. Translated by John H. S. Burleigh. Philadelphia: Westminster, 1953.

Augustine. *The Immortality of the Soul. The Magnitude of the Soul. On Music. The Advantage of Believing. On Faith in Things Unseen*. Translated by L. Schopp, J. J. McMahon, R. C. Taliaferro, L. Meagher, O.S.B., R. J. Deferrari, and M. F. McDonald, O.P. Washington, DC: Catholic University of America Press, 1947.

Augustine. *Letters 100–155 (Epistulae)*. Edited by Boniface Ramsey, O.P. Translated by Roland Teske. Hyde Park, NY: New City Press, 2003.

Augustine. *The Literal Meaning of Genesis*. Translated by John Hammond Taylor, S.J. New York: Newman Press, 1982.

Augustine. *On Christian Teaching*. Translated by R. P. H. Green. Oxford: Oxford University Press, 1997.

Augustine. *On the Trinity: Books 8–15*. Translated by Gareth B. Matthews. Cambridge: Cambridge University Press, 2002.

Ausonius. Translated by Hugh G. Evelyn-White. 2 vols. Cambridge, MA: Harvard University Press, 2014.

Bacht, Heinrich. "'Meditatio' in den ältesten Mönchsquellen." *Geist und Leben* 28 (1955): 360–73.

Baier, Karl. "Meditation and Contemplation in High and Late Medieval Europe." In *Yogic Perception, Meditation and Altered States of Consciousness*, edited by Eli Franco, 325–49. Vienna: Austrian Academy of Sciences Press, 2009.

Baillet, Adrien. *La vie de Monsieur Descartes*. Paris: Chez D. Horthemels, 1691.

Barthes, Roland. *Sade Fourier Loyola*. Translated by Richard Miller. New York: Hill and Wang, 1976.

Basil of Caesarea. *Ascetical Works*. Translated by Monica Wagner. Washington, DC: Catholic University of America Press, 1962.
Basil of Caesarea and Rufinus von Aquileia. *Nosce te ipsum . . . animum tuam . . . Deum. Predigt 3 des Basilius Caesariensis in der Übersetzung des Rufinus*. Edited and translated by Heinrich Marti. Berlin: De Gruyter, 2012.
Bauer, Gerhard. *Claustrum Animae. Untersuchungen zur Geschichte der Metapher vom Herzen als Kloster*. Munich: W. Fink, 1973.
Bäumert, Norbert. "Zur 'Unterscheidung der Geister.'" *Zeitschrift für katholische Theologie* 111 (1989): 183–95.
Beck, L. J. *The Metaphysics of Descartes: A Study of the Meditations*. Oxford: Clarendon Press, 1965.
Becker, Ottfrid. *Das Bild des Weges und verwandte Vorstellungen im frühgriechischen Denken*. Berlin: Weidmann, 1937.
Beierwaltes, Werner. "Lux intelligibilis: Untersuchung zur Lichtmetaphysik der Griechen." PhD diss., Ludwig-Maximilians-Universität München, 1957.
Beierwaltes, Werner. "Die Metaphysik des Lichtes in der Philosophie Plotins." *Zeitschrift für philosophische Forschung* 15 (1961): 334–62.
Belin, Christian. *La conversation intérieure. La méditation en France au XVII siècle*. Paris: Champion, 2002.
Benedict of Nursia. *The Rule of Saint Benedict*. Edited and translated by Bruce L. Venarde. Cambridge, MA: Harvard University Press, 2011.
Bengson, John, and Marc A. Moffett, eds. *Knowing How: Essays on Knowledge, Mind and Action*. New York: Oxford University Press, 2011.
Benjamin, Walter. *Gesammelte Schriften*. Edited by Rolf Tiedemann and Hermann Schweppenhäuser. Frankfurt: Suhrkamp, 1991.
Benveniste, Emile. *Problems in General Linguistics*. Translated by Mary Elizabeth Meek. Coral Gables, FL: University of Miami Press, 1971.
Ben-Yami, Hanoch. *Descartes' Philosophical Revolution: A Reassessment*. London: Palgrave Macmillan, 2015.
Bermudez, J. L. "The Originality of Cartesian Scepticism: Did It Have Ancient or Medieval Antecedents?" *History of Philosophy Quarterly* 17 (2000): 333–60.
Bernard of Clairvaux. *Five Books on Consideration: Advice to a Pope*. Translated by John Anderson and Elizabeth Kennan. Kalamazoo, MI: Cistercian Publications, 1976.
Bernard of Clairvaux. *Selected Works*. Translated by Gillian R. Evans. New York: Paulist Press, 1987.
Beyssade, Jean-Marie. "The Idea of God and the Proofs of His Existence." In *The Cambridge Companion to Descartes*, edited by John Cottingham, 174–99. New York: Cambridge University Press, 1992.
Bicknell, Jeanette. "Descartes's Rhetoric: Roads, Foundations, and Difficulties in Method." *Philosophy and Rhetoric* 36 (2003): 22–38.

Bloom, Harold. *The Anxiety of Influence: A Theory of Poetry*. New York: Oxford University Press, 1973.
Blumenberg, Hans. "Licht als Metapher der Wahrheit. Im Vorfeld der philosophischen Begriffsbildung." In *Ästhetische und metaphorische Schriften*, edited by Anselm Haverkamp, 139–71. Frankfurt: Suhrkamp, 2001.
Böckmann, Aquinata. "Discretio im Sinn der Regel Benedikts und ihrer Tradition." *Erbe und Auftrag* 52 (1976): 362–73.
Boland, Paschal, O.S.B. *The Concept of Discretio Spirituum in John Gerson's "De Probatione Spirituum" and "De Distinctione Verarum Visionum a Falsis."* Washington, DC: Catholic University of America Press, 1959.
Bonaventure. *The Journey of the Mind to God*. Edited by Stephen F. Brown. Translated by Philotheus Boehner, O.F.M. Indianapolis, IN: Hackett, 1993.
Boyle, Deborah. "Descartes' Natural Light Reconsidered." *Journal of the History of Philosophy* 37 (1999): 601–12.
Boyle, Deborah. *Descartes on Innate Ideas*. London: Continuum, 2009.
Brockliss, L. W. B. *French Higher Education in the Seventeenth and Eighteenth Centuries: A Cultural History*. Oxford: Clarendon Press, 1987.
Brodsky Lacour, Claudia. *Lines of Thought: Discourse, Architectonics, and the Origin of Modern Philosophy*. Durham, NC: Duke University Press, 1996.
Brooke, Christopher. *Philosophic Pride: Stoicism and Political Thought from Lipsius to Rousseau*. Princeton, NJ: Princeton University Press, 2012.
Brown, Deborah. "Augustine and Descartes on the Function of Attention in Perceptual Awareness." In *Consciousness: From Perception to Reflection in the History of Philosophy*, edited by S. Heinämaa, V. Lähteenmäki, and P. Remes, 153–75. Berlin: Springer, 2007.
Brown, Rachel Fulton. "My Psalter, My Self; or How to Get a Grip on the Office according to Jan Mombaer (d.c. 1501): An Exercise in Training the Attention for Prayer." *Spiritus: A Journal of Christian Spirituality* 12 (2012): 75–105.
Brown, Saskia. "The Childhood of Reason: Pedagogical Strategies in Descartes's *La recherche de la vérité par la lumière naturelle*." *Romanic Review* 87 (1996): 465–80.
Browne, Alice. "Descartes's Dreams." *Journal of the Warburg and Courtauld Institutes* 40 (1977): 256–73.
Buckle, Stephen. "Descartes, Plato and the Cave." *Philosophy* 82 (2007): 301–37.
Buckley, Michael, S.J. "Discernment of Spirits." *The Way*, Supplement 20 (1973): 19–37.
Bull, Reinhard. *Das grosse Buch vom Wachs. Geschichte, Kultur, Technik*. Munich: Callwey, 1977.
Butzer, Günter. *Soliloquium. Theorie und Geschichte des Selbstgesprächs in der europäischen Literatur*. Munich: Fink, 2008.

Caciola, Nancy. *Discerning Spirits. Divine and Demonic Possession in the Middle Ages*. Ithaca, NY: Cornell University Press, 2002.

Campe, Rüdiger. "Shapes and Figures: Geometry and Rhetoric in the Age of Evidence." *Monatshefte* 102 (2010): 285–99.

Campe, Rüdiger. "Vor Augen Stellen. Über den Rahmen rhetorischer Bildgebung." In *Poststrukturalismus. Herausforderung an die Literaturwissenschaft*, edited by G. Neumann, 208–25. Stuttgart: J. B. Metzler, 1997.

Carraud, Vincent. "De la connaissance intuitive de dieu selon A.T., V, pp. 136–139." In *La biografia intellettuale di Rene Descartes attraverso la* Correspondance, edited by Jean-Robert Armogathe, Giulia Belgioioso, and Carlo Vinti, 287–315. Naples: Vivarium, 1999.

Carriero, John. "Painting and Dreaming in the First Meditation." In *Norms and Modes of Thinking in Descartes*, edited by Tuomo Aho and Mikko Yrjönsuuri, 13–46. Helsinki: Societas Philosophica, 1999.

Carriero, John. "The Second Meditation and the Essence of the Mind." In *Essays on Descartes' Meditations*, edited by Amélie Oskenberg Rorty, 199–221. Berkeley: University of California Press, 1986.

Carruthers, Mary. *The Book of Memory: A Study of Memory in Medieval Culture*. Cambridge: Cambridge University Press, 1990.

Carruthers, Mary. *The Craft of Thought: Meditation, Rhetoric, and the Making of Images, 400–1200*. Cambridge: Cambridge University Press, 1998.

Carruthers, Mary, and Jan M. Ziolkowski, eds. *The Medieval Craft of Memory: An Anthology of Texts and Pictures*. Philadelphia: University of Pennsylvania Press, 2002.

Cassian, John. *The Conferences*. Translated by Boniface Ramsey, O.P. New York: Paulist Press, 1997.

Cavaillé, Jean-Pierre. "L'itinéraire onirique de Descartes: De l'âge des songes aux temps du rêve." In *Les* Olympiques *de Descartes: Ètudes et textes*, edited by Fernand Hallyn, 73–90. Geneva: Libr. Droz, 1995.

Cicero. *De Oratore I–II*. Translated by E. W. Sutton and H. Rackham. Cambridge, MA: Harvard University Press, 1988.

Cicero. *De Oratore III. De Fato. Paradoxa Stoicorum. De Partitione Oratoria*. Translated by H. Rackham. Cambridge, MA: Harvard University Press, 1992.

Cicero. *On the Republic—On the Laws*. Translated by Clinton Walker Keyes. Cambridge, MA: Harvard University Press, 2006.

Clarke, Desmond M. *Descartes' Philosophy of Science*. Manchester: Manchester University Press, 1982.

Cole, John R. *The Olympian Dreams and Youthful Rebellion of René Descartes*. Urbana: University of Illinois Press, 1992.

Constable, Giles. *The Reformation of the Twelfth Century*. Cambridge: Cambridge University Press, 1998.

Constable, Giles. "Twelfth-Century Spirituality and the Late Middle Ages." *Medieval and Renaissance Studies* 5 (1971): 27–60.

Coolahan, Marie-Louise. "Redeeming Parcels of Time: Aesthetics and Practice of Occasional Meditation." *Seventeenth Century* 22 (2007): 124–43.

Coolidge, John S. *The Pauline Renaissance in England: Puritanism and the Bible.* Oxford: Clarendon, 1970.

Cooper, John M. "Justus Lipsius and the Revival of Stoicism in Late Sixteenth-Century Europe." In *New Essays on the History of Autonomy*, edited by Natalie Brender and Larry Krasnoff, 7–29. Cambridge: Cambridge University Press, 2004.

Copeland, Clare, and Jan Machielsen, eds. *Angels of Light? Sanctity and Discernment of Spirits in the Early Modern Period.* Leiden, Netherlands: Brill, 2013.

Cottingham, John. *Cartesian Reflections: Essays on Descartes's Philosophy.* Oxford: Oxford University Press, 2008.

Cottingham, John. "The Desecularization of Descartes." In *The Persistence of the Sacred in Modern Thought*, edited by Nathan Jacobs and Chris Firestone, 15–37. Notre Dame, IN: University of Notre Dame Press, 2012.

Cottingham, John. *Philosophy and the Good Life: Reason and the Passions in Greek, Cartesian and Psychoanalytic Ethics.* Cambridge: Cambridge University Press, 1998.

Crowe, Michael B. *The Changing Profile of the Natural Law.* The Hague: Nijhoff, 1977.

Cunning, David. "*Semel in vita*: Descartes' Stoic View on the Place of Philosophy in Human Life." *Faith and Philosophy* 24 (2007): 165–84.

Curley, Edwin. "Analysis in the *Meditations*: The Quest for Clear and Distinct Ideas." In *Essays on Descartes' Meditations*, edited by Amélie Oskenberg Rorty, 153–76. Berkeley: University of California Press, 1986.

Curley, Edwin. "Spinoza as an Expositor of Descartes." In *Speculum Spinozanum*, edited by Siegfried Hessing, 133–42. London: Routledge and Kegan Paul, 1977.

Daniel, Gabriel. *A Voyage to the World of Cartesius: Written Originally in French, and Now Translated into English.* London: Thomas Bennet, 1692.

Daniel, Stephen H. "Descartes' Treatment of 'lumen naturale.'" *Studia Leibnitiana* 10 (1978): 92–100.

Dante Aleghieri. *The Divine Comedy.* Translated by Charles S. Singleton. Princeton, NJ: Princeton University Press, 1975.

David, Joannes. *Veridicus Christianus.* Antwerp: Ex officina Plantiniana 1601.

De Nicolas, Antonio T. *Powers of Imagining: Ignatius de Loyola.* Albany: State University of New York Press, 1986.

Dear, Peter. *Mersenne and the Learning of the Schools.* Ithaca, NY: Cornell University Press, 1988.

Dekoninck, Ralph. *Ad imaginem: Statuts, fonctions et usages de l'image dans la littérature spirituelle jésuite du XVIIe siècle.* Geneva: Droz, 2005.
Derrida, Jacques. "Is There a Philosophical Language?" In *Points . . . Interviews, 1974–1994*, edited by Elisabeth Weber, translated by Peggy Kamuf and others, 216–27. Stanford, CA: Stanford University Press, 1995.
Derrida, Jacques. "Le langue et le discourse de la méthode." *Recherches sur la philosophie et la langage* 3 (1983): 35–51.
Derrida, Jacques. *The Margins of Philosophy.* Translated by Alan Bass. Chicago: University of Chicago Press, 1982.
Derrida, Jacques. *Writing and Difference.* Translated by Alan Bass. Chicago: University of Chicago Press, 1978.
Descartes, René. *The Correspondence between Princess Elisabeth of Bohemia and René Descartes.* Edited and translated by Lisa Shapiro. Chicago: University of Chicago Press, 2007.
Descartes, René. *Descartes' Conversations with Burman.* Translated by John Cottingham. Oxford: Clarendon Press, 1976.
Descartes, René. *Oeuvres de Descartes.* Edited by Charles Adam and Paul Tannery. 12 vols. Paris: Vrin, 1964–76.
Descartes, René. *The Philosophical Writings of Descartes.* Edited by John Cottingham, Robert Stoothoff, Dugald Murdoch, and Anthony Kenny. 3 vols. Cambridge: Cambridge University Press, 1984–91.
Descartes, René. *Regulae ad directionem ingenii—Cogitationes privatae. Lateinisch—Deutsch.* Edited and translated by Christian Wohlers. Hamburg: Felix Meiner Verlag, 2011.
Didi-Huberman, Georges. "The Order of Material: Plasticities, *Malaises*, Survivals." In *Sculpture and Psychoanalysis*, edited by Brandon Taylor, 195–211. Aldershot, UK: Ashgate, 2006.
Dingjan, Dr. Fr., O.S.B. *Discretio: Les origines patristiques et monastiques de la doctrine sur la prudence chez saint Thomas d'Aquin.* Assen, Netherlands: Van Gorcum, 1967.
Diogenes Laertius. *Lives of Eminent Philosophers, Books VI–X.* Translated by R. D. Hicks. Cambridge, MA: Harvard University Press, 1931.
Drever, Matthew. *Image, Identity, and the Forming of the Augustinian Soul.* New York: Oxford University Press, 2013.
Dunn, Kevin. "'A Great City Is a Great Solitude': Descartes's Urban Pastoral." *Yale French Studies* 80 (1991): 93–107.
Dyson, Henry. *Prolepsis and Ennoia in the Early Stoa.* Berlin: Walter de Gruyter, 2009.
Edelman, Nathan. "The Mixed Metaphor in Descartes." *Romanic Review* 41 (1950): 167–78.

Elliott, Dyan. "Seeing Double: John Gerson, the Discernment of Spirits, and Joan of Arc." *American Historical Review* 112 (2002): 26–54.

Endean, Philip. "The Ignatian Prayer of the Senses." *Heythrop Journal* 31 (1990): 391–418.

Epictetus. *Discourses as Reported by Arrian: Books I–II*. Translated by W. A. Oldfather. Cambridge, MA: Harvard University Press, 2000.

Epictetus. *Discourses, Books III–IV: The Encheiridion*. Translated by W. A. Oldfather. Cambridge, MA: Harvard University Press, 2000.

Evans, Christopher, ed. *Writings on the Spiritual Life: A Selection of Works of Hugh, Adam, Achard, Richard, Walter and Godfrey of St. Victor*. Turnhout, Belgium: Brepols, 2013.

Fabre, Pierre-Antoine. *Ignace de Loyola. Le lieu de l'image*. Paris: Librairie Philosophique J. Vrin, 1992.

Feuling, D. "Discretio." *Benediktinische Monatsschrift* 7 (1925): 241–58, 349–66.

Foucault, Michel. *Folie et déraison: Historie de la folie à l'âge classique*. Paris: Librairie Plon, 1961.

Foucault, Michel. *The Hermeneutics of the Subject: Lectures at the Collège de France, 1981–82*. Edited by Frédéric Gros. Translated by Graham Burchell. New York: Palgrave Macmillan 2005.

Foucault, Michel. "My Body, This Paper, This Fire." In *Aesthetics, Method, and Epistemology*, edited by James D. Faubion, 393–417. New York: New Press, 1998.

Francis de Sales. *Treatise on the Love of God*. Translated by Henry Benedict Mackey, O.S.B. Grand Rapids, MI: Christian Classics Ethereal Library, 2000.

Freccero, John. *Dante: The Poetics of Conversion*. Cambridge, MA: Harvard University Press, 1988.

Frede, Michael. "Stoic Epistemology." In *The Cambridge History of Hellenistic Philosophy*, edited by Keimpe Algra, Jonathan Barnes, Jaap Mansfeld, and Malcolm Schofield, 295–322. Cambridge: Cambridge University Press, 1999.

Frede, Michael. "Stoics and Sceptics on Clear and Distinct Impressions." In *Essays in Ancient Philosophy*, by Michael Frede, 151–76. Oxford: Clarendon Press, 1987.

Freedberg, David. *The Power of Images: Studies in the History and Theory of Response*. Chicago: University of Chicago Press, 1989.

Futrell, John Carroll, S.J. "Ignatian Discernment." *Studies in the Spirituality of the Jesuits* 2 (1970): 47–88.

Gabbey, Alan, and Robert E. Hall. "The Melon and the Dictionary: Reflections on Descartes' Dreams." *Journal of the History of Ideas* 59 (1998): 651–68.

Gamble, Harry Y. *Books and Readers in the Early Church: A History of Early Christian Texts*. New Haven, CT: Yale University Press, 1995.

Garber, Daniel. *Descartes Embodied: Reading Cartesian Philosophy through Cartesian Science*. Cambridge: Cambridge University Press, 2001.
Garber, Daniel, and Lesley Cohen. "A Point of Order: Analysis, Synthesis, and Descartes's Principles." *Archiv für Geschichte der Philosophie* 64 (1982): 135–47.
Gaukroger, Stephen. *Descartes: An Intellectual Biography*. Oxford: Clarendon Press, 1995.
Gehl, Paul F. "*Competens Silentium*: Varieties of Monastic Silence in the Medieval West." *Viator* 18 (1987): 125–60.
Gerson, Jean. *Early Works*. Translated by Brian Patrick McGuire. New York: Paulist Press, 1998.
Gigon, Olof. "Antike Erzählungen über die Berufung zur Philosophie." *Museum Helveticum* 3 (1946): 1–21.
Gilbert, Neal W. *Renaissance Concepts of Method*. New York: Columbia University Press, 1963.
Gilson, Etienne. *The Christian Philosophy of Saint Augustine*. New York: Octagon Books, 1988.
Gilson, Etienne. *The Philosophy of St. Bonaventure*. Paterson, NJ: St. Anthony Guild Press, 1965.
Glouberman, Mark. "Cogito: Inference and Certainty." *Modern Schoolman* 70 (1993): 81–98.
Glouberman, Mark. "Descartes's Wax and the Typology of Early Modern Philosophy." *Modern Schoolman* 74 (1997): 117–41.
Göttler, Christine. "'Seelen in Wachs': Material, Mimesis und Memoria in der religiösen Kunst um 1600." In *Ebenbilder: Kopien von Körpern—Modelle des Menschen*, edited by Jan Gerchow, 83–96. Ostfieldern-Ruit, Germany: Hatje Cantz, 2002.
Göttler, Christine. "Wachs und Interdisziplinarität: Giovanni Bernadino Azzolinos 'Vier Letzte Dinge.'" In *Zwischen den Disziplinen. Perspektiven der Frühneuzeitforschung*, edited by Helmut Puff and Christopher J. Wild, 103–48. Göttingen: Wallstein, 2003.
Goudriaan, Aza. *Philosophische Gotteserkenntnis bei Suárez und Descartes im Zusammenhang mi der niederländischen reformierten Theologie und Philosophie des 17. Jahrhunderts*. Leiden, Netherlands: Brill, 1999.
Gouhier, Henri. *Les premieres pensées de Descartes. Contribution a l'histoire de l'anti-Renaissance*. Paris: J. Vrin, 1958.
Graf, Fritz. "Ekphrasis: Die Entstehung der Gattung in der Antike." In *Beschreibungskunst - Kunstbeschreibung. Ekphrasis von der Antike bis zur Gegenwart*, edited by Gottfried Boehm and Helmut Pfotenhauer, 143–55. Munich: Brill, 1995.
Grafton, Anthony. *Traditions of Conversion: Descartes and His Demon*. Berkeley: University of California Press, 2000.

Greene, Robert A. "Instinct of Nature: Natural Law, Synderesis, and the Moral Sense." *Journal of the History of Ideas* 58 (1997): 173–98.
Greene, Robert A. "Synderesis, the Spark of Conscience, in the English Renaissance." *Journal of the History of Ideas* 52 (1991): 195–219.
Gregory the Great. *Dialogues*. Translated by Odo John Zimmermann, O.S.B. Washington, DC: Catholic University Press, 1959.
Gregory, Stephan. "Lumen naturale: Licht und Wahrheit bei Descartes." *Zeitschrift für Kulturphilosophie* 8 (2014): 261–78.
Greiffenberg, Catharina Regina von. *Des Allerheiligst- und Allerheilsamsten Leidens und Sterbens Jesu Christi Zwölf andächtige Betrachtungen*. Neustadt an der Aysch, Germany: Drechsler, 1683.
Gueroult, Martial. *Descartes's Philosophy Interpreted according to the Order of Reasons*. Minneapolis: University of Minnesota Press, 1984–85.
Hadot, Pierre. "Conversio." In *Historisches Wörterbuch der Philosophie*, edited by Joachim Ritter, 1:1033–36. Basel: Schwabe, 1971–2007.
Hadot, Pierre. "Un dialogue interrompu avec Michel Foucault. Convergences et divergences." In *Exercices spirituels et philosophie antique*, by Pierre Hadot, 305–11. Paris: A. Michel, 2002.
Hadot, Pierre. *Exercices spirituels et philosophie antique*. Paris: A. Michel, 2002.
Hadot, Pierre. *Philosophie als Lebensform: Antike und moderne Exerzitien der Weisheit*. Frankfurt: Fischer, 2002.
Hadot, Pierre. *Philosophy as a Way of Life: Spiritual Exercises from Socrates to Foucault*. Edited by Arnold Davidson. Translated by Michael Chase. Oxford: Blackwell, 1995.
Hadot, Pierre. *Plotinus, or the Simplicity of Vision*. Translated by Michael Chase. Chicago: University of Chicago Press, 1998.
Hadot, Pierre. *The Present Alone Is Our Happiness: Conversations with Jeannie Carlier and Arnold I. Davidson*. Stanford, CA: Stanford University Press, 2011.
Haines, C. R., ed. and trans. *Marcus Aurelius*. Cambridge, MA: Harvard University Press, 2003.
Hallyn, Fernand. "*Olympica*: Les songes du jeune Descartes." in *Le songe a la Renaissance*, edited by Françoise Charpentier, 41–51. Saint-Etienne: Université de Saint-Etienne, 1987.
Hatfield, Gary. "Descartes's *Meditations* as Cognitive Exercises." *Philosophy and Literature* 9 (1985): 41–58.
Hatfield, Gary. "The Senses and the Fleshless Eye: The *Meditations* as Cognitive Exercises." In *Essays on Descartes' Meditations*, edited by Amélie Oksenberg Rorty, 45–76. Berkeley: University of California Press, 1986.
Hausherr, Irénée. *The Name of Jesus*. Translated by Charles Cummings, OCSO. Kalamazoo, MI: Cistercian, 1978.

Hays, Peter. *The Limping Hero: Grotesques in Literature.* New York: New York University Press, 1971.
Heider, Fritz. "Thing and Medium." *Psychological Issues* 1 (1959): 1–34.
Heller-Roazen, Daniel. *The Inner Touch: Archaeology of a Sensation.* New York: Zone Books, 2007.
Hennig, Boris. "Cartesian *Conscientia*." *British Journal for the History of Philosophy* 15 (2007): 454–84.
Hennig, Boris. "Conscientia bei Descartes." *Zeitschrift für philosophische Forschung* 60 (2006): 21–36.
Hennig, Boris. *"Conscientia" bei Descartes.* Freiburg: Verlag Karl Alber, 2006.
Hermans, Michel, and Michel Klein. "Ces *Exercices spirituels* que Descartes aurait pratiqués." *Archives de philosophie* 59 (1996): 427–40.
Hettche, Matt. "Descartes and the Augustinian Tradition of Devotional Meditation: Tracing a Minim Connection." *Journal of the History of Philosophy* 48 (2010): 283–311.
Heyd, Michael. *"Be Sober and Reasonable": The Critique of Enthusiasm in the Seventeenth and Early Eighteenth Centuries.* Leiden, Netherlands: Brill, 1995.
Hijmans, B. L. *ΑΣΚΗΣΙΣ. Notes on Epictetus' Educational System.* Assen, Netherlands: Van Gorcum, 1959.
Hintikka, Jaako. "Cogito, Ergo Sum: Inference or Performance?" *Philosophical Review* 71 (1962): 3–32.
Hintikka, Jaako. "A Discourse on Descartes's Method." In *Descartes: Critical and Interpretive Essays*, edited by Michael Hooker, 74–88. Baltimore: Johns Hopkins University Press, 1978.
Hintikka, Jaako. "Plato on Knowing How, Knowing That, and Knowing What." In *Knowledge and the Known: Historical Perspectives on Epistemology*, 31–49. Dordrecht: Reidel, 1974.
Horn, Christoph. "Welche Bedeutung hat das augustinische Cogito? (Buch XI. 26)." In *Augustinus, De civitate dei*, edited by Christoph Horn, 109–29. Berlin: De Gruyter, 1997.
Horowitz, Maryanne Cline. *Seeds of Virtue and Knowledge.* Princeton, NJ: Princeton University Press, 1998.
Hoye, William. *Actualitas omnium actuum: Man's Beatific Vision of God as Apprehended by Thomas Aquinas.* Meisenheim, Germany: Hain, 1975.
Hoye, William. "Gotteserkenntnis per essentiam im 13. Jahrhundert." In *Die Auseinandersetzungen an der Pariser Universität im XIII. Jahrhundert*, edited by Albert Zimmermann, 269–84. Berlin: De Gruyter, 1976.
Hugh of Saint Victor. *The Didascalicon of Hugh of Saint Victor: A Medieval Guide to the Arts.* Translated by Jerome Taylor. New York: Columbia University Press, 1961.
Hugh of Saint Victor. *Selected Spiritual Writings.* London: Faber, 1962.

Huntley, Frank Livingstone, ed. *Bishop Joseph Hall and Protestant Meditation in Seventeenth-Century England: A Study with the Texts of* The Art of Divine Meditation *(1606) and* Occasional Meditations *(1633)*. Binghampton, NY: Center for Medieval and Renaissance Studies, 1981.

Ignatius of Loyola. *The Constitutions of the Society of Jesus*. Translated by George E. Ganss, S.J. St. Louis: Institute of Jesuit Sources, 1970.

Ignatius of Loyola. *Personal Writings:* Reminiscences, Spiritual Diary, *Select Letters—including the Text of* The Spiritual Exercises. Translated by Joseph A. Munitiz and Philip Endean. London: Penguin Books, 1996.

Ioppolo, Anna-Maria. "Presentation and Assent: A Physical and Cognitive Problem in Early Stoicism." *Classical Quarterly* 40 (1990): 423–49.

Jacobson, Roman. "Shifters, Verbal Categories, and the Russian Verb." In *Selected Writings II: Word and Language*, 130–47. The Hague: Mouton, 1971.

Jacquette, Dale. "Descartes' Lumen Naturale and the Cartesian Circle." *Philosophy and Theology* 9 (1996): 273–320.

Jaeger, Werner. *Paideia: The Ideals of Greek Culture*. New York: Oxford University Press, 1943.

Jolley, Nicholas. *The Light of the Soul: Theories of Ideas in Leibniz, Malebranche, and Descartes*. Oxford: Clarendon, 1998.

Jones, Matthew L. *The Good Life in the Scientific Revolution: Descartes, Pascal, Leibniz, and the Cultivation of Virtue*. Chicago: University of Chicago Press, 2006.

Jones, W. T. "*Somnio Ergo Sum*: Descartes's Three Dreams." *Philosophy and Literature* 4 (1980): 145–66.

Jordan, Mark D. "The Intelligibility of the World and the Divine Ideas in Aquinas." *Review of Metaphysics* 38 (1984): 17–32.

Kamlah, Wilhelm. "Der Anfang der Vernunft bei Descartes—autobiographisch und historisch." *Archiv für Geschichte der Philosophie* 43 (1961): 70–84.

Karnes, Michelle. *Imagination, Meditation, and Cognition in the Middle Ages*. Chicago: University of Chicago Press, 2017.

Keefer, Michael H. "The Dreamer's Path: Descartes and the Sixteenth Century." *Renaissance Quarterly* 49 (1996): 30–76.

Keevak, Michael. "Descartes's Dreams and Their Address for Philosophy." *Journal of the History of Ideas* 53 (1992): 373–96.

Kemmann, Andreas. "Evidentia, Evidenz." In *Historisches Wörterbuch der Rhetorik*, edited by Gert Ueding, 3:33–47. Tübingen: Niemeyer, 1996.

Kenney, John Peter. *Contemplation and Classical Christianity: A Study of Augustine*. Oxford: Oxford University Press, 2013.

Kennington, Richard. "Descartes' 'Olympica.'" *Social Research* 28 (1961): 171–204.

Kerstiens, Ludwig. "Kontemplation." In *Historisches Wörterbuch der Philosophie*, edited by Joachim Ritter, 4:1024–26. Basel: Schwabe, 1971–2007.

Kitzinger, Ernst. "The Cult of Images in the Age before Iconoclasm." *Dumbarton Oaks Papers* 8 (1954): 83–150.
Klein, R. Julie. "Memory and the Extension of Thinking in Descartes's *Regulae*." *International Philosophical Quarterly* 42 (2002): 23–40.
Kobusch, Theodor. "Descartes' *Meditations*: Practical Metaphysics: The Father of Rationalism in the Tradition of Spiritual Exercises." In *Philosophy as a Way of Life: Ancients and Moderns: Essays in Honor of Pierre Hadot*, edited by Michael Chase, Stephen R. L. Clark, and Michael McGhee, 167–83. Chichester, UK: Wiley, 2013.
Koschorke, Albrecht. "System. Die Ästhetik und das Anfangsproblem." In *Grenzwerte des Ästhetischen*, edited by Robert Stockhammer, 146–63. Frankfurt: Suhrkamp, 2002.
Koschorke, Albrecht. "Zur Logik kultureller Gründungserzählungen." *Zeitschrift für Ideengeschichte* I/2 (2007): 5–12.
Kosman, L. Aryeh. "The Naïve Narrator: Meditation in Descartes' *Meditations*." In *Essays on Descartes'* Meditations, edited by Amélie Oskenberg Rorty, 21–43. Berkeley: University of California Press, 1986.
Kreuzer, Johann. *Pulchritudo: Vom Erkennen Gottes bei Augustin. Bemerkungen zu den Büchern IX, X und XI der Confessiones*. Munich: W. Fink Verlag, 1995.
Kruger, Steven F. *Dreaming in the Middle Ages*. Cambridge: Cambridge University Press, 2005.
Ladner, Gerhart. "Homo Viator: Mediaeval Ideas on Alienation and Order." In *Images and Ideas in the Middle Ages: Selected Studies in History and Art*, by Gerhart Ladner, 937–74. Rome: Edizioni di storia e letteratura, 1983.
Lagrée, Jacqueline. "Constancy and Coherence." In *Stoicism: Traditions and Transformations*, edited by Steven K. Strange and Jack Zupko, 148–76. Cambridge: Cambridge University Press, 2004.
Lakoff, George, and Mark Johnson. *Metaphors We Live By*. Chicago: University of Chicago Press, 1980.
Largier, Niklaus. "Inner Senses—Outer Senses: The Practice of Emotions in Medieval Mysticism." In *Codierungen von Emotionen im Mittelalter / Emotions and Sensibilities in the Middle Ages*, edited by Stephen Jaeger and Ingrid Kasten, 3–15. Berlin: De Gruyter, 2003.
Largier, Niklaus. "Praying by Numbers: An Essay on Medieval Aesthetics." *Representations* 103 (2008): 73–91.
Largier, Niklaus. "Rhetorik des Begehrens. Die 'Unterscheidung der Geister' als Paradigma mittelalterlicher Subjektivität." In *Inszenierungen von Subjektivität in der Literatur des Mittelalters*, edited by Martin Baisch, Jutta Eming, Hendrikje Haufe, and Andrea Sieber, 249–70. Königstein, Germany: Helmer, 2005.

Lausberg, Heinrich. *Handbuch der literarischen Rhetorik. Eine Grundlegung der Literaturwissenschaft.* Munich: M. Heuber, 1960.
Leclercq, Jean. "Pour l'histoire de l'expression 'philosophie chrétienne.'" *Mélanges de science religieuse* 9 (1952): 221–26.
Leibniz, Gottfried Wilhelm. *Philosophische Schriften.* Berlin: Akademie Verlag, 1999.
Leibniz, Gottfried Wilhelm. *Theodicy: Essays on the Goodness of God, the Freedom of Man, and the Origin of Evil.* Edited by Austin Farrer. Translated by E. M. Huggard. La Salle, IL: Open Court, 1985.
Levi, Anthony, S.J. *French Moralists: The Theory of Passions, 1585 to 1649.* Oxford: Clarendon, 1964.
Lieb, Ludger. "Emblematische Experimente. Formen und Funktionen der frühen Jesuiten-Emblematik am Beispiel der Emblembücher Jan Davids." In *The Jesuits and the Emblem Tradition*, edited by John Manning and Marc van Vaeck, 307–21. Turnhout, Belgium: Brepols, 1999.
Lienhard, Joseph T., S.J. "On 'Discernment of Spirits' in the Early Church." *Theological Studies* 41 (1980): 505–29.
Light of the World: An Anthology of Seventeenth-Century Dutch Religious and Occasional Poetry. Translated by Christopher Levenson. Windsor, ON: Netherlandic Press, 1982.
Lipsius, Justus. *On Constancy.* Edited by John Sellars. Translated by Sir John Stradling (1594). Exeter: Liverpool University Press, 2006.
Long, A. A., and D. N. Sedley. *The Hellenistic Philosophers.* Cambridge: Cambridge University Press, 1987.
Long, Anthony A. "Representation and the Self in Stoicism." In *Stoic Studies*, by Anthony A. Long, 264–85. Berkeley: University of California Press, 2001.
Luhmann, Niklas. *Art as Social System.* Stanford, CA: Stanford University Press, 2000.
Lumpe, Adolf. "Kontemplation." In *Reallexikon für Antike und Christentum*, edited by Georg Schöllgen, 21:485–98. Stuttgart: Hiersemann, 2006.
Luther, Martin. *Selections from His Writings.* Translated by John Dillenberger. Garden City, NY: Doubleday, 1961.
Luther, Martin. *Werke. Kritische Gesamtausgabe.* Weimar: Herman Böhlau, 1883.
Luther, W. "Wahrheit, Licht, Sehen und Erkennen im Sonnengleichnis von Platons Politeia: Ein Ausschnitt aus der Lichtmetaphysik der Griechen." *Studium Generale* 18 (1963): 479–96.
Lyons, John D. "The Cartesian Reader and the Methodic Subject." *L'esprit createur* 21 (1981): 37–47.
Lyons, John D. "Subjectivity and Imitation in the *Discours de la méthode.*" *Neophilologus* 66 (1982): 508–24.
Maia Neto, José R. "Charron's *Epoché* and Descartes' *Cogito*: The Sceptical Base of

Descartes' Refutation of Scepticism." In *The Return of Scepticism from Hobbes and Descartes to Bayle*, edited by Gianni Paganini, 81–113. Dordrecht: Kluwer Academic Publishers, 2003.

Marcus Aurelius. *Meditations*. Translated by Martin Hammond. London: Penguin, 2006.

Marion, Jean-Luc. *Cartesian Questions: Method and Metaphysics*. Chicago: University of Chicago Press, 1999.

Marno, David. *Death Be Not Proud: The Art of Holy Attention*. Chicago: University of Chicago Press, 2016.

Marno, David. "Easy Attention: Ignatius of Loyola and Robert Boyle." *Journal of Medieval and Early Modern Studies* 44 (2014): 135–61.

Marshall, John. *Descartes's Moral Theory*. Ithaca, NY: Cornell University Press, 1998.

Martin, A. Lynn. *The Jesuit Mind: The Mentality of an Elite in Early Modern France*. Ithaca, NY: Cornell University Press, 1988.

Martz, Louis L. *The Poetry of Meditation: A Study in English Religious Literature of the Seventeenth Century*. New Haven, CT: Yale University Press, 1962.

Matthews, Gareth B. "Knowledge and Illumination." In *The Cambridge Companion to Augustine*, edited by Eleonore Stump and Norman Kretzmann, 171–85. Cambridge: Cambridge University Press, 2002.

Matthews, Gareth. *Thought's Ego in Augustine and Descartes*. Ithaca, NY: Cornell University Press, 1992.

McCrea, Adriana. *Constant Minds: Political Virtue and the Lipsian Paradigm in England, 1584–1650*. Toronto: University of Toronto Press, 1997.

McGinn, Bernard. "*Visio Dei*: Seeing God in Medieval Theology and Mysticism." In *Envisaging Heaven in the Middle Ages*, edited by Carolyn Muessig and Ad Putter, 15–33. New York: Routledge, 2007.

McGinn, Bernard. "Visions and Visualizations in the Here and Hereafter." *Harvard Theological Review* 98 (2005): 227–46.

McGushin, Edward F. *Foucault's Askēsis: An Introduction to the Philosophical Life*. Evanston, IL: Northwestern University Press, 2007.

McGushin, Edward F. "Foucault's Cartesian Meditations." *International Philosophical Quarterly* 45 (2005): 41–59.

McMahon, Robert. *Understanding the Medieval Meditative Ascent: Augustine, Anselm, Boethius, and Dante*. Washington, DC: Catholic University of America Press, 2006.

McRae, Robert. "'Idea' as a Philosophical Term in the Seventeenth Century." *Journal of the History of Ideas* 26 (1965): 175–90.

Mehl, Edouard. "Les méditations stoïcennes de Descartes: Hypothèses sur l'influence du stoïcisme dans la constitution de la pensée cartésienne

(1629–1637)." In *Le stoïcisme au XVIe et au XVIIe siècle*, edited by P.-F. Moreau, 251–80. Paris: A. Michel, 1999.

Melion, Walter S. *The Meditative Art: Studies in the Northern Devotional Print, 1550–1625*. Philadelphia: St. Joseph's University Press, 2009.

Meltzer, Françoise. "Descartes' Dreams and Freud's Failure, or the Politics of Originality." In *The Trial(s) of Psychoanalysis*, edited by Françoise Meltzer, 81–102. Chicago: University of Chicago Press, 1988.

Menn, Stephen. *Descartes and Augustine*. Cambridge: Cambridge University Press, 1998.

Mercer, Christia. "Descartes' Debt to Teresa of Ávila, or Why We Should Work on Women in the History of Philosophy." *Philosophical Studies* 174 (2017): 2539–55.

Mercer, Christia. "The Methodology of the *Meditations*: Tradition and Innovation." In *The Cambridge Companion to Descartes' Meditations*, edited by David Cunning, 1–22. Cambridge: Cambridge University Press, 2014.

Mersch, Dieter. *Medientheorien*. Hamburg: Junius, 2006.

Mesnard, Pierre. "L'arbre de la sagesse." In *Descartes. Cahiers de Royaumont, Philosophie, no. 2*, 336–59. Paris: Éditions de Minuit, 1957.

Migne, Jacques-Paul, ed. *Patrologiae Cursus Completus: Series Latina*. Paris: Garnier, 1844–90.

Mijuskovic, Ben. "Descartes's Bridge to the External World: The Piece of Wax." *Studi internazionali di filosofia* 3 (1971): 65–81.

Miles, Margaret. "Vision: The Eye of the Body and Eye of the Mind in Saint Augustine's *De Trinitate* and *Confessions*." *Journal of Religion* 63 (1983): 125–42.

Minahan, Charles D. "The Turbulent Dream-Vision of Descartes's 'Olympian' Experience." In *Dreams in French Literature: The Persistent Voice*, edited by Tom Conner, 65–84. Amsterdam: Rodopi, 1995.

Morford, Mark. *Stoics and Neostoics: Rubens and the Circle of Lipsius*. Princeton, NJ: Princeton University Press, 1991.

Morris, John. "Descartes' Natural Light." *Journal of the History of Philosophy* 11 (1973): 169–87.

Moser, Christian. *Buchgestützte Subjektivität: Literarische Formen der Selbstsorge und der Selbsthermeneutik von Platon bis Montaigne*. Tübingen: Niemeyer, 2006.

Murakami, Katsuzo, Megura Sasaki, and Tetsuichi Nishimura, eds. *Concordance to Descartes' Meditationes de Prima Philosophia*. Hildesheim, Zürich: Olms-Weidmann, 1995.

Nancy, Jean-Luc. "Larvatus pro Deo." *Glyph* 2 (1977): 14–36.

Nash, Ronald H. *The Light of the Mind: St. Augustine's Theory of Knowledge*. Lexington: University Press of Kentucky, 1969.

Nash, Ronald H. "Some Philosophic Sources of Augustine's Illumination Theory." *Augustinian Studies* 2 (1971): 47–66.
Nelson, Alan. "Cartesian Innateness." In *A Companion to Descartes*, edited by Janet Broughton and John Carriero, 319–33. Oxford: Oxford University Press, 2007.
Newman, Robert J. "*Cotidie meditare*: Theory and Practice of the *meditatio* in Imperial Stoicism." *Aufstieg und Niedergang der römischen Welt* 36 (1989): 1473–1517.
Nicol, Martin. *Meditation bei Luther*. Göttingen: Vandenhoeck and Ruprecht, 1984.
Nightingale, Andrea. *Once out of Nature: Augustine on Time and the Body*. Chicago: University of Chicago Press, 2011.
Nightingale, Andrea. *Spectacles of Truth in Classical Greek Philosophy: Theoria in Its Cultural Context*. Cambridge: Cambridge University Press, 2004.
Nolan, Lawrence. "The Ontological Argument as an Exercise in Cartesian Therapy." *Canadian Journal of Philosophy* 35 (2005): 521–62.
Nolan, Lawrence. "The Third Meditation: Causal Arguments for God's Existence." In *The Cambridge Companion to Descartes' Meditations*, edited by David Cunning, 127–48. Cambridge: Cambridge University Press, 2014.
Nolan, Lawrence, and Alan Nelson. "Proofs for the Existence of God." In *The Blackwell Guide to Descartes' Meditations*, edited by Stephen Gaukroger, 104–21. Malden, MA: Blackwell, 2006.
Nolte, Ulrich. *Philosophische Exerzitien bei Descartes: Aufklärung zwischen Privatmysterium und Gesellschaftsentwurf*. Würzberg: Königshausen and Neumann, 1995.
O'Meara, Dominic J. "Eriugena and Aquinas on Beatific Vision." In *Eriugena redivivus: Zur Wirkungsgeschichte seines Denkens im Mittelalter und im Übergang zur Neuzeit*, edited by Werner Beierwaltes, 224–36. Heidelberg: C. Winter, 1987.
O'Rourke Boyle, Marjorie. "Angels Black and White: Loyola's Spiritual Discernment in Historical Perspective." *Theological Studies* 44 (1983): 241–57.
O'Rourke Boyle, Marjorie. *Loyola's Acts: The Rhetoric of Self*. Berkeley: University of California Press, 1997.
O'Rourke Boyle, Marjorie. *Senses of Touch: Human Dignity and Deformity from Michelangelo to Calvin*. Leiden, Netherlands: Brill, 1998.
Oestreich, Gerhard. *Neostoicism and the Early Modern State*. Cambridge: Cambridge University Press, 1982.
Olin, John C. "The Idea of Pilgrimage in the Experience of Ignatius Loyola." *Church History* 48 (1979): 387–97.
Ossa-Richardson, Anthony. "Gijsbert Voet and *Discretio Spirituum* after Descartes." In *Angels of Light? Sanctity and the Discernment of Spirits in the Early*

Modern Period, edited by Clare Copeland and Jan Machielsen, 235–53. Leiden, Netherlands: Brill, 2013.

Pacho, Julian. "Über einige erkenntnistheoretische Schwierigkeiten des klassischen Rationalismus." *Zeitschrift für Philosophische Forschung* 38 (1984): 561–81.

Palmer, Martin E., S.J., ed. and trans. *On Giving the Spiritual Exercises: The Early Jesuit Manuscript Directories and the Official Directory of 1599*. St. Louis, MO: Institute of Jesuit Sources, 1996.

Papy, Jan. "Lipsius' (Neo-)Stoicism: Constancy between Christian Faith and Stoic Virtue." *Grotiana* 22/23 (2001–2): 47–72.

Park, Katherine. "Impressed Images: Reproducing Wonders." In *Picturing Science, Producing Art*, edited by Caroline A. Jones and Peter Galison, 254–71. New York: Routledge, 1998.

Penkett, Robert. "Discerning the Divine and the Demonic in the *Life of Antony*." *Reading Medieval Studies* 24 (1998): 79–94.

Peperzak, Adriaan. "Life, Science, and Wisdom according to Descartes." *History of Philosophy Quarterly* 12 (1995): 133–53.

Pereboom, Derk. "Stoic Psychotherapy in Descartes and Spinoza." *Faith and Philosophy* 11 (1994): 592–625.

Perler, Dominik. "Was ist ein frühneuzeitlicher philosophischer Text? Kritische Überlegungen zum Rationalismus/Empirismus-Schema." In *Zwischen den Disziplinen? Perspektiven der Frühneuzeitforschung*, edited by Helmut Puff and Christopher Wild, 55–80. Göttingen: Wallstein, 2003.

Perler, Dominik. "Was there a 'Pyrrhonian Crisis' in Early Modern Philosophy? A Critical Notice of Richard Popkin." *Archiv für Geschichte der Philosophie* 86 (2004): 209–20.

Plato. *The Republic of Plato*. Translated by Allan Bloom. New York: Basic Books, 1991.

Plato. *The Theaetetus of Plato*. Edited by Myles Burnyeat. Translated by M. J. Levett. Indianapolis, IN: Hackett, 1990.

Platt, Verity. "Burning Butterflies: Seals, Symbols, and the Soul in Antiquity." In *Pagans and Christians: From Antiquity to the Middle Ages*, edited by Lauren Gilmour, 89–99. Oxford: Archeopress, 2007.

Platt, Verity. "Making an Impression: Replication and the Ontology of the Graeco-Roman Seal Stone." *Art History* 29 (2006): 233–57.

Pliny. *Natural History Books 8–11*. Translated by H. Rackham. Cambridge, MA: Harvard University Press, 2006.

Plotinus. *Porphyry on Plotinus, Ennead I*. Translated by A. H. Armstrong. Cambridge, MA: Harvard University Press, 1989.

Popkin, Richard. *The History of Scepticism: From Savonarola to Bayle*. Oxford: Oxford University Press, 2003.

Portman, Karel. "Cats' Concept of the Emblem and the Role of Occasional Meditation." *Emblematica* 6 (1991): 65–82.
Potts, Timothy C. *Conscience in Medieval Philosophy*. Cambridge: Cambridge University Press, 1980.
Poulet, Georges. *Studies in Human Time*. Translated by Elliott Coleman. Baltimore: Johns Hopkins University Press, 1956.
Pranger, Burcht. *Eternity's Ennui: Temporality, Perseverance and Voice in Augustine and Western Literature*. Leiden, Netherlands: Brill, 2010.
Puff, Helmut, Ulrike Strasser, and Christopher Wild, eds. *Cultures of Communication: Theologies of Media in Early Modern Europe and Beyond*. Toronto: University of Toronto Press, 2017.
Quintilian. *The Institutio Oratoria of Quintilian*. Translated by H. E. Butler. Cambridge, MA: Harvard University Press, 1980.
Quiring, Heinrich. "Der Traum des Descartes. Eine Verschlüsselung seiner Kosmologie, seiner Methodik und der Grundlage seiner Philosophie." *Kant-Studien* 46 (1954–55): 135–56.
Raabe, A. M. "Discernment of Spirits in the Prologue to the *Rule* of Benedict." *American Benedictine Review* 23 (1972): 397–423.
Rabbow, Paul. *Seelenführung: Methodik der Exerzitien in der Antike*. Munich: Kösel-Verlag, 1954.
Ragazzi, Grazia Mangano. *Obeying the Truth: Discretion in the Spiritual Writings of Saint Catherine of Siena*: Oxford: Oxford University Press, 2014.
Rahner, Hugo, S.J. "Die 'Anwendung der Sinne' in der Betrachtungsmethode des Hl. Ignatius von Loyola." In *Meditation in Religion und Psychotherapie*, edited by Wilhelm Bitter, 58–83. Stuttgart: E. Klett, 1958.
Rahner, Hugo, S.J. *Ignatius the Theologian*. Translated by Michael Barry. London: Geoffrey Chapman, 1990.
Ranea, Alberto Guillermo. "A 'Science for *honnêtes hommes*': *La recherche de la vérité* and the Deconstruction of Experimental Knowledge." In *Descartes' Natural Philosophy*, edited by Stephen Gaukroger, John Schuster, and John Sutton, 313–29. London: Routledge, 2000.
Reynolds, Philip L. "Spiritual Cognition in Thomas Aquinas." *The Thomist* 67 (2003): 505–38.
Rich, Antony D. *Discernment in the Desert Fathers: Διάκρισις in the Life and Thought of Early Egyptian Monasticism*. Milton Keynes, UK: Pater Noster, 2007.
Richard of St. Victor. *The Twelve Patriarchs, The Mystical Ark, and Book Three of the Trinity*. Translated by Grover A. Zinn. New York: Paulist Press, 1979.
Richeome, Louis. *The Pilgrime of Loreto. Performing His Vow Made to the Glorious Virgin Mary Mother of God. Conteyning Divers Devout Meditations upon*

the Christian and Catholic Doctrine. Translated by E. W. Paris: English College Press, 1630.

Ritter, Joachim. "Methode." In *Historisches Wörterbuch der Philosophie*, edited by Joachim Ritter, 5:1304–13. Basel: Schwabe, 1971–2007.

Rodis-Lewis, Geneviève. *Descartes: His Life and Thought*. Translated by Jane Marie Todd. Ithaca, NY: Cornell University Press, 1998.

Rönnegård, Per. "Melétē in Early Christian Ascetic Texts." In *Meditation in Judaism, Christianity and Islam: Cultural Histories*, edited by Halvor Eifring, 79–92. London: Bloomsbury Academic, 2013.

Roochnik, David. *Of Art and Wisdom: Plato's Understanding of Techne*. University Park: Pennsylvania State University Press, 1996.

Rorty, Amélie Oksenberg. "Experiments in Philosophical Genre: Descartes' *Meditations*." *Critical Inquiry* 9 (1983): 545–64.

Rorty, Amélie Oksenberg. "The Structure of Descartes' *Meditations*." In *Essays on Descartes' Meditations*, edited by Amélie Oskenberg Rorty, 1–20. Berkeley: University of California Press, 1986.

Roth, Cornelius. *Discretio spirituum. Kriterien geistlicher Unterscheidung bei Johannes Gerson*. Würzburg: Echter, 2001.

Rothkamm, Jan. "Lichtmetaphorik bei Francis Bacon, Rene Descartes, Thomas Hobbes und Baruch de Spinoza." *Archiv für Begriffsgeschichte* 52 (2010): 73–92.

Rouse, Richard, and Mary Rouse. "The Vocabulary of Wax Tablets." In *Vocabulaire du livre e de l'écriture au moyen age*, edited by Olga Weijers, 220–30. Turnhout, Belgium: Brepols, 1989.

Rouse, Richard, and Mary Rouse. "Wax Tablets." *Language and Communication* 9 (1989): 175–91.

Rubidge, Bradley. "Descartes's *Meditations* and Devotional Meditations." *Journal of the History of Ideas* 51 (1990): 27–49.

Russell, D. A., and M. Winterbottom, eds. and trans. *Classical Literary Criticism*. Oxford: Oxford University Press, 1989.

Rutherford, Donald. "On the Happy Life: Descartes vis-à-vis Seneca." In *Stoicism: Traditions and Transformations*, edited by Steven K. Strange and Jack Zupko, 177–97. Cambridge: Cambridge University Press, 2004.

Rutherford, Donald. "Reading Descartes as a Stoic: Appropriate Action, Virtue, and the Passions." *Philosophie antique* 14 (2014): 129–55.

Ryle, Gilbert. "Knowing How and Knowing That." *Proceedings of the Aristotelian Society* 46 (1946): 1–16.

Sandbach, F. H. "Phantasia Kataleptike." In *Problems in Stoicism*, edited by A. A. Long, 9–21. London: Athlone Press, 1971.

Scaglione, Aldo. *Liberal Arts and the Jesuit College System*. Amsterdam: John Benjamins, 1986.

Schechtman, Anat. "Descartes' Argument for the Existence of the Idea of an Infinite Being." *Journal of the History of Philosophy* 52, no. 3 (2014): 487–518.

Schildknecht, Christiane. "Erleuchtung und Tarnung. Überlegungen zur literarischen Form bei René Descartes." In *Literarische Formen der Philosophie*, edited by Gottfried Gabriel and Christiane Schildknecht, 92–120. Stuttgart: J. B. Metzler, 1990.

Schmidt, Andreas. *Göttliche Gedanken: Zur Metaphysik der Erkenntnis bei Descartes, Malebranche, Spinoza und Leibniz*. Frankfurt: Klostermann, 2009.

Schmitter, Amy. "The Wax and I: Perceptibility and Modality in the Second Meditation." *Archiv für Geschichte der Philosophie* 82 (2000): 178–201.

Scholz, Bernhard F. "Ekphrasis and Enargeia in Quintilian's *Institutionis oratoriae libri XII*." In *Rhetorica movet: Studies in Historical and Modern Rhetoric in Honour of Heinrich F. Plett*, edited by Peter L. Oesterreich and Thomas O. Sloane, 3–24. Leiden, Netherlands: Brill, 1999.

Schreiner, Susan. *Are You Alone Wise? The Search for Certainty in the Early Modern Era*. Oxford: Oxford University Press, 2012.

Sellars, John. "Justus Lipsius's *De constantia*: A Stoic Spiritual Exercise." *Poetics Today* 28 (2007): 339–62.

Seneca. *Epistles 66–92*. Translated by Richard M. Gummere. Cambridge, MA: Harvard University Press, 2006.

Seneca. *Epistles 93–124*. Translated by Richard M. Gummere. Cambridge, MA: Harvard University Press, 2006.

Seneca. *Moral Essays*. Translated by John W. Basore. Cambridge, MA: Harvard University Press, 1935.

Sepper, Dennis L. "Descartes and the Eclipse of the Imagination, 1618–1630." *Journal of the History of Philosophy* 27 (1989): 379–403.

Sepper, Dennis L. *Descartes's Imagination: Proportion, Images, and the Activity of Thinking*. Berkeley: University of California Press, 1996.

Sepper, Dennis L. "The Texture of Thought: Why Descartes' *Meditationes* Is Meditational, and Why It Matters." In *Descartes' Natural Philosophy*, edited by Stephen Gaukroger, John A. Schuster, and John Sutton, 736–50. London: Routledge, 2000.

Severus, Emmanuel von. "Das Wort 'Meditari' im Sprachgebrauch der Heiligen Schrift." *Geist und Leben* 26 (1953): 365–75.

Sextus Empiricus. *Against the Logicians*. Translated by Richard Bett. Cambridge: Cambridge University Press, 2005.

Shapin, Steven. "Descartes the Doctor: Rationalism and Its Therapies." *British Journal for the History of Science* 33 (2000): 131–54.

Sievert, Donald. "The Importance of Descartes's Wax Example." *Ratio* 21 (1979): 73–85.

Sluhovsky, Moshe. *Becoming a New Self: Practices of Belief in Early Modern Catholicism.* Chicago: University of Chicago Press, 2017.

Sluhovsky, Moshe. *Believe Not Every Spirit: Possession, Mysticism, and Discernment in Early Modern Catholicism.* Chicago: University of Chicago Press, 2007.

Smith, Courtney Weiss. *Empiricist Devotions: Science, Religion, and Poetry in Early Eighteenth-Century England.* Charlottesville: University of Virginia Press, 2016.

Smith, Jeffrey Chips. *Sensuous Worship: Jesuits and the Art of the Early Catholic Reformation in Germany.* Princeton, NJ: Princeton University Press, 2002.

Stallybrass, Peter. "Books and Scrolls: Navigating the Bible." In *Books and Readers in Early Modern England,* edited by Jennifer Andersen and Elizabeth Sauer, 42–79. Philadelphia: University of Pennsylvania Press, 2002.

Staubach, Nikolaus. "L'influence victorine sur la dévotion moderne." In *L'école de Saint-Victor de Paris: Influence et rayonnement du moyen âge à l'époque moderne,* edited by Dominique Poirel, 583–99. Turnhout, Belgium: Brepols, 2010.

Stewart, Columba. *Cassian the Monk.* New York: Oxford University Press, 1988.

Stewart, Columba. "John Cassian on Unceasing Prayer." *Monastic Studies* 15 (1984): 159–77.

Stock, Brian. *After Augustine: The Meditative Reader and the Text.* Philadelphia: University of Pennsylvania Press, 2001.

Stock, Brian. *Augustine the Reader: Meditation, Self-Knowledge and the Ethics of Interpretation.* Cambridge, MA: Harvard University Press, 1996.

Stohrer, Walter John. "Descartes and Ignatius Loyola: La Flèche and Manresa Revisited." *Journal of the History of Philosophy* 17 (1979): 11–27.

Stolz, Anselm. "Anselm's Theology in the *Proslogion.*" In *The Many-Faced Argument: Recent Studies on the Ontological Argument for the Existence of God,* edited by John Hick and Arthur C. McGill, 183–206. New York: Macmillan, 1967.

Störmer-Caysa, Uta. *Gewissen und Buch. Über den Weg eines Begriffes in die deutsche Literatur des Mittelalters.* Berlin: De Gruyter, 1998.

Sucquet, Antoine. *Via vitae aeternae. Iconibus Illustrata per Boëtium A Bolswert.* Antwerp: Typis Martini Nutij, 1620.

Summa, Gerd. *Geistliche Unterscheidung bei Johannes Cassian.* Würzburg: Echter, 1992.

Thomas Aquinas. *Summa Theologiae.* Edited by John Mortenson and Enrique Alarcón. Translated by Fr. Laurence Shapcote, O.P. Lander, WY: Aquinas Institute, 2012.

Thomsen, Dirko. *"Techne" als Metapher und als Begriff der sittlichen Einsicht. Zum Verhältnis von Vernunft und Natur bei Platon und Aristoteles.* Freiburg: K. Alber, 1990.

Thomson, Arthur. "Ignace de Loyola et Descartes. L'influence des exercices spirituels sur les oeuvres philosophiques de Descartes." *Archives de philosophie* 35 (1972): 61–81.
Timmermans, Benoit. "The Originality of Descartes's Conception of Analysis as Discovery." *Journal of the History of Ideas* 60 (1999): 433–47.
Toner, Jules. *A Commentary on St. Ignatius'* Rules for Discernment of the Spirits. St. Louis, MO: Institute of Jesuit Sources, 1982.
Trottmann, Christian. *La vision béatifique: Des disputes scolastiques à sa définition par Benoît XII*. Rome: Ecole Française de Romer, 1995.
Van De Pitte, Frederick. "Intuition and Judgement in Descartes' Theory of Truth." *Journal of the History of Philosophy* 26 (1988): 453–70.
Van der Horst, Pieter W. "*Sortes*: Sacred Books as Instant Oracles in Late Antiquity." In *The Use of Sacred Books in the Ancient World*, edited by L. V. Rutgers, P. W. van der Horst, H. W. Havelaar, and L. Teugels, 143–74. Leuven, Belgium: Peeters, 1998.
Van Engel, John. *Sisters and Brothers of the Common Life: The* Devotio Moderna *and the World of the Later Middle Ages*. Philadelphia: University of Pennsylvania Press, 2008.
Van Fleteren, Frederick. "Ascent of the Soul." In *Augustine through the Ages: An Encyclopedia*, edited by Allan Fitzgerald, O.S.A., 63–67. Grand Rapids, MI: William B. Eerdmans, 1999.
Van Leeuwen, Evert. "Method, Discourse, and the Act of Knowing." In *Essays on the Philosophy and Science of René Descartes*, edited by Stephen Voss, 224–41. Oxford: Oxford University Press, 1993.
Vasari, Georgio. *The Lives of the Artists*. Translated by Julia Conaway Bondanella and Peter Bondanella. Oxford: Oxford University Press, 1998.
Vasoli, Cesare. "Le rapport entre les *Olympica* et la culture de la Renaissance." In *Descartes et la Renaissance*, edited by Emmanuel Faye, 187–208. Paris: H. Champion, 1999.
Vélez, Karin Annalise. "Resolved to Fly: The Virgin of Loreto, the Jesuits, and the Miracle of Portable Catholicism in the Seventeenth-Century Atlantic World." PhD diss., Princeton University, 2008.
Vendler, Zeno. "Descartes' Exercises." *Canadian Journal of Philosophy* 19 (1989): 193–224.
Vielhauer, Philipp. "*Oikodome*. Das Bild vom Bau in der christlichen Literatur vom Neuen Testament bis Clemens Alexandrinus." In *Aufsätze zum Neuen Testament*, by Philipp Vielhauer, 1–168. Munich: C. Kaiser, 1979.
Vinci, Thomas C. *Cartesian Truth*. Oxford: Oxford University Press, 1998.
Von Arnim, Hans, ed. *Stoicorum veterum fragmenta*. Leipzig: B. G. Teubneri, 1903–24.

Wagner, Stephen I. "Descartes' Wax: Discovering the Nature of Mind." *History of Philosophy Quarterly* 12 (1995): 165–83.
Walsh, James. "Application of the Senses." *The Way*, Supplement 27 (1976): 59–68.
Walter, H. "Die benediktinische Discretio." In *Einsicht und Glaube*, edited by Josef Ratzinger and H. Fries, 209–15. Freiburg: Herder, 1962.
Waterschoot, Werner. "*Veridicus Christianus* and *Christeliiken Waersegghers* by Joannes David." In *Emblemata sacra: Rhétorique et herméneutique du discours sacré dans la littérature en image*, edited by Ralph Dekoninck and Agnès Guiderdoni-Bruslé, 527–34. Turnhout, Belgium: Brepols, 2007.
Watson, Richard. *Cogito, Ergo Sum: The Life of René Descartes*. Boston: David R. Godine, 2002.
Wells, Norman J. "Descartes' *Idea* and Its Sources." *American Catholic Philosophical Quarterly* 67 (1993): 513–35.
Wild, Christopher J. "*Apertio Libri*: Codex and Conversion." In *Literary Studies and the Pursuits of Reading*, edited by Eric Downing, Richard Benson, and Jonathan Hess, 17–39. Rochester, NY: Camden House, 2012.
Wild, Christopher J. "1609—The Munich Production of Jakob Bidermann's *Cenodoxus* Effects the Conversion of Fourteen Nobles from the Bavarian Court: Jesuit Theater and the Blindness of Self-Knowledge." In *A New History of German Literature*, edited by David Wellbery, 270–75. Cambridge, MA: Harvard University Press, 2004.
Wild, Christopher J. "'Weder mit worten und rutten': The Force of Gryphius' Examples." *Germanic Review* 76, no. 2 (2001): 99–118.
Woolf, Raphael. "Shaggy Soul Story: How Not to Read the Wax Tablet Model in Plato's *Theatetus*." *Philosophy and Phenomenological Research* 69 (2004): 573–604.
Zabarella, Jacopo. *On Methods*. Edited and translated by John P. McCaskey. Cambridge, MA: Harvard University Press, 2013.
Zittel, Claus. "*Mirabilis scientiae fundamenta*. Die Philosophie des jungen Descartes (1619–1628)." In *Seelenmaschinen. Gattungstraditionen, Funktionen und Leistungsgrenzen der Mnemotechniken vom späten Mittelalter bis zum Beginn der Moderne*, edited by Jörg Jochen Berns and Wolfgang Neuber, 309–62. Vienna: Böhlau, 2001.
Zittel, Claus. *Theatrum philosophicum. Descartes und die Rolle ästhetischer Formen in der Wissenschaft*. Berlin: Akademie Verlag, 2009.

Index

Abbe Isaac, 204
acies mentis, 123, 213, 247, 252, 254, 305n63
action. *See* practice (meditation and philosophy as)
advertere, 88, 192, 219–21, 278n31. *See also* attention; intentionality
affect. *See* emotion
Agamben, Giorgio, 78
Albertus Magnus, 172
allegory, 23–24, 81–83, 169–81, 185, 213, 242–43
allegory of the cave, 9, 30, 34, 74, 77, 100, 132, 213, 226–27, 229
Ambrose (Saint), 239–40
analysis, 115, 117–19, 164
animadvertere, 219, 221, 278n31
anime separatae, 175–77
Anselm (Saint), 117, 238–39
Antony (Saint), 34, 49, 58, 135–37, 200
anxiety of influence, 18–19, 108, 281n74
applicatio sensuum, 167, 291n10
a priori, 115
Aquinas, Thomas, 52, 137, 172, 179, 225, 241, 246, 249, 256
Arendt, Hannah, 266n49
Aristotle, 7, 92, 106, 125, 172–73, 180, 185–86, 227, 293n35. *See also* Scholasticism
Arnauld, Antoine, 79
Ars poetica (Horace), 124
Art of Divine Meditation (Hall), 165
askēsis, 98–99, 261n8
Assmann, Aleida, 159–60
Athanasius, 135, 200

attention, 22–24, 75–81, 88–93, 113–18, 135–36, 143–44, 159, 165–66, 190–221, 295n8. *See also* orientation (intellectual); temporality
Augustine (Saint): attention and, 204–9, 218–20, 297n22; *cogito* of, 18–19; contemplation and, 228–31, 234, 237, 239–41, 244–45, 303n49; conversion experience of, 1–2, 8–9, 21–22, 31–33, 38, 57–58, 60–62, 64–66, 69–70, 77–79, 106–7, 188–89, 208, 223, 225, 271n55; Ignatius and, 40; judgment and, 52, 54; meditation and, 17, 72
"Augustine and Descartes on the Function of Attention" (Brown), 298n33
Ausonius, 57–58, 64–71, 146, 267n10
Autobiography (Ignatius), 39–40
autonomy, 19, 65–66, 70, 82, 107–8, 118–20, 276n11
autopsy, 127–28, 134, 215–16, 227
aversion, 100, 121–23, 188–89, 192–93, 219–20, 247–48. *See also* conversion; universal doubt
Azzolino, Giovanni Bernardino, 176

Bahnung, 97, 279n54
Baillet, Adrien, 12, 21, 29, 37, 44, 51
Basil of Caesarea, 172, 199–200
Bass, Alan, 279n54
Beck, L. J., 190
Benedict (Saint), 34, 137, 200–201
Benjamin, Walter, 169, 185

Benjamin major and minor (Richard of Saint Victor), 233–35, 245–46
Benveniste, Emile, 116–17
Bernard of Clairvaux, 1–2, 44, 231–32
Bérulle, Pierre de, 12–13
bibliomancy, 51, 57, 66. See also *sortilegia*
Bidermann, Jakob, 263n19
Boethius, 14, 269n29
Bolswert, Boetius à, 40, *41, 43, 129*
Bonaventure (Saint), 1–2, 39, 52–53, 223, 231, 234–35, 246, 257
Brodsky Lacour, Claudia, 276n12
Brown, Deborah, 298n33
Burman, Frans, 119

Carruthers, Mary, 20, 85–86, 102–3, 211, 238, 269n29, 280n69
Cartesian method, 9, 21–22, 55, 74, 86–95, 103–4, 112, 122, 204, 221, 255. See also *cogito*; conversion; discernment of spirits; innate ideas; *lumen naturale*; meditation; *methodos*; rules; universal doubt
Casaubon, Meric, 27
Cassian, John, 10, 22, 135–37, 139, 146, 148, 201–2, 208, 219–20
causality, 189–90
Cenodoxus (Bidermann), 263n19
ceroplasticity, 166, 169–85, 293n36. See also wax
certainty, 2, 82, 90, 112–13. See also epistemology; skepticism
Chadwick, Henry, 208–9
Charron, Pierre, 14
chrēsis tōn phantasiōn, 132–36, 145, 149, 198, 286n17
Christianity: in early modern Europe, 9–17; philosophy and, 3–9
Christina of Sweden, 16
Chrysippus, 134, 292n27
Cicero, 54–55, 92, 127, 172, 226, 229
cogito: Augustine's version of, 18–19; Descartes's dreams and, 36, 73; discovery of, 22–23, 145–50, 212; evidence and, 153–60, 184; *gnōthi seauton* and, 6; intuition and, 115, 249–51, 282n89; malicious demon and, 23; meditation and, 152–70, 256–57; methodological arrival at, 122–24; performativity and, 115–16, 218–19; receptive intellect and, 249–50; self-evidence and, 6–7, 19, 77, 251; Stoic roots of, 14–15; wax and, 161–70
cognition: attention and, 22–24, 75–81, 88–93, 113–18, 135–36, 143–44, 159, 165–66, 190–221, 295n8; deduction and, 90–94, 193–98, 212–18, 222–23, 249; emotion and, 20, 127, 137–39, 158; imagination and, 22–23, 54, 104, 124–28, 166–67, 177; the intellect and, 25, 32, 53–58, 88–90, 100–102, 109–11, 122–25, 149–52, 177–80, 196, 222–29, 241–52; intelligibility and, 75, 115, 173, 184, 220, 227–30, 240–47, 254; intentionality and, 6, 60, 66, 139, 210, 219, 224; intuition and, 90–93, 110–15, 193–95, 213–19, 223–24, 232–33, 239–41, 247–57, 282n89; memory and, 83–86, 135, 171–72, 177, 196–98, 214–16; practical habituation and, 19–22, 71–73, 80–86, 91–104, 123–30, 144, 152, 221–39, 282n89, 284n3; representationalism and, 20, 102–4, 123–30, 132–59, 181–86. See also *acies mentis*; *obtutus mentis*
College of La Flèche, 12–13, 17, 19, 23, 30, 45, 47, 62, 167
Colvius, 18–19, 282n90
Commentary on Ecclesiastes (Hugh of Saint Victor), 232–33
Commentary on Ezekiel (Jerome), 52
Commentary on the Gospel of Luke (Ambrose), 239–40
common sense, 177–78
communication (of conversive practice), 22, 99, 105–20. See also conversion; *methodos*; practice (meditation and philosophy as); rules
conceptual metaphorics. See metaphorics (conceptual)

Conferences (Cassian), 135, 201–5, 208, 297n19
Confessions (Augustine), 32, 57–58, 78–79, 188–89, 208, 230, 237, 244
Congregation of the French Oratory, 12
consolations, 14, 48, 71–72, 141–44
Constable, Giles, 235
constantia, 14, 75–81, 92–93, 202–3
Constitutions (Society of Jesus), 40
contemplatio Dei, 24, 122–23, 136, 189, 222–26, 233, 238–57, 305n63
contemplation, 23–24, 122–23, 136, 189, 222–57, 305n63. *See also theoria*
Conversation with Burman (Descartes), 119
conversion: as art of turning, 21–22, 28–29, 37–38, 40–45, 74–81, 86–93, 100–107, 121–23, 213, 226–27, 256–57; attention and, 24, 206–21; aversion and, 100, 121–23, 147, 188–89, 192–93, 219–20, 247–48; communication of, 22, 99, 105–20; *contemplatio Dei* and, 223–26; definitions of, 8–9; divine call and, 49–50, 56–70, 78–79, 106–7, 116–17; dreams and, 8, 29–30, 35–70, 266n2, 268n21; emotional ductus and, 50, 71–72, 85–86; evidence and, 27–35, 72, 106, 126–27, 153–60; foundations and, 31–37, 82–83, 121–23, 144, 201–2, 269n29; maintenance of, 13, 34–35, 74–81, 91–93, 96, 99–104, 202–3; media's assistance with, 23–24, 78–79, 107–8; meditation and, 8–11, 238–39, 270n39; paradigm cases of, 30–33, 36, 53, 57–62, 66, 106–7, 223, 240, 269n29, 271n53; performativity and, 71, 76–77, 93; perversion and, 42, 49, 57, 74–75, 145; as philosophy's goal, 3–9, 27–35; reading and, 10, 113–16, 197–98; self-sufficiency and autonomy and, 19, 65–66, 70, 82, 107–8, 276n11; spiritual practices and, 10–11, 27–35, 71–73, 132–52. *See also* meditation; metaphorics (conceptual); philosophy; spirituality

Corpus omnium veterum poetarum latinorum (des Brosses), 274n86
The Craft of Thought (Carruthers), 20
creatio continua, 34

Davidius, John, 57–58, 61–62, *63–64*, 130, *131*
De anima (Aristotle), 125–26, 173
De civitate Dei (Augustine), 18–19, 205–6
De consideratione (Bernard of Clairvaux), 232
De constantia (Lispius), 14
deduction, 24, 90–93, 193–94, 197–98, 212–18, 222–23, 249. *See also* cognition; temporality
deiformity, 51, 54, 74, 180–81, 247–48, 256–57
De la sagesse (Charron), 14
De meditatione (Hugh of Saint Victor), 301n26
demonstration, 127, 163, 187, 192–97, 217, 282n92. *See also* evidence
Derrida, Jacques, 6, 109, 284n2
Des Allerheiligst- und Allerheilsamsten Leidens und Sterbens Jesu Christi (Greiffenberg), *154–55*
des Brosses, Pierre, 274n86
Descartes, René: art of turning of, 21, 74–81, 88–93; attention and, 211–21; contemplation and, 222–26, 247–57; conversion and, 27–70, 81–86, 106–7; dreams of, 8, 22, 35–70, 74, 150–51; historical context of, 9–17, 51, 289n48; images of, *253*; religious education of, 1–3, 12–14, 17–19, 23, 29–30, 40, 45, 47, 50–51, 62, 91–92, 167, 232, 254–55, 267n9, 269n29; scholarly debates over, 2–3, 6–7, 17–25; thinking practices of, 94–104. *See also specific works*
desolations, 48, 71–72, 141–42
De spiritualibus ascensionibus (Zerbolt), 10
De Trinitate (Augustine), 206–7, 218, 230
De vera religione (Augustine), 244
De veritate (Aquinas), 52

334   *Index*

De vita beata (Seneca), 16
De vivendo Deo (Augustine), 239
devotio moderna, 9–10, 98–99, 236
Didascalicon (Hugh of Saint Victor), 46, 232
Didi-Huberman, Georges, 181–82
Diogenes Laertius, 30, 173, 182, 292n27
discernment of spirits, 22–23, 29, 46–53, 71–73, 107–8, 132–52, 188–89, 203–4, 271n49, 271n54, 287n34, 288n41, 289n45
Discourse on the Method (Descartes), 18, 21, 28–30, 35, 65, 70–95, 103–16, 237–38, 252–55, 275n9, 277n30, 278n46, 279n49
Discourses (Epictetus), 197–98, 277n22
discretion, 136–37
distensio, 209–11, 297n28
distraction, 37, 46, 75, 135, 139, 194–212, 216–21. *See also* attention; discernment of spirits
divertissement, 37–38, 40–46, 266n2
Dominic (Saint), 48
doubt. *See* skepticism; universal doubt
dreams and dreaming: Descartes's conversion and, 29–30, 35–70, 268n21; painting and, 22–23, 123–30; waking's distinction from, 21–22, 46–47, 50–52, 56–70, 138–39
ductus, 50, 71–72, 85–86
du Vair, Guillaume, 14–15

edification, 81–86, 103–4, 201–2, 276n12, 276n17
education, 30, 32–33, 74–76, 105–20, 198–99, 254–55. *See also* conversion; Descartes, René; practice (meditation and philosophy as)
Ejercitatorio de la vida spiritual (Garcia de Cisneros), 10
Elisabeth of Bohemia, 16, 25, 96, 275nn6–7, 289n45
emotion: conversion and, 32, 202, 291n14; discernment and, 127, 137–39,

158; ductus and, 50, 71–72, 85–86; representations and, 20
empeiria, 79–80
enargeia, 127, 133–34, 174
enthusiasm, 27, 54, 146, 300n1
Epictetus, 13, 22, 98, 103, 133–34, 197–99, 277n22
epimeleia heautou, 4–6, 98, 262n8
epistemology: certainty as goal of, 2, 82, 90, 112–13; evidence and, 126–30, 134, 141–48, 153–63, 173–74, 184–98, 213–19; foundations and, 29, 31–37, 67–70, 82–83, 121–23, 144, 201–2, 269n29; practical knowledge and, 78–80, 98–129, 162–70, 280n71; representationalism and, 20, 102–4, 123–30, 152–59, 181–86; *theoria* and, 226–31, 237, 241–43, 257; universal doubt and, 21–23, 82, 100, 112–13, 121–23, 132–52, 157–58. *See also* conversion; illumination; *methodos;* perception; rationalism; Stoicism
errancy, 65–67, 71–73, 88–89, 233–34, 244–47
Eustratius, 92
evidence, 6, 19, 27–35, 72, 112–20, 126–34, 141–63, 173–74, 184–98, 213–19. *See also* deduction; intuition; self-evidence
evil spirits, 46–51, 73, 132–52, 157, 196, 271n49, 289n45. *See also* discernment of spirits

First Letter to the Corinthians (Paul), 84
form, 20, 78, 109, 180–81, 183–86, 189–90, 280n67, 293n35, 294n43
Foucault, Michel, 3–4, 6–7, 20, 30–31, 93, 97–98, 284n2
foundations, 29, 31–37, 67–70, 82–83, 121–23, 144, 201–2, 269n29. *See also* conversion; edification; epistemology
Francis of Assisi (Saint), 58, 234–35
Francis of Sales (Saint), 12–13, 48, 236–37
Freud, Sigmund, 97

Galilei, Gallileo, 1–2
Galle, Cornelius, 130
Garcia de Cisneros, 10, 236
Gassendi, Pierre, 161
genius malignus. See discernment of spirits; evil spirits
genre, 1–3, 8–9, 20–21, 23, 76–77, 108–12. *See also* demonstration; meditative ascent; performativity
Gerson, Jean, 22, 137–39, 144, 150–51, 235–36, 287n34
Gilbert, Neal, 92
Gilson, Etienne, 301n23
gnōthi seauton, 4–6
God: beatific visions of, 2, 25, 32, 208, 239–42, 248–50, 255–57, 303n49; contemplation of, 23–24, 122–23, 136, 189, 222–26, 233, 238–57, 305n63; divine call of, 49–50, 56–70, 78–79, 106–7, 116–17; grace of, 33, 46, 58, 77, 84, 135, 142–43, 231, 234–37, 241–51, 289n45; illumination and, 14, 25, 53, 67, 74, 95–96, 105, 146, 225–26, 247–57, 305n66; proofs of, 23–24, 101, 124, 148–49, 157–58, 187–98, 222–23, 296n9, 298n36. *See also* conversion
Gonçalves de Câmara, Luis, 49
Good Life in the Scientific Revolution (Jones), 18
Göttler, Christine, 175
grace, 33, 46, 58, 77, 84, 135, 142–43, 228–32, 234–37, 241–51, 289n45
Grafton, Anthony, 21, 27, 31, 268n23
Gregory the Great, 137
Greiffenberg, Catharina Regina von, 153, *154–55*, 156
Grosseteste, Robert, 92
Gueroult, Martial, 17

habituation, 96, 99–104, 117–18, 187–88, 214–16, 252, 254–55. *See also* attention; conversion; practice (meditation and philosophy as)
Hadot, Pierre, 3–4, 6, 20, 77–78, 104, 109, 197, 201, 262n11, 279n63, 296n15

Hall, Joseph, 11, 165–66
Hall, Robert, 291n7
Harrison, Timothy, 266n2
Harsdörffer, Georg Philipp, 291n7
Hausherr, Irénée, 98
Heider, Fritz, 183–84, 306n70
Hermeneutics of the Subject (Foucault), 4, 30–31, 97–98
Hettche, Matt, 13
Hintikka, Jaako, 116
History of Madness (Derrida), 6
Hobbes, Thomas, 180
Hohenburg, Herwart von, 31
Horace, 124
Hortensius (Cicero), 229
Hugh of Saint Victor, 46, 231–33, 235–36, 301n26
Huygens, Constantjin, 164, 197–98
hylomorphism. *See* form; mediality

ideas (mental images): ceroplasticity and, 166, 169–73, 177–85, 293n36; clear and distinct, 122–23, 132–52, 161–70, 189–95, 212, 220–21, 254–55; contemplation and, 247–57; discernment of spirits and, 20–23, 29, 46–53, 71–73, 107–8, 132–52, 188–89, 203–4, 271n49, 271n54, 287n34, 288n41, 289n45, 289nn45–46; imagination and, 22–23, 54, 104, 124–28, 166–67, 177; impressions and imprinting and, 53–55, 152–60, 170–86, 223–26, 256–57, 292n27; innate, 8, 20, 110, 124, 149, 180, 192–93, 212, 216–17, 247–57, 299n54.; memory and, 83–86, 135, 171–72, 177, 196–98, 214–16; painting and, 22–23, 123–30, 152, 284n3; purgation of, 21–23, 36–37, 82, 100, 112–13, 121–23, 132–52, 157–58; representationalism and, 123–30, 153–60, 280n67, 288n41; self-presentation and, 153–60
Idylls (Ausonius), 57
Ignatius of Loyola (Saint): consolation and desolation and, 139–46, 148;

contemplation and, 236; conversion experience of, 8–9, 11, 21–22, 31–33, 36, 39, 44–45, 47–49, 58, 60–61, 71–72, 126, 269n29, 271n53; evidentiary practices and, 126–27; influences on, 10; spiritual exercises of, 11, 17, 22–23, 30, 36–37, 47–49, 59, 78, 85–86, 91–92, 99, 101, 114, 139–40, 267n9, 279n63, 289n48

illumination, 53–55, 71–74, 89–96, 105, 127, 146, 224–26, 240–46, 248–57, 304n58, 306n68. *See also* cognition; God; *lumen naturale;* meditation

imagination, 22–23, 54, 104, 124, 127–28, 166–67, 177

immission, 148–49

immortality of the soul, 2–3, 8, 100, 149, 228–29, 270n39

imprinting, 53–55, 152–60, 170–71, 177–86, 223–26, 256–57, 292n27. *See also* cognition; ideas (mental images); mediality; wax

in-formation, 173–74, 179–80, 189–90, 207. *See also* wax

innate ideas, 8, 20, 110, 124, 149, 180, 192–93, 212, 216–17, 247–57, 299n54. *See also* cognition; ideas (mental images)

intellect, 25, 32, 53–58, 88–90, 100–102, 109–11, 122–25, 149–52, 177–80, 196, 222–29, 240–57

intelligibility, 75, 115, 173, 184, 220, 227–30, 240–57

intentio, 297n22. *See also* attention; Augustine (Saint)

intentionality, 6, 60, 66, 139, 210, 219, 224

Introduction to the Devout Life (Saint Francis of Sales), 13

intuition, 90–93, 110–15, 193–95, 213–19, 223–24, 232–33, 239–41, 247–57, 282n89

itinerancy, 65–67, 71–73, 88–89, 233–34, 244–47

Jaeger, Werner, 30

Jerome (Saint), 52, 98–99
Jesuit order, 10–14, 17–18, 29–30, 39–40, 50, 61–62, 78–79, 236
Jolley, Nicholas, 305n66
Jones, Matthew, 18, 87, 298n36
The Journey of the Mind to God (Bonaventure), 39, 52–53, 234–35, 246
judgment, 96, 150, 158–59, 170–72, 184–85. *See also* discernment of spirits

Kant, Immanuel, 2
kataleptic presentations, 133–34, 157, 173–74
Kenney, John Peter, 228–29, 231
Kircher, Athanasius, 31
Klein, Julie, 214
Koren-Bloemen (Huygens), 164
Koschorke, Albrecht, 268n23

Leclercq, Jean, 5, 231
Legenda aurea (Voragine), 48
Leibniz, Gottfried Wilhelm von, 18, 57–58, 61–62, 89, 267n10, 273n74
The Life of the Mind (Arendt), 266n49
Light of the Soul (Jolley), 305n66
L'immortalité de l'âme (Silhon), 248
Lipsius, Justus, 14–15, 170
Literal Meaning of Genesis (Augustine), 240, 245
Ludolf of Saxony, 48
Luhmann, Niklas, 183
lumen naturale, 25, 53, 67, 74, 95–96, 105, 146, 225–26, 247–57, 305n66. *See also* God; illumination
L'usage de la raison (Mersenne), 13
Luther, Martin, 8–10, 31, 99, 289n48
Luyken, Jan, 164
Lyons, John, 115, 282n92, 282n96

Macrobius, 29
Manuale Sodalitatis (Véron), 17
Marcus Aurelius, 13, 168, 198–99
mathematics, 94–95, 104
matter. *See* form; in-formation; mediality
Matthew (Saint), 11, 47

Mauburnus, Johannes, 10
McMahon, Robert, 117
mediality: attention and, 220–21; conversion and, 23–24, 78; deduction and, 249–50; ideas and, 152–70, 256–57, 280n67; practices and, 100–105; *tabula* view of the mind and, 123–30, 152–53, 156; wax and, 23, 161–86. *See also* deduction; ideas (mental images); symbolic notation
meditation: attention and, 24, 197–221, 295n8; Augustinian versions of, 17, 72; *cogito* of, 152–70; communication of, 105–20; contemplation and, 221–57, 305n63; conversion and, 8–11, 115–20, 270n39; discernment of spirits and, 22–23, 29, 46–53, 71–73, 107–8, 132–52, 188–89, 203–4, 271n49, 271n54, 287n34, 288n41, 289n45; habituation and, 17, 96–104; illumination and, 247–57; locational memory and, 85–86, 127–28, 166–67; mediality and, 100–104, 113, 115–16, 161–86; *methodos* and, 67, 89–93, 96–97, 115, 237, 247, 251–55, 277n29; occasional, 23, 164–70, 290n4; painting and, 22–23, 123–30, 156–60, 291n14; prayer and, 51, 75, 91, 201–2; reading and, 10, 113–16, 197–98; representationalism and, 102–4; the senses and, 167–68, 291n10; as spiritual practice, 1–10, 187–88; temporality and, 116–18, 206–11; thinking and, 91–93; wax as object of, 23, 161–70. *See also contemplatio Dei;* conversion; ductus; *lumen naturale;* mediality; thinking (as practice)
Meditations (Descartes): attention and, 211–21; *cogito* in, 22, 110–12, 115–16; contemplation and, 237, 247–57; conversion and, 8–9, 34–35, 50–73, 76–77, 82–83, 90, 100–104, 121–23, 147; Foucault on, 6; genre and, 109–12, 114–23; mental practice in, 6–7, 20–21, 94–104; preface to, 1–2, 101, 122; proofs of God in, 24, 101, 124, 148–49, 157–58, 187–98, 222–23, 296n9, 298n36; scholarly debates over, 17–25; self-sufficiency and autonomy and, 19, 65–66, 70, 82, 107, 115, 118–20
Meditations (Marcus Aurelius), 168
Meditations on the Passion (Greiffenberg), 153
meditative ascent, 24, 123, 189, 201–2, 206–8, 217–18, 221–39, 247–57
meditative matrix, 23, 128, 144, 149, 153, 157, 169–70, 289n48
meletē, 4, 97–99, 279n61. *See also* meditation
Melion, Walter, 130
memory, 83–86, 135, 171–72, 177, 196–98, 214–16
Mersch, Dieter, 184
Mersenne, Marin, 12–13, 18–19, 100–101, 119, 179, 254–55, 294n38, 300n1
Mesnard, Pierre, 17
metanoia, 38, 49–50
metaphorics (conceptual), 266n50; definition of, 20, 276n11, 303n44; edification and, 81–86, 104, 201–2, 276n12, 276n17; equestrian, 166; itinerancy and, 65–67, 71–73, 88–89, 233–34, 244–45, 247; *methodos* and, 89–93, 96, 115, 237, 247, 254–55, 277n29; natural light and spark of the soul and, 25, 52–53, 55–56, 71–74, 89–93, 95–96, 105, 146, 224, 240–44, 247–57, 305n66, 306n68; orientation and, 22, 42–45, 65–73, 80–93; painting and, 22–23, 123–30, 144, 152, 284n3; pilgrimage and, 30, 38–39; seeds and, 53–56, 95; turning and, 37–38, 100–104; wax and, 23, 162–81, 292n16, 293n36
method. *See* Cartesian method; communication (of conversive practice); orientation (intellectual); practice (meditation and philosophy as); rules

methodos, 67, 89–93, 96–97, 115, 237, 247, 251, 254–55, 277n29
Metrodorus of Scepsis, 172
mind. *See cogito;* cognition; imagination; intellect; meditation; memory; perception; thinking (as practice); wax
mind-body distinction, 161–70, 177
mirabilis scientiae fundamenta, 29, 45, 59, 65–70, 74, 89, 94, 110–11
mnēmē theou, 75, 135, 139, 172, 202–4, 280n69. *See also* memory
monasticism, 13, 17, 34, 58, 75–78, 85–86, 98–99, 110, 135–37, 200–201, 211, 231–32
Montaigne, Michel de, 145
Mountain of Contemplation (Gerson), 235–36
Mystical Ark (Richard of Saint Victor), 233

narration, 115–16. *See also* evidence; genre; performativity
Natural History (Pliny), 181–82
navigation. *See* orientation (intellectual)
Nelson, Alan, 294n46
Neoplatonism, 38, 228. *See also* Plotinus
Neostoicism, 13–14, 16–17. *See also specific philosophers*
Nicomachean Ethics (Aristotle), 92
Nightingale, Andrea, 209, 226, 297n28, 297n30
Nolan, Lawrence, 189
Notre Dame of Loretto, 30, 38, 40

obtutus mentis, 220, 247, 305n63
occasional meditations, 23, 164–70, 290n4
Occasional Meditations (Hall), 11
Odyssey (Homer), 59
Olin, John, 39
Olympica (Descartes), 28–32, 35, 53, 76, 82, 89, 237–38
On Christian Teaching (Augustine), 72

"On Distinguishing True from False Revelations" (Gerson), 137
On Memory and Recollection (Aristotle), 172
On the Immortality of the Soul (Augustine), 229
On the Teacher (Augustine), 229–30
Opera Philosophica (Descartes), 253
Orbita probitatis, 62, 63, 130, 131
orientation (intellectual), 22, 42–45, 65–73, 80–81, 86–93, 97–104, 106, 136, 256–57
orthopraxis, 103, 280n71
Ossa-Richardson, Anthony, 288n41

painting, 22–23, 123–30, 152, 284n3
Park, Katherine, 174
Pascal, Blaise, 18
Passions of the Soul (Descartes), 21, 298n33, 300n5
pathfinding. *See* orientation (intellectual)
Paul (Saint), 11, 21, 32, 36, 47, 53, 60, 70, 84–85, 106, 134, 141, 169, 237, 276nn17–18
perception: attention and, 197–211; of God, 1–2, 53, 203–4, 207, 222–26, 237–57; intuition and, 90–93, 110–15, 193–95, 213–14, 223–24, 247–57; meditation and, 153–60, 222–26, 257; mental gaze and, 123, 213, 247, 252, 254, 305n63; passivity and activity of, 177–78, 207, 249, 255; seeing the place and, 85–86, 127–28, 166–67; sensory, 159, 167–68, 177, 198–99, 240–41, 247–57, 291n14, 293n36, 294n43. *See also* cognition; imagination; *lumen naturale*
performativity, 71, 76, 88–89, 93, 99–100, 115–17, 121–23, 218–19. *See also* genre
perversion, 42, 49, 57, 74–75, 145
Petrarch, 58, 60
Phaedrus (Plato), 78, 92
phantasia, 132–35, 145, 173, 286n17
Philo of Alexandria, 261n4
philosophy: conversion and, 27–35, 74–

81; definitions of, 5–8; institutionality and, 9–10, 77–79; modern secularization of, 1–2; spirituality and, 3–9, 13–14, 16, 27–35, 76–77, 86–93; as spiritual practice, 3–9, 77–78, 86–105, 164, 213, 226–27
pilgrimage, 30, 38–40
Pilgrim of Loreto (Richeome), 236
pineal gland, 177
Plato, 8–9, 30–31, 77, 79–80, 98, 100, 105–6, 170–73, 213, 220–29, 234–44, 292n16
Pliny the Elder, 181–82
Plotinus, 213, 228, 243–44
practice (meditation and philosophy as): attention and, 197–221; communication of, 103, 105–20, 280n71; *constantia* and, 14, 75–81, 92–93, 202–3; contemplation as, 231–57; conversion and, 3–9, 27–35, 57–61, 65, 71–81, 91–93, 202–3, 256–57; discernment of spirits and, 22–23, 29, 46–53, 71–73, 107–8, 132–52, 188–89, 203–4, 271n49, 271n54, 287n34, 288n41, 289n45; doubting as, 112–13; in early modern Europe, 9–17; God's will and, 57–60, 62, 65–66; habituation and, 96–99, 117–18, 187–88, 214–16, 252, 254–55; knowledge and, 78–80, 98–99, 102–20, 162–70, 280n71; memory and, 171–80; orientation and, 22, 42–45, 65–73, 97–104, 106, 136; perception and, 153–60; representationalism and, 20, 123–30, 132–52; rules and, 77–79, 86–104, 203–4, 211–21, 231–39, 278n46; thinking as, 19–20, 22, 71–73, 80–86, 91–104
Praeambula (Descartes), 30, 47, 56
prayer, 51, 75, 91, 201–2
Principia philosophiae (Descartes), 7, 21, 80–81, 107, 119, 221, 225, 252, 295n8, 299n47
Progymnasmata (Nicolaos of Myra), 127
proofs of God, 23–24, 101, 124, 148–49, 157–58, 187–98, 222–23, 296n9, 298n36
Proslogion (Anselm), 117, 238
prosochē, 24, 197–211. *See also* attention
Pyrrhonianism, 14
"A Pythagorean Reflection on the Difficulty of Choosing One's Lot in Life" (Ausonius), 67

Quintilian, 126–27

rationalism, 1, 27, 56, 77, 89
Reformation, 9–10
Replies (Descartes), 100–101, 108, 114, 161–62, 179–80, 187–89, 195, 219–20, 248, 251, 280n67, 283n104
representationalism, 20, 102–4, 123–30, 132–59, 181–86, 288n41. *See also* cognition; epistemology; ideas (mental images)
Republic (Plato), 9, 30–31, 226, 242–43. *See also* allegory of the cave
Rhetorica ad Herennium, 83, 292n19
Richard of Saint Victor, 231–36, 245–46
Richeome, Louis, 236
Rönnegård, Per, 98
Rosetum exercitiorum spirtualium (Mauburnus), 10
Rouse, Mary and Richard, 182
Rufinus of Aquileia, 200–201
The Rule of Saint Benedict, 137
rules, 77–79, 86–120, 141–43, 203–4, 231–39
Rules for the Direction of the Mind (Descartes), 18–22, 54–55, 65–69, 86–88, 95–110, 177–79, 193–94, 211–26, 248–54

Sanches, Francisco, 145
Scholasticism, 5–8, 51, 53, 56, 87, 105–6, 118–20, 125–26, 172, 241, 249, 261n6
Schreiner, Susan, 137, 288n39
scientific method (modern understanding of), 2, 18, 21–22, 27–35, 86–87, 217–18

scintilla animae, 25, 53, 95–96, 146, 220–21, 257. *See also* sparks
scintilla conscientiae, 52–55
scintilla rationis, 54, 67, 69
Scriver, Christian, 291n7
"The Scrubbing Brush" (Huygens), 164
The Search for Truth by Means of the Natural Light (Descartes), 119–20, 125, 152–53, 252, 283n108
seeds, 53–56, 71–73, 95. *See also semina scientiae*
self-evidence, 6, 19, 27–28, 32, 143, 190, 195, 214–16, 218–19, 299n54. *See also* evidence; innate ideas
self-presentations, 157–60, 173–74. *See also cogito*; representationalism
self-reflexivity, 23, 102, 138
self-sufficiency, 19, 65–66, 70, 82, 107, 115, 118–20, 276n11
semina scientiae, 54–55, 95. *See also* seeds
Seneca, 13–14, 16, 22, 54, 198–99
senses: *applicatio sensuum* and, 167, 291n10; passivity of, 177–78, 207, 249, 255. *See also* cognition; discernment of spirits; perception; representationalism
serious sayings, 56–70
Sermons on the Song of Songs (Bernard), 44
Silhon, Jean de, 112, 248
skepticism, 2, 14, 21–23. *See also* epistemology
Socrates, 22, 31, 74, 76, 78, 106
Soliloquies (Augustine), 244
Sophist (Plato), 80
Sorbonne, 1–2, 77, 197, 223
sortilegia, 59, 62. *See also* bibliomancy
Soul in Heaven, 176
Soul in Purgatory, 175
sparks, 53–56, 71–73, 95–96, 105. *See also scintilla animae*
spirits (discernment of), 22–23, 29, 46–54, 71–73, 107–8, 132–52, 188–89, 203–4, 271n49, 271n54, 287n34, 288n41, 289n45

Spiritual Exercises (Ignatius), 11, 17, 22–23, 39–40, 47–49, 78, 85–86, 91–92, 99, 126–28, 139–40, 145, 167, 189, 236
spirituality: attention and, 24, 197–211; in early modern Europe, 9–17; enthusiasm and, 27, 146, 300n1; foundationalism and, 32–35; institutionality and, 9–10, 77–79; Jesuit education and, 10–14, 17; philosophy and, 3–9, 13–14, 16, 27–35; practical exercises and, 3–17, 94–104, 199–201. *See also* conversion
Steno, 58–59
Stoicism, 13–17, 23–24, 54, 92–101, 133–36, 140–41, 149, 173–74, 197–99, 292n27. *See also specific stoics and neostoics*
Sucquet, Antoine, 40, *41, 42, 43,* 128, *129*
Summa Theologiae (Aquinas), 179, 246, 256
syllogisms, 195–96
symbolic notation, 215–16
synderesis, 50–56, 235, 272n57
synthesis, 118

Tacitus, 13
technē, 30, 72–74, 79–80, 92–93, 96, 99–106, 110. *See also* practice (meditation and philosophy as)
temporality, 116–18, 141–43, 152, 168–69, 195–206, 208–21
Theaetetus (Plato), 170–72, 292n16
Theodicy (Leibniz), 57–58
theology (discipline of), 5
theoria, 226–31, 237, 241–43, 257
Thesaurus hieroglyphicus (Hohenburg), 31
thinking (as practice), 19–20, 22–23, 71–73, 77–104, 123–30, 144, 152, 162–70, 221–39, 282n89, 284n3. *See also* cognition; conversion; intuition; metaphorics (conceptual); rules
Traité de la constance (du Vair), 14
Treatise on Man (Descartes), 177
Treatise on the Love of God (Francis of Sales), 236–37

Twelve Patriarchs (Richard of Saint Victor), 233
typosis, 174–75

universal doubt, 21–23, 82, 100, 112–13, 121–23, 132–52, 157–58. *See also* conversion; discernment of spirits; skepticism
University of Paris, 232

vanity (of things), 23–24, 75, 164–70. *See also* occasional meditations; Stoicism; wax
Vatier, Antoine, 284n1
Veridicus Christianus (Davidius), 57–58, 61–62, *63–64*, 130, *131*
Véron, François, 17

Via vitae aeternae (Sucquet), 40, *41*, 42, *43*, 128, *129*
Victorine spirituality, 17–18
visio beatifica, 2, 25, 32, 208, 239–42, 248–50, 255–57, 303n49
Vita Antonii (Athanasius), 135, 200
Vita Christi (Ludolf of Saxony), 48
Volvelle, 62, *64*
Voragine, Jacobus de, 48

wax, 23, 161–86, 292n16, 293n36
wisdom (as goal of philosophy), 5–8, 228
Wisdom of Simple Christians, 61–62

Zabarella, Jacopo, 92–93, 96–97
Zerbolt, Gerard, 10

Cultural Memory in the Present

Raúl E. Zegarra, *A Revolutionary Faith: Liberation Theology Between Public Religion and Public Reason*
Helmut Puff, *The Antechamber: Toward a History of Waiting*
David Simpson, *Engaging Violence: Civility and the Reach of Literature*
Michael P. Steinberg, *The Afterlife of Moses: Exile, Democracy, Renewal*
Alain Badiou, *Badiou by Badiou*, translated by Bruno Bosteels
Eric B. Song, *Love against Substitution: Seventeenth-Century English Literature and the Meaning of Marriage*
Niklaus Largier, *Figures of Possibility: Aesthetic Experience, Mysticism, and the Play of the Senses*
Mihaela Mihai, *Political Memory and the Aesthetics of Care: The Art of Complicity and Resistance*
Ethan Kleinberg, *Emmanuel Levinas's Talmudic Turn: Philosophy and Jewish Thought*
Willemien Otten, *Thinking Nature and the Nature of Thinking: From Eriugena to Emerson*
Michael Rothberg, *The Implicated Subject: Beyond Victims and Perpetrators*
Hans Ruin, *Being with the Dead: Burial, Ancestral Politics, and the Roots of Historical Consciousness*
Eric Oberle, *Theodor Adorno and the Century of Negative Identity*
David Marriott, *Whither Fanon? Studies in the Blackness of Being*
Reinhart Koselleck, *Sediments of Time: On Possible Histories*, translated and edited by Sean Franzel and Stefan-Ludwig Hoffmann
Devin Singh, *Divine Currency: The Theological Power of Money in the West*
Stefanos Geroulanos, *Transparency in Postwar France: A Critical History of the Present*
Sari Nusseibeh, *The Story of Reason in Islam*
Olivia C. Harrison, *Transcolonial Maghreb: Imagining Palestine in the Era of Decolonialization*
Barbara Vinken, *Flaubert Postsecular: Modernity Crossed Out*
Aishwary Kumar, *Radical Equality: Ambedkar, Gandhi, and the Problem of Democracy*
Simona Forti, *New Demons: Rethinking Power and Evil Today*
Joseph Vogl, *The Specter of Capital*
Hans Joas, *Faith as an Option*
Michael Gubser, *The Far Reaches: Ethics, Phenomenology, and the Call for Social Renewal in Twentieth-Century Central Europe*
Françoise Davoine, *Mother Folly: A Tale*
Knox Peden, *Spinoza Contra Phenomenology: French Rationalism from Cavaillès to Deleuze*

Elizabeth A. Pritchard, *Locke's Political Theology: Public Religion and Sacred Rights*
Ankhi Mukherjee, *What Is a Classic? Postcolonial Rewriting and Invention of the Canon*
Jean-Pierre Dupuy, *The Mark of the Sacred*
Henri Atlan, *Fraud: The World of Ona'ah*
Niklas Luhmann, *Theory of Society, Volume 2*
Ilit Ferber, *Philosophy and Melancholy: Benjamin's Early Reflections on Theater and Language*
Alexandre Lefebvre, *Human Rights as a Way of Life: On Bergson's Political Philosophy*
Theodore W. Jennings, Jr., *Outlaw Justice: The Messianic Politics of Paul*
Alexander Etkind, *Warped Mourning: Stories of the Undead in the Land of the Unburied*
Denis Guénoun, *About Europe: Philosophical Hypotheses*
Maria Boletsi, *Barbarism and Its Discontents*
Sigrid Weigel, *Walter Benjamin: Images, the Creaturely, and the Holy*
Roberto Esposito, *Living Thought: The Origins and Actuality of Italian Philosophy*
Henri Atlan, *The Sparks of Randomness, Volume 2: The Atheism of Scripture*
Rüdiger Campe, *The Game of Probability: Literature and Calculation from Pascal to Kleist*
Niklas Luhmann, *A Systems Theory of Religion*
Jean-Luc Marion, *In the Self's Place: The Approach of Saint Augustine*
Rodolphe Gasché, *Georges Bataille: Phenomenology and Phantasmatology*
Niklas Luhmann, *Theory of Society, Volume 1*
Alessia Ricciardi, *After* La Dolce Vita: *A Cultural Prehistory of Berlusconi's Italy*
Daniel Innerarity, *The Future and Its Enemies: In Defense of Political Hope*
Patricia Pisters, *The Neuro-Image: A Deleuzian Film-Philosophy of Digital Screen Culture*
François-David Sebbah, *Testing the Limit: Derrida, Henry, Levinas, and the Phenomenological Tradition*
Erik Peterson, *Theological Tractates*, edited by Michael J. Hollerich
Feisal G. Mohamed, *Milton and the Post-Secular Present: Ethics, Politics, Terrorism*
Pierre Hadot, *The Present Alone Is Our Happiness, Second Edition: Conversations with Jeannie Carlier and Arnold I. Davidson*
Yasco Horsman, *Theaters of Justice: Judging, Staging, and Working Through in Arendt, Brecht, and Delbo*
Jacques Derrida, *Parages*, edited by John P. Leavey
Henri Atlan, *The Sparks of Randomness, Volume 1: Spermatic Knowledge*
Rebecca Comay, *Mourning Sickness: Hegel and the French Revolution*
Djelal Kadir, *Memos from the Besieged City: Lifelines for Cultural Sustainability*
Stanley Cavell, *Little Did I Know: Excerpts from Memory*

for a complete listing of titles in this series, visit the Stanford University Press website, sup.org

The authorized representative in the EU for product safety and compliance is:
Mare Nostrum Group
B.V Doelen 72
4831 GR Breda
The Netherlands

www.ingramcontent.com/pod-product-compliance
Lightning Source LLC
Chambersburg PA
CBHW031754220426

43662CB00007B/396